Kieran Hall, Nicole Benbow, Felicity Gladwin, Marcus Wilson, Brenda Grubb, Ally Benbow

Published in Australia by Alison Benbow (HYAUST)
PO Box 2580, Regency Park SA 5942
1300 400 444
info@ashes06.com
www.ashes06.com

This publication is an official licenced product of Cricket Australia.

First Published Jun 2006.
Copyright © 2006.
Printing and binding in Australia by Five Star.

All rights reserved. No part of this publication may be reproduced in any form or by any means electronic, mechanical, photocopying or otherwise without prior written permission of the publisher.

The National Library of Australia Cataloguing-in-Publication entry;

Hall, Kieran.
The Ashes dowununder 06/07 : essential souvenir travel guide.

ISBN 0 9775482 0 1.

1. Test matches (Cricket) - Australia. 2. Cricket - Tournaments - Australia. 3. Test matches (Cricket) - England. I. Benbow, Nicole Anne, 1978- . II. Gladwin, Felicity. III. Title.

796.358650994

ACKNOWLEDGMENTS
This publication could not have been produced without the assistance given by the state cricket associations, tourism associations and transport authorities in QLD, SA, WA, Victoria and NSW. Thank you also to the staff at Cricket Australia, including Chris Loftus-Hills, David Steinhardt and Samantha Burn. Finally, thank you to all those who supported the production of this publication, including Richard Benbow, Helen Benbow, Melissa Benbow, Sarah Hall, Ian Carlson, Casey Hall, Brendan Hall, Sally Rainsford and Andrew Sullivan.

DISCLAIMER
Every effort has been made to ensure that this book is free from errors. However, the publisher, and its respective employees or agents, shall not accept responsibility for injury, loss or damage occasioned to any person acting or refraining from action as a result of material in this book whether or not such injury, loss or damage is in any way due to any negligent act or omission, breach of duty or default on the part of the publisher and its respective employees or agents.

CONTENTS

1ST TEST BRISBANE 9

The Gabba.................................12
Match day information..........13
Transport................................16
Getting to the Gabba.............21
Accommodation....................22
Restaurants...........................28
Pubs & Clubs........................31
Attractions............................42
Suggested itineraries............44
Directory...............................45

2ND TEST ADELAIDE 49

Adelaide Oval........................52
Match day information..........53
Transport................................56
Getting to Adelaide Oval.......59
Accommodation....................60
Restaurants...........................66
Pubs & Clubs........................68
Attractions............................78
Suggested itineraries............80
Directory...............................81

3RD TEST PERTH 83

The WACA............................86
Match day information..........87
Transport................................90
Getting to the WACA............95
Accommodation....................96
Restaurants..........................102
Pubs & Clubs.......................105
Attractions...........................116
Suggested itineraries...........119
Directory..............................120

4TH TEST MELBOURNE 123

Melbourne Cricket Ground....126
Match day information.........127
Transport..............................130
Getting to the MCG..............135
Accommodation...................136
Restaurants..........................141
Pubs & Clubs.......................144
Attractions...........................157
Suggested itineraries...........160
Directory..............................161

5TH TEST SYDNEY 163

Sydney Cricket Ground..........166
Match day information.........167
Transport..............................171
Getting to the SCG...............178
Accommodation...................181
Restaurants..........................188
Pubs & Clubs.......................192
Attractions...........................213
Suggested itineraries...........216
Directory..............................218

ASHES HISTORY 2

History of the Ashes................................2
Famous Ashes series..............................4
The last time they met: 2005 6
Ashes Honour Board...............................7

EXTRAS 221

2006/07 Cricket Calendar....................222
Ashes 2006/07 Scorecards..................223
Cricket ticket refunds..........................228
Ashes urn returns 229
2007 One-Day Schedule 230
Domestic Cricket Down Under 232
ICC World Cup: West Indies 2007.......234
Howzat! Trivia Challenge 236
Aussie Slang..238
New Year's Eve 2006...........................240
Beer Drinker's Guide to Oz 243
Discount Offers....................................245

ashes06.com

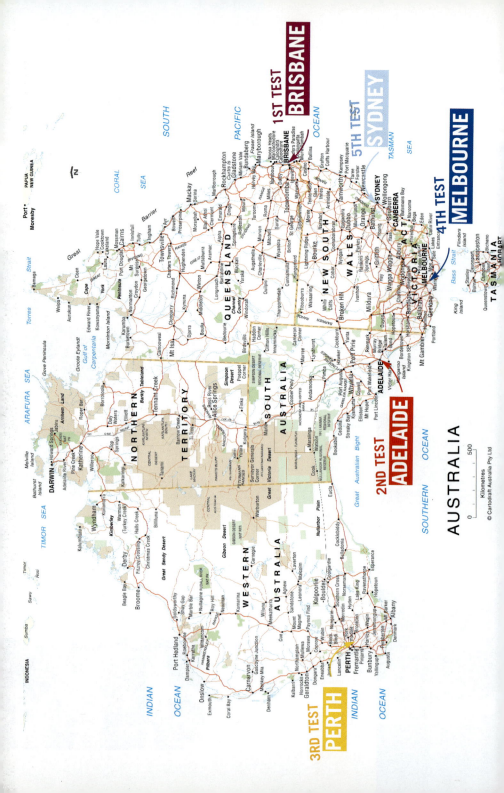

INTRODUCTION

When you land in a city you've never been to before it can be daunting not knowing where to stay, where to eat or simply where to find a good pub to have a cold beer!

But for Australians travelling interstate and English fans making the trip for the 2006/07 Ashes series, it doesn't have to be daunting at all.

The Ashes Down Under 06/07 is a comprehensive travel guide designed specifically for cricket followers, featuring great tips on accommodation, restaurants, pubs, transport and local attractions in all five Test cities - Brisbane, Adelaide, Perth, Melbourne and Sydney.

The Ashes Down Under 06/07 is a comprehensive travel guide designed specifically for cricket followers, featuring great tips on accommodation, restaurants, pubs, transport and local attractions in all five Test cities - Brisbane, Adelaide, Perth, Melbourne and Sydney.

It contains lots of detailed maps to help you get around, a wide-ranging contacts directory for each city containing useful phone numbers and websites, plus a stack of special discount offers to redeem during your stay.

Want to know what type of beer is available at a particular Test or where to place a bet inside the stadium? Look no further than *The Ashes Down Under 06/07*, which features key match day information for spectators, including gate times and entry restrictions.

As well as a dedicated Ashes history, the guide also contains information on the one-day series between Australia, England and New Zealand, plus a preview of the 2007 World Cup in the West Indies.

Throw in a review of Aussie slang and a "Beer Drinker's Guide to Oz" *(do you know the difference between a "pot" and a "middy"?)* and everything you need for a memorable Ashes holiday is right at your fingertips!

HISTORY
OF THE ASHES

Australia and England vie for "The Ashes" in a biennial Test cricket contest, which stands as the sport's fiercest and most celebrated rivalry.

But just how did the Ashes come about in the first place?

The first Test match between Australia and England was played in 1877, however the Ashes story only dates back to 1882 when the Aussies won in England for the first time. In the aftermath of the shock loss, *The Sporting Times* published the following satirical obituary:

"IN AFFECTIONATE REMEMBRANCE of ENGLISH CRICKET, Which died at the Oval, on 29th August, 1882. Deeply lamented by a large circle of sorrowing friends and acquaintances. R.I.P.

N.B. - The body will be cremated, and the ashes taken to Australia."

In the lead-up to the following series between the countries in 1882/83, the English press dubbed the tour to Australia as "the quest to regain The Ashes".

Upon England's 2-1 series win, the English team - led by Ivo Bligh - was presented with a small terracotta urn reputed to contain a set of burnt bails, symbolising "the ashes of English cricket".

The Australians appeal for an English wicket during the 2005 Ashes series. Photo: Getty Images.

www.ashes06.com

A poem was also presented to Bligh with the urn, which read:

When Ivo goes back with the urn, the urn;
Studds, Steel, Read and Tylecote return, return;
The welkin will ring loud,
The great crowd will feel proud,
Seeing Barlow and Bates with the urn, the urn;
And the rest coming home with the urn.

And so the tradition began, which has since seen Australia win 30 Ashes series over the past 124 years compared to England's 27. There have also been six drawn series, however only once has England retained the Ashes due to a deadlocked result (in 1972 following a 2-2 series in England).

This year sees the 64th staging of the Ashes and is the first time England has defended the urn since 1989, a series which saw Australia prevail on English soil 4-0.

THE URN

The precious Ashes urn has come to symbolise the series between Australia and England, however it is not physically awarded as the trophy for the winning side.

Since 1998/99, a Waterford crystal trophy has been presented to the victorious team, while the treasured urn remains in the MCC Cricket Museum at Lord's.

The urn has only ever been back to Australia once, in January 1988 for a museum tour as part of Australia's bicentennial celebrations, however it returns Down Under this year for a special exhibition as part of the highly anticipated 2006/07 series.

See tour dates on page 229.

Andrew Symonds (middle) celebrates a wicket with his Australian teammates. Photo: Getty Images.

HISTORY OF THE ASHES
...continued from page 3.

FAMOUS ASHES SERIES

While every Ashes series is special, the following battles stand out in history:

1932/33: BODYLINE

England's famous "Bodyline" tour of Australia in 1932/33 will long be remembered as one of the most ferocious series ever played.

Mindful of the Aussies' potent batting line-up, which included the legendary Don Bradman, English captain Douglas Jardine instructed his pacemen to bowl at the bodies of the Australian batsmen, with the goal of forcing them to defend their bodies with their bats and provide easy catches to a stacked leg side field. The tactic caused much controversy and resulted in a 4-1 series win to England. Jardine reportedly remarked at the time: "I've not travelled 6,000 miles to make friends. I'm here to win the Ashes."

1948: THE INVINCIBLES

Undefeated in 36 matches during their 1948 tour of England, the Australians were dubbed "The Invincibles" after winning the Ashes 4-0. Led by 39-year-old Don Bradman in his last appearance for Australia, the visitors stunned the English side with their sheer dominance.

The series will also be remembered for one of the most poignant moments in cricket history. In the Fifth Test at The Oval, Bradman needed just four runs in his final innings or remain not out to maintain a career batting average of 100. However, Eric Hollies bowled him for a second-ball duck, sending the great man into

(L-R) Simon Katich, Ricky Ponting, Justin Langer, Glenn McGrath and Matthew Hayden appeal during the 2005 Ashes series in England.
Photo: Getty Images.

www.ashes06.com

retirement with a career batting average of 99.94.

1981: BOTHAM'S ASHES

Taking a 1-0 lead going into the Third Test at Headingly, Australia was on target for an easy win midway through the match, prompting Australian players Dennis Lillee and Rod Marsh to lay a small bet with an English bookmaker who was offering odds of 500-1 for an England victory.

This seemingly harmless punt soon came back to haunt Lillee and Marsh who watched on as Ian Botham dragged his side back into the contest with an unbeaten 149 in the second innings. Needing 130 to win, the Aussies were then bundled out for 111 as fast bowler Bob Willis finished with figures of 8/43 to give England a miraculous win.

Botham was at his best once again in the Fourth Test at Edgbaston, inspiring another England comeback, but this time with the ball. He took 5/11 in Australia's second innings of 121 to give his side victory by 29 runs. England went on to win the Fifth Test at Old Trafford to retain the Ashes.

2005: ENGLISH REVIVAL

When Australia easily won the First Test at Lord's in 2005, high hopes of England breaking its 16-year Ashes drought seemed dashed. But what followed in the remaining four matches turned a potential whitewash into one of the greatest and most evenly-fought series of all time.

A two-run victory in the Second Test at Edgbaston - the smallest runs victory margin in Ashes history - catapulted the home side back into contention, before a classic draw was played out in the Third Test at Old Trafford when Australian tailenders Brett Lee and Glenn McGrath outlasted England's bowlers in a pulsating finish.

The tide turned in England's favour in the Fourth Test at Trent Bridge, with Michael Vaughan's men triumphant by three wickets in another superb contest. England then drew the Fifth Test at The Oval to win the series 2-1 and finally reclaim the Ashes.

The England team celebrates a long-awaited triumph over Australia in 2005 - the country's first Ashes win since 1986/87.
Photo: Getty Images.

HISTORY OF THE ASHES
...continued from page 5.

AUSTRALIA VS ENGLAND

The last time they met... 2005

1st TEST... Lord's (July 21-24, 2005)

Australia 190 (Harmison 5/43) **& 384** (Clarke 91, Katich 67, Martyn 65)
England 155 (Pietersen 57, McGrath 5/53) **& 180** (Pietersen 64*)

RESULT
AUSTRALIA WON
BY 239 RUNS

2nd TEST... Edgbaston (August 4-7, 2005)

England 407 (Trescothick 90, Pietersen 71, Flintoff 68)
& 182 (Flintoff 73, Warne 6/46)
Australia 308 (Langer 82, Ponting 61) **& 279**

RESULT
ENGLAND WON
BY 2 RUNS

3rd TEST... Old Trafford (August 11-15, 2005)

England 444 (Vaughan 166, Trescothick 63, Bell 59)
& 6/280 declared (Strauss 106, Bell 65, McGrath 5/115)
Australia 302 (Warne 90, S. Jones 6/53) **& 9/371** (Ponting 156)

RESULT
MATCH DRAWN

4th TEST... Trent Bridge (August 25-28, 2005)

England 477 (Flintoff 102, G. Jones 85, Trescothick 65, Vaughan 58) **& 7/129**
Australia 218 (S. Jones 5/44) **& 387** (Langer 61, Katich 59, Clarke 56)

RESULT
ENGLAND WON
BY 3 WICKETS

5th TEST... The Oval (September 8-12, 2005)

England 373 (Strauss 129, Flintoff 72, Warne 6/122)
& 335 (Pietersen 158, Giles 59, Warne 6/124)
Australia 367 (Hayden 138, Langer 105, Flintoff 5/78) **& 0/4**

RESULT
MATCH DRAWN

SERIES RESULT: **ENGLAND WON 2-1**
Players of the Series: Andrew Flintoff & Shane Warne

www.ashes06.com

ASHES HONOUR BOARD

SEASON	VENUE	TESTS	AUST WINS	ENG WINS	DRAWS	SERIES RESULT	SEASON	VENUE	TESTS	AUST WINS	ENG WINS	DRAWS	SERIES RESULT
1882-83	Australia	3	1	2	0	ENGLAND 2-1	1946-47	Australia	5	3	0	2	AUSTRALIA 3-0
1884	England	3	0	1	2	ENGLAND 1-0	1948	England	5	4	0	1	AUSTRALIA 4-0
1884-85	Australia	5	2	3	0	ENGLAND 3-2	1950-51	Australia	5	4	1	0	AUSTRALIA 4-1
1886	England	3	0	3	0	ENGLAND 3-0	1953	England	5	0	1	4	ENGLAND 1-0
1886-87	Australia	2	0	2	0	ENGLAND 2-0	1954-55	Australia	5	1	3	1	ENGLAND 3-1
1887-88	Australia	1	0	1	0	ENGLAND 1-0	1956	England	5	1	2	2	ENGLAND 2-1
1888	England	3	1	2	0	ENGLAND 2-1	1958-59	Australia	5	4	0	1	AUSTRALIA 4-0
1890	England	3	0	2	1	ENGLAND 2-0	1961	England	5	2	1	2	AUSTRALIA 2-1
1891-92	Australia	3	2	1	0	AUSTRALIA 2-1	1962-63	Australia	5	1	1	3	DRAWN
1893	England	3	0	1	2	ENGLAND 1-0	1964	England	5	1	0	4	AUSTRALIA 1-0
1894-95	Australia	5	2	3	0	ENGLAND 3-2	1965-66	Australia	5	1	1	3	DRAWN
1896	England	3	1	2	0	ENGLAND 2-1	1968	England	5	1	1	3	DRAWN
1897-98	Australia	5	4	1	0	AUSTRALIA 4-1	1970-71	Australia	7	0	2	5	ENGLAND 2-0
1899	England	5	1	0	4	AUSTRALIA 1-0	1972	England	5	2	2	1	DRAWN
1901-02	Australia	5	4	1	0	AUSTRALIA 4-1	1974-75	Australia	6	4	1	1	AUSTRALIA 4-1
1902	England	5	2	1	2	AUSTRALIA 2-1	1975	England	4	1	0	3	AUSTRALIA 1-0
1903-04	Australia	5	2	3	0	ENGLAND 3-2	1977	England	5	0	3	2	ENGLAND 3-0
1905	England	5	0	2	3	ENGLAND 2-0	1978-79	Australia	6	1	5	0	ENGLAND 5-1
1907-08	Australia	5	4	1	0	AUSTRALIA 4-1	1981	England	6	1	3	2	ENGLAND 3-1
1909	England	5	2	1	2	AUSTRALIA 2-1	1982-83	Australia	5	2	1	2	AUSTRALIA 2-1
1911-12	Australia	5	1	4	0	ENGLAND 4-1	1985	England	6	1	3	2	ENGLAND 3-1
1912	England	3	0	1	2	ENGLAND 1-0	1986-87	Australia	5	1	2	2	ENGLAND 2-1
1920-21	Australia	5	5	0	0	AUSTRALIA 5-0	1989	England	6	4	0	2	AUSTRALIA 4-0
1921	England	5	3	0	2	AUSTRALIA 3-0	1990-91	Australia	5	4	1	0	AUSTRALIA 4-1
1924-25	Australia	5	4	1	0	AUSTRALIA 4-1	1993	England	6	4	1	1	AUSTRALIA 4-1
1926	England	5	0	1	4	ENGLAND 1-0	1994-95	Australia	5	3	1	1	AUSTRALIA 3-1
1928-29	Australia	5	1	4	0	ENGLAND 4-1	1997	England	6	3	2	1	AUSTRALIA 3-2
1930	England	5	2	1	2	AUSTRALIA 2-1	1998-99	Australia	5	3	1	1	AUSTRALIA 3-1
1932-33	Australia	5	1	4	0	ENGLAND 4-1	2001	England	5	4	1	0	AUSTRALIA 4-1
1934	England	5	2	1	2	AUSTRALIA 2-1	2002-03	Australia	5	4	1	0	AUSTRALIA 4-1
1936-37	Australia	5	3	2	0	AUSTRALIA 3-2	2005	England	5	1	2	2	ENGLAND 2-1
1938	England	5	1	1	3	DRAWN							

allout cricket

THE MAGAZINE THE PLAYERS READ

SUBSCRIBE AT WWW.ALLOUTCRICKET.CO.UK

THE SUNSHINE STATE

The Gabba · www.thegabba.org.au

NOVEMBER 23-27, 2006

1ST TEST
BRISBANE

BRISBANE CITY OVERVIEW

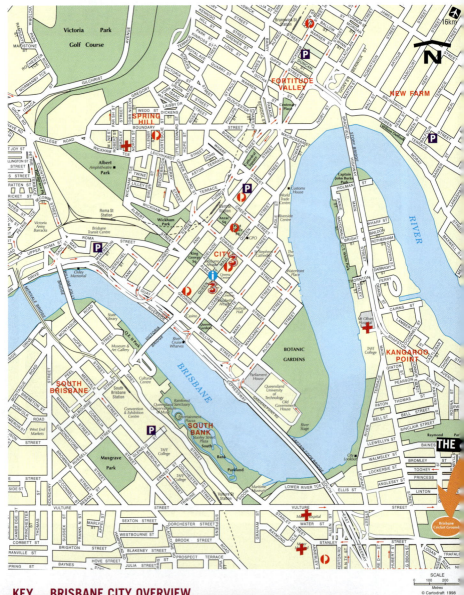

KEY... BRISBANE CITY OVERVIEW

- 3 store
- Hospital
- Police
- Post Office
- Tourist information
- Airport

Queensland State Map

© Cartodraft 1998

www.ashes06.com

WELCOME TO
-BRISBANE, QUEENSLAND

While you're in Brisbane...

For a city that has more sunny days than Florida and warmer winter days than the Bahamas, it's easy to see why Brisbane is one of Australia's hottest tourist destinations.

The Queensland capital has an average summer temperature of 28°C (and 21°C in winter) and in recent times has come of age to be recognised as one of Down Under's most progressive centres. No wonder many people now call it "BrisVegas"!

and home to 1.8 million residents who live in near perfect climate all year round, Brisbane has a sophisticated but friendly charm which visitors love.

Located in the south-eastern corner of Queensland, compact Brisbane is experiencing a boom in top-class hotels, restaurants and cafes, with some of the best alfresco dining spots in the land.

Featuring fashionable districts outside the city centre such as

> For a city that has **more sunny days than Florida** and warmer winter days than the Bahamas, it's easy to see **why Brisbane is one of AUSTRALIA'S HOTTEST** tourist destinations.

As the third largest city in Australia, Brisbane has thrived since wowing international visitors in 1982 for the Commonwealth Games and again in 1988 for the World Expo. A lively, cosmopolitan metropolis

Paddington, Fortitude Valley, South Bank and New Farm, Brisbane also acts as the gateway to a host of premier tourist sites, including the Gold Coast, Sunshine Coast, the Whitsundays and the Great Barrier Reef.

Eat: Moreton Bay bugs. Also known as "Bay lobsters", Moreton Bay bugs are a local delicacy found along the entire coast of the northern half of Australia. Despite their name, they are not bugs at all, rather saltwater crustaceans with succulent flesh reminiscent of lobsters. An ideal addition to the barbecue!

Drink: XXXX. No, it's not an outrageously inappropriate movie for the kids, it's Queensland's iconic beer. Try the full-strength XXXX Bitter or the increasingly popular XXXX GOLD mid-strength offering. And if you're after something stronger, home-grown Bundaberg Rum is widely acclaimed as Australia's number one spirit.

See: Australia Zoo - Home of the Crocodile Hunter. Get up close and personal with all sorts of Australian wildlife and you might even bump into the "Crocodile Hunter" himself Steve Irwin. Australia Zoo houses more than 750 animals, including 100 fresh and saltwater crocodiles - crikey, it's a beauty!

Do: Ride Brisbane River. Get on board the high-speed CityCats and spend the day cruising up and down Brisbane River. With a TransLink daily pass, you can hop on and off and check out attractions such as New Farm, Riverside and Eagle Street Pier precinct, as well as trendy South Bank.

STATE FACTS... QUEENSLAND
- Founded: 1859
- Population: 3.6 million (Brisbane = 1.8 million)
- Colours: Dark blue & gold (Unofficial: Maroon)
- Floral emblem: Cooktown Orchid
- Faunal emblems: Koala & Brolga
- Average summer temperature: 28°C
- Average winter temperature: 21°C
- Time zone: GMT + 10 hours
- Domestic cricket team: Queensland Bulls

The Gabba. Photo: Queensland Cricket: www.bulls.com.au

THE GABBA

What's in a name?
The Gabba derives its name from the suburb Woolloongabba in which it is situated. An Aboriginal word, there are two theories about the meaning of Woolloongabba, some believing it means "whirling waters" while others say it represents "fight talk place".

The Gabba will once again kick-start the Australian summer of cricket through its customary role as host of the First Test.

Located at Woolloongabba, hence the name, the Gabba is situated 2km from Brisbane city centre and is home to the Queensland Bulls in the domestic cricket competition, as well as the Brisbane Lions in Australian Rules football.

The ground dates back to 1895 when the land was first designated as a cricket site, however the first Test match wasn't played at the venue until 1931 when Australian batting legend Don Bradman made 226 against South Africa, which remarkably, still stands as the highest individual score in a Test played in Brisbane.

In the 1950s and '60s, the Gabba hosted a number of English First Division football matches featuring the likes of Blackpool, Everton and Manchester United, while in more recent times, the venue was used during the 2000 Olympic Games.

Regular upgrades over the past decade, including a new $40 million (£16 million) fully seated grandstand completed in 2005, have entrenched the Gabba as Brisbane's premier sports stadium.

The record attendance stands at 47,096 when Australia played Great Britain in the Second Rugby League Test in 1954, however reconfigurations over the years mean the current crowd capacity is slightly lower at 42,000.

Spanning 171 x 150 metres (slightly larger than the MCG), the ground itself boasts a state-of-the-art playing surface, which is now completely bordered by grandstands providing first-class corporate, media and public facilities.

www.ashes06.com

MATCH DAY INFORMATION

1ST TEST:
AUSTRALIA vs ENGLAND

The Gabba, Nov 23-27, 2006

Gates:
Gates open at 8.30am on all five days of the Test. Public entry gates are located on Vulture St (Gates 4 and 7) and on Stanley St (Gates 2 and 9).

Match times:
FIRST SESSION:	10.00am - 12noon
Lunch:	12noon - 12.40pm
SECOND SESSION:	12.40pm - 2.40pm
Tea:	2.40pm - 3.00pm
THIRD SESSION:	3.00pm - 5.00pm

*Note: Times are subject to change.

[BE WARNED! Gabba ground management reserve the right to implement bag and body searches and may refuse entry at its discretion.]

Parking:
Parking around the Gabba on any match day is restricted to 15 minutes unless otherwise signed. All day parking is available at the South Bank Parklands underground car park or the Brisbane Convention Centre for $10 to ticket-holders. Patrons can then catch a free shuttle to and from the Gabba, leaving from the South Bank or Cultural Centre Busway stations.

For up-to-date information, visit bulls.com.au or phone (07) 3292 3100.

Prohibited items:
- Deliveries from external caterers
- Large eskies
- Folding chairs
- Crockery
- Alcohol
- Cans, opened bottles, glass containers
- Flares, fireworks, laser pointers
- Horns and whistles
- Flags displaying political/offensive messages
- Knives, chains, studded belts

Bag/Container restrictions:
- Coolers, eskies, bags and other belongings must be stored under your seat.
- Oversized items will not be permitted into the venue.
- No facilities for the storage of items are available.

General information:
- Public food and beverage outlets, parents' rooms and toilets are easily accessible and have been designed to reduce waiting times for patrons.
- You can access cash at EFTPOS at various locations around the ground, including Gate 7 at the Vulture St end of the ground, and Bays 39 and 76, which are both situated between the members area and the main scoreboard.
- First-aid facilities are scattered throughout the venue at Gates 2, 4, 7 and 9.
- Public phones are in abundance at the Gabba, but if you're in a hurry, go straight to Gate 2, 4, 7 or 9 or Bay 12, 32, 44, 51 or 74.
- Wheelchair seating areas have been allocated in Bays 2, 7, 49, 64 and 71.
- Match day offices are spread evenly around the ground at Gates 2, 4, 5, 7 and 9.

continued overpage...

MATCH DAY INFORMATION
...continued from page 13.

Food & beverage:
Fast food outlets can be found around the ground, which sell all the basic stadium fare such as meat pies, pasties, sausage rolls, hot chips, hotdogs and chiko rolls. Chicken, fish and calamari are also available, as are an assortment of sandwiches, salads, fruit salads, pitta wraps and Turkish breads.

As Lion Nathan is the major sponsor of the venue during the cricket, XXXX GOLD (mid-strength) and Hahn Premium Light will be the only beers available in public areas during the Test, with XXXX Bitter (full-strength) and Heineken only available in the members.

Smoking:
The Gabba is a non-smoking venue, with smoking banned within the stadium and within four metres from each entry point to the ground.

[SCALPING:]
It is an offence to re-sell any tickets to any Test match in Australia at a premium or to use any of them for advertising, promotional or other commercial purposes without the prior written consent of Cricket Australia or the relevant state cricket association.

If the ticket is sold or used in contravention of this condition, the bearer of the ticket will be denied admission to the venue.

TAB/Betting:
TAB and sports betting facilities are available at the Vulture St end of the ground in Bay 4 on the lower tier, just next to the members area.

The Gabba. Photos: Queensland Cricket: www.bulls.com.au

www.ashes06.com

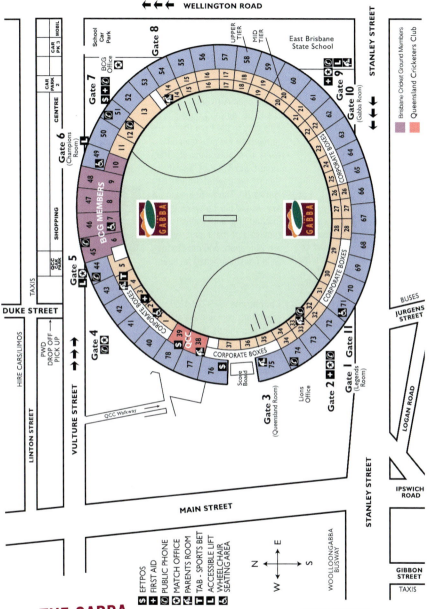

THE GABBA
-SEATING PLAN

[TRANSPORT

By Plane...
Australian carriers **Qantas**, **Jetstar** and **Virgin Blue** operate interstate routes to and from Brisbane Airport, which is located 16km north-east of the city centre at Eagle Farm.

All the major international airlines fly through Brisbane, as do a number of smaller airlines which operate up and down the Queensland coast and interstate. So if you get to Brisbane and decide you want to explore other parts of the state, such as the Gold Coast, Cairns or the Great Barrier Reef, check out:
Alliance Airlines:
(07) 3212 1212, allianceairlines. com.au (Brisbane/Mt Isa/Townsville/ Cairns);

Australian Airlines: 13 13 13, australianairlines.com.au (Cairns/Gold Coast);

Macair: 13 13 13, macair.com.au (Outback);

Sunshine Express: 13 13 13, sunshineexpress.com.au (Brisbane/Sunshine Coast/Maryborough/Hervey Bay)

And if you need to book your flight between Brisbane and Adelaide for the Second Test, a one-way fare with Qantas or Virgin Blue will set you back around $190 (£80).

To/from Airport...
There are a number of door-to-door services from Brisbane Airport to the city (and the Gold Coast and Sunshine Coast) for visitors to access. The air-conditioned **Airtrain** (13 12 30, airtrain.com.au) is the best way to get from the terminal to the city, running every 15 minutes between the airport and Roma St Transit Centre and Central Station ($10/4.20). The Airtrain also acts as the link between the international and domestic terminals of the airport, which are 2km apart, and runs to the Gold Coast every half an hour as well.

Coachtrans (07 3238 4700, coachtrans.com.au) operates its **Skytrans** shuttle bus between the airport and all hotels in the CBD, meeting all major flights seven days a week. One-way trips cost $11 (£4.50). Coachtrans also operates direct services between the airport and the Gold Coast from Sanctuary Cove to Coolangatta, while **Sun-air** (07 5478 2811, sunair.com.au) has daily services every hour to the Sunshine Coast for around $42 (£17.50).

Car hire is available through numerous airport operators, including **Avis** (13 63 33, avis.com.au), **Budget** (1300 794 344, budget.com.au), Europcar (1300 131 390, europcar.com.au), Hertz (13 30 39, hertz.com.au) and **Thrifty** (1300 367 227, thrifty.com.au), or jump in a cab which will cost you $35-$40 (£14-£17) for the airport-city trip.

By Train... (INTERSTATE)
Queensland Rail's **Traveltrain** (13 22 32, traveltrain.com.au) operates a number of services throughout Queensland, with the **Roma St Transit Centre** the hub for all long distance train services.

> And if you need to book your flight between Brisbane and Adelaide for the Second Test, a one-way fare with Qantas or Virgin Blue will set you back around $190 (£80).

CountryLink (13 22 32, countrylink.info) connects Brisbane and Sydney with prices for the 15-hour trip starting at around $115 (£48), while four main services operate within Queensland. The Brisbane to Cairns run forms the main line and is serviced by the **Tilt Train** - a high-speed connection that operates three times a week (25 hours, $280/£116) - and the more leisurely **Sunlander** which has four services a week (30 hours, $190/£80). Inland services between Brisbane and Charleville are catered for by the **Westlander** (16 hours, $90/£38), while the Brisbane to Longreach via Rockhampton route is serviced by the **Spirit of the Outback** (24 hours, $165/£69).

By Bus... (INTERSTATE)
The **Roma St Transit Centre** in Brisbane can assist you with all your long distance bus and train requirements.

continued overpage...

www.ashes06.com

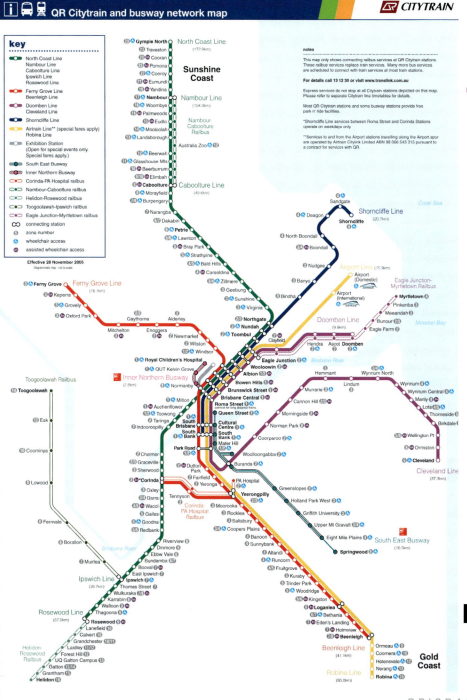

[TRANSPORT
...continued from page 16.

As Australia's largest bus company, **Greyhound Australia** (13 14 99, greyhound.com.au) will not only get you from city to city during the Ashes series, it can also take you to many Queensland towns from Brisbane.

The Cairns route which travels up the coast on the Bruce Hwy is one of the most popular, and costs around $200 (£84) for the 29-hour journey.

Premier Motor Service (13 34 10, premierms.com.au) is another option, covering the route between Sydney, Brisbane and Cairns. The company has fewer services than Greyhound but you'll probably get a cheaper fare.

As a guide, the 16-hour bus ride from Brisbane to Sydney will cost you around $100 (£42). If you're travelling directly to Adelaide for the cricket, a 40-hour route costing around $290 (£120) is available, but flying is probably your best bet for this leg of your trip.

PUBLIC TRANSPORT...

Brisbane has a reliable public transport system, with a new integrated ticketing system called **TransLink** (13 12 30, translink.com.au) standardising fares, concessions and ticket types and zones across bus, train and ferry modes of public transport.

There are 23 travel zones in total across the south-east Queensland region, however the city centre and its immediate surrounds all fall within Zone 1, so a standard **Single** ticket for this region will only cost you $2.10 (88p).

Daily tickets are available for between $4.20-$7.40 (£1.75-£3.10) depending on the number of zones you travel, and give you unlimited transport on buses, trains and ferries all day.

Off-peak daily tickets can also be purchased for $3.20-$5.60 (£1.30-£2.30) for travel on weekends and between 9am-3.30pm and after 7pm on weekdays, with the price again depending on the number of zones travelled.

And if you think you'll spend a bit of time on public transport, a wise move is to buy a **Ten Trip Saver** for $16.80-$29.60 (£7-£12.30) which gives you 10 trips for the price of eight.

By Public Bus...
The downtown **Loop** is a free bus service that circles the city, operating every 10 minutes on weekdays between 7am-5.50pm and stopping at the Queensland University of Technology, Queen St Mall, City Hall, Central Station and Riverside.

The main stop for local buses is the underground Queen St Mall station in the Myer Centre, which also houses an information centre for visitors. Buses run at frequent intervals on weekdays between 5am-6pm, however be mindful that services are reduced on Saturday afternoons and Sundays.

By Public Train...
The **Citytrain** network has seven lines which service the metropolitan area, running as far north as Gympie North (for Sunshine Coast travellers) and as far south as Nerang (for Gold Coast travellers).

All trains go through Roma St, Central Station and Brunswick St Station.

By Public Ferry...
For river commuting, the **CityCat** catamarans operate from the University of Queensland, in the city's south-west, to Bretts Wharf in the north-east every 20-30 minutes between 5.50am-10.30pm. North Quay (for those wanting

The CityCat on Brisbane River. Photo: Tourism Queen

to visit Queen St Mall), South Bank, Riverside (for CBD visitors) and New Farm are among the many stops along the route.

The **Inner City Ferries** also service river commuters (as do a number of smaller cross-river ferries), travelling back and forth across the river between North Quay and Mowbray Park. Services run regularly every day. For more information on routes and timetables, contact the **Trans-Info Service** (13 12 30, transinfo.com.au), the **Brisbane Visitor Information Centre** (corner Albert/Queen Sts), the **Bus Station Information**

Centre (Queen St Mall) or the adjacent **Queensland Rail Travel Centre**.

By Bicycle...

Brisbane has a network of bike paths that wind along either side of the river and through parks and gardens in both the inner city and suburban areas.

To hire a bike (which will cost you around $20/£8 for the day), ask your hotel concierge, or contact:

Valet Cycle Hire & Tours: 0408 003 198, cyclebrisbane.com;

Brisbane Bicycle Sales/Hire: (07) 3229 2433, brizbike.com;

Riverlife Adventure Centre: (07) 3891 5766, riverlife.com.au

By Taxi...

There are licensed ranks across Brisbane or simply call:
Black & White Cabs ...13 10 08
Yellow Cabs..................13 19 24
Brisbane Cabs.............13 22 11

A maximum of four passengers applies per cab, however five-seater and 11-seater MaxiTaxis are available on request. Luxury and wheelchair-compatible options are also available.

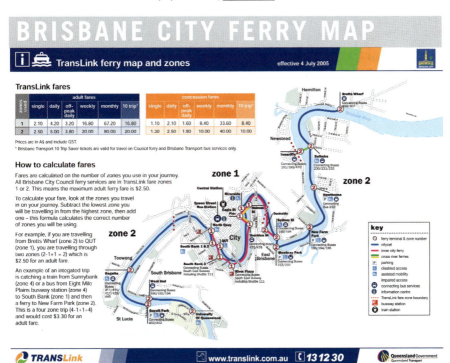

BRISBANE BUS ZONE MAP

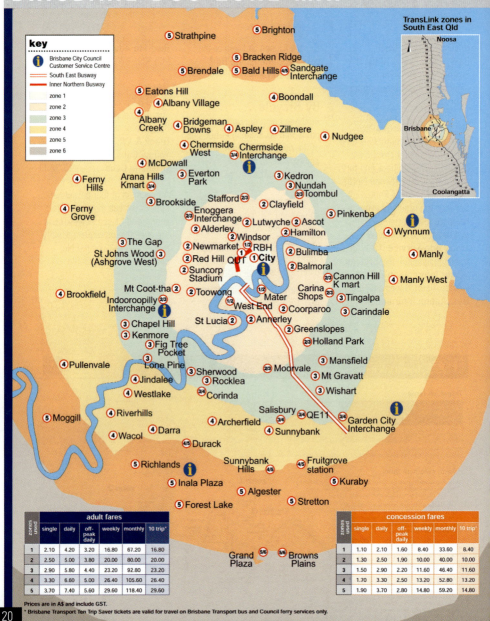

GETTING TO THE GABBA

If you've bought your Gabba Test ticket through Ticketmaster you're eligible for free travel to and from the match on Brisbane Transport buses and QR Citytrain rail services. All you need to do is flash your ticket!

Free shuttle buses will leave from outside Roma St Station (bus stop 125) for the Gabba at 5-10-minute intervals, picking up at Adelaide St opposite City Hall (bus stop 42A), then all busway stations to the Gabba, setting down in Stanley St outside Gates 1 and 2. At the conclusion of play for up to an hour, the free buses will leave Stanley St, between Wellington Rd and Ipswich Rd (opposite Gates 2 and 9), returning to the city (including South Bank and Roma St rail stations).

Ticketmaster ticket-holders will also be able to travel to the Gabba for free on specially chartered buses at 15-minute intervals from the Eight Mile Plains, Carindale and Chermside interchanges. These chartered buses will return via the same route after the match, leaving from platforms 1 and 2 of the Woolloongabba busway station and Main St (stop 9) respectively.

On Foot...
Located on Vulture St in Woolloongabba in southern Brisbane, the Gabba is a fair old hike from the city centre, so it's easier and quicker to take advantage of the public transport system which will be fully geared for the First Test.

As you approach the ground, remember that public entry is via Gates 4 and 7 at the Vulture St end of the venue, and Gates 2 and 9 at the Stanley St end.

By Bus...
The Gabba is serviced by two major bus stops, the Woolloongabba stop on Stanley St and the Woolloongabba stop on Logan Rd. Both terminals are only a two-minute walk to the gates of the Gabba and form part of the "Fiveways" road intersection.

Buses from all over Brisbane service these bus stops regularly, including every 15-20 minutes from the Myer Centre. From stop 41 on the corner of Adelaide/Albert St, look out for buses 116, 117, 124, 125, 230 and 235, while from stop 38 on the corner of Adelaide/Edward St hail buses 174, 175 and 204 to get to the ground.

By Train...
The nearest train stop to the Gabba is the Vulture St Station at South Bank, which is about a 15-minute walk to the ground (1.5km).

Only the Cleveland, Robina and Beenleigh lines have regular services to the ground, with all other lines connecting to Vulture St via Central Station.

By Taxi...
There are licensed ranks across Brisbane which will get you to the ground, as well as on Wellington Rd between Vulture St and Stanley St (eastern side of the Gabba) which will take you from the ground.
Otherwise call:
Yellow Cabs 13 19 24
Black & White Cabs..13 10 08
Brisbane Cabs............13 22 11

By Car...
If you bought your Brisbane Test ticket from Ticketmaster, all day parking is available for $10 (£4.20) in the South Bank Parklands underground car park or the Brisbane Convention Centre car park. Patrons can then catch a free shuttle to and from the ground, leaving from the South Bank or Cultural Centre Busway stations.

The Gabba is located south of Brisbane's city centre. Photo: Tourism Queensland.

BRISBANE

BRISBANE -ACCOMMODATION

The Conrad Treasury is one of Brisbane's finest hotels. Photo: Tourism Queensland.

HOSTELS

LOW-RANGE: < $100 (£42)

BRISBANE BACKPACKERS RESORT (pp34-35)
$22-$69 (£9-£29)
110 Vulture St, West End
1800 626 452 (free call within Australia) OR **(07) 3844 9956**
brisbanebackpackers.com.au

Brisbane Backpackers Resort is located near South Bank in the CBD, just a few minutes walk from the Brisbane Exhibition and Convention Centre and the Queensland Gallery of Modern Art. The Gabba is also within walking distance from the hostel (2.5km). The resort has great facilities, including a communal kitchen, laundry, restaurant, bar with big screen projector, pool with spa and a tennis court. Room rates are competitive - air-conditioned dorm rooms with ensuite bathroom start from $22 (£9) and double rooms with ensuite bathroom cost $69 (£28) per night.

BRISBANE CITY BACKPACKERS (pp34-35)
$17-$85 (£7-£35)
380 Upper Roma St, Brisbane
1800 062 572 (free call within Australia) OR **(07) 3211 3221**
citybackpackers.com

Brisbane City Backpackers is conveniently located in the city centre, just 400m from the Brisbane Transit Centre. And the Gabba is only 3km away. City Backpackers has excellent facilities including a roof-top swimming pool, a fully equipped communal kitchen, 24-hour laundry and internet access. The hostel also has a pub called The Fiddler's Elbow that offers great entertainment every night. City Backpackers has a broad range of accommodation available to suit every budget. The cheapest is in

www.ashes06.com

[**NOTE:** Hostels can be booked via www.hostelbookers.com or www.hostelworld.com. Hotels, motels and apartments can be booked via www.wotif.com.]

the big dorm rooms costing $17 (£7) per night, but if you're after comfort and privacy, you can book a single or double with ensuite, air-conditioning, TV and fridge from $85 (£35) per night.

CLOUD 9 BACKPACKERS RESORT (pp34-35)
$17-$71 (£7-£30)
350 Upper Roma St, Brisbane
1800 256 839 (free call within Australia) OR **(07) 3236 2300**
cloud9backpackers.com

Cloud 9 Backpackers Resort is the newest hostel Brisbane has to offer and is located in the heart of the city. If you're arriving or departing by interstate bus, it's only a five-minute walk from the Brisbane Transit Centre. The Gabba is also within 3km. The hostel has great facilities including a communal kitchen (open from 6am to midnight, seven days a week), laundromat with new washers and dryers, free luggage storage and 24-hour access so you are free to come and go as you please. Cloud 9 has various room types to suit all budgets. Prices range from the cheapest dorm beds at $17 (£7) per night to the more expensive twin deluxe air-conditioned with ensuite rooms from $71 (£30) per night.

PALACE BACKPACKERS
(pp34-35)
$23-$28 (£9-£12)
308 Edward St, Brisbane
1800 676 340 (free call within Australia) OR **(07) 3211 2433**
palacebackpackers.com.au

Palace Backpackers is housed in a heritage building and located only a block away from Brisbane's famous Queen St Mall, so you'll be able to check out Brisbane's premier shopping district as you make your way to the Gabba, which is also within walking distance (3km). Palace Backpackers has excellent facilities including a self-catering kitchen, laundry, internet access, TV rooms with satellite and a roof deck. The hostel offers a range of room types for all budgets. Dorm beds start at $23 (£9) per night and double bed privates cost $28 (£11) per person per night.

SOMEWHERE TO STAY (pp34-35)
$19-$67 (£8-£28)
47 Brighton Rd, Highgate Hill
1800 812 398 (free call within Australia) OR **(07) 3846 2858**
somewheretostay.com.au

Somewhere to Stay hostel is located in the cosmopolitan West End district, close to cafes, bookshops and restaurants, and only a short walk from the central South Bank Parklands and CBD. You'll find the Gabba is also within close distance (2.5km). Somewhere to Stay is a family run hostel with a great view of Brisbane's skyline. Nestled in lovely surrounds including a tropical garden and saltwater pool, the hostel has friendly staff and offers cable TV, internet access and luggage storage. The hostel has a variety of rooms with prices suiting all budgets. Room

types range from dorms - with beds starting at $19 (£8) per night - to deluxe double rooms (containing ensuite, TV and fridge) costing $67 (£28) per night.

HOTELS, MOTELS & APARTMENTS

LOW-RANGE: < $100 (£42)

LEOPARD LODGE (pp34-35)
$95-$200 (£40-£83)
41 Leopard St, Kangaroo Point
(07) 3392 0714
Reservations via email:
accom@leopardlodge.com.au

The **Leopard Lodge** is housed in a lovely heritage building located close to the scenic Kangaroo Point cliffs. The Gabba is conveniently only a block away (500m). The Leopard Lodge offers modest but comfortable accommodation. Rooms contain air-conditioning, large beds and internet access. Rates are very reasonable with queen rooms starting from $95 (£40) per night. Three-bedroom apartments (sleeping six people) are also available from $200 (£83) per night.

IL MONDO BOUTIQUE HOTEL
(pp34-35)
$99-$265 (£41-£110)
25-35 Rotherham St, Kangaroo Point
(07) 3891 5777
ilmondo.com.au

Il Mondo Boutique Hotel is located in the fashionable dockside precinct of Kangaroo Point and within walking distance of the Gabba (1.5km). The hotel's position also provides easy access to Brisbane's South Bank

continued overpage…

[ACCOMMODATION
...continued from page 23.

Parklands and the CBD. The hotel offers nice facilities that include a restaurant and wine bar. Il Mondo has a range of affordable boutique accommodation with great facilities. Standard rooms cost $99 (£41) per night, studio apartments cost $135 (£56) per night and two-bedroom apartments cost $265 (£110). Each room contains air-conditioning, TV with cable, ensuite bathroom and internet access.

MATER HILL PLACE (pp34-35)
$85-$120 (£35-£50)
1 Allen St, South Brisbane
1800 787 743 (free call within Australia) OR **(07) 3846 3144**
Reservations via email:
matermotel@iprimus.com.au

Mater Hill Place offers great value self-contained units in a nice location close to the attractions of Brisbane's South Bank. The Gabba is also conveniently within walking distance (500m). The apartments feature TV, kitchenettes, fridge, microwave and ensuite bathrooms. Single suites start from $85 (£35) per night, double suites start at $95 (£39) per night, twin suites start at $99 (£41) per night, while family suites are from $120 (£50) per night.

THE BROADWAY HOTEL
$11-$40 (£4-£17)
93 Logan Rd, Woolloongabba
(07) 3217 3469

The Broadway Hotel is within easy walking distance to the riverside restaurants and cafes of Brisbane's South Bank and only a stone's throw from the Gabba (900m). The Broadway Hotel has good facilities including a restaurant, bar, laundry, internet access, large beer garden, pool tables and travel desk. Room rates provide excellent value and suit all budgets dorm rooms start at $11 (£4.50) per night, double bed privates from $25 (£10.50) per person per night, while single privates will set you back $40 (£16.50) per night.

A1 MOTEL BRISBANE (pp34-35)
$75-$100 (£31-£42)
650 Main St, Kangaroo Point
(07) 3391 6222
a1motel.com.au

A1 Motel Brisbane is located in nice surrounds, adjacent a large inner city park, and close enough to the river to watch climbers scale the Kangaroo Point cliffs. The Gabba is also conveniently close by (500m) - a five-minute walk down main street will get you there.
A1 Motel Brisbane offers great value accommodation: doubles start from $75 (£31) per night, twins from $90 (£38) per night and triples from $100 (£42). All rooms contain air-conditioning, ensuite, TV and mini fridge.

SAPPHIRE RESORT (pp34-35)
$85-$109 (£35-£46)
55 Boundary St, South Brisbane
(07) 3217 2588
Reservations via email:
sapphireresort@iinet.net.au

The **Sapphire Resort** is located in South Brisbane conveniently close to the Brisbane Exhibition and Convention Centre, the restaurants and cafes of South Bank and the Museum and Art Gallery. You'll find the Gabba is also within manageable walking distance (2.5km). The Sapphire is a resort-style complex offering serviced rooms, complimentary off-street undercover parking, laundry, swimming pool and a restaurant.
Rooms contain good standard facilities, including reverse cycle air-conditioning, ensuite bathroom and TV. Rates are great value: twin rooms cost $85 (£35), while family suites and triple rooms start from $109 (£46).

HOTELS, MOTELS & APARTMENTS

MID-RANGE: $100-$200 (£42-£84)

DOCKSIDE CENTRAL APARTMENT HOTEL (pp34-35)
$165-$180 (£68-£75)
44 Ferry St, Kangaroo Point
(07) 3891 6644
stellaresorts.com.au

Dockside Central Apartment Hotel complex provides fantastic views of the Brisbane River and city. It's also close to the Kangaroo Point cliffs and Riverlife Adventure Centre. The Gabba is easily accessible on foot (1.5km). Dockside Central offers spacious one and two-bedroom apartments and has great hotel facilities, including conference rooms, outdoor pool, tennis court and restaurants. Room amenities are high quality and include air-conditioning, TV and self-contained kitchen. Apartment rates are good value: one-bedroom apartments start at

$165 (£68) per night, with two-bedroom apartments from $180 (£75) per night.

THE POINT BRISBANE
(pp34-35)
$148-$260 (£61-£108)
21 Lambert St, Kangaroo Point
1800 088 388 (free call within Australia) OR **(07) 3240 0888**
thepointbrisbane.com.au

The **Point Brisbane** is one of Brisbane's newest hotels. It is located in the city's south, with great views of the Brisbane River and scenic Kangaroo Point. The Gabba is conveniently close by and within easy walking distance (1km). The Point offers the latest in hotel services and facilities, including 24-hour reception and room service, travel desk, gym, heated swimming pool, tennis court and restaurant. The Point has a wide range of accommodation types to suit different budgets. Studio hotel rooms (1-2 people) start from $148 (£61) per night, one-bedroom apartments (1-2 people) start at $190 (£79) per night, while two-bedroom apartments (up to four people) cost $260 (£108) per night. Hotel rooms and apartments contain high quality amenities, including kitchenette, air-conditioning, mini bar, broadband internet access and satellite TV.

KANGAROO POINT HOLIDAY APARTMENTS (pp34-35)
$88-$175 (£36-£73)
819 Main St, Kangaroo Point
1800 676 855 (free call within Australia) OR **07 3391 6855**
kangaroopoint.com

Kangaroo Point Holiday Apartments offer affordable yet stylish self-contained apartments conveniently situated within easy walking distance of the Gabba (200m), the Kangaroo Point cliffs and the cafes and restaurants of South Bank. The apartments are fitted with high quality facilities, including air-conditioning, living room, TV, fully equipped kitchen, internet access and a pool. One-bedroom apartments at 3-4-star quality (1-2 people) start at $88 (£36) per night, two-bedroom apartments (1-5 people) start from $121 per night (£50), while four-bedroom apartments (1-7 people) start at $175 (£73) per night. Kangaroo Point Holiday Apartments also offer four-star, two-bedroom apartments (1-4 people) from $132 (£55) per night.

QUEST BRIDGEWATER
(pp34-35)
$140-$320 (£58-£133)
55 Baildon St, Kangaroo Point
(07) 3391 5300
questbridgewater.com.au

The **Quest Bridgewater** is a luxury apartment complex found in a lush tropical garden. Its great position also provides access to

continued overpage...

Brisbane at night. Photo: Tourism Queensland.

BRISBANE

ACCOMMODATION
...continued from page 25.

the Kangaroo Point entertainment district and the Gabba, which is just a short stroll away (1.5km). The Quest Bridgewater features great facilities including a lagoon style pool, spa, sauna, gym and barbecue area. Apartments contain fully equipped kitchens, laundry, air-conditioning, fax/modem phone line and TV. Apartments and suites are great value: studio apartments (two people) start at $140 (£58) per night, one-bedroom apartments (two people) start at $175 (£73) per night, two-bedroom apartments (four people) start at $225 (£94) per night, while three-bedroom apartments (six people) start at $320 (£133) per night.

RYANS ON THE RIVER (pp34-35)
$89-$159 (£37-£66)
269 Main St, Kangaroo Point
(07) 3391 1011
Reservations via email:
reservations@ryans.com.au
ryans.com.au

Ryans On The River is a boutique hotel located on the banks of the Brisbane River, offering gorgeous views of the city and surrounds. Its location close to the city centre, the cafes and restaurants of thriving New Farm and the Gabba (1km) make it a convenient choice. Ryans' quality hotel facilities include a saltwater pool with a unique breakfast restaurant on the pool deck, a tour desk, laundry, babysitting service and private lounge. Ryans' has rooms to suit all budgets: budget rooms start at $89 (£37) per night, standard rooms start at $139 (£58) per night, while Riverview rooms start at $159 (£66) per night. All rooms contain air-conditioning, TV, ensuite and key card security access.

HOTELS, MOTELS & APARTMENTS

HIGH-RANGE: $200+ (£84+)

CONRAD TREASURY MARRIOTT (pp34-35)
$400-$1300 (£166-£541)
130 William St, Brisbane
1800 506 889 (free call within Australia) OR **(07) 3306 8888**
conrad.com.au

Conrad Treasury Marriott offers the ultimate in luxury and style. One of Brisbane's finest hotels, it can be found in a great location at the top of Queen St Mall with fantastic views of the Brisbane River. The Gabba is within close proximity (2.4km), as is the Brisbane Convention and Exhibition Centre and restaurants of fashionable South Bank. The Conrad Treasury is an award-winning hotel containing five separate restaurants offering a variety of choices from five-star silver service to low-key café dining. Rooms at the Conrad offer state-of-the-art facilities, including air-conditioning, TV, lavish private bathroom, bar and refrigerator. Room types and accommodation rates range from deluxe king rooms starting at $400 (£166) per night to the Parkview Gallery Suite at $1300 (£541) per night.

PACIFIC INTERNATIONAL APARTMENTS (pp34-35)
$230-$360 (£95-£150)
570 Queen St, Brisbane
1800 224 584 (free call within Australia) OR **(07) 3234 8888**
pacificinthotels.com

Pacific International Apartments can be found in a fantastic location right in the heart of Brisbane's CBD. It is close to the entertainment and dining options in the thriving city centre and within walking distance to Fortitude Valley - the cultural heart of Brisbane. A short taxi ride taking in the pleasant Botanic Gardens and Brisbane River will get you to the Gabba. The Pacific International offers spacious and stylish apartments and suites featuring fully equipped kitchens, large bathrooms, air-conditioning and internet access. Hotel and apartment rates are very affordable: hotel rooms start at $230 (£95) per night, one-bedroom apartments start at $270 (£112) per night and two-bedroom apartments from $360 (£150) per night.

STAMFORD PLAZA BRISBANE
(pp34-35)
$520-$3500 (£216-£1458)
Cnr Edward & Margaret Sts, Brisbane
(07) 3221 1999
Reservations via email:
sales@spb.stamford.com.au
stamford.com.au

Stamford Plaza Brisbane is one of Brisbane's premier luxury hotels. You'll find it in a stunning location, metres from the Botanic Gardens on the banks of the Brisbane River. The Gabba is also within walking distance (2km), as is the city centre. All rooms at the Stamford Plaza offer superb views of the city skyline, the Brisbane River and the Kangaroo Point cliffs. Each are fitted with high quality facilities, including large beds, lavish marble bathrooms, cable TV, laundry service and broadband internet access. The hotel itself boasts several restaurants with a range of fine to less formal dining options. The Stamford Plaza offers ongoing specials so it's worth checking out their website (stamford.com.au). Superior king/twin rooms start at $520 (£216) per night, deluxe king rooms $570 (£237) per night, junior suites $790 (£329) per night, while the Presidential Suite will cost you $3500 (£1458) per night.

RYDGES SOUTH BANK (pp34-35)
$350-$545 (£146-£227)
9 Glenelg St, South Bank
1300 857 922 (free call within Australia) OR **(02) 9261 4929**
rydges.com

As the name suggests, the **Rydges South Bank** is located in Brisbane's South Bank, the heart of the flourishing entertainment and arts districts of the West End, just a few metres from the Brisbane Exhibition and Convention Centre. You'll also be able to walk the short distance to the Gabba (1.5km) through the scenic parklands. Rydges South Bank has undergone a $6.5 million (£2.7 million) refurbishment so you can expect high quality facilities, including a fitness area containing gym, spa and sauna. The hotel also features a variety of dining and bar areas. Rooms are well presented and contain remote control TV, air-conditioning, refrigerator and mini bar. Standard queens start at $350 (£146) per night, superior queens $370 (£154) per night and one-bedroom suites $545 (£227) per night.

SOFITEL BRISBANE (pp34-35)
$432-$576 (£180-£240)
249 Turbot St, Brisbane
(07) 3835 3535 sofitel.com

You'll find the **Sofitel Brisbane**, one of the city's finest hotels, situated just minutes from the entertainment and shopping precinct of the Queen St Mall and the restaurants and bars of the Eagle St Pier, which also has an arts and crafts market every Sunday. The Gabba is also just 3km away. The Sofitel has first-rate hotel facilities, including a fitness room, outdoor swimming pool, sauna, spa and a dry cleaning service. It also boasts three separate bar areas and a restaurant famous for its fresh seafood and international cuisine. Rooms contain the latest amenities including air-conditioning, satellite TV and mini bar. Room rates suit different budgets: a classic king starts at $432 (£180) per night, a Sofitel club king room costs $497 (£207) per night, while the top of the range Sofitel suite will set you back $576 (£240) per night.

Enjoy a drink at the Story Bridge Hotel while you're in Brisbane. Photo: Tourism Queensland.

Brisbane offers excellent riverside dining. Photo: Tourism Queensland.

[BRISBANE -RESTAURANTS

NORTH OF THE GABBA

> The Breakfast Creek Hotel has earned iconic status as Brisbane's most well-known pub eatery. This is largely to do with the groundbreaking nature of the pub's history. It was the first hotel to incorporate beer garden style dining in the late 1940s and the first to construct a drive-through bottle shop in the 1960s. Of course, the thing it's most famous for is being the first pub in Brisbane to introduce an outdoor kitchen in the late 1960s, where customers could choose their own steaks from a chilled cabinet and have them barbecued. Pay a visit to the Breakfast Creek and you'll see that this tradition remains today, as patrons line up to have an aged fillet superbly char-grilled in an open kitchen.
**2 Kingsford Smith Dve, Breakfast Creek
(07) 3262 5988
Mains $17-$25 (£7-£10)**

> The Bow Thai Restaurant is located in flourishing Fortitude Valley, close to the boutiques and designer dress shops of Brunswick St Mall. Relocation to larger premises in 1999 helped the Bow Thai make it into the Thai Restaurant Association's top 10 Australian restaurants in 2000, and it has maintained this high standard ever since. The Bow Thai serves authentic Thai cuisine at affordable prices, making it a favourite among Fortitude Valley locals. The restaurant offers BYO for bottled wine and beer and charges corkage of $1.50 (60p) per person.
Shop 14 Cathedral Place

www.ashes06.com

(Cnr Wickham St/Gipps St),
Fortitude Valley
(07) 3216 1700
(pp34-35)
Mains $12-$20 (£5-£8)

The multi award-winning **Cha Cha Char Wine Bar & Grill** is commonly regarded as Australia's superlative steak restaurant. You'll find it located on the Eagle St Pier - Brisbane's veritable heartland of refined restaurant dining. Cha Cha Char specialises in beef and prides itself on delivering steak perfection. You are guaranteed a unique dining experience as staff expertly inform you of a steak's breed, age and the feeding regime it was raised on. Cha Cha Char also caters for patrons preferring non-beef dishes with a large selection of vegetarian and seafood meals.
Eagle St Pier, Brisbane
(07) 3211 9944
(pp34-35)
Mains $27-$50 (£11-£21)

> **Customs House Restaurant** offers excellent international inspired cuisine amid elegant surrounds inside the heritage-registered Customs House building. Dating back to 1888, Customs House has been fully restored to its former architectural glory thanks to the financial backing of the University of Queensland. Aside from the high quality restaurant, Customs House also encompasses boardrooms,

function rooms and an exquisite ballroom, which you can view on a guided tour. You'll find Customs House right on the waterfront, providing delightful views of the Brisbane River and conveniently just a block away from Queen St Mall.
399 Queen St, Brisbane
(07) 3365 8921
(pp34-35)
Mains $25-$35 (£10-£14)

> **Il Centro Restaurant and Bar** is a local and national award-winner located on the fashionable Eagle St Pier. You'll have excellent views of the Brisbane River and Story Bridge whether you dine alfresco or indoor. Il Centro serves tantalising modern Italian cuisine but maintains a commitment to using fresh Australian produce. Il Centro also incorporates a fantastic bar, added during renovations in 2000, which is frequented by the after-work crowd.
Eagle St Pier, Brisbane
(07) 3221 6090
(pp34-35)
Mains $12-$40 (£5-£16)

> A great way to enjoy the stunning views of the Brisbane River and the city scape while enjoying a high quality buffet, is to book your place on one of the **Kookaburra River Queens**. Soak up the sights on a lunch cruise which leaves Eagle St Pier at 12pm (returns 2pm), or if you prefer bright lights, reserve a

spot on the dinner cruise which departs at 7pm (returns 10.30pm).
Eagle St Pier, Brisbane
(07) 3221 1300
(pp34-35)
Mains $25-$75 (£10-£31)

If you're looking for a modern Australian menu infused with European influences, then try the award-winning **Vino's Restaurant & Bar** located on the popular Eagle St Pier. Vino's features a 180-degree balcony that offers fantastic views overlooking the Brisbane River and beyond, with the venue priding itself on using primarily fresh local produce to create dishes that are exceptional in taste. Sunday nights are always a great time to drop in to hear some fantastic jazz numbers and sample a few mouth-watering tapas.
Eagle St Pier, Brisbane
(07) 3221 0811
(pp34-35)
Mains $25-$43 (£10-£17)

WEST
OF THE GABBA

> **Gambaro Restaurant** is a well-established seafood restaurant and winner of six American Express Gold Plate Awards. You'll find it located on thriving Caxton St - the home of the popular Caxton St Seafood & Wine Festival, which draws huge crowds eager to sample the

continued overpage...

[RESTAURANTS

...continued from page 29.

fantastic food and enjoy the great entertainment. Gambaro Restaurant offers delicious seafood dishes; you'll be able to sample Queensland's famous Moreton Bay bugs or green lobster chosen directly from the tank. The huge seafood platter accompanied by Gambaro's renowned seafood sauce is also a firm favourite amongst patrons.
33 Caxton St, Milton
(07) 3369 9500
(pp34-35)
Mains $20-$40 (£8-£16)

> Sitar Indian Restaurant, located in Brisbane's funky West End, is a first-rate Indian restaurant that forms part of the Sitar chain - a popular choice for many Brisbane locals. Using tried and tested methods, chefs recapture the great flavours of traditional North Indian cuisine. Depending on your mood, you can enjoy a mild korma or spicy vindaloo.
195 Melbourne St, West End
(07) 3846 7271
(pp34-35)
Mains $15-$19 (£6-£8)

> Chinese restaurant, the Wang Dynasty, is a dining hot spot for Brisbane's locals. Located in the thriving entertainment precinct of South Bank, the Wang Dynasty features an outdoor terrace and dining room that provides fabulous views of the Brisbane River and city. The Wang Dynasty serves a delicious variety of dishes that incorporate traditional Chinese flavours. Vegetarians aren't disappointed either with fantastic non-meat options, but if you're after a Chinese and Australian blend - and feel daring - try the kangaroo or crocodile dishes.
Riverside Restaurant Building,
South Bank Parklands,
South Brisbane
(07) 3844 8318
(pp34-35)
Mains $15-$25 (£6-£10)

Brisbane is big on alfresco areas. Photo: Tourism Queensland.

Cru Bar & Cellar in Fortitude Valley. Photo: Tourism Queensland.

BRISBANE -PUBS & CLUBS

PUBS

NORTH OF THE GABBA

The Story Bridge Hotel is one of Brisbane's last remaining family-owned and operated hotels. Established in 1886, it was originally called the Kangaroo Point Hotel, but underwent a name change in 1940 to mark the opening of the Story Bridge. Today, it is an icon, tempting patrons from all walks of life. The Story Bridge Hotel offers three separate bar areas to suit different tastes. These include the trendy Corner Bar which serves a wide selection of beers, wines and cocktails, the relaxed Outback Bar containing a beer garden and dining area, and the suave Shelter Bar, uniquely placed directly under the Story Bridge and containing five plasma screen TVs - so you'll be able to catch all the Ashes highlights!
200 Main St, Kangaroo Point
(pp34-35) **(07) 3391 2266**

The Pineapple Hotel was built in 1864 amongst the pineapple plantations of Kangaroo Point. Today, it's a thriving venue featuring four distinct pub areas, including the recently refurbished Lounge Bar, which serves great Australian pub fare, and the Sports Bar which contains a heap of memorabilia, TAB and seven TV screens. Joe's Bar upstairs is fitted with comfy lounges, a big screen TV and pool tables, while the hotel also features a relaxed undercover beer garden. Another attraction is the venue's award-winning Steakhouse, which never ceases to attract an abundance of diners.
706 Main St, Kangaroo Point
(pp34-35) **(07) 3393 1111**

Not to be confused with the Regatta Hotel's St Arnou Street Café is the sophisticated St Arnou Beer Café found on the fashionable Eagle St Pier overlooking stunning views of the Brisbane River. Located right in the heart of the city, St Arnou Beer Café has a restaurant that

continued overpage…

PUBS AND CLUBS
...continued from page 31.

serves modern Australian cuisine in a pleasant and relaxed setting. At the bar you can sample premium "Australian-brewed European styled" beers, including the entire St Arnou range featuring St Arnou Pale Ale, St Arnou St Cloud, St Arnou Kildara, St Arnou Premium Blonde and St Arnou Pilsner. You'll also be able to try a comprehensive assortment of Australian and imported beers on tap or in the bottle.
Upper Level, Eagle St Pier, Brisbane
(pp34-35) **(07) 3229 0922**

Union Jack's Ale House incorporates a British theme and is the place to go in Brisbane if you're a Barmy Army fan. The pub is split into four different sections, with memorabilia representing England, Ireland, Scotland and Wales. Union Jack's Ale House has a great selection of beers including 12 UK brews on tap. You'll also be able to catch up on all the Premier League action and results from all European sports, not to mention the Ashes highlights on the large screen TVs.
127 Charlotte St, Brisbane
(pp34-35) **(07) 3210 1172**

SOUTH
OF THE GABBA

Cavill's Norman Hotel, which was built in the late 1880s, is run by the Cavill family and has a reputation for serving top quality steaks. Aside from its famous steakhouse, you will also find it incorporates great hotel facilities, including a gaming room and drive-through bottle shop. Cavill's has three excellent bar areas. You can take your pick from the newly refurbished Cav's Bar, which always shows live sport so you'll be able to view all the Ashes highlights, the popular Top Bar where you'll find cold beer on tap and great coffees and desserts, or if you're looking to dine alfresco in the gorgeous Queensland sun, try the ultra-modern Garden Bar.
102 Ipswich Rd, Woolloongabba
(07) 3391 5022

WEST
OF THE GABBA

The stylish **Chalk Hotel** is a newly established bar conveniently located just a few blocks from the Gabba. It boasts three floors and features several chic areas for socialising, plus indoor and alfresco dining. Depending on your mood, you can choose between five different bars, including the vibrant Sticks bar and restaurant located at the front of the hotel. The comfortable Stumps bar and restaurant found at the rear of the hotel is also good value, as is the upstairs Powder Room for a more low-key, intimate setting. Cocktails are also served in Dust, which boasts an extensive drinks menu sure to please.
735 Stanley St, Woolloongabba
(pp34-35) **(07) 3896 6565**

The **Normanby Hotel** is an architecturally stunning, heritage-registered hotel steeped in rich colonial history. Once constructed as a centre for horse-drawn tram traffic, it also served as a station on Brisbane's first suburban rail line. Today, it easily stands out as one of the best value pubs Brisbane has to offer, making it a popular venue for locals to enjoy a tasty pub meal and quiet drink with friends. Recent renovations have also seen it emerge as a premier venue for functions.
1 Musgrave Rd, Red Hill
(pp34-35) **(07) 3831 3353**

The **Regatta Hotel** is a heritage-registered pub, named in honour of the rowing regattas that took place on the Brisbane River during the 1840s. If you visit the hotel you can experience its rich history with a 30-minute guided tour, which will take you back through time to the rowing regattas, the destructive floods of 1893 and 1974, the feminist protests of the 1960s and the colonial past of the suburb of Toowong. The Regatta Hotel incorporates two distinct dining areas - the Boatshed Restaurant which serves modern Australian fare and St Arnou Street Café which serves delicious meals in a relaxed alfresco atmosphere.
543 Coronation Dve, Toowong
(07) 3871 9595

www.ashes06.com

Having fun on Brisbane River. Photo: Tourism Queensland.

CLUBS
NORTH OF THE GABBA

The Zoo started life in 1992 as merely a café and pool hall. Today, it is one of Brisbane's ultimate live music venues. Located in Fortitude Valley, and close to the avant-garde suburb of New Farm, The Zoo caters for all tastes, playing host to some fantastic local and international acts. The Zoo presents a diverse range of music, including jazz, pop, reggae, electronic and hip-hop every Wednesday, Saturday and some Sunday nights. The Zoo also features a dance club so you can get down to the wee hours of the morning.
711 Ann St,
Fortitude Valley
(pp34-35) **(07) 3854 1381**

The Family Nightclub is Brisbane's ultimate party venue, voted best Australian club for the past three years by *Australian Bartender Magazine*. It consists of four levels where you can choose between techno, house, R & B or chilled retro, so you'll have no problem finding the right beats to suit your mood. Family opens at 9pm and doesn't close until 5am on Friday and Saturday nights. Entry costs around $8-$15 (£3-£7). The dress code is casual - you'll be admitted wearing jeans and trainers - so you can happily leave the suit at home!
8 McLachlan St,
Fortitude Valley
(pp34-35) **(07) 3852 5000**

Another fantastic club located in Brisbane's vibrant Valley district is Monastery Nightclub. Recent renovations have made Monastery a favourite venue for clubbers, particularly as it regularly attracts big name DJs from Australia and all over the world. Monastery oozes style with its swish lounge areas and booths, large dance arena, modern observation deck and curved bar incorporating eye-catching stained glass windows. Monastery has a $10-$15 cover charge (£4-£7) and is open until 5am on Thursday, Friday, Saturday and Sunday nights.
621 Ann St, Fortitude Valley
(pp34-35) **(07) 3257 7081**

BRISBANE CITY MAP

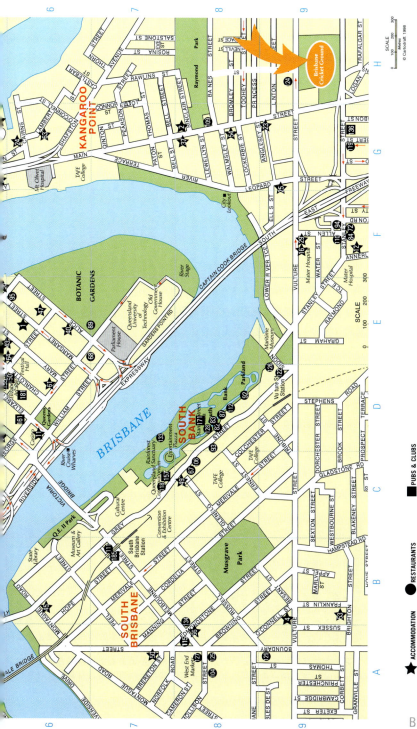

BRISBANE CITY MAP (pp34-35)

- Denotes multiple venue

ACCOMMODATION KEY

#	Ref	Name	Address	Phone	Website	$ Cost per night	RATE Star rating	OVAL Kilometres from GABBA
1	E6	212 on Margaret	212 Margaret St, Brisbane, 4000	07 3012 8020	www.212margaretst.com.au	185-280	*****	3.26
2	G7	A1 Motel Brisbane	650 Main St, Kangaroo Point, 4169	07 3391 6222	www.a1motel.com.au	75-100	***	1.08
3	D3	Astor Apartments	35 Astor Tce, Spring Hill, 4000	07 3839 9022	www.astorapartments.com.au	110-200	****	3.56
4	B9	Brisbane Backpackers Resort	110 Vulture St, West End, 4101	07 3844 9956	www.brisbanebackpackers.com.au	20-69		3.41
5	A5	Brisbane City Backpackers	380 Upper Roma St, Brisbane, 4000	07 3844 9956	www.brisbanebackpackers.com.au	17-85		4.64
6	A5	Brisbane City YHA Lodge	392 Upper Roma St, Brisbane, 4000	07 3236 1004	www.yha.com	24-81		4.66
7	F2	Bunk Brisbane	11-21 Gipps St, Fortitude Valley, 4006	07 3257 3644	www.bunkbrisbane.com.au	18-140		3.55
8	C5	Carlton Crest Hotels	Cnr Roma & Ann St, Brisbane, 4000	07 3229 9111	www.carltonhotels.com.au	155-255	*****	3.21
9	G2	Central Brunswick Apartment Hotel	455 Brunswick St, Fortitude Valley, 4006	07 3852 1411	www.centralbrunswickhotel.com.au	140	****	4.13
10	A5	Cloud 9 Backpackers Resort	350 Upper Roma St, Brisbane, 4000	07 3236 2333	www.cloud9backpackers.com.au	17-71		4.57
11	D6	Conrad Treasury Brisbane	130 William St, Brisbane, 4000	07 3306 8888	www.conradtreasury.com.au	400-1300	******	3.26
12	F9	Diana Plaza Hotel	12 Annerley Rd, Woolloongabba, 4102	07 3391 2911	www.dianaplaza.com	145-225	****	1.60
13	G5	Dockside Central Apartment Hotel	44 Ferry St, Kangaroo Point, 4169	07 3891 6644	www.central-apartments.com.au	165-240		2.18
14	C5	Explorers Inns	63 Turbot St, Brisbane, 4000	07 3211 3488	www.explorers.com.au	109-150	***	3.54
15	F2	FV 4006 Apartments	Berwick St, Fortitude Valley, 4006	07 3251 1200	www.fv4006.com.au	180		3.47
16	F9	Hillcrest Central	311 Vulture St, South Brisbane, 4101	07 3846 3000	www.central-apartments.com.au	140-295	****	2.42
17	D5	Hilton International	190 Elizabeth St, Brisbane, 4000	07 3234 2000	www.hilton.com	147-410	******	3.68
18	C5	Holiday Inn	Roma St, Brisbane, 4000	03 3238 2222	www.holiday-inn.com	270-310	****	4.59
19	C3	Hotel Grand Chancellor	23 Leichhardt St, Brisbane, 4000	07 3831 4055	www.ghihotels.com	165	****	4.73
20	C5	Hotel Ibis Brisbane	27-35 Turbot St, Brisbane, 4000	07 3237 2333	www.accorhotels.com.au	99-169		3.16
21	B3	Hotel Watermark	551 Wickham Tce, Spring Hill, 4000	07 3831 3111	www.hotelwatermark.com.au	145-180	****	5.07
22	G4	Il Mondo Boutique Hotel	25-35 Rotherham St, Kangaroo Point, 4169	07 3891 5777	www.ilmondo.com.au	99-265	****	2.23
23	G8	Kangaroo Point Holiday Apartments	819 Main St, Kangaroo Point, 4169	07 3391 6855	www.kangaroopoint.com	88-230	****	0.68
24	G6	Lagoon Apartments	26 Cairns St, Kangaroo Point, 4169	07 3392 2700	www.lagoonapartments.com.au	175-240	****	1.79
25	G9	Leopard Lodge	41 Leopard St, Kangaroo Point, 4169	07 3392 0714	www.leopardlodge.com.au	95-200		1.04
26	E4	Lexicon Apartments	Cnr Ann & Wharf St, Brisbane, 4000	07 3222 4999	www.theoaksgroup.com.au	190-280	****	4.76
27	E5	MacArthur Chambers Heritage Apart.	201 Edward St, Brisbane, 4000	07 3221 9229	www.macarthurchambers.com.au	140-517	*****	4.57
28	E3	Marriott Brisbane	515 Queen St, Brisbane, 4000	07 3303 8000	www.marriott.com	225-565	******	4.49
29	F9	Mater Hill Place Motel	1 Allen St, South Brisbane, 4101	07 3846 3144	www.goldenchain.com.au	85-120		1.76
30	F2	Medina Serviced Apartments	15 Ivory Lane, Brisbane, 4000	07 3218 5800	www.medina.com.au	170-730		3.29
31	C5	Mercure Hotel Brisbane	85-87 North Quay, Brisbane, 4000	07 3237 2300	www.mercurebrisbane.com.au	135-409	****	3.11
32	C4	Metro Hotel Tower Mill	239 Wickham Tce, Brisbane, 4000	07 3832 1421	www.towermill.com.au	99-129	****	3.69
33	B5	North Quay Apartments	293 North Quay, Brisbane, 4000	07 3236 1440	www.theoaksgroup.com.au	125-280	****	4.89
34	D3	Novotel Brisbane	200 Creek St, Brisbane, 4000	07 3309 3309	www.novotelbrisbane.com	165-315		4.38
35	E3	Pacific International Hotels	570 Queen St, Brisbane, 4000	07 3234 8888	www.pacificinthotels.com	230-360	****	3.61
36	D4	Palace Backpackers	308 Edward St, Brisbane, 4000	07 3211 2433	www.palacebackpackers.com.au	20-56		4.29
37	G8	Paramount Motel & Serviced Apart.	649 Main St, Kangaroo Point, 4169	07 3393 1444	www.paramountmotel.com.au	72-85		1.08
38	E2	Prince Consort Backpackers	230 Wickham St, Fortitude Valley, 4006	07 3257 2252	www.princeconsort.com.au	24-30		3.64
39	D4	Quality Hotel The Inchcolm	73 Wickham Tce, Spring Hill, 4000	07 3226 8888	www.inchcolmhotel.com.au	170-220	****	4.47

www.ashes06.com

#	Map	Name	Address	Phone	Web	Rooms	Stars	Rating
40	E6	Quay West Suites	132 Alice St, Brisbane, 4000	07 3853 6000	www.mirvachotels.com.au	251-315	*****	3.41
41	G4	Quest Bridgewater	55 Baildon St, Kangaroo Point, 4169	07 3391 5300	www.questbridgewater.com.au	140-320	****	2.38
42	G5	Quest on Story Bridge	85 Deakin St, Kangaroo Point, 4169	07 3249 8400	www.queststorybridge.com.au	165-260	****	2.25
43	E6	Quest River Park Central	120 Mary St, Brisbane, 4000	07 3838 1000	www.questriverparkcentral.com.au	195-260	*****	3.38
44	D4	Rendezvous Hotel Brisbane	255 Ann St, Brisbane, 4000	07 3001 9888	www.rendezvoushotels.com.au	132-270	****	3.22
45	B6	Riverside Hotel Southbank	20 Montague Rd, South Brisbane, 4101	07 3846 0577	www.riversidehotel.com.au	125-225	****	4.61
46	E4	Rothbury on Ann	301 Ann St, Brisbane, 4000	07 3239 8888	www.rothburyhotel.com	189-270	*****	4.90
47	E6	Royal on the Park	Cnr Alice & Albert St, Brisbane, 4000	07 3221 3411	www.royalonthepark.com.au	150-215	*****	3.69
48	G5	Ryans on the River	269 Main St, Kangaroo Point, 4169	07 3391 1011	www.ryans.com.au	89-159	****	2.00
49	C8	Rydges South Bank	Grey St, South Bank, 4101	07 3364 0800	www.rydges.com	250-545	*****	2.93
50	A7	Sapphire Resort	55 Boundary St, South Brisbane, 4101	07 3217 2588	www.sapphireresort.com.au	85-109	*****	4.78
51	E1	Snooze Inn Fortitude Valley	383 St Pauls Tce, Fortitude Valley, 4004	07 3620 4800	www.snoozeinn.com.au	79-115	***	3.96
52	D4	Sofitel Brisbane	249 Turbot St, Brisbane, 4000	07 3835 3535	www.sofitelbrisbane.com.au	430-576	*****	4.00
53	B9	Somewhere to Stay	47 Brighton Rd, Highgate Hill, 4101	07 3846 2858	www.somewheretostay.com.au	19-67	****	3.51
54	G8	Southern Cross Motel	721 Main St, Kangaroo Point, 4169	07 3391 2881	www.constellationhotels.com	75-170		0.90
55	D1	Spring Hill Terraces	260 Water St, Spring Hill, 4004	07 3854 1048	www.springhillterraces.com	65-120	****	4.23
56	E5	Stamford Plaza Brisbane	Cnr Edward & Margaret St, Brisbane, 4000	07 3221 1999	www.stamford.com.au	520-3500	*****	3.43
57	G5	Story Bridge Motor Inn	321 Main St, Kangaroo Point, 4169	07 3393 1433		76-190	***	1.80
58	C3	Summit Central Apartments	32 Leichhardt St, Spring Hill, 4006	07 3839 7000	www.centralgroup.com.au	145-250	****	4.73
59	C4	Terraces on Wickham	345 Wickham Tce, Brisbane, 4000	07 3831 6177	www.accorhotels.com.au	99-263		4.73
60	D5	The Chifley at Lennons, Brisbane	66 Queen St Mall, Brisbane, 4000	07 3222 3222	www.chifleyhotels.com	345-391	*****	2.64
61	D6	The Chifley on George, Brisbane	103 George St, Brisbane, 4000	07 3221 6044	www.chifleyhotels.com	311-368	****	3.13
62	D4	The Manor Apartment Hotel	289 Queen St, Brisbane, 4000	07 3319 4700	www.manorapartments.com.au	160-300	****	4.13
63	G6	The Point Brisbane	21 Lambert St, Kangaroo Point, 4169	07 3240 0888	www.thepointbrisbane.com.au	148-260	*****	1.69
64	E6	The Sebel Suites Brisbane	Cnr Albert & Charlotte St, Brisbane, 4000	07 3224 3500	www.mirvachotels.com.au	171-207	*****	4.03
65	C5	Tinbilly Travellers	462 George St, Brisbane, 4000	07 3238 5888	www.tinbilly.com	27-28		4.01
66	B8	Westend Central	220 Melbourne St, West End, 4101	07 3011 8333	www.central-apartments.com.au	155-295	*****	4.62

continued overpage...

BRISBANE MAPS

BRISBANE CITY MAP (pp34-35)

RESTAURANTS KEY

#	Ref	Name	Address	Phone	Website	Cuisine	$ Cost of main meal	BYO
67	C8	CBD Café Bar	Grey St, South Brisbane, 4101	07 3364 0877	www.rydges.com	Modern Australian	14-34	N
73	E5	Arnou Beer Café	Eagle St Pier, Brisbane, 4000	07 3229 0922	www.starnoubeercafe.com.au	Modern Australian	18-30	N
68	E6	Augustines on George	40 George St, Brisbane, 4000	07 3221 9365	www.brisbane.citysearch.com.au	A la carte	28-33	N
69	F1	Bar Soma	4/22 Constance St, Fortitude Valley, 4006	07 3252 9550	www.barsoma.com	French/Modern Aus	24-28	N
70	E5	Belgian Beer Café	Cnr Edward & Mary St, Brisbane, 4000	07 3221 0199	www.belgianbeercafebrussels.com.au	Modern Australian	22-32	N
71	F2	Belushi's	336 Brunswick St, Fortitude Valley, 4006	07 3252 3424	www.belushis.com.au	International	7-17	Y
72	F9	Bengal Curry Restaurant	609 Stanley St, Woolloongabba, 4102	07 3891 1034		Indian	11-16	Y
44	D4	Berkley's on Ann	255 Ann St, Brisbane, 4000	07 3220 1022	www.berkleys.com.au	A la carte	22-35	N
11	D6	Blackjacks	Treasury Casino, Brisbane, 4000	07 3306 8888	www.conrad.com.au	Modern Australian	11-26	N
66	E2	Bombay Dhaba	220 Melbourne St, South Brisbane, 4101	07 3846 6662		Indian	10-25	Y wine-$1pp corkage
76	E2	Bow Thai	Cathedral Place, Fortitude Valley, 4006	07 3216 1700		Thai	12-20	Y beer & wine-corkage
77	E5	Brasserie on the River	Margaret St, Brisbane, 4000	07 3221 1999	www.stamford.com.au	Modern Australian	17-35	N
9	G2	Bravo Wine Bar & Bistro	455 Brunswick St, Fortitude Valley, 4006	07 3852 3533		Spanish/Modern Aus	20-30	N
79	G5	Butter Bistro	15 Goodwin St, Kangaroo Point, 4169	07 3891 7005	www.butterbistro.com	Modern Australian	26-33	N
80	E2	BYO Vietnamese Rest.	194 Wickham St, Fortitude Valley, 4006	07 3252 4112		Vietnamese	11-17	Y beer & wine-$2 corkage
11	D6	Café 21	Treasury Casino, Brisbane, 4000	07 3306 8795	www.conrad.com.au	Hot/cold buffet	20-27	N
82	D8	Café Dell'Ugo	182 Grey St, South Brisbane, 4101	07 3844 0500	www.cafedellugo.com.au	Italian	25-35	Y wine-$5pp corkage
83	D8	Café San Marco	Stanley St, South Brisbane, 4101	07 3846 4334	www.cafesanmarco.com.au	Mediterranean	16-29	Y
84	F9	CC's Restaurant	601 Stanley St, Woolloongabba, 4102	07 3891 1011		Modern Australian	9-20	N
85	C5	Cerello's Bar Café	325 George St, Brisbane, 4000	07 3308 0736	www.cerellos.com	Café/Steak	15-26	N
86	E5	Cha Cha Char	Eagle St Pier, Brisbane, 4000	07 3211 9944	www.chachachar.com.au	Steak	27-50	N
87	D8	Chez Laila	South Bank Parklands, South Brisbane, 4101	07 3846 3402	www.chezlaila.com.au	Lebanese	8-35	Y wine-$2pp corkage
88	E3	Circa Restaurant	483 Adelaide St, Brisbane, 4000	07 3832 4722	www.circarestaurant.com.au	Modern Australian	30-42	N
89	E6	City Gardens Café	Botanic Gardens, Alice St, Brisbane, 4000	07 3229 1554	www.citygardens.com.au	Modern Australian	9-23	N
90	G1	Cru Bar and Cellars	22 James St, Fortitude Valley, 4006	07 3252 2400	www.crubar.com	Modern Australian	24-30	N
91	E4	Customs House Rest.	399 Queen St, Brisbane, 4000	07 3365 8921	www.customshouse.com.au	Modern Australian	25-35	N
92	D8	Decks	South Bank Parklands, South Brisbane, 4101	07 3846 4036		Seafood/Steak	14-35	N
93	D8	Ellysium	167 Grey St, South Brisbane, 4101	07 3846 6033	www.ellysium.com.au	Modern Australian	12-25	N
94	F9	Fiasco's Steakhouse	640 Stanley St, Woolloongabba, 4102	07 3391 1413		Modern Aust/Steak	12-29	N
95	E6	Fix Restaurant & Bar	Edward St, Brisbane, 4000	07 3210 6016	www.portofficehotel.com.au	Modern Australian	15-30	N
96	E5	Fridays Club Terrace	123 Eagle St, Brisbane, 4000	07 3832 2122	www.fridays.com.au	Modern Australian	15-35	N
97	A4	Gambaro's Seafood Rest.	33 Caxton St, Brisbane, 4000	07 3369 9500	www.gambaros.com.au	Seafood	20-40	Y wine-$10 corkage
98	H3	Himalayan Café	640 Brunswick St, New Farm, 4005	07 3358 4015		Nepalese	12	N
99	G5	Icons on Main	180 Main St, Kangaroo Point, 4169	07 3895 8311		Modern Australian	25	Y wine-$4pp corkage
100	E5	Il Centro Rest. & Bar	Eagle St Pier, Brisbane, 4000	07 3221 6090	www.il-centro.com.au	Modern Australian	12-40	N
101	E5	Kookaburra River Queens	Eagle St Pier, Brisbane, 4000	07 3254 1300	www.kookaburrariverqueens.com	Hot/cold buffet	25-75	N
102	G1	Lunar Lounge	79 James St, Fortitude Valley, 4006	07 3254 1996	www.lunarlounge.com.au	Modern Australian	25-36	N
103	A3	Normanby	1 Musgrave Rd, Red Hill, 4059	07 3831 3353	www.thenormanby.com.au	Modern Australian	12-43	N
104	A8	Ottoman Cafe	37 Mollison St, South Brisbane, 4101	07 3846 3555		Turkish	15	Y wine-$2pp corkage

Denotes multiple venue

www.ashes06.com

#	Grid	Name	Address	Phone	Website	Cuisine	Price	BYO	
105	E2	Oyama Restaurant	115 Wickham St, Fortitude Valley, 4006	07 3257 0738		Japanese	16-27	N	
106	C8	Parklands Bar and Grill	Grey St, South Brisbane, 4101	07 3364 0800	www.rydges.com	Seafood/Steak	65	N	
8	C5	Picasso's	Cnr Roma & Ann St, Brisbane, 4000	07 3222 1128	www.carltonhotels.com.au	Mediterranean	17-34	N	
108	E5	Pier Nine Restaurant	Eagle St Pier, Brisbane, 4000	07 3226 2100	www.piernine.com.au	Modern Australian	29-42	N	
109	G8	Pineapple Hotel	706 Main St, Kangaroo Point, 4169	07 3393 1111	www.pineapplehotel.com.au	Modern Australian	15-33	N	
110	F9	Presidential Rest. & Bar	616-618 Stanley St, Woolloongabba, 4102	07 3255 2257		Modern Australian	18-28	N	
111	C7	Punjabi Palace	15 Melbourne St, South Brisbane, 4101	07 3846 3884	www.punjabipalace.com.au	Indian	13-18	Y wine
112	D8	River Canteen	South Bank Parklands, South Brisbane, 4101	07 3846 1880	www.rivercanteen.com.au	Modern Australian	15-32	Y wine-$4pp corkage
113	A3	Romeo's Italian	216 Petrie Tce, Brisbane, 4000	07 3367 0955	www.romeos.com.au	Italian	27-35	N	
22	G4	Savini	25 Rotherham St, Kangaroo Point, 4169	07 3891 5777	www.ilmondo.com.au	Modern Australian	26-32	Y wine-$4pp corkage
115	A8	Sitar Indian Restaurant	195 Melbourne St, West End, 4101	07 3846 7271	www.sitar.com.au	Indian	15-19	N	
116	F1	societe Bar Bistro	332 Brunswick St, Fortitude Valley, 4006	07 3252 7140		Modern Australian	10-24	Y beer & wine-corkage
117	E5	St Arnou Beer Café	Eagle St Pier, Brisbane, 4000	07 3229 0922	www.starnoubeercafe.com.au	Modern Australian	20-28	N	
118	C7	Star Café & Bar	166 Grey St, South Bank, 4101	07 3844 8448	www.starcafe.com.au	Café/Modern Aus	14-24	N	
119	G9	Sticks	735 Stanley St, Woolloongabba, 4102	07 3896 6565	www.chalkhotel.com.au	Modern Australian	19-33	N	
120	G5	Story Bridge Hotel	200 Main St, Kangaroo Point, 4169	07 3391 2266	www.storybridgehotel.com.au	Modern Australian	14-28	N	
121	F2	Sunbar	367 Brunswick St, Fortitude Valley, 4006	07 3257 4999	www.thesunbar.com	International	8-26	N	
122	E9	Tastes of India	Sidon St, South Bank, 4101	07 3846 1866		Indian	12-20	N	
123	F2	Thai-Wi-Rat	20 Duncan St, Fortitude Valley, 4006	07 3257 0884		Thai	10-13	Y wine-corkage
124	H9	The German Club	416 Vulture St, East Brisbane, 4169	07 3391 2434		German	10-16	N	
125	A8	The Gun Shop Café	53 Mollison St, West End, 4101	07 3844 2241	www.thegunshopcafe.com	Modern Australian	14-25	Y wine-$5pp corkage
126	E9	The Ship Inn	Stanley St, South Brisbane, 4101	07 3844 8000		Modern Aus/Seafood	18-24	N	
127	A8	Three Monkeys	58 Mollison St, West End, 4101	07 3844 6045	www.threemonkeys.com.au	International	10-13	Y wine-$1pp corkage
128	D8	Toscanis	Little Stanley St, South Bank, 4101	07 3846 1000	www.toscanis.com.au	Italian	16-31	Y	
129	A9	Tukka	145B Boundary St, West End, 4101	07 3846 6333	www.tukkarestaurant.com.au	Native Australian	25-35	N	
130	E5	Venice Café Bar	501 Queen St, Brisbane, 4000	07 3831 1400		Modern Australian	10-34	N	
131	E5	Vino's Restaurant & Bar	Eagle St Pier, Brisbane, 4000	07 3221 0811	www.vinos.com.au	Modern Australian	25-43	N	
132	G1	Vroom Café	46 James St, Fortitude Valley, 4006	07 3257 4455	www.vroomcafe.com.au	Modern Aust/Asian	10-25	Y beer & wine-$3 corkage
133	D7	Wang Dynasty	Riverside Promenade, South Brisbane, 4101	07 3844 8318	www.wangdynasty.com	Asian Chinese	15-25	N	
134	B8	West End Garden	190 Melbourne St, South Brisbane, 4101	07 3844 1368	www.westendgarden.com.au	Chinese/Vietnamese	14-18	Y	
135	D4	Zen Bar	215 Adelaide St, Brisbane, 4000	07 3211 2333	www.zenbar.com.au	Asian	15-29	N	

continued overpage....

BRISBANE MAPS

39

BRISBANE

BRISBANE CITY MAP (pp34-35)

PUBS & CLUBS KEY

■ Denotes multiple venue

FOX Sports Bar | B/R Bistro/Restaurant | TAB Betting facilities | OVAL Kilometres from the GABBA

#	Ref	Name	Address	Phone	Website	Closing Time	FOX	B/R	TAB	OVAL
136	G9	Australian National Hotel	867 Stanley St, Woolloongabba, 4102	07 3391 3964	www.beachhousebargrill.com	Daily: 11pm	Y	Y	Y	0.68
137	D5	Beachhouse Bar & Grill	Albert St, Brisbane, 4000	07 3003 0017	www.beachhousebargrill.com	Daily: til late	Y	Y	N	3.49
70	E5	Belgian Beer Café	Cnr Edward & Mary St, Brisbane, 4000	07 3221 0199	www.belgianbeercafebrussels.com.au	Mon-Sat: til late	N	Y	N	3.93
139	F2	Birdee Num Num	608 Ann St, Fortitude Valley, 4006	07 3257 3644	www.bunkbrisbane.com.au	Mon-Sun: 1am	N	N	N	3.62
140	D5	Brisbane Underground	235 Edward St, Brisbane, 4000	07 3220 1477	www.brisbaneunderground.com.au	Thu-Sat: 5am	N	N	N	4.45
141	A4	Casablanca	52 Petrie Tce, Brisbane, 4000	07 3369 6969	www.casablanca.com.au	Tues-Thurs: 3am, Fri-Sat: 5am, Sun: 3am	Y	Y	N	4.85
142	D5	Cesars nightclub	15 Adelaide St, Brisbane, 4000	07 3221 5099	www.cesars.com.au	Thurs-Sat: 3am	N	N	N	3.54
119	G9	Chalk Hotel	735 Stanley St, Woolloongabba, 4102	07 3896 6565	www.chalkbar.com.au	Daily: 3am	Y	Y	Y	1.19
144	E5	Chill on Queen	255 Queen St, Brisbane, 4000	07 3229 1444	www.chillonqueen.com.au	Tues-Thurs: Midnight, Fri-Sat: 2am	Y	Y	N	4.57
84	F9	Clarence Corner Hotel	601 Stanley St, Woolloongabba, 4101	07 3891 1011		Mon-Sat: 3am, Sun: Midnight	Y	Y	Y	1.70
146	D5	Criterion Tavern	Adelaide St, Brisbane, 4000	07 3221 7411		Mon-Thurs: 10pm, Fri-Sat: 2am	Y	Y	N	3.52
147	F2	Dooleys Hotel	394 Brunswick St, Fortitude Valley, 4006	07 3252 4344	www.dooleyshotel.com.au	Mon-Sun: 5am	Y	Y	N	3.60
148	E5	Embassy Hotel	Elizabeth St, Brisbane, 4000	07 3221 7616		Mon-Sun: Midnight	Y	Y	N	3.73
149	E5	Exchange Hotel	Edward St, Brisbane, 4000	07 3229 3522	www.theexchange.com.au	Daily: 3am	Y	Y	Y	3.84
150	D6	Fat Louies's Karaoke	124 Albert St, Brisbane, 4000	07 3229 7031		Sun-Thurs: 2am, Fri-Sat: 3am	N	N	N	3.44
151	D4	Finelly's Arms Hotel	270 Ann St, Brisbane, 4000	07 3220 2061	www.grandcentralhotel.com.au	Mon-Thurs & Sun: Midnight, Fri-Sat: 2am	Y	Y	Y	4.37
152	E4	Fridays Riverside	123 Eagle St, Brisbane, 4000	07 3832 2122	www.fridays.com.au	Mon-Tues: 11pm, Wed-Sat: 5am	Y	Y	N	4.08
153	F1	Fringe Bar	Constance St, Fortitude Valley, 4006	07 3252 9833	www.fringebar.net	Mon: 1am, Tues-Sun: 5am	N	N	N	3.80
150	D5	Gilhooleys Irish Pub	Charlotte St, Brisbane, 4000	07 3229 0672	www.gilhooleys.com	Mon-Wed: Midnight, Thurs: 1am, Fri-Sat: 3am	Y	Y	Y	4.03
155	D5	Good Knight Bar	18 Charlotte St, Fortitude Valley, 4000	07 3221 6433	www.pancakemanor.com.au	Mon-Sun: Midnight	Y	Y	N	3.63
156	F1	GPO Hotel	740 Ann St, Fortitude Valley, 4006	07 3252 1322	www.gpohotel.com.au	Mon-Sun: 2am	N	Y	N	3.79
157	C7	Greystone Bar & Cellar	166 Grey St, South Brisbane, 4101	07 3846 6990	www.greystonebar.com.au	Sun-Thurs: 1am, Fri-Sat: 3am	N	Y	N	2.57
158	A4	Hotel L.A.	68 Petrie Tce, Brisbane, 4000	07 3368 2560	www.hotella.com.au	Thurs: 3am, Fri-Sat: til late	Y	Y	N	4.86
159	E3	Hotel Orient	560 Queen St, Brisbane, 4101	07 3839 4625	www.orienthotel.com.au	Mon-Wed: Midnight, Thurs: 1am, Fri-Sat: 3am	N	N	N	3.61
100	E5	Il Centro	Eagle St Pier, 1 Eagle St, Brisbane, 4000	07 3221 6090	www.il-centro.com.au	Daily: til late	Y	Y	N	4.93
11	D6	Irish Murphy's	175 George St, Brisbane, 4000	07 3221 4377	www.irishmurphys.com.au	Sun-Tues: 2am, Wed-Sat: 3am	Y	Y	Y	3.26
161	D6	Jade Buddha	Eagle Pier St, Brisbane, 4000	07 3221 2888	www.jadebuddha.com.au	Sun-Wed: Midnight, Thurs: 1am, Fri-Sat: 3am	N	Y	N	3.32
162	E5	Kitty O'Shea's Irish Bar	25 Caxton St, Brisbane, 4000	07 3368 1933		Thurs-Sun: 2am	N	N	N	3.80
163	A4	Live Wire Bar	130 William St, Brisbane, 4000	07 3306 8888	www.conrad.com.au	Mon-Sun: Open 24 hrs	Y	Y	N	4.93
165	D5	Mick O'Malleys Irish Pub	Queen St Mall, Brisbane, 4000	07 3211 9881	www.omalleysirishpub.com.au	Mon-Sat: 3am, Sun: Midnight	Y	Y	Y	3.26
166	F2	Monastery Nightclub	621 Ann St, Fortitude Valley, 4006	07 3257 7081	www.monastery.com.au	Mon-Sun: 5am	N	N	N	4.51
94	F9	Morrison Hotel	640 Stanley St, Woolloongabba, 4101	07 3391 1413		Mon-Tues: 11pm, Wed: Midnight, Thurs-Sat: 1am	Y	Y	Y	3.56
103	A3	Normanby Hotel	1 Musgrave Rd, Red Hill, 4059	07 3831 3353	www.thenormanby.com.au	Mon-Sun: 2am	Y	Y	N	1.52
169	E4	Pig 'n' Whistle	123 Eagle St, Brisbane, 4000	07 3832 9099	www.pignwhistle.com	Daily: til late	Y	Y	N	5.50
109	G8	Pineapple Hotel	706 Main St, Kangaroo Point, 4169	07 3393 1111	www.pineapplehotel.com.au	Mon-Sun: Midnight	Y	Y	Y	0.98

www.ashes06.com

BRISBANE MAPS

Ref	Name	Address	Phone	Website	Hours			
171 D8	Plough Inn Tavern	South Bank Parklands, South Brisbane, 4101	07 3844 7777	www.ploughinn.com.au	Mon-Thurs: 10.30pm, Fri-Sat: Midnight, Sun: 11pm	Y	N	2.70
95 E6	Port Office Hotel	Edward St, Brisbane, 4000	07 3221 0072		Mon-Wed: Midnight, Thurs-Fri: 3am, Sat: 5am	Y	N	3.43
173 F2	Press Club	339 Brunswick St, Fortitude Valley, 4006	07 3852 4000	www.pressclub.com.au	Mon-Tues: 3am, Wed-Sun: 5am	N	N	3.44
174 H1	Q A on James	64 James St, Fortitude Valley, 4006	07 3358 2799		Mon-Wed: Midnight, Thurs-Sat: 2am, Sun: 9pm	Y	N	4.10
175 F2	Royal George Hotel	327 Brunswick St, Fortitude Valley, 4006	07 3252 2524	www.qahotel.com	Mon-Wed & Sun: Midnight, Thurs-Sat: 3am	Y	N	3.45
176 C3	Spring Hill Tavern	447 Wickham Tce, Spring Hill, 4004	07 3839 4866		Mon-Sun: 2am	N	N	4.59
117 E5	St Arnou Beer Café	Eagle St Pier, Eagle St, Brisbane, 4000	07 3229 0922	www.starnoubeercafe.com.au	Thurs-Sat: 1am	N	Y	3.80
178 D3	St Pauls Tavern	Leichhardt St, Spring Hill, 4004	07 3831 8288		Mon-Sun: 11pm	Y	N	4.89
120 G5	Story Bridge Hotel	200 Main St, Kangaroo Point, 4169	07 3391 2266	www.storybridgehotel.com.au	Mon-Sun: til late	Y	N	2.18
180 D5	Strike Bowling Bar	Wintergarden, Queen St, Brisbane, 4000	1300 787 453	www.strikebowlingbar.com	Fri-Sat: 2am, Sun-Thurs: Midnight	N	N	3.60
181 D6	The Brewhouse	Level 1/142 Albert St, Brisbane, 4000	07 3003 0098	www.thebrewhouse.com.au	Daily: 1am	Y	N	3.48
182 A4	The Caxton Hotel	38 Caxton St, Brisbane, 4000	07 3369 5544	www.caxton.com.au	Sun-Thu: 2am, Fri-Sat: 5am	Y	Y	5.08
38 E2	The Elephant & Wheelbarrow	230 Wickham St, Fortitude Valley, 4006	07 3252 4136		Mon-Sun: til late	Y	N	3.64
184 F2	The Family Nightclub	8 McLachlan St, Fortitude Valley, 4006	07 3852 5000	www.thefamily.com.au	Fri-Sun: 5am	N	N	3.26
185 B7	The Fox Hotel	Melbourne St, South Brisbane, 4101	07 3844 2883	www.thefox.com.au	Mon-Thurs: 10pm, Fri-Sat: 11pm	N	Y	4.15
126 E9	The Ship Inn	Sidon St, South Brisbane, 4101	07 3844 8000		Mon-Fri: 10pm, Sat-Sun: Midnight	N	N	2.27
187 E4	The Tank Hotel	371 Queen St, Brisbane, 4000	07 3229 6261		Mon-Thurs: 7pm, Fri: Midnight, Sat: 5pm	Y	Y	4.22
188 E5	The Victory Hotel	Charlotte St, Brisbane, 4000	07 3221 0444	www.thevictory.com.au	Mon-Wed & Sun: Midnight, Thurs-Sat: 3am	Y	Y	3.84
189 F1	The Zoo	711 Ann St, Fortitude Valley, 4006	07 3854 1381	www.thezoo.com.au	Wed-Sun: 1am	N	N	3.89
65 C5	Tinbilly Traveller's Bar	462 George St, Brisbane, 4000	07 3238 5888	www.tinbilly.com	Mon-Sun: Open 24 hrs	Y	N	4.02
191 F1	Troubadour The	322 Brunswick St, Fortitude Valley, 4006	07 3252 2626	www.thetroubadour.com.au	Thurs-Sun: 2am	N	N	3.45
192 E5	Union Jacks Ale House	127 Charlotte St, Brisbane, 4000	07 3210 1172	www.unionjacks.com.au	Mon-Wed: Midnight, Fri: 2am, Sat: 4am	Y	Y	3.96
131 E5	Vino's Restaurant & Bar	Eagle St Pier, Eagle St, Brisbane, 4000	07 3221 0811		Mon-Sun: 1am	N	N	3.80
194 F1	Wickham Hotel	308 Wickham St, Fortitude Valley, 4006	07 3852 1301	www.thewickham.com.au	Sun-Mon: Midnight, Tues-Thurs: 3am, Fri-Sat: 5am	N	N	3.84
135 D4	Zenbar	215 Adelaide St, Brisbane, 4000	07 3211 2333	www.zenbar.com.au	Mon-Sat: 12.30am	Y	N	4.46
36 D4	Zi Bar	308 Edward St, Brisbane, 4000	07 3211 2433		Mon-Thurs: 10pm, Fri: Midnight, Sat-Sun: 2pm	Y	N	4.29

The "Corkscrew" at Sea World. Photo: Tourism Queensland.

BRISBANE ATTRACTIONS

Organised tours... Walk About Brisbane (0431 025 077, walkaboutbrisbane.com.au) is a great way of learning about the city on foot from a local guide, while Coachtrans Australia (07 5500 8999, coachtrans.com.au) provides coach transfers between Brisbane and the Gold Coast.
These are just two of many tour operators to choose from, with the full rundown of tour options available from the Brisbane Visitor Information Centre in the Queen St Mall (07 3006 6290).

XXXX Brewery

For an authentic taste of Brisbane, check out the famed XXXX Brewery in Milton, which produces XXXX Bitter and the highest selling mid-strength beer in Australia, XXXX GOLD.

An Australian institution since being established 128 years ago, the XXXX Brewery offers comprehensive visitor tours including an all-important taste-testing in the Ale House Bar.

Open Monday to Friday, the brewery is accessible by bus and train from the city, with tours costing $18 (£7.50).

Views from Mt Coot-tha

For a spectacular view over Brisbane, head up to the Mt Coot-tha lookout 8km west of the city. You can see as far as the Glass House Mountains to the north, the Gold Coast hinterland to the south and Moreton and Stradbroke Islands to the east.

Mt Coot-tha is also an ideal place for a trek, with various trails allowing walkers to take full advantage of the beautiful views. Visitors can also walk along an Aboriginal art trail which features tree carvings and rock paintings along the way. To get to Mt Coot-tha, hop on the City Heights Tour in Adelaide St or jump on bus 471 at the corner of Adelaide St and Albert St between 9.15am-3.15pm. Remember though, the last bus back from the mountain leaves at 3.50pm.

Conrad Treasury Casino

Based in the superb sandstone Treasury Building at the top of Queen St, Conrad Treasury Casino is not only a great place for a bet, but also an ideal meeting place for dinner or a few drinks.

Open 24 hours and featuring more than 80 gaming tables

www.ashes06.com

and over 1300 gaming machines, the casino has four restaurants and seven bars split over three levels.

Throw in live music and stand-up comedy and you have Brisbane's premier entertainment precinct - perfect for a post-Test match gathering.

Theme parks

Queensland is renowned for its theme parks, with four absolute beauties located within an hour's drive from Brisbane.

Dreamworld is the largest theme park and is home to some of the world's tallest and fastest rides, **Warner Bros Movie World** features amazing stunt shows and street parades, **Wet 'n' Wild Water World** is ideal for hot days, while **Sea World** offers a brilliant array of dolphin, shark and seal shows.

Perfect for couples, groups and families, all four theme parks are open every day from 10am-5pm.

South Bank

You can swim in the lagoon, see movies in the parklands or be wowed by artists and performers at South Bank.

You can also take part in free outdoor activities such as tai chi, yoga and aqua aerobics, or get a few friends together for a picnic or barbecue.

Shops, cafes, restaurants, galleries, theatres, museums and market stalls give the precinct a truly diverse mix of entertainment and leisure options, making it a popular gathering place for locals and tourists alike.

Moreton Island

Located 35km from the Brisbane CBD, Moreton Island is one of the largest sand islands in the world and a great day-trip option.

Regarded as an "aquatic playground", the island consists of white sandy beaches, clear sparkling water and freshwater lakes, and is a favourite among campers, fishermen, bushwalkers and naturalists.

To get there, hop on the OceanXplorer - a fast, inflatable rubber craft - from South Bank and be whisked along the river to Moreton Island in 50 exhilarating minutes.

Riverlife Adventure Centre

If you're up for a spot of abseiling, rock climbing or kayaking, visit the Riverlife Adventure Centre on the banks of the Brisbane River, 10 minutes from the city centre.

Located beneath the 200 million-year-old Kangaroo Point Cliffs, the Riverlife Adventure Centre not only gives customers an adrenalin-pumping experience, but enables you to admire the city, Story Bridge and Botanic Gardens from a completely different viewpoint.

The centre is open every day and might be the ideal tonic to get you going again after a few lazy days at the cricket!

Australia Zoo - The Crocodile Hunter

Crikey, if you love animals then the "Crocodile Hunter" Steve Irwin's Australia Zoo is a must-see destination.

Just an hour's drive north of Brisbane, Australia Zoo offers a blend of relaxation and exciting adventure all based on a wildlife theme.

With 14 shows daily, you can see crocodiles being fed from alarmingly close range, a free flight bird show featuring macaws and wedge-tailed eagles, and a host of weird and wonderful animals from koalas and snakes to tigers and elephants. And make sure you say hello to "Harriet", the zoo's amazing Galapagos tortoise who hatched in 1830 and is the world's oldest living resident!

Moreton Island. Photo: Tourism Queensland.

[SUGGESTED -ITINERARIES

[If you've got some time before or after the First Test in Brisbane, here are some ideas to help you plan your stay:]

A day...

Take the floating "River Walk" from New Farm to the CBD and then spend the morning acquainting yourself with Brisbane life in Queen St Mall.

After scoring the best view in town from the top of City Hall's 85-metre clock tower, grab some picnic rations and set yourself up for lunch - and maybe a quick nap - in the beautiful Botanic Gardens.

In the afternoon, head out to the world famous XXXX Brewery and sample the beers on offer before dinner in one of the many restaurants in picturesque South Bank.

And if you're up for a big night, check out the Conrad Treasury Casino, head to one of the many pubs or go clubbing at Family, recognised as one of Australia's hottest nightspots.

A few days...

After spending your first day taking in the urban sights of Brisbane, get an overview of the entire city by heading to the top of Mt Coot-tha, just 8km west of the CBD. There are also some wonderful walking trails, including an Aboriginal art trail featuring tree carvings and rock paintings.

Queensland is known for its theme parks so spend a day on rides, rollercoasters and waterslides at either Dreamworld, Warner Bros Movie World, Wet 'n' Wild Water World or Sea World, which are all located less than an hour's drive from Brisbane.

And for an adrenalin rush of a different kind, check out Australia Zoo on your final day. Home of Steve Irwin, the "Crocodile Hunter", Australia Zoo houses more than 750 animals, including 100 fresh and saltwater crocodiles.

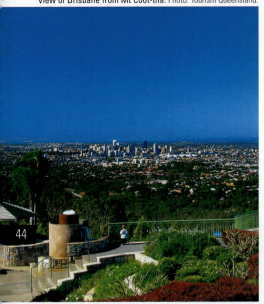

View of Brisbane from Mt Coot-tha. Photo: Tourism Queensland.

A week...

Brisbane is the gateway to many of the country's most recognisable tourist destinations, so if you've got a week to spare consider a trip along the coast.

A short journey south will take you to Surfers Paradise on the world famous Gold Coast, or head north to idyllic Noosa Heads and nearby Fraser Island, which features freshwater lakes and its own beach highway.

Hervey Bay is another pleasant spot, well worth the five-hour train ride from Brisbane, and if you're lucky you might see a humpback whale while you stroll along the flawless shoreline.

If you're really keen though, keep travelling north along the coast to the hip town of Airlie Beach or Cairns, where you can base yourself while you explore the breathtaking Whitsunday Islands and Great Barrier Reef.

www.ashes06.com

BRISBANE DIRECTORY

CRICKET
Cricket Australia: ....(03) 9653 9999, cricket.com.au
Queensland Cricket: ....(07) 3292 3100, bulls.com.au

EMERGENCY
Ambulance: 000
Fire: 000
Police: 000
Police (non-emergency): ....(07) 3224 4444
RACQ Roadside Service: ....13 19 05, racq.com.au
Brisbane Sexual Assault Service: ....(07) 3636 5206

HEALTH
Brisbane Private Hospital: ....(07) 3834 6111
Princess Alexandra Hospital (Woolloongabba):
....(07) 3240 2111
Mater Misericordiae (South Brisbane): .....(07) 3840 8111
Royal Brisbane Hospital: ....(07) 3636 8111
St Andrew's Hospital (Spring Hill): ....(07) 3831 6660
Travellers Medical Service: ....(07) 3221 3611
Disability Information Awareness Line: ....(07) 3224 8444

INTERNET ACCESS
BRA Travel & Internet Centre: ......158 Roma St, Brisbane
Cyber Room: ....25 Adelaide St, Brisbane
Inferno Internet Lounge: ....65 Adelaide St, Brisbane
DIALUP cyber lounge: ....126 Adelaide St, Brisbane
Netparadise: ....198 Adelaide St, Brisbane
Cyberlounge Internet Café: ....
....43 Queen St Mall, Brisbane
The Bunker: ....62 Queen St Mall, Brisbane
Global Gossip: ....288 Edward St, Brisbane
Internet City: ....132 Albert St, Brisbane
The Hub Internet Café: ....125 Margaret St, Brisbane
Central City Library: ....69 Ann St, Brisbane
South Bank Visitor Information Centre: ....
....Stanley St Plaza, South Bank
State Library of QLD: ....Stanley St, South Bank
The Computer Café: ....107 Latrobe Tce, Paddington
Hot Web: ....70 Jephson St, Toowong

continued overpage…

Overlooking Brisbane. Photo: Tourism Queensland.

BRISBANE

BRISBANE DIRECTORY

MONEY
American Express: ....1300 139 060, ...americanexpress.com.au
Travelex: ....1800 637 642, travelex.com.au

PHONE/MOBILE
3 mobile: ....131 681, three.com.au
International code to UK: ....
............0011 (or 0018) + 44 + Area Code + Local Number
Country Direct (reverse charge/credit to UK): ....
...................1800 881 440, 1800 881 441, 1800 881 417
Directory Assistance: ....
..................1223 (local/national) or 1225 (international)

POST
City GPO (Queen St): ....13 13 18, austpost.com.au

TOURISM
Tourism Queensland (30 Makerston St): ....13 88 33, ...tq.com.au, queenslandtravel.com
Brisbane Visitor Information Centre...........(07) 3006 6290 (cnr Albert St/Queen St):.............experiencebrisbane.com
South Bank Visitor Information Centre:......(07) 3867 2051
Gold Coast Visitor Information: 1300 309 540

Sunshine Coast Visitor Information:...........(07) 5422 255
Brisbane Cruises: ....(07) 3630 266
....brisbanecruises.com.a
Coachtrans Australia: ....(07) 3238 4700
....coachtrans.com.a
Hughies Grape & Golf Tours: ....(07) 3879 609
OceanXplorer: ....(07) 3820 7957, oceanxplorer.co
River City Cruises: ......0428 278 473, rivercitycruises.co
Tour Spots Online:...................................(07) 3352 7249
....tourspotsaustralia.cor
Walk About Brisbane:................................0431 025 07
....walkaboutbrisbane.com.a

TRANSPORT
PLANE
Brisbane Airport: ....(07) 3406 3000, bne.com.a
Qantas: ....13 13 13, qantas.com.a
Jetstar: ....131 538, jetstar.com.a
Virgin Blue:............................13 67 89, virginblue.com.a
Alliance Airlines:(07) 3212 1212, allianceairlines.com.a
Australian Airlines:....13 13 13, australianairlines.com.a
Macair: ....13 13 13, macair.com.a
Sunshine Express:.......13 13 13, sunshineexpress.com.a

Botanic Gardens. Photo: Tourism Queensla

King George Square and Brisbane City Hall. Photo: Tourism Queensland.

BUS - LOCAL
TransLink: ....13 12 30, translink.com.au
Trans-Info Service:...................13 12 30, transinfo.com.au
Coachtrans (airport to city): ....(07) 3238 4700,
....coachtrans.com.au

BUS - INTERSTATE
Greyhound Australia: ....13 14 99, greyhound.com.au
Premier Motor Service:.........13 34 10, premierms.com.au

TRAIN - LOCAL
TransLink: ....13 12 30, translink.com.au
Trans-Info Service:...................13 12 30, transinfo.com.au
Airtrain (airport to city):.............13 12 30, airtrain.com.au

TRAIN - REGIONAL/INTERSTATE
Queensland Rail Travel Centre: 1800 627 655
Traveltrain:............................13 22 32, traveltrain.com.au
CountryLink: ....13 22 32, countrylink.info

FERRY
TransLink (CityCat):.................13 12 30, translink.com.au
Trans-Info Service:...................13 12 30, transinfo.com.au

TAXI
Black & White Cabs:...13 10 08
Yellow Cabs: 13 19 24
Brisbane Cabs: 13 22 11

CAR HIRE
Avis: ....13 63 33, avis.com.au
Budget:..............................1300 794 344, budget.com.au
Europcar: ....1300 131 390, europcar.com.au
Hertz: ....13 30 39, hertz.com.au
Thrifty:..................................1300 367 227, thrifty.com.au
Metro Rent A Car:......................................1800 236 459,
....metrorentacar.com.au
Ace Rental Cars: ....1800 620 408, acerentals.com.au
Priority Car Rental:......................................1800 682 176,
....prioritycarrental.com.au
Airport Rent A Car: 1800 673 067,
....airportrentacar.com.au

MOTORCYCLE/SCOOTER HIRE
Ozmoto:..................................1300 724 680, ozmoto.com
Big Kahuna Scooter Hire (Sunshine Coast): ....
...................................(07) 5446 4703, bigkahuna.net.au

BICYCLE HIRE
Valet Cycle Hire & Tours:............................0408 003 198,
....cyclebrisbane.com
Brisbane Bicycle Sales & Hire:.................(07) 3229 2433,
....brizbike.com
Riverlife Adventure Centre: ....(07) 3891 5766,
....riverlife.com.au

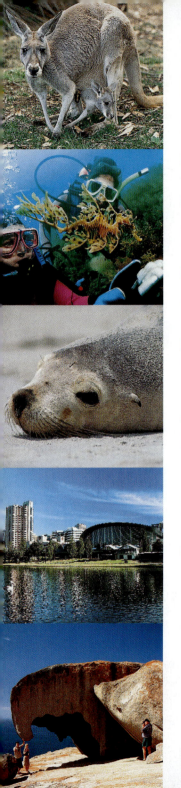

SEE SOUTH AUSTRALIA.
It'll Bowl You Over!

South Australia might have one of the world's most picturesque cricket grounds but it also has so much more to offer. Our tours will knock you for a six!

KANGAROO ISLAND HIGHLIGHTS DAY TOUR
See the best of the best sights on this full day coach tour with lunch. Ex Adelaide **$218**

KANGAROO ISLAND COAST TO COAST
This fantastic 2 day/1 night tour explores Australia's finest nature-based destination. Visit a series of stunning and unique locations including National Parks, Seal Bay, beautiful unspoiled beaches and some local cottage industries. Ex Adelaide from **$383**

KANGAROO ISLAND ADVENTURE TOUR
See more, do more, go for the adventure! 2 days of walking trails, searching for native wildlife and exploring some of Kangaroo Island's most spectacular locations. Overnight farmstay accommodation with all meals included. **$365^**

KANGAROO ISLAND BEACH WILDERNESS ADVENTURE
The ultimate Kangaroo Island escape. This 3 day/2 night tour is the best value Kangaroo Island Package around. Plenty of time to explore this incredible island and see the wildlife with 2 nights accommodation at the Penneshaw YHA. **$245^**

ADELAIDE SIGHTSEEING
See more of South Australia. City Highlights **$53**, Mt Lofty/Hahndorf **$56**, Victor Harbor **$79**, Barossa Valley **$105**, Coorong Adventure Cruise **$145**, Flinders Ranges **$297**, River Murray Highlights Cruise **$114**.
All tours include hotel pick-ups.

FREE City Sights Tour when booking Barossa Valley and Kangaroo Island Highlights Tour or Barossa Valley and Coorong Adventure Cruise.

Call 13 13 01 Open 7 days to 9pm
www.sealink.com.au or bookings@sealink.com.au

City Centre Travel – 75 King William Street
Sightseeing & Travel Centre – 211 Victoria Square
Sealink Travel Centre – 440 King William Street

SEALINK
Travel Group

All prices are per person and valid to 31st March 2007. Accommodation where applicable on a twin share basis. ^Dormitory style accommodation. Self drive packages available. All tours include pick-up from selected Adelaide accommodation. *Conditions apply. ABN 69 007 367 TTA 64062

THE FESTIVAL STATE

Adelaide Oval. Photo: South Australian Cricket Association.

DECEMBER 1 - 5, 2006

**2ND TEST
ADELAIDE**

ADELAIDE CITY OVERVIEW

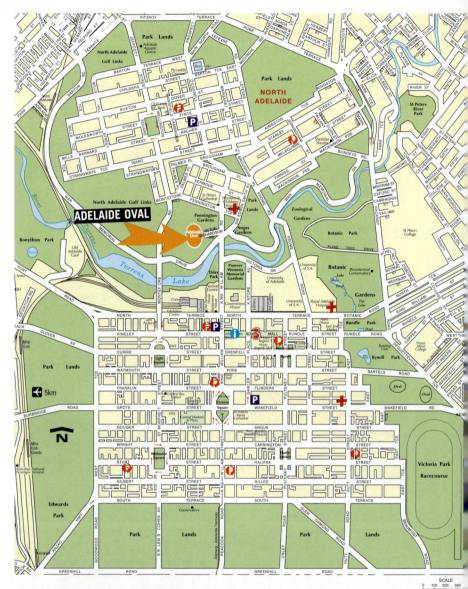

KEY... ADELAIDE CITY OVERVIEW

- 3 store
- Hospital
- Police
- Post Office
- Tourist information
- Airport

South Australia State Map

www.ashes06.com

WELCOME TO
-ADELAIDE, SOUTH AUSTRALIA

Think world-class wines, arts festivals, warm weather and white sandy beaches. Think Adelaide.

Named in honour of Queen Adelaide, wife of King William IV, South Australia's capital city is one of the country's best-kept secrets; hip and elegant, yet laidback and unassuming. Home to 1.2 million residents, the "city of churches" has a vibrant outdoor food and wine scene and boasts an impressive cross-section of pubs from upmarket bars to typical Aussie watering holes.

With an average summer temperature of 28°C and little rain to speak of, Adelaide is known as the "20-minute city" because it never takes much more than 20 minutes to get from one place to the next.

And within an hour of the capital you can experience some of Australia's finest tourist hot spots. Enjoy a wine tasting in the Barossa Valley, go whale watching at Victor Harbor, water ski on the mighty Murray River or visit the nation's oldest German settlement at Hahndorf.

STATE FACTS... SOUTH AUSTRALIA

Founded: 1836
Population: 1.5 million (Adelaide = 1.2 million)
Colours: Red, blue & gold
Floral emblem: Sturt Desert Pea
Faunal emblems: Hairy Nosed Wombat & Piping Shrike
Average summer temp: 28°C
Average winter temp: 16°C
Time: GMT + 10 hours, 30 minutes
Domestic cricket team: West End Redbacks

While you're in Adelaide...

Eat: A "pie floater". Available from "pie carts" outside SkyCity Adelaide Casino on North Tce and alongside the GPO in Victoria Square, this famous SA dish comprises an upside down meat pie covered in green pea soup and tomato sauce. Sounds weird but it's been a favourite among late-night revellers for over 130 years!

Drink: Coopers Pale Ale. As Australia's only remaining family-owned brewery, Coopers is quintessentially South Australian. Pale Ale is clearly its most popular beer, however Coopers Sparkling Ale and Premium Lager are also worth a taste.

See: Kangaroo Island. The perfect place to escape the hustle and bustle of city living, this unspoilt natural wonder off the SA coast is seven times the size of Singapore and literally crawling with wildlife, including seals, echidnas, goannas, wallabies and kangaroos. Catch a plane from Adelaide or take the SeaLink ferry from Cape Jervis.

Do: Tram to Glenelg. Jump on a tram in Victoria Square in the heart of the city and enjoy a 30-minute journey taking you to cosmopolitan Glenelg beach. The "Bay" is full of restaurants, pubs, shopping, markets and amusements... and of course a great beach!

Adelaide Oval. Photo: South Australian Cricket Association.

ADELAIDE OVAL

Adelaide Oval is one of the most picturesque cricket grounds in the world, combining modern facilities with a heritage charm.

Located just a stone's throw from the River Torrens (a short stroll from the city centre), Adelaide Oval is home to the West End Redbacks in the Australian domestic competition and remains a favourite among players and spectators alike.

Established in 1871, Adelaide Oval has preserved its aesthetic appeal over the years, in particular, the elegant Edwardian scoreboard on the northern mound continues to stand the test of time. Celebrating its 95th birthday this year, the scoreboard doubles as a popular meeting point for cricket goers, although to be fair, the Scoreboard Bar is probably what attracts most!

Spanning 190 x 125 metres, the ground hosted its first Test match in 1884, which saw England defeat Australia by eight wickets.

The record cricket crowd stands at 50,962, recorded on the Saturday of the Bodyline Test in January 1933, however bigger attendances have been recorded at Australian Rules football games which are also played at the venue. Today, the crowd capacity for cricket matches is 32,500.

There are four main grandstands at Adelaide Oval: the two-tiered Sir Donald Bradman Stand at the southern end, the single level western stand combining the Sir Edwin Smith, George Giffen and Mostyn Evan Stands, and the two new Chappell Stands on the eastern side of the ground, which were constructed in 2003. There is also the smaller Clem Hill Stand for a limited number of spectators.

The rest of the ground comprises a grassed hill, as well as several rows of seating near the boundary fence, while modern light towers and a large video screen suitably complement the traditional values of the venue.

www.ashes06.com

MATCH DAY INFORMATION

2ND TEST:
AUSTRALIA vs ENGLAND

Adelaide Oval, Dec 1-5, 2006

Gates:
Gates open at 8.00am.
Public entry via the Clarrie Grimmett Gates (northern entrance) and Victor Richardson Gates (eastern entrance).

Match times:
FIRST SESSION:	11.00am - 1.00pm
Lunch:	1.00pm - 1.40pm
SECOND SESSION:	1.40pm - 3.40pm
Tea:	3.40pm - 4.00pm
THIRD SESSION:	4.00pm - 6.00pm

*Note: Times are subject to change.

BE WARNED! Gate staff will conduct bag searches on entry to check for prohibited items. In the event prohibited items are found, patrons will be asked to dispose of the items prior to entering the ground.

Office hours:
The ground's administration office (located inside the southern gates) will be open from 8.00am-6.00pm on each day of the Test. The match office (located at the top of the George Giffen Stand on the western side of the ground) is open from 9.00am to the close of play.

For up-to-date information, visit saca.com.au or phone (08) 8300 3800.

Prohibited items:
- Glass containers, bottles and cans
- Alcohol
- Hard eskies
- Offensive signs and banners
- Weapons, guns and knives
- Trumpets and horns
- Push bikes
- Pets
- Any item deemed dangerous

Permitted items:
- Video/still cameras (non-commercial use only).
- Chairs (only in outer and concourse areas) as long as they do not restrict the view of other patrons or restrict walkways.
- Signs/banners as long as they do not contain offensive wording or restrict the view of other patrons or ground/fence signage.
- Umbrellas, but should not restrict the view of other patrons.

General information:
- ATMs are located outside the Members Bar on the western side of the ground, behind the Sir Donald Bradman Stand at the southern end of the venue and behind the Chappell Stands on the eastern side (adjacent to the Victor Richardson Gates).
- Public telephones are located outside the Members Bar and behind the Sir Donald Bradman Stand.
- St John's First-Aid is located underneath the Sir Donald Bradman Stand.
- Disability car parks are adjacent the northern and southern gates.
- All undercover and seated areas of Adelaide Oval are smoke-free.
- A minimum standard dress of neat casual applies in the members' enclosure at all times.

continued overpage...

MATCH DAY INFORMATION
...continued from page 53.

Food & beverage:
Fast food outlets and bars in the public section of the ground include the Scoreboard Bar on the northern mound, the Cathedral Bar & Kiosk and River Bar & Kiosk behind the Chappell Stands on the eastern side of the ground.

Mid-strength XXXX GOLD and Hahn Premium Light are again likely to be the only beers available in the outer, with full-strength offerings West End Draught and Tooheys Extra Dry only available in the members.

Smoking:
Smoking is banned in all grandstand undercover seating areas and outdoor seated areas at Adelaide Oval. Thoroughfares and walkways around the ground, all food outlets, dining rooms and administration areas are also smoke-free.

TAB/Betting:
If you want to place a bet on the cricket, a TAB operates on the boundary road behind the Scoreboard Bar on the northern mound.

Parking:
Car parking around Adelaide Oval is governed by Adelaide City Council. Parking in the northern car park, which opens at 7.00am, costs $10 (£4). Pinky Flat, south-west of the ground along the River Torrens, opens when the northern car park is full.
Note: The southern car park is not available for public use.

Fans flock to the "hill" at Adelaide Oval... and the Scoreboard Bar! Photo: South Australian Cricket Association.

www.ashes06.com

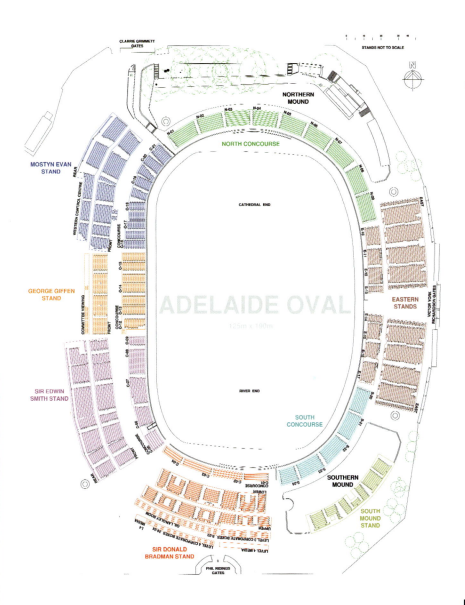

ADELAIDE OVAL
-SEATING PLAN

TRANSPORT

By Plane...
Five airlines operate scheduled international flights through Adelaide Airport, including Qantas, Air New Zealand, Singapore Airlines, Malaysia Airlines, Cathay Pacific and Garuda Indonesia. British Airways also provides international access to Adelaide through code-shared services with Qantas.

Qantas (13 13 13, qantas.com.au), **Virgin Blue** (13 67 89, virginblue.com.au) and **Jetstar** (131 538, jetstar.com.au) operate interstate routes including Test cities Brisbane, Perth, Melbourne and Sydney.

To/from Airport...
Skylink Airport Shuttle (08 8332 0528, skylinkadelaide.com) runs frequent shuttles between Adelaide Airport and the city centre for $7.50 one way (£3).

Shuttles from the airport go via the interstate train station at Keswick and most major hotels in the CBD, and run from 6.15am to 9.40pm daily. Shuttles from the city back to the airport start at 5.30am and operate until 9pm.

The **Adelaide Airport Flyer** (1300 856 444) also makes regular runs to and from the airport to outer suburban regions, but bookings are necessary.

A public *Jet* **Bus** service is available too, which links the airport and city through to the north-eastern suburbs of Adelaide, including connections to rail and other bus routes. Services from the airport run daily every 15 minutes from 5.20am to 11.35pm, while services to the airport begin at 4.50am and run past midnight to 12.05am. Single trip tickets cost around $3.50 (£1.50).
For more information, visit adelaidemetro.com.au.

Car hire is available through numerous airport operators, including **Avis** (08 8234 4558, avis.com.au), **Budget** (08 8234 4111, budget.com.au), **Europcar** (13 13 90, europcar.com.au), **Hertz** (08 8234 4566, hertz.com.au) and **Thrifty** (1300 367 227, thrifty.com.au), or simply hail a cab which will cost you around $17 (£7) for the 15-minute airport-city trip.

By Train...
Great Southern Railways (13 21 47, gsr.com.au) operates three major interstate train services from its Adelaide station at Keswick, which is conveniently serviced by the Skylink Airport Shuttle for passengers continuing on into the city or airport.

The **Indian Pacific** operates regularly between Sydney, Adelaide and Perth. A trip from Adelaide to Sydney (25 hours) will set you back $245 (£100), while the Adelaide to Perth route (39 hours) costs $340 (£145).

The **Ghan** operates between Adelaide, Alice Springs and Darwin, while the **Overland** links Adelaide and Melbourne. A one-way Overland fare to Melbourne (11 hours) costs $65 (£28).

By Bus...
Adelaide's **Central Bus Station** on Franklin St has terminals and ticket offices for all major statewide and interstate bus companies, including **Firefly Express** (1300 730 740, fireflyexpress.com.au), **Greyhound Australia** (13 14 99, greyhound.com.au), **Premier Stateliner** (08 8415 5555, premierstateliner.com.au) and **V/Line** (13 61 96, vline.com.au).

The respective bus companies and **Bus SA** (bussa.com.au) have fare and timetable information on their websites. As a guide, prices for a one-way trip to Melbourne (11 hours) range from $50-$65 (£22-£28) and Sydney (24 hours) around $125 (£52).

PUBLIC TRANSPORT...

The **Adelaide Metro** (adelaidemetro.com.au) operates the city's bus, train and tram network, with two of its most popular services being the free **City Loop (99C)** and **Bee Line (99B)** bus services.

The City Loop service takes you around the city via North Tce, the East End, the Adelaide Central Market and Hindley St. It runs every 15 minutes on weekdays from 8am to 6.15pm (9.15pm Fridays), and every 30 minutes on Saturdays from 8.15am to 5.45pm and Sundays from 10am to 5.45pm.

The Bee Line takes you through the centre of the city via North Tce, King William St and Victoria Square, stopping at Rundle Mall, the Adelaide Town Hall and the Adelaide Central Market. It runs every five minutes on weekdays from 7.40am to 6pm (9.20pm Fridays), every 15 minutes on Saturdays from 8.27am to 5.35pm and every 15 minutes on Sundays from 10am to 5.30pm.

The City Loop and Bee Line (which both include wheelchair access) connect with services for the Glenelg Tram, Adelaide Railway Station, O-Bahn and *Jet* Bus (airport).

Tickets are required for other public transport services and can be purchased at the **Adelaide Metro Information Centre** on the corner of King William St and Currie St in the city. Tickets are also available in convenience stores, newsagents, staffed train stations or when you board (with the exception of multitrip tickets which must be purchased in advance).

Daytrip tickets for $7.20 (£3) are a popular choice for many travellers, as are the two-hour peak ($3.80/£1.60) and off-peak ($2.30/96p) singletrip tickets. Peak travel time is before 9am and after 3pm. And remember, you must validate your ticket in the blue stamping machines each time you board a service! A favourite service for late-night revellers is the **Wandering Star,** which for just $6 (£2.50) can pick you up from designated nightspots around town and deliver you to your front door with a designated Star Zone, whether you're staying in the city or suburbs. The service operates every Saturday and Sunday morning from 12.30am to 5am and is a cheap and safe means of getting home after a big night!

If you're commuting between Adelaide and Glenelg, the **Glenelg Tram** is your best bet. It operates between Moseley Square on the beach and Victoria Square in the city, and runs approximately every 15 minutes from 6am to 11.50pm.

For train passengers, five metropolitan routes are available to and from the **Adelaide Railway Station** on North Tce, including Belair via Goodwood and Blackwood, Gawler via North Adelaide and Ovingham, Noarlunga via Goodwood, Marion, Brighton and Seacliff, Outer Harbour via Port Adelaide, Glanville and Largs, and the Grange line.

The Adelaide City Council (adelaide.sa.gov.au) also runs a free **Adelaide Connector** bus service linking North Adelaide to the city. Daily services operate from 8am to 6pm Monday to Thursday, 8am to 9.30pm on Fridays, and 10am to 5pm on weekends.

By Taxi...

There are licensed ranks across the city or call:
Adelaide Independent..13 22 11
Suburban Taxis............13 10 08
Yellow Cabs..................13 22 27

For people with a disability, **Adelaide Access Taxis** (1300 360 940) are available around the clock. Fares to Adelaide Oval from most locations within the CBD are less than $10 (£4.20).

By Bicycle...

If cycling is more your thing, the Adelaide City Council provides free bicycle hire (up to two hours) for roaming the city. Bikes are available between 8am and 6pm daily from **Bicycle SA** (46 Hurtle Square, Adelaide) and **Cannon St Backpackers** (110 Franklin St, Adelaide - opposite the Central Bus Station).

The Bee Line (99B) is a free bus service for inner city commuting. Photo: South Australian Tourism Commission.

[GETTING TO ADELAIDE OVAL

And if **you're approaching** from **O'Connell St** in **NORTH** ADELAIDE, make sure you **take advantage** of the **view of the Adelaide Hills**.

By Bus...
Since Adelaide Oval is only a short walk from the city centre, there are numerous buses which will take you to within walking distance of the ground depending on which direction you are coming from (see adelaidemetro.com.au).

On Foot...
Adelaide Oval is situated on the northern edge of the city centre and is within easy walking distance of the main shopping and entertainment precincts of Rundle Mall and Hindley St.

For those staying in one of the numerous hotels on North Tce, the ground is just a five-minute stroll down King William St, past the Adelaide Festival Centre and Elder Park on the left and over the River Torrens which takes you to the south-eastern corner of the ground.

And if you're approaching from O'Connell St in North Adelaide, make sure you take advantage of the view of the Adelaide Hills as you make your way down from the prestigious suburb. That's if one of the cosy little pubs doesn't take your eye first!

If you're staying in the city during the Test, a clever option might be to take a free City Loop or Bee Line service (see page 57) which have drop points on North Tce.

By Train...
For train passengers on any of the five metropolitan routes to the **Adelaide Railway Station** on North Tce, including the Belair, Gawler, Noarlunga, Outer Harbour and Grange lines, it only takes five minutes to walk to the ground from the terminal.

By Taxi...
There are licensed taxi ranks across the city. Fares to Adelaide Oval from most locations within the CBD should cost you less than $10 (£4.20).
Adelaide Independent..13 22 11
Suburban Taxis 13 10 08
Yellow Cabs...................13 22 27

Tourists enjoying Adelaide.
Photo: South Australian Tourism Commission.

ADELAIDE

[ADELAIDE
-ACCOMMODATION

The Hyatt Regency Adelaide is just a five-minute walk from Adelaide Oval.
Photo: South Australian Tourism Commission.

[**NOTE:** Hostels can be booked via www.hostelbookers.com or www.hostelworld.com. Hotels, motels and apartments can be booked via www.wotif.com]

HOSTELS

LOW-RANGE: < $100 (£42)

ANNIE'S PLACE (pp70-71)
$17.95-$35.75 (£7.50-£15)
239 Franklin St, Adelaide
1800 818 011 (free call within Australia) OR **(08) 8212 2668**
anniesplace.com.au

Annie's Place Adelaide is a well-established hostel located near the Adelaide Central Markets and Gouger St's diverse and popular restaurant district. Adelaide Oval isn't too far away either - around a 20-minute walk

(2km) or quicker by taxi. All rooms contain air-conditioning, heating and television. The hostel itself is a heritage-listed building and contains a travel desk and bar.
It also offers useful facilities such as laundry and internet access. Dorm rooms and doubles/twins are available to suit all budgets. Dorm beds start at $17.90 per night (£7.50), while twin/double rooms with ensuite cost $35.75 (£15).

BLUE GALAH BACKPACKERS HOSTEL (pp70-71)
$25-$66 (£10.50-£27.50)
Level 1, 62 King William St, Adelaide **1800 555 322** (free call within Australia) OR **(08) 8231 9295**
bluegalah.com.au

Blue Galah Backpackers Hostel is a central hostel located only a few metres from the entertainment and shopping precincts of Rundle Mall and

www.ashes06.com

Hindley St. Adelaide Oval is also within easy walking distance (1km). The hostel has very modern and clean facilities, including a large multi-bay kitchen, internet, email and coin-operated laundry. You'll be able to relax on the large outdoor balconies or in the licensed bar that remains open until 3am. Dorm beds start from $25 per night (£10.50) and twin rooms, with shared bathroom, cost $66 per person per night (£27.50).

CANNON ST BACKPACKERS
(pp70-71)
$22 (£9)
110 Franklin St, Adelaide
(08) 8410 1218

Cannon St Backpackers is conveniently located opposite Adelaide's Central Bus Station (interstate arrivals and departures) and is just a block away from the Adelaide Central Market. You'll also be able to walk the short journey to Adelaide Oval (1km). The hostel has good facilities including restaurant, bar, internet access, laundry and luggage storage. All dorm rooms contain four beds and cost $22 per night (£9).

MY PLACE ADELAIDE
BACKPACKERS (pp70-71)
$22-$32 (£9-£13)
257 Waymouth St, Adelaide
1800 221 529 (free call within Australia) OR **(08) 8221 5299**
hostelworld.com

My Place Adelaide Backpackers Hostel is a good value hostel with very friendly and helpful staff. It is close to China Town, the Adelaide Central Market and Gouger St restaurants. You can walk to Adelaide Oval from the hostel in about 20 minutes or grab a taxi for the 2km journey. The hostel has been recently refurbished with new bathrooms and also contains table tennis facilities and a sauna for guests' use. It even operates a free bus shuttle to the beach! Rooms are air-conditioned with dorm beds costing $22 per night (£9) and double bed privates from $32 per person per night (£13).

SHAKESPEARE BACKPACKERS INTERNATIONAL HOSTEL
(pp70-71)
$19 (£8)
123 Waymouth St, Adelaide
1800 555 322 (ask for Shakespeare Backpackers - free call within Australia) OR **(08) 8231 7655** bluegalah.com.au

Shakespeare Backpackers International Hostel is located about three blocks from the pubs and bars of the funky west end of Hindley St. Adelaide Oval isn't too far away either and can be easily reached on foot (1.5km). The hostel is a restored 19th century mansion and contains a travel desk, laundry facilities and internet. Accommodation is simple but comfortable, with a cheap dorm bed rate of $19 per night (£8).

TATT'S BACKPACKERS ADELAIDE (pp70-71)
$18-$29 (£7.50-£12)
17 Hindley St, Adelaide
(08) 8410 8461
hostelsadelaide.com

Tatt's Backpackers Adelaide is a small hostel conveniently located on bustling Hindley St above the Tattersall's hotel. It's a great location and you won't need to go far to get a pint as you admire the views of Hindley St and Rundle Mall from the outdoor terrace. And Adelaide Oval is an easy 10-minute walk away (1km). The hostel's facilities include laundry, restaurant and internet access, and you'll receive complimentary transfers to the hostel from the interstate train station, bus station or airport if you book for three or more days. Dorm beds start from $18 per night (£7.50), while a twin private with shared bathroom costs $29 per person (£12).

HOTELS, MOTELS & APARTMENTS

LOW-RANGE: < $100 (£42)

ADELAIDE PARINGA MOTEL
(pp70-71)
$95 (£40)
15 Hindley St, Adelaide
1800 088 202 (free call within Australia) OR **(08) 8231 1000**
Reservations via email:
paringa@senet.com.au

The **Adelaide Paringa Motel** is a well-priced hotel situated on Hindley St opposite Rundle Mall. This great location provides close access to the Adelaide Festival Centre, SkyCity Adelaide Casino and, of course, Adelaide Oval, which is only a stone's throw away (1km). The hotel offers a 24-hour desk, restaurant, room service and a tour desk. All rooms have TV, air-conditioning, ensuite and mini fridge. Standard rooms start from $95 per night (£40).

continued overpage...

[ACCOMMODATION
...continued from page 61.

AMBASSADORS' HOTEL
(pp70-71)
$60-$80 (£25-£33)
107 King William St, Adelaide
1800 882 995 (free call within Australia) OR **(08) 8231 4331**
Reservations via email:
ambhotel@senet.com.au

The **Ambassadors' Hotel** offers inexpensive accommodation and is well located in the city centre. Just a block away you'll find the entertainment and shopping precincts of Rundle Mall and Hindley St. Adelaide Oval is within walking distance (1km) and you can easily take a taxi down King William St to reach the ground. All rooms are fitted with ensuite bathrooms, air-conditioning and TV.

Ambassadors' room rates are great value: single rooms cost $60 per night (£25) and double rooms $80 (£33).

DIRECTOR'S STUDIO (pp70-71)
$92-$120 (£38-£50)
259 Gouger St, Adelaide
1800 804 224 (free call within Australia) OR **(08) 8213 2500**
Reservations via email:
directors.info@shg.com.au
savillesuites.com

Director's Studio offers comfortable and affordable hotel or suite accommodation and is located on Gouger St, one of Adelaide's premier dining strips. Adelaide Oval can be reached on foot (2km) or by a five-minute taxi ride. The studios themselves contain kitchenette facilities, TV and air-conditioning. Director's Studio hotel rooms start at $92 per night (£38) while studio rooms/apartments start at $120 (£50).

MOTEL ADJACENT CASINO
(pp70-71)
$70-$200 (£29-£83)
25 Bank St, Adelaide
(08) 8231 8881
Reservations via email:
reception@motel adjacentcasino.com.au
moteladjacentcasino.com.au

The **Motel Adjacent Casino** is located on Bank St and, as the name suggests, sits opposite SkyCity Adelaide Casino. This great location also puts it close to the hub of Adelaide's entertainment districts. Adelaide Oval is close by and within easy walking distance (1km). The Motel Adjacent Casino offers modest but comfortable accommodation. Rooms are serviced daily and contain reverse cycle air-conditioning, TV and ensuite. Single rooms start from $70 per night (£29), double rooms $80 (£33), and triple share rooms $110 (£46). Apartments start from $200 per night (£83).

Hotel Richmond. Photo: South Australian Tourism Commission.

www.ashes06.com

ACCOMMODATION

PRINCES LODGE MOTEL
(pp70-71)
$49-$89 (£20-£37)
73 Lefevre Tce, North Adelaide
(08) 8267 5566
Reservations via email:
princeslodge@senet.com.au
princeslodge.com.au

The **Princes Lodge Motel** lies in a picturesque location alongside architecturally beautiful homes and parklands. It is within close walking distance to North Adelaide's restaurants and pubs, while Adelaide Oval is just a short walk (1.5km) or taxi ride. The Princes Lodge Motel suits the budget traveller, with single rooms starting from $49 (£20), standard double rooms from $70 (£29) and deluxe doubles from $89 (£37). All rooms include private ensuite, air-conditioning and TV.

HOTELS, MOTELS & APARTMENTS

MID-RANGE: $100-$200 (£42-£84)

BEST WESTERN O'CONNELL INN (pp70-71)
$105-$150 (£44-£62)
197-199 O'Connell St,
North Adelaide **(08) 8239 0766**
Reservations via email:
reservations@
oconnellinn.com.au

The **Best Western O'Connell Inn** is located on stylish O'Connell St in North Adelaide. Close to cafés, pubs, bars and boutique shops, you'll have plenty to do, before and after a day's play during the Test. You can walk (1.5km) or catch a taxi from O'Connell St to Adelaide Oval, passing beautiful St Peter's Cathedral on the way. All rooms feature reverse cycle air-conditioning, private ensuite and TV with satellite. The O'Connell Inn offers standard rooms ($105/£44), deluxe rooms ($115/£48) and spa rooms ($160/£67). You can also book apartments, with a one-bedroom starting from $125 (£52) and a three-bedroom from $150 (£62).

HOTEL RICHMOND (pp70-71)
$145-$190 (£60-£79)
128 Rundle Mall, Adelaide
(08) 8223 4044
hotelrichmond.com.au

The **Hotel Richmond** is nestled within the shopper's paradise of Rundle Mall. This great location gives you easy access to the lively East End, the Art Gallery of South Australia and the South Australian Museum. To get to Adelaide Oval (1km), enjoy a walk along the River Torrens, past charming Adelaide University. A redevelopment in 2000 has resulted in chic yet comfortable guest rooms. Room facilities are high quality and include Sony flat-screen TVs, ensuite bathrooms, room safes and opening windows. Standard guest rooms start from $145 per night (£60), with the higher range executive suites starting from $190 (£79).

MAJESTIC ROOF GARDEN HOTEL ADELAIDE (pp70-71)
$149 (£62)
55 Frome St, Adelaide
(08) 8100 4400
majestichotels.com.au

The **Majestic Roof Garden Hotel Adelaide** is the place to stay if you want to be close to Adelaide's cosmopolitan East End. As the name suggests, the hotel has a unique roof garden that provides superb views of the city. Rooms are high quality with excellent facilities, such as large-screen TV with satellite, sizeable private bathrooms, air-conditioning and mini-bar. The Majestic Roof offers business class rooms starting from $149 (£62). It's worth looking at their website as you can view discount rates and check out other Majestic hotels and serviced apartments in Adelaide.

MERCURE GROSVENOR HOTEL ADELAIDE
(pp70-71)
$99-$190 (£41-£79)
125 North Tce, Adelaide
1800 888 222 (free call within Australia) OR **(08) 8407 8888**
mercuregrosvenorhotel.com.au

The **Mercure Grosvenor Hotel Adelaide** is a well-priced hotel given its ideal location on North Tce. Not only is it situated opposite SkyCity Adelaide Casino and Adelaide Festival Centre, Adelaide Oval is conveniently within walking distance (1km) so you won't need to go far to catch all the Test action. The Mercure Grosvenor has a range of rooms with good standard facilities such as centralised air-conditioning and ensuite bathroom. Room prices suit different budgets and range from economy at $99 twin share (£41) to the deluxe spa suites at $190 twin share (£79).

continued overpage…

ACCOMMODATION
...continued from page 63.

QUEST MANSIONS SERVICED APARTMENTS (pp70-71)
$165 (£69)
21 Pulteney St, Adelaide
(08) 8232 0033
Reservations via email:
questmansions@questapartments.com.au
questmansions.com.au

The **Quest Mansions Serviced Apartments** are nicely priced apartments in a great location adjoining Rundle Mall - and just metres from the boutiques and restaurants of Rundle St! You can easily walk to Adelaide Oval (1km) along the newly redeveloped North Tce frontage. All apartments have been refurbished and contain fully equipped kitchens, air-conditioning, TVs and large living rooms. A one-bedroom apartment costs $165 per night (£69).

HOTELS, MOTELS & APARTMENTS

HIGH-RANGE: $200+ (£84+)

HILTON ADELAIDE (pp70-71)
$210 (£88)
233 Victoria Square, Adelaide
(08) 8217 2000 hilton.com

The **Hilton Adelaide** is located in the heart of the city and overlooks the open green spaces of Victoria Square. Trams to historic Glenelg leave from Victoria Square regularly, so you can arrive at one of Adelaide's premier beach areas in around 30 minutes. Guest room rates generally start at $210 twin share per night (£88). All rooms contain queen-sized beds, large opening windows, air-conditioning, separate bathroom, TV and Sony PlayStation. You can walk or take a taxi north along King William St to Adelaide Oval, which is less than 2km away.

HYATT REGENCY ADELAIDE (pp70-71)
$260 (£108)
North Tce, Adelaide
13 12 34 OR **(08) 8231 1234**
adelaide.regency.hyatt.com

The **Hyatt Regency Adelaide** is arguably Adelaide's foremost luxury hotel. Situated in a prime location on North Tce, it is flanked by SkyCity Adelaide Casino and the Adelaide Convention Centre. Looking north, Adelaide Oval is visible on the other side of the River Torrens, making the Hyatt an impressive part of the riverbank promenade. Every room is fitted with high quality facilities including air-conditioning, TV with satellite, marble bathroom with bathtub and separate shower. The hotel complex itself contains three restaurants, lounge bar and a nightclub. Twin/double room rates start from $260 (£108).

Swimming with dolphins. Photo: South Australian Tourism Commission.

www.ashes06.com

ACCOMMODATION

MEDINA GRAND ADELAIDE TREASURY (pp70-71)
$271-$420 (£113-£175)
2 Flinders St, Adelaide
1300 633 462 OR **(08) 8112 0000**
medinaapartments.com.au

The **Medina Grand Adelaide Treasury** in the centre of town offers a range of one and two-bedroom serviced apartments and studio rooms overlooking picturesque Victoria Square. This convenient location allows easy walking access to the retail and restaurant areas of Rundle Mall, Hindley St and Gouger St. And Adelaide Oval is less than 2km away. The studios and apartments feature fully equipped kitchens, bathrooms, separate lounge and dining areas. Studio rooms (1-2 persons) cost $271 per night (£113). A one-bedroom apartment (1-2 persons) costs $315 (£131) and a two-bedroom apartment (2-4 persons) costs $420 (£175).

PACIFIC INTERNATIONAL APARTMENTS (pp70-71)
$250-$540 (£104-£225)
88 Frome St, Adelaide
1800 224 584 (free call within Australia) OR **(08) 8223 9000**
pacificinthotels.com

The **Pacific International Apartments** complex is located metres from Adelaide's chic and thriving East End.
You can easily walk to Adelaide Oval (1km) along lovely tree-lined North Tce, taking in the beautifully maintained Victorian buildings of Adelaide University, the Art Gallery of South Australia and the South Australian Museum.
The Pacific International Apartments offer spacious studios costing $250 per night (£104). One-bedroom apartments cost $270 (£113), two-bedroom apartments $350 (£146) and three-bedroom apartments $540 (£225).

RADISSON PLAYFORD HOTEL & SUITES ADELAIDE (pp70-71)
$160-$220 (£67-£92)
120 North Tce, Adelaide
(08) 8213 8888
radisson.com/adelaideau

The **Radisson Playford Hotel and Suites Adelaide** is an elegant boutique hotel located on North Tce, just a stone's throw from the Adelaide Festival Centre, Adelaide SkyCity Casino and Adelaide Railway Station. Adelaide Oval is also conveniently within walking distance (1km). The Radisson has comfortable, high quality amenities in each room, including deluxe private bathroom, TV and kitchenette. You can take advantage of the hotel's "hot deals", which will get you a twin share guest room for around $160 (£67) by booking in advance. Otherwise, guest rooms generally start at around $220 per night (£92).

Barossa Valley. Photo: South Australian Tourism Commission.

ADELAIDE

[ADELAIDE -RESTAURANTS

Adelaide has restaurants for all tastes. Photo: South Australian Tourism Commission.

EAST
OF ADELAIDE OVAL

> Amalfi Pizzeria Risorante, named in honour of the gorgeous Italian seaside village, has been serving up wood-fired pizzas in Adelaide's funky East End for over 20 years. Amalfi is packed with locals just about every night and it's not difficult to see why it's such a popular spot when you sample the tasty Italian fare on offer.
29 Frome St, Adelaide
(08) 8223 1948
(pp70-71)
Mains $15-$30 (£6-£13)

> The Botanic Café provides an appealing alternative to the traditional restaurant dining experience. While it has always been trendy and modern, the Botanic has reached a stylish peak since undergoing a facelift in 2003. Enjoy an alfresco lunch where you can admire the beautiful Botanic Gardens and parklands located opposite. At night and on weekends the Botanic becomes a favourite night spot for Adelaide's young and fashionable.
4 East Tce, Adelaide
(08) 8232 0626
(pp70-71)
Mains $20-$30 (£8-£13)

> The Jasmin Indian Restaurant has earned the much-deserved reputation of being the best Indian restaurant in Adelaide. One of the oldest family run restaurants, the Jasmin has been going strong for almost 25 years. In cosy surrounds, enjoy the sublime flavours of traditional North Indian dishes. If you like it hot, try the fiery, mouth-watering beef vindaloo, or for those who like something a little less explosive but no less tasty, consider the chicken masala which consists of a boneless chicken curry in a mild sauce with herbs and spices.
31 Hindmarsh Square, Adelaide (08) 8223 7837
(pp70-71)
Mains $20-$30 (£8-£13)

NORTH
OF ADELAIDE OVAL

> Adelaide is renowned for its superb Thai restaurants and the award-winning Amarin is one of the best the city has to offer.

www.ashes06.com

Tucked away in a little side street adjacent to lively O'Connell St in North Adelaide (if you didn't know it was there you could easily walk past it), Amarin's food is divine. The Miang Kum in particular is highly recommended, consisting of steamed prawns and cashews in coconut and ginger, wrapped in a fresh betel leaf.
108 Tynte St, North Adelaide
(08) 8239 0026
(pp70-71)
Mains under $20 (£8)

SOUTH
OF ADELAIDE OVAL

The award-winning Alphütte restaurant is the place to go to enjoy Swiss and European style cuisine. When ordering your main course it's hard to go past the traditional Swiss "roschti" as an accompaniment, which consists of grated potatoes arranged into a pancake shape and fried with other ingredients such as bacon, onion and cheese. Alphütte has maintained a consistent level of quality service for the past 20 years.
242-244 Pulteney St, Adelaide
(08) 8223 4717 alphutte.com.au
(pp70-71)
Mains $25-$30 (£10-£13)
Fully licensed (no BYO)

If you crave elegant yet comfortable surroundings to heighten your dining experience, consider Auge Ristorante. Start the night by sampling an aperitif at the bar, then move into the dining room to enjoy Auge's lush, authentic Italian fare (honoured as South Australia's "Best Restaurant" in 2005).
22 Grote St, Adelaide
(08) 8410 9332
(pp70-71)
Mains $24-$32 (£10-£13)

Jerusalem Sheshkabab House is the place to go for the best Middle Eastern cuisine in Adelaide. Located on lively Hindley St, the Jerusalem Sheshkabab House is a lovely little family run restaurant with loads of character. The interior of the restaurant is charming, with a tented ceiling and traditional music playing in the background enhancing your dining enjoyment. Atmosphere aside, the food is delicious - just don't forget to bring your own bottle of wine as the restaurant does not serve alcohol!
131b Hindley St, Adelaide
(08) 8212 6185
(pp70-71)
Mains $10-$20 (£4-£8)

South Australia is the home of King George whiting and Paul's Seafood on Gouger is the place to go for a nicely grilled or battered piece. Paul's doesn't only stand out for its lovely whiting, it also serves a range of delicious seafood including snapper, oysters, prawns, calamari - indeed, the list is seemingly endless! Paul's is also fantastic value for money.
79 Gouger St, Adelaide
(08) 8410 0268
(pp70-71)
Mains under $10 (£4)

Gaucho's Argentinian Restaurant barely has enough wall space to fit the multiple awards for excellence it has won. Gaucho's, the first Argentinian restaurant in Australia, specialises in char-grilled meats and seafood and offers a unique dining experience which allows you to select your own fresh cuts of meat.
91 Gouger St, Adelaide
(08) 8231 2299
(pp70-71)
Mains $25-$35 (£10-£15)

WEST
OF ADELAIDE OVAL

There is no better place to sample some genuine Australian cuisine than at the Red Ochre restaurant, which is simply first-rate. Situated in a wonderful location on the banks of Adelaide's River Torrens, you'll enjoy a scenic view of both the river and city skyline, while enjoying a wonderfully authentic Australian meal made from indigenous Australian ingredients.
War Memorial Dve,
North Adelaide
(08) 8211 8555
(pp70-71)
Mains $20-$35 (£8-£15)

The Radisson Playford Hotel on North Tce is just a short stroll from Adelaide Oval. Photo: South Australian Tourism Commission.

ADELAIDE PUBS & CLUBS

PUBS

EAST
OF ADELAIDE OVAL

The Exeter Hotel is a popular pub in the city's East End that attracts a laidback "university" crowd. Friday and Saturday nights are particularly busy with patrons literally spilling out the front door. The front and lounge bars open from 11am until late, and the enclosed beer garden to the rear of the pub features live bands every night at 9pm. The Exeter has so much character from the classic old wooden bar fridges to its famous curry nights on the balcony every Wednesday and Thursday (be sure to book).
246 Rundle St, Adelaide
(pp70-71) **(08) 8223 2623**

The old Kent Town Hotel, now affectionately called The Tap Inn, is the ultimate hotel for the golf enthusiast. Featuring an indoor driving range and a rooftop putting green, The Tap Inn offers a kitsch alternative to enhance your pub and dining experience. Exquisite main meals consisting of delicious tapas are a highlight, but if it's just a beer or two you're after, the venue offers a vast collection of brews on tap. Oh, and if you don't have a ticket to Adelaide Oval for the Test, you can watch all the 3 mobile Ashes action on wide-screen TVs in the "Sand Bunker" beer garden.
76 Rundle St, Kent Town
(pp70-71) **(08) 8362 2116**

A relatively recent addition to Adelaide's pub scene is the authentic Belgian Beer Café – Oostende, located in the vibrant East End. For beer connoisseurs, a visit to the Belgian Beer Café is a must, with a tantalising selection of specialty imported beers. You'll be impressed with the traditional beer pouring ritual which sees bar staff wash, rinse and chill your glass before delicately pouring the beer and smoothing off the overflow with a head cutter. The Belgian Beer Café also serves top quality traditional Belgian fare - try the delicious mussels and pomme frites with mayonnaise.
27-29 Ebenezer Place, Adelaide
(pp70-71) **(08) 8359 2233**

For a great British pub check out The Elephant just off Rundle St in the East End. The faux medieval exterior certainly gives the pub an enchanting yesteryear feel and the interior is equally charming with authentic looking décor; hearty pub meals and a large range of imported beers on tap.
1 Cinema Place, Adelaide
(pp70-71) **(08) 8227 1633**

www.ashes06.com

PUBS AND CLUBS

NORTH
OF ADELAIDE OVAL

After a $4 million (£1.7 million) revamp, the **Archer Hotel** on thriving O'Connell St is easily one of the best Aussie pubs in Adelaide. The Archer is truly a hybrid, providing two very distinct bar areas. Downstairs you'll find an Australian Outback style bar dubbed "Larrikins" and upstairs you'll find a sophisticated cocktail bar serving premium spirits. To attest to the Archer's unique appearance and high quality service, the hotel was named joint winner of the state's "Best Bar Presentation and Service Award" in 2003.
**60 O'Connell St,
North Adelaide**
(pp70-71) **(08) 8361 9300**

The Lion Hotel has undergone many incarnations since its days as a 19th century brewery. In the early 20th century it was an aerated water manufactory (fizzy pop makers), but in the 1970s it was renamed the "Old Lion" and became a popular entertainment venue. After extensive renovations in the late 1990s, it morphed into its present stylish guise as "The Lion". Nowadays, it generally attracts a large, trendy crowd each Friday and Saturday night, serving great local beers and cocktails. You can also enjoy a top-notch meal in the restaurant or beer garden.
**161 Melbourne St,
North Adelaide**
(pp70-71) **(08) 8367 0222**

The Queen's Head Hotel is a popular little pub tucked away on a lovely residential street in North Adelaide. Housed in a charming bluestone heritage-listed building, it is one of the oldest hotels in SA. Many locals choose the Queen's Head as the place to go to enjoy a pint after a day's cricket at Adelaide Oval.

Just follow the throngs when stumps are called.
**117 Kermode St,
North Adelaide**
(pp70-71) **(08) 8267 1139**

SOUTH
OF ADELAIDE OVAL

Visit the **Coopers Alehouse** at the Earl of Aberdeen Hotel and you'll get the best of both local and international beer worlds. You can sample the entire Coopers range (South Australia's foremost local brewery) or indulge in the numerous imported and boutique beers available. The Alehouse has a lovely interior where you can relax on luxury suede seating, marvel at the enormous brass fan, enjoy good music and catch all the Ashes highlights on the large plasma screen TVs.
316 Pulteney St, Adelaide
(pp70-71) **(08) 8223 6433**

CLUBS

EAST
OF ADELAIDE OVAL

For a fantastic cocktail lounge in Adelaide, try **Fumo Blu** on Rundle St in the city. Hidden below street level, head downstairs and be impressed when you enter a stylish bar that oozes class. After you order from the extensive cocktail menu, grab one of the large comfy booths. Remember strict dress codes apply - avoid shorts, thongs or trainers.
270 Rundle St, Adelaide
(pp70-71) **(08) 8232 2533**

SOUTH
OF ADELAIDE OVAL

In recent times, Adelaide has seen a surge of groovy lounge bars pop up throughout the city. **Savvy Bar & Lounge** is certainly a popular addition to this trend. The newly renovated Savvy is at the height of club lounge sophistication, with a combination of cosy couches and chilled beats. Savvy remains a firm favourite with locals looking to unwind with friends.
149 Waymouth St, Adelaide
(pp70-71) **(08) 8221 6030**

GLENELG
SOUTH-WEST OF CITY

If you feel like getting out of the city, head down to the **Stamford Grand** at Glenelg. Aside from being a high quality luxury hotel situated right on the beachfront, it also boasts a popular bar and nightclub. On a busy Saturday night the line-up can be quite long as hip young things wait patiently to get inside. The music is a mixture of the latest chart toppers, R & B, soul and dance beats.
**Moseley Square, Glenelg
(08) 8376 1222**

ADELAIDE CITY MAP

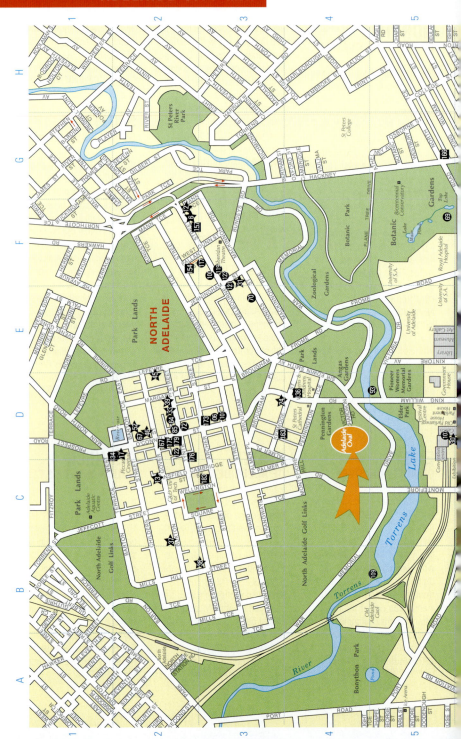

ADELAIDE MAPS

continued overpage...

ADELAIDE CITY MAP (pp70-71)

■ Denotes multiple venue

ACCOMMODATION KEY

#	Ref	Name	Address	Phone	Website	$ Cost per night	RATE Star rating	OVAL Kilometres from Adelaide Oval
1	C7	Adelaide Central YHA	135 Waymouth St, Adelaide, 5000	08 8414 3010	www.yha.com.au	27-111	***	1.93
2	E8	Adelaide City Park Motel	471 Pulteney St, Adelaide, 5000	08 8223 1444	www.citypark.com.au	104-122	***	2.91
3	D6	Adelaide Paringa Motel	15 Hindley St, Adelaide, 5000	08 8231 1000		95-150	****	1.09
4	G8	Adelaide Parklands City Townhouse	376 South Tce, Adelaide, 5000	08 8223 1832		120		3.90
5	F8	Adelaide Parklands Heritage Cottage	15 McLaren St, Adelaide, 5000	08 8223 1832		120		3.25
6	F2	Adelaide Regent Apartments	55 Melbourne St, North Adelaide, 5006	08 8267 8888	www.adelaideregent.com.au	143-169	****	1.66
7	E8	Adelaide Regent Apartments	Cnr Gilles & Hutt Sts, Adelaide, 5000	08 8224 8888	www.adelaideregent.com.au	132-169	****	3.36
8	E7	Adelaide Regent Apartments	177 Angas St, Adelaide, 5000	08 8224 8888	www.adelaideregent.com.au	169-194	****	2.45
9	E8	Adelaide Regent Aparts-Chelsea	188 Carrington St, Adelaide, 5000	08 8224 8888	www.adelaideregent.com.au	195-221	****	2.58
10	E8	Adelaide Regent Aparts-Windsor	Cnr Pulteney & Gilles St, Adelaide, 5000	08 8224 0753	www.adelaideregent.com.au	175	****	2.82
11	F8	Adelaide Traveller's Inn	220 Hutt St, Adelaide, 5000	08 8224 8888		20-65		3.32
12	F2	All Seasons Adelaide Meridien	21 Melbourne St, North Adelaide, 5006	08 8267 3033	www.adelaidemeridien.com.au	119-260	****	1.77
13	C2	Aman & Gurny Lodge Apartments	190 Gover St, North Adelaide, 5006	08 8267 2500		69-110		1.68
14	D6	Ambassadors Hotel	107 King William St, Adelaide, 5000	08 8231 4331		60-80		1.29
15	C7	Annie's Place Adelaide	239 Franklin St, Adelaide, 5000	08 8212 2668	www.anniesplace.com.au	18-36		2.67
16	C6	Best Western Adelaide Riviera	31 North Tce, Adelaide, 5000	08 8231 8000	www.adelaideriviera.com.au	100-205	****	1.77
17	D2	Best Western O'Connell Inn	197 O'Connell St, North Adelaide, 5006	08 8239 0766	www.oconnellinn.com.au	105-160		1.68
18	D6	Blue Galah Backpackers Resort	Lvl 1, 62 King William St, Adelaide, 5000	08 8231 9295	www.bluegalah.com.au	25-66		1.10
19	C7	Cannon St Backpackers	110 Franklin St, Adelaide, 5000	08 8410 1218	www.cannonst.com.au	19-57		2.17
20	E8	Chifley on South Terrace	226 South Tce, Adelaide, 5000	08 8223 4355	www.chifleyhotels.com	142-203	****	3.00
21	B7	Director's Studios Adelaide	259 Gouger St, Adelaide, 5000	08 8213 2500	www.savillesuites.com	92-120	****	2.71
22	D6	Festival City Hotel Motel	140 North Tce, Adelaide, 5000	08 8212 7877		90-135	***	1.25
23	D7	Franklin Central Apartments	36 Franklin St, Adelaide, 5000	08 8221 7050	www.franklinapartments.com.au	109-380	****	1.68
24	D3	Greenways Apartments	45 King William Rd, North Adelaide, 5006	08 8267 5903	www.greenwaysapartments.com	80-200	***	0.79
25	D7	Hilton Adelaide	233 Victoria Square, Adelaide, 5000	08 8217 2000	www.hilton.com	185-535	*****	2.00
26	D6	Holiday Inn Adelaide	65 Hindley St, Adelaide, 5000	08 8231 5552	www.holiday-inn.com	145-250	****	1.24
27	E8	Hotel 208 by Constellation	208 South Tce, Adelaide, 5000	08 8223 2800	www.constellationhotels.com	131-149	****	2.79
28	D6	Hotel Grand Chancellor Adelaide	18 Currie St, Adelaide, 5000	08 8112 8888		180-230	****	1.23
29	E6	Hotel Richmond	128 Rundle Mall, Adelaide, 5000	08 8223 4044	www.hotelrichmond.com.au	145-270	****	1.99
30	D5	Hyatt Regency Adelaide	North Tce, Adelaide, 5000	08 8231 1234	www.adelaide.regency.hyatt.com	260	*****	1.16
31	F3	Majestic Old Lion Apartments	9 Jerningham St, North Adelaide, 5006	08 8334 7799	www.majestichotels.com.au	149-258	****	1.38
32	F6	Majestic Roof Garden Hotel	55 Frome St, Adelaide, 5000	08 8100 4400	www.majestichotels.com.au	149-264	****	1.84
33	D2	Majestic Tynte St Apartments	82 Tynte St, North Adelaide, 5006	08 8334 7783	www.majestichotels.com.au	117-136	****	1.43
34	D7	Medina Grand Adelaide Treasury	2 Flinders St, Adelaide, 5000	08 8112 0000	www.medinaapartments.com.au	271-420	****	1.46
35	D6	Mercure Grosvenor Hotel	125 North Tce, Adelaide, 5000	08 8407 8888	www.mercuregrosvenorhotel.com.au	99-210	****	1.17
36	C7	My Place Adelaide Backpackers	257 Waymouth St, Adelaide, 5000	08 8221 5299	www.hostelworld.com	22-32		2.05
37	C2	North Adelaide Heritage Aparts	Buxton St, North Adelaide, 5006	08 8272 1355	www.adelaideheritage.com	180-220	*****	2.01
38	B3	Nth Adel Heritage Aparts	82 Molesworth St, North Adelaide, 5006	08 8272 1355	www.adelaideheritage.com	295	*****	1.97
39	D2	Nth Adelaide Heritage Apartments	78 Tynte St, North Adelaide, 5006	08 8272 1355	www.adelaideheritage.com	240-350	****	1.44

40	D6	Oaks Embassy Hotel	96 North Tce, Adelaide, 5000	08 8124 9900	www.theoaksgroup.com.au	185-500	*****	1.44
41	C6	Oaks Horizons Adelaide	104 North Tce, Adelaide, 5000	08 8210 8000	www.theoaksgroup.com.au	155-550	*****	1.48
42	F6	Pacific International Apartments	88 Frome St, Adelaide, 5000	08 8223 9000	www.pacificinthotels.com	250-540	****	1.98
43	E6	Pacific International Suites	55-67 Hindmarsh Square, Adelaide, 5000	08 8412 3333	www.pacificinthotels.com	189-334	*****	2.02
44	D6	Plaza Hotel	85 Hindley St, Adelaide, 5000	08 8231 6371	www.plazahotel.com.au	75-85	***	1.30
45	D2	Princes Lodge Motel	73 Lefevre Tce, North Adelaide, 5006	08 8267 5566	www.princeslodge.com.au	49-126	**,	1.68
46	D2	Quality Hotel Old Adelaide	160 O'Connell St, North Adelaide, 5006	08 8267 5066	www.oldadelaideinn.com.au	129-219	*****	1.52
47	C6	Quality Hotel Rockford Adelaide	164 Hindley St, Adelaide, 5000	08 8211 8255	www.rockfordhotels.com.au	118-245	*****	1.59
48	E6	Quest Mansions	21 Pulteney St, Adelaide, 5000	08 8232 0033	www.questmansions.com.au	140-190	****	1.51
49	D6	Quest on King William	82 King William St, Adelaide, 5000	08 8217 5000	www.questapartments.com.au	145-240	****	1.15
50	D8	Quest on Sturt	14 Sturt St, Adelaide, 5000	08 8416 4200	www.questapartments.com.au	185	*****	2.34
51	D6	Radisson Playford Hotel and Suites	120 North Tce, Adelaide, 5000	08 8213 8888	www.radisson.com	160-500	*****	1.61
52	D2	Regal Park Motor Inn	44 Barton Tce East, North Adelaide, 5006	08 8267 3222	www.regalpark.com.au	100-155	***	1.72
53	D6	Rendezvous Allegra Hotel Adelaide	55 Waymouth St, Adelaide, 5000	08 8115 8888	www.rendezvous.com.au	340-650	*****	1.51
54	H6	Royal Coach Motor Inn	24 Dequetteville Tce, Kent Town, 5067	08 8362 5676	www.royalcoach.com.au	125-195	****	3.13
55	B8	Rydges South Park Adelaide	Cnr South & West Tces, Adelaide, 5000	08 8212 1277	www.rydges.com	130-230	*****	3.61
56	C6	Saville City Suites Adelaide	255 Hindley St, Adelaide, 5000	08 8217 2500	www.savillesuites.com	135-165	****	1.87
57	D6	Shakespeare Backpackers Int.	123 Waymouth St, Adelaide, 5000	08 8231 7655	www.bluegalah.com.au	19-66		1.73
58	D6	Stamford Plaza Adelaide	150 North Tce, Adelaide, 5000	08 8461 1111	www.stamford.com.au	180-987	****	0.95
59	D6	Tatts Backpackers Adelaide	17 Hindley St, Adelaide, 5000	08 8231 3225	www.hostelsadelaide.com	18-58		1.09
60	D6	The Motel Adjacent Casino	25 Bank St, Adelaide, 5000	08 8231 8881	www.moteladjacentcasino.com.au	70-200	***	1.12
61	F9	Tiffins on the Park	176 Greenhill Rd, Adelaide, 5000	08 8271 0444	www.tiffinsonthepark.com.au	139-219	****	4.00

continued overpage...

ADELAIDE CITY MAP (pp70-71)

RESTAURANTS KEY

■ Denotes multiple venue
$ Cost of main meal

#	Ref	Name	Address	Phone	Website	Cuisine	$	BYO
62	E7	Alphutte	242 Pulteney St, Adelaide, 5000	08 8223 4717	www.alphutte.com.au	Modern Australian	25-30	N
63	F6	Amalfi Pizzeria	29 Frome St, Adelaide, 5000	08 8223 1948		Italian	15-30	Y wine -$10 corkage
64	D2	Amarin Thai	108 Tynte St, North Adelaide, 5006	08 8239 0026		Thai	15-20	Y wine -$8 corkage
65	D7	Auge Ristorante	22 Grote St, Adelaide, 5000	08 8410 9332	www.auge.com.au	Italian	24-44	Y wine -$15 corkage
66	F6	Belgian Beer Cafe	27-29 Ebenezer Pl, Adelaide, 5000	08 8359 3400	www.oostende.com.au	Belgian	20-28	N
67	D2	Beyond India	170 O'Connell St, North Adelaide, 5006	08 8267 3820		Indian	14	Y wine -$6 corkage
68	F6	Botanic Cafe	4 East Tce, Adelaide, 5000	08 8223 0626		Bistro/Cafe, Italian	20-30	Y wine -$15 corkage
69	F5	Botanic Gardens	North Tce, Adelaide, 5000	08 8223 3526	www.botanicgardenrestaurant.com.au	Modern Australian	40-52	Y wine -$7.50 corkage
70	E3	British Hotel	58 Finniss St, North Adelaide, 5006	08 8267 2188		Modern Australian	18-25	Y wine -$15 corkage
71	E6	Cafe Michael	204 Rundle St, Adelaide, 5000	08 8223 3519		Thai	15-25	Y wine -$8 corkage
72	D2	Café Paesano	100 O'Connell St, North Adelaide, 5006	08 8239 0655		Italian	15	Y wine -$7 corkage
73	F6	Caffe Primo	300 Rundle St, Adelaide, 5000	08 8232 4246		Italian	10-14	N
74	F8	Chianti Classico	160 Hutt St, Adelaide, 5000	08 8232 7955	www.chianticlassico.com.au	Modern Italian	22-45	Y wine -$15 corkage
75	F6	Chopstix on Rundle	287 Rundle St, Adelaide, 5000	08 8223 7575		Asian	12-17	Y wine -$10 corkage
76	D8	Citi Zen Chinese	King William St, Adelaide, 5000	08 8212 6383	www.zenrestaurant.com.au	Chinese	14-30	Y wine -$15 corkage
77	F6	Citrus	199 Hutt St, Adelaide, 5000	08 8224 0100	www.citrus.net.au	Varied	18-32	Y wine -$15 corkage
78	E6	Comix Comedy Cellar	68 Grenfell St, Adelaide, 5000	08 8232 5688	www.comedycellar.com.au	Varied	40-60	N
79	E6	Coopers Alehouse	316 Pulteney St, Adelaide, 5000	08 8232 6433	www.earlofab.com.au	Modern Australian	20-28	N
80	D6	Cos Bar & Restaurant	18 Leigh St, Adelaide, 5000	08 8231 7611	www.justcos.com.au	Modern Australian	15-29	Y wine only
81	F8	Enoteca Cucina	262 Carrington St, Adelaide, 5000	08 8227 0766	www.enotecacucina.com.au	Italian	21-51	N
82	E6	Eros Ouzeri	277 Rundle St, Adelaide, 5000	08 8223 4022	www.erosouzeri.com.au	Greek	25-28	Y wine -$10 corkage
83	E6	Everest Cafe	187 Rundle St, Adelaide, 5000	08 8223 2243	www.everestcafe.com.au	Café style food	10-20	N
84	E7	Fasta Pasta	131 Pirie St, Adelaide, 5000	08 8224 0320	www.fastapasta.com.au	Italian	9-18	N
85	D2	Fellini Café	102 O'Connell St, North Adelaide, 5006	08 8239 2235		Italian	18	N
86	C7	Gaucho's Argentinian	91-93 Gouger St, Adelaide, 5000	08 8231 2299	www.gauchos.com.au	Argentinian	28-35	Y wine -$15 corkage
87	F8	Goodlife Modern Organic	170 Hutt St, Adelaide, 5000	08 8223 2618	www.goodlifepizza.com	Organic Pizza	15-35	Y wine -$10 corkage
88	C7	Gouger Fish Cafe	98-100 Gouger St, Adelaide, 5000	08 8231 2320		Seafood	20	Y wine -$15 corkage
89	C7	Great River Korean BBQ	103 Gouger St, Adelaide, 5000	08 8211 6866		Korean	20-22	Y wine -$6 corkage
90	F7	House Of Chow	82 Hutt St, Adelaide, 5000	08 8223 6181	www.houseofchow.com.au	Chinese	15-20	N
91	E6	Jasmin Indian	31 Hindmarsh Sq, Adelaide, 5000	08 8223 7837	www.jasmin.com.au	Indian	20-30	N
92	C6	Jerusalem Sheshkabab	131a-131b Hindley St, Adelaide, 5000	08 8212 6185		Lebanese	10-20	Y wine -$1.50 corkage
93	D5	Jolleys Boathouse	Jolleys La, Adelaide, 5000	08 8223 2891	www.jolleysboathouse.com	Modern Australian	23-38	N
94	D8	Kings Head Hotel	357 King William St, Adelaide, 5000	08 8212 6657	www.kingsheadhotel.com.au	Modern Australian	18-28	Y wine -$8 corkage
95	C7	La Trattoria	346 King William St, Adelaide, 5000	08 8212 3327	www.latratt.com.au	Fine Italian	15-25	N
75	F6	Lemongrass Thai Bistro	289 Rundle St, Adelaide, 5000	08 8223 6627	www.lemongrassbistro.com.au	Modern Thai	13-20	Y wine -$6 corkage
97	D7	Lime & Lemon Thai Cafe	89 Gouger St, Adelaide, 5000	08 8231 8876	www.limelemon.com.au	Asian Thai	13-25	Y
98	C7	Matsuri Japanese	167 Gouger St, Adelaide, 5000	08 8231 3494	www.matsuri-sa.com.au	Japanese	20	N
99	D7	Maya Indian	10 Market St, Adelaide, 5000	08 8231 1177		Indian	15	Y wine -$6.50 corkage
100	F3	Montezuma's	134 Melbourne St, North Adelaide, 5006	08 8239 0949	www.montezumas.com.au	Mexican	12-20	Y wine -$7 corkage

www.ashes06.com

#	Grid	Name	Address	Phone	Website	Cuisine	Price	Corkage
101	D3	Ned Kelly's Retreat	24 O'Connell St, North Adelaide, 5006	08 8361 9994	www.nedkellysretreat.com	Modern Australian	20-25	Y wine -$10 corkage
102	C6	Night Train Entertainment	9 Light Sq, Adelaide, 5000	08 8231 2252	www.nighttrain.com.au	Modern Australian	74	N
103	C7	Nu's Thai	117 Gouger St, Adelaide, 5000	08 8410 2288		Thai	13-30	Y wine -$12 corkage
104	F6	P.J.O'Brien's Irish Pub	14 East Tce, Adelaide, 5000	08 8232 5111	www.pjobriens.com.au	Irish	10-17	N
97	D7	Paul's Seafood	79 Gouger St, Adelaide, 5000	08 8231 9778		Seafood	10	Y wine -$7 corkage
106	D3	Pink Pig Wine Bar	50 O'Connell St, North Adelaide, 5006	08 8267 2139	www.pinkpig.com.au	Steak/Seafood	18-30	N
107	D5	Pullman	Adelaide Casino, Adelaide, 5000	08 8218 4273	www.skycityadelaide.com.au	Buffet	25-40	N
108	D6	Quiet Waters Lebanese	75 Hindley St, Adelaide, 5000	08 8231 3637		Lebanese	15-30	Y wine -$2 corkage
78	E6	Red Rock Noodle	187 Rundle St, Adelaide, 5000	08 8223 6855	www.redrocknoodlebar.com.au	Asian	12-27	N
109	B4	Red Ochre	War Memorial Dve, North Adelaide, 5006	08 8211 8555	www.redochre.com.au	Modern Australian	20-35	N
110	F6	Rundle Spices Noodle	278a Rundle St, Adelaide, 5000	08 8232 9288		Asian	14-22	N
110	F6	Scoozi Caffe Bar	272 Rundle St, Adelaide, 5000	08 8232 4733	www.scoozi.com.au	Italian	12-20	Y
112	C7	Stanley's Fish Café	76 Gouger St, Adelaide, 5000	08 8410 0909		Seafood	20-30	N
113	D7	Star Of Siam	67 Gouger St, Adelaide, 5000	08 8231 3527		Thai	12-20	Y wine -$10 corkage
114	E7	Sumo Station	172 Pulteney St, Adelaide, 5000	08 8232 0188	www.sumostation.com.au	Sushi	12-24	Y wine -$6 corkage
115	F6	Taj Tandoor	290 Rundle St, Adelaide, 5000	08 8359 2066	www.tajtandoor.com.au	Indian	15-22	Y wine -no corkage
116	F8	The Blanc	Shop 28, 240 Hutt St, Adelaide, 5000	08 8232 1188	www.blanc.com.au	Modern Seafood	24-30	Y wine -$12.50 corkage
117	F3	The Elephant Walk	76 Melbourne St, North Adelaide, 5006	08 8267 2006		Coffee Lounge	10-15	N
25	D7	The Grange	Adelaide Hilton, Adelaide, 5000	08 8217 2000	www.adelaide.hilton.com	Modern Australian	105-159	N
119	F3	The Greedy Goose	153 Melbourne St, North Adelaide, 5006	08 8267 2385	www.greedygoose.com.au	European	27	Y wine -$12 corkage
120	E8	The Greek On Halifax	75-79 Halifax St, Adelaide, 5000	08 8223 3336	www.thegreek.com.au	Greek	18-28	N
121	E3	The Lion	161 Melbourne St, North Adelaide, 5006	08 8367 0222	www.thelionhotel.com	Modern Australian	25-32	N
122	D2	The Manse	142 Tynte St, North Adelaide, 5006	08 8267 4636	www.manserestaurant.com.au	Australian/French	29-35	N
123	F3	The Store	Melbourne St, North Adelaide, 5006	08 8361 6999	www.thestore.com.au	Modern Australian	18	Y wine -$6 corkage
75	F6	Universal Wine Bar	285 Rundle St, Adelaide, 5000	08 8232 5000	www.universalwinebar.com.au	Modern Australian	20-26	N
125	C7	Vietnam Palace	132 Gouger St, Adelaide, 5000	08 8212 1968		Vietnamese	10-15	Y wine -$6 corkage

continued overpage....

ADELAIDE CITY MAP (pp70-71)

PUBS & CLUBS KEY

■ Denotes multiple venue

FOX Sports Bar B/R Bistro/Restaurant TAB Betting facilities OVAL Kilometres from the Adelaide Oval

#	Ref	Name	Address	Phone	Website	Closing Time	FOX	B/R	TAB	OVAL
126	E8	Astor Hotel	437 Putney St, Adelaide, 5000	08 8223 2442	www.theastor.com.au	Mon-Sat: Midnight	Yes	Yes	No	2.78
107	D5	Balcony Bar	North Terrace, Adelaide, 5000	08 8218 4111	www.skycityadelaide.com.au	Mon-Fri: 4am, Sat-Sun: 6am	Yes	Yes	Yes	1.00
65	D7	Belgian Beer Cafe	27-29 Ebenezer Pl, Adelaide, 5000	08 8359 2233	www.oostende.com.au	Mon: Midnight, Fri-Sat: 2am	Yes	Yes	No	2.00
129	D6	Berkeley Hotel	58 Hindley St, Adelaide, 5000	08 8231 3236		Daily: 24 hours	No	No	No	1.23
66	F6	Botanic Bar	North Terrace, Adelaide, 5000	08 8227 0799		Mon-Sat: til late	No	Yes	No	2.00
131	D8	Brecknock Hotel	401 King William St, Adelaide, 5000	08 8231 5467	www.brecknockhotel.com.au	Mon-Thurs: Midnight, Fri-Sat: 3am	Yes	Yes	Yes	2.10
70	E3	British Hotel	58 Finniss St, North Adelaide, 5000	08 8267 2188	www.britishhotel.com.au	Mon-Wed & Sun: 10pm	No	Yes	No	1.26
133	D6	Bull & Bear Alehouse	89 King William St, Adelaide, 5000	08 8231 5795		Mon-Wed: 8pm, Fri-Sat: Midnight	Yes	Yes	Yes	1.20
134	D1	Caledonian Hotel	219 O'Connell St, North Adelaide, 5006	08 8267 1375	www.caledonianhotel.com.au	Mon-Thurs: Midnight, Fri-Sat:1am, Sun:11pm	No	Yes	No	1.65
135	C6	Cargo Club	213 Hindley St, Adelaide, 5000	08 8231 2327	www.cargoclub.com.au	Wed-Sun: 3am	No	No	No	1.77
136	D4	Cathedral Hotel	45 Kermode St, North Adelaide, 5006	08 8267 2197		Sun-Thurs: 10pm, Fri-Sat: 1am	Yes	Yes	No	0.30
137	E6	Church	9 Synagogue Pl, Adelaide, 5000	08 8223 4233	www.churchthenightclub.com.au	Fri-Sat: 5am	No	No	No	1.71
138	C6	Colonel Light Hotel	141 Currie St, Adelaide, 5000	08 8231 4044	www.coloniallighthotel.com.au	Mon-Thurs: Midnight, Fri-Sat: 5am	No	Yes	No	1.65
79	E8	Coopers Alehouse	316 Pulteney St, Adelaide, 5000	08 8223 6433	www.earlobab.com	Mon-Thurs: Midnight, Fri-Sat: 1am, Sun: 10pm	Yes	Yes	Yes	2.59
140	F6	Crown & Anchor Hotel	196 Grenfell St, Adelaide, 5000	08 8223 3212		Mon-Wed: 3am, Thurs-Sat: 4am, Sun: Midnight	No	No	No	1.85
141	D8	Crown & Sceptre Hotel	308 King William St, Adelaide, 5000	08 8112 4159	www.sceptre.com.au	Mon-Thurs & Sun: 2am, Fri-Sat: 4am	Yes	Yes	No	2.03
142	C4	Cumberland Arms Hotel	205 Waymouth St, Adelaide, 5000	08 8231 3577		Mon-Sat: til late	Yes	Yes	No	2.09
21	B7	Directors Hotel	247 Gouger St, Adelaide, 5000	08 8231 8484	www.thed.com.au	Mon-Thurs & Sun: Midnight, Fri-Sat: 3am	Yes	Yes	Yes	2.82
144	D6	Duke of York	82 Currie St, Adelaide, 5000	08 8231 4088	www.dukeofyork.com.au	Mon-Sat: til late	Yes	Yes	No	1.30
145	F6	Exeter Hotel	246 Rundle St, Adelaide, 5000	08 8223 2623		Daily: til late	No	Yes	No	1.85
2	E8	Frostbites	471 Pulteney St, Adelaide, 5000	08 8232 3252		Mon-Sat: 5am	Yes	No	No	2.91
110	F6	Fumo Blu	270 Rundle St, Adelaide, 5000	08 8232 2533	www.fumoblu.com.au	Tues-Sat: 3am, Sun: 2am	Yes	Yes	No	1.93
148	C6	Garage	163 Waymouth St, Adelaide, 5000	08 8212 9577		Mon-Wed: 6pm, Thurs-Fri: Midnight, Sat: 1am	Yes	Yes	Yes	2.20
149	F8	General Havelock Hotel	162 Hutt St, Adelaide, 5000	08 8223 3680		Mon-Sun: Midnight, Sun: 10pm	Yes	Yes	No	3.22
150	D8	Gilbert St Hotel	88 Gilbert St, Adelaide, 5000	08 8231 9909		Mon-Sun: 2am	No	Yes	No	3.00
151	C6	Grace Emily Hotel	232 Waymouth St, Adelaide, 5000	08 8231 5500	www.graceemilyhotel.com	Mon-Sat: 2am, Sun: Midnight	No	Yes	No	1.78
152	E6	Griffins Head Tavern	38 Hindmarsh Square, Adelaide, 5000	08 8223 7954	www.griffinshead.com	Mon-Wed: 10pm, Thurs: Midnight, Fri-Sat til late	Yes	Yes	No	1.76
153	E6	Historian Hotel	18 Coromandel Pl, Adelaide, 5000	08 8223 3300	www.historianhotel.com.au	Mon-Thurs: Midnight, Fri-Sat: 2am	Yes	Yes	No	1.50
154	F2	Kentish Arms Hotel	23 Stanley St, North Adelaide, 5006	08 8267 1173		Mon-Thurs: 10.30pm, Fri-Sat: Midnight	Yes	Yes	No	1.93
94	D8	Kings Head Hotel	353 King William St, Adelaide, 5000	08 8212 6657	www.kingsheadhotel.com.au	Daily: til late	Yes	Yes	Yes	1.73
156	D6	London Tavern	175 North Terrace, Adelaide, 5000	08 8231 5464		Mon-Thurs: 7.30pm, Fri-Sat: 11pm, Sat: 5am	Yes	Yes	Yes	1.21

www.ashes06.com

ADELAIDE MAPS

Map	Name	Address	Phone	Website	Hours				
157 F2	Lord Melbourne Hotel	63 Melbourne St, North Adelaide, 5006	08 8267 1157		Mon-Sun: 2am	Yes	Yes	No	1.65
158 D7	Metropolitan Hotel	46 Grote St, Adelaide, 5000	08 8231 5471		Mon: 10pm, Fri-Sat: Midnight	Yes	Yes	No	2.02
159 E7	Moon under Water	76 Wakefield St, Adelaide, 5000	08 8223 1622		Mon-Fri: 11pm, Sat: 3am	Yes	Yes	No	1.92
160 C6	Moskva Vodka Bar	192 Hindley St, Adelaide, 5000	08 8211 9007		Fri-Sat: 5am	No	No	No	1.68
104 F6	P.J.O'Brien's Irish Pub	14 East Terrace, Adelaide, 5000	08 8232 5111		Sun-Tues: 1am, Wed-Thurs: 3am, Fri-Sat: 4am	Yes	Yes	No	1.98
162 C8	Prince Albert Hotel	254 Wright St, Adelaide, 5000	08 8212 7912	www.princealberthotel.com.au	Mon-Sat: Midnight	Yes	Yes	No	1.96
163 D3	Queen's Head Hotel	117 Kermode St, North Adelaide, 5006	08 8267 1139	www.queenshead.com.au	Mon-Sun: Midnight	Yes	Yes	No	0.50
164 D7	Raglans Hotel	109 Waymouth St, Adelaide, 5000	08 8231 4602	www.raglans.com.au	Sun-Thurs: Midnight, Fri-Sat: 5am	Yes	Yes	No	1.69
165 C6	Rosemont Hotel	160 Hindley St, Adelaide, 5000	08 8221 5156		Mon-Sun: 6am	Yes	Yes	Yes	1.58
166 G5	Royal Hotel Kent Town	2 North Terrace, Kent Town, 5067	08 8363 4888		Mon-Thurs & Sun: Midnight, Fri-Sat: 2am	Yes	Yes	Yes	2.30
167 D2	Royal Oak Hotel	123 O'Connell St, North Adelaide, 5006	08 8267 2488	www.royaloakhotel.com.au	Daily: til late	No	Yes	No	1.30
168 E8	Saracen's Head Tavern	82 Carrington St, Adelaide, 5000	08 8223 4449		Mon-Thurs: Midnight, Fri-Sat: 3am	Yes	No	No	2.29
169 C7	Savvy Bar & Lounge	149 Waymouth St, Adelaide, 5000	08 8221 6030	www.savvybarlounge.com	Thurs: 2am, Fri-Sat: 5am	No	No	No	1.84
170 F7	Seven Stars Hotel	187 Angas St, Adelaide, 5000	08 8223 6879		Mon-Thurs: 11pm, Fri-Sat: 1am	Yes	Yes	No	2.48
171 F6	Stag Hotel	299 Rundle St, Adelaide, 5000	08 8223 2934	www.staghotel.com.au	Mon-Thurs & Sun: Midnight, Fri-Sat: 3am	Yes	Yes	No	1.90
172 C7	Talbot Hotel	104 Gouger St, Adelaide, 5000	08 8231 9780		Mon-Thurs: 3am, Fri-Sat: 5am	No	Yes	Yes	2.29
173 D3	The Archer Hotel	60 O'Connell St, North Adelaide, 5006	08 8361 9300	www.archerhotel.com.au	Mon-Thurs & Sun: Midnight, Fri-Sat: 2am	Yes	Yes	No	1.20
174 F6	The Austral	205 Rundle St, Adelaide, 5000	08 8223 4660	www.theaustral.com	Sun-Thurs: Midnight, Fri-Sat: 3am	Yes	Yes	No	1.57
175 D2	The Banque Wine Bar	107 O'Connell St, North Adelaide, 5006	08 8267 6999		Mon-Thurs & Sun: Midnight, Fri-Sat: 2am	No	No	No	1.30
176 D2	The Daniel O'Connell	165 Tynte St, North Adelaide, 5006	08 8267 4032	www.danieloconnell.com.au	Mon-Sun: 1am	Yes	Yes	No	1.43
177 F6	The Elephant	1 Cinema Place, Adelaide, 5000	08 8227 1633	www.theelephant.com.au	Sun-Wed: 1am, Thurs-Sat: 3am	Yes	Yes	No	1.80
121 E3	The Lion Hotel	161 Melbourne St, North Adelaide, 5006	08 8367 0222	www.thelionhotel.com	Mon-Sat: Midnight	Yes	Yes	No	1.10
179 D2	The Oxford Hotel	101 O'Connell St, North Adelaide, 5006	08 8267 2652		Sun-Thurs: 2am, Fri-Sat: 3am	No	Yes	No	1.30
96 G6	The Tap Inn	79 Rundle St, Kent Town, 5067	08 8362 2166	www.thetapinn.com.au	Daily: til late	Yes	Yes	No	3.13
180 C6	The Woolshed	94 Hindley St, Adelaide, 5000	08 8231 3023		Daily: til late	Yes	Yes	No	1.34
34 D7	Treasury	144 King William St, Adelaide, 5000	08 8212 0499		Mon-Sat: 1am	No	Yes	No	1.42
182 D6	Union Hotel	70 Waymouth St, Adelaide, 5000	08 8231 2114		Mon-Fri: 2am	Yes	Yes	No	1.58
183 C3	Wellington Hotel	36 Wellington Sq, North Adelaide, 5006	08 8267 1322	www.wellingtonhotel.com.au	Mon-Thurs: 10pm, Fri-Sat: Midnight	Yes	Yes	Yes	1.71
184 C6	Worldsend Hotel	208 Hindley St, Adelaide, 5000	08 8231 9137	www.worldsendhotel.com.au	Daily: til late	Yes	No	No	1.40

ADELAIDE

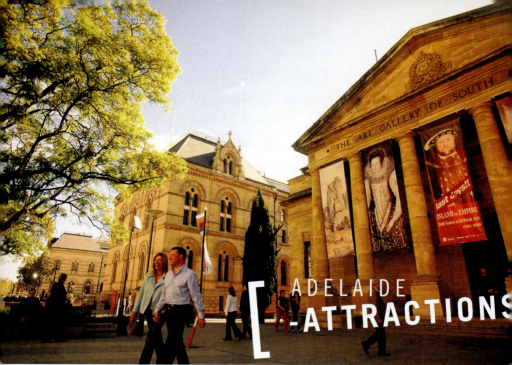

The Art Gallery of South Australia on North Tce. Photo: South Australian Tourism Commission.

ADELAIDE ATTRACTIONS

Winery tours

The Barossa Valley, McLaren Vale, Clare Valley, Coonawarra, Riverland and the Adelaide Hills… South Australia is blessed with many of the country's iconic wine regions and they're all just a short drive from Adelaide!

Join one of the many organised tours available (such as Barossa Experience Tours - phone **08 8563 3248** or visit **barossavalleytours.com**) and enjoy the sensational cellar doors where you can meet the maker and taste world-class wines.

Swim with dolphins

Just 20 minutes from the city centre, you can swim with dolphins on a Temptation Sailing cruise at Glenelg.

Relax on a 17-metre (55ft) catamaran as you sail up and down Adelaide's glorious coastline where over 1000 common and bottlenose dolphins roam. And if on the odd chance the dolphins decide not to come out and play, Temptation Sailing offers a money-back guarantee. Prices start from $19 per person (£8) for a 90-minute trip. Visit **dolphinboat.com.au** or phone **0412 811 838**.

Port Willunga

The beach at Port Willunga is as good as any you will find in Australia and it's also home to one of the best dining spots in the state, **The Star of Greece**.

Perched on cliffs overlooking the sea, The Star of Greece (named after a cargo ship that ran aground in 1888) is all about good food and good times. Open for lunch and dinner everyday throughout summer, the restaurant/kiosk combination has wowed visitors for years. Be warned though, you'll need to book! Phone **(08) 8557 7420**.

Organised tours… There are a variety of sightseeing tours you can take in and around Adelaide, including the air-conditioned Adelaide Explorer hop-on hop-off bus. It travels in a circuit and stops at a number of popular destinations, including Glenelg and the Adelaide Zoo. Departures are from the corner of King William St and Rundle Mall in the city at 9.05am, 10.30am and 1.30pm daily. Day tickets cost $30 (£12.50). Phone **(08) 8293 2966**.

w w w . a s h e s 0 6 . c o m

The Star of Greece at Port Willunga.
Photo: South Australian Tourism Commission.

Adelaide Central Market.
Photo: South Australian Tourism Commission.

Adelaide Hills
If you want a bird's eye view of the city then take a short trip up to the Adelaide Hills and marvel at the vista from the Mount Lofty scenic lookout.

And while you're in the area, cuddle a koala and take a guided night walk among 120 species of native animals at Cleland Wildlife Park (which boasts the world's biggest bird aviary) or experience the German charms of Hahndorf – all less than an hour's drive from the city!

Adelaide Central Market
Buzzing with sounds, colours and exotic smells, the Adelaide Central Market is one of the city's most popular tourist destinations, especially for those who love their food!

Located between Grote St and Gouger St, the market is home to an eclectic range of stalls offering fresh fruit, vegetables, meat, fish and gourmet delights.

Open every Tuesday (7am-5.30pm), Thursday (9am-5.30pm), Friday (7am-9pm) and Saturday (7am-3pm), parking is available in the U-Park directly above the stalls.

North Terrace
Adelaide's "cultural boulevard" is home to many of the city's great institutions, including the South Australian Museum, Migration Museum, Art Gallery of South Australia and State Library.

Parliament House, Government House and the University of Adelaide are also located on leafy North Tce, making it the ideal starting point for any cultural experience in SA.

DISCOUNT CARDS!

The **Discover Adelaide Card** offers 14 sightseeing experiences, providing eight passes to use at your choice of attractions. From nature's wonders at the Warrawong Earth Sanctuary to arts and crafts at the JamFactory, the Discover Adelaide Card offers up to 50% off the price of admission, as well as bonus offers at selected attractions. Cards cost $48 (£20) and can be purchased online at bass.net.au or by phoning BASS on 131 246. Visit adelaidecard.com.au.

For wine lovers, the **Cellar Door Pass** comes highly recommended, offering over $300 (£125) value for just $99 (£41). Among a host of benefits, the pass entitles two people to six bottles of wine, as well as premium wine tastings and winery tours throughout South Australia. To purchase your pass visit cellardoorpass.com.

View of Adelaide from Mt Lofty scenic lookout. Photo: South Australian Tourism Commission.

SUGGESTED -ITINERARIES

[If you've got some time before or after the Second 3 mobile Ashes Test in Adelaide, here are some ideas to help you plan your stay:]

A day...

Visit the Adelaide Central Market and stock up on fresh produce and gourmet specialties for a delicious lunch or dinner. Then head out on a walking tour of Adelaide where you can take in the sights and sounds of this elegant city.

After lunch visit the Adelaide Zoo and Botanical Gardens or take a walk along North Tce, making sure you stop in at the South Australian Museum and Art Gallery of South Australia on the way.

After a long day, head over to nearby Rundle St for a refreshing beer in one of the great pubs along the cosmopolitan strip, such as the Exeter or Austral, or if wine is your fancy, wander further east along North Tce to the National Wine Centre for an educational experience followed by a sumptuous dinner.

A few days...

A wine tour is a must! Choose from a range of world-class regions, including the Barossa Valley, McLaren Vale, Clare Valley or Coonawarra. Spend the day going from winery to winery, sampling exquisite reds and whites from welcoming cellar doors.

And what better way to treat a hangover than by spending the next day lying on the beach. Glenelg is the closest and most popular coastal suburb and offers a host of shops, restaurants, pubs and amusements for visitors. You can also swim with the dolphins on a Temptation Sailing cruise from nearby Holdfast Shores Marina.

To conclude your stay, head into the Adelaide Hills and marvel at the city view from the Mount Lofty lookout before getting back to nature at Cleland Wildlife Park. Reflect on your experiences with a cold beer in German-influenced Hahndorf or return to Adelaide for a delicious meal on Gouger St.

A week...

Kangaroo Island is one of South Australia's premier tourist destinations and should be considered compulsory sightseeing, especially for wilderness buffs.

With its coastline stretching 509km, "KI" is the third largest island in Australia and is located 110km south-west of Adelaide (accessible by ferry or plane). Approximately 4,000 people live on the island, which sees tens of thousands of visitors explore its natural wonders, beaches, conservation parks and wildlife sanctuaries every year.

Coach packages (including accommodation, hotel pick-ups and transfers) are available, using air-conditioned tour buses and local drivers who provide excellent commentaries on the Island's unique attractions. Or why not hire a car and take advantage of a self-drive package.
For more information visit tourkangarooisland.com.au or sealink.com.au.

A sea lion at Kangaroo Island's Seal Bay.
Photo: South Australian Tourism Commission.

www.ashes06.com

ADELAIDE DIRECTORY

CRICKET
Cricket Australia:..............(03) 9653 9999, cricket.com.au
SACA:..................................(08) 8300 3800, saca.com.au

EMERGENCY
Ambulance: 000
Fire:..000
Police: 000
Police (non-emergency):..................................131 444
RAA Emergency Roadside Assistance: 13 11 11
Rape & Sexual Assault Service:................(08) 8226 8787

HEALTH
Emergency dentist: ....(08) 8272 8111
Late night chemist (Cnr West Tce/Waymouth St,
Adelaide):..(08) 8231 6333
Queen Elizabeth Hospital (Woodville South):..(08) 8222 6000
Royal Adelaide Hospital: ....(08) 8222 4000
Women's & Children's Hospital (North Adelaide): ....(08) 8161 7000

INTERNET ACCESS
Adelaide City Council: ....25 Pirie St, Adelaide
State Library of SA:..Cnr North Tce/Kintore Ave, Adelaide
hq central: ....7 Ebenezer Plc (Rundle St), Adelaide
The Zone Internet Café:...............238 Rundle St, Adelaide
Kosher Coffee & Wireless Café: ....53 Hindley St, Adelaide
Cybersurfer Internet Café:.........Holdfast Shores, Glenelg
Net-Lan Internet & PC Games Centre: ....Westfield Marion, Oaklands Park
Norwod Oz Net Café:...............160 Magill Rd, Norwood
The Generals Lounge: ....503 Goodwood Rd, ...Colonel Light Gardens

MONEY
American Express: 1300 139 060
....americanexpress.com.au
Travelex: ....1800 637 642, travelex.com.au

PHONE/MOBILE
3 mobile: ....131 681, three.com.au
Country Direct (reverse charge/credit to UK): ....
.....................1800 881 440, 1800 881 441, 1800 881 417
International code to UK:..
............0011 (or 0018) + 44 + Area Code + Local Number

POST
Adelaide GPO: ....13 13 18, austpost.com.au

TOURISM
South Australian Tourism Commission Visitor & Travel
Centre (18 King William St, Adelaide): 1300 655 276
....southaustralia.com
Adelaide Explorer Tours (Keswick): ....(08) 8293 2966
....adelaideexplorer.com.au
Adelaide Sightseeing:................................(08) 8231 4144
....adelaidesightseeing.com.au
SeaLink: ....13 13 01, sealink.com.au
Cellar Door Pass: .... cellardoorpass.com
Discover Adelaide Card:.................. adelaidecard.com.au
Tourabout Adelaide (Kent Town): ....(08) 8333 1111
....touraboutadelaide.com.au

TRANSPORT
PLANE
Adelaide Airport:.....................(08) 8308 9211, aal.com.au
Qantas: ....13 13 13, qantas.com.au
Virgin Blue:.................................13 67 89, virginblue.com.au
Jetstar: ....131 538, jetstar.com.au

continued overpage...

View of Adelaide from the north. Photo: South Australian Tourism Commission.

[DIRECTORY
...continued from page 81.

Glenelg. Photo: South Australian Tourism Commis[sion]

BUS - LOCAL
Adelaide Airport Flyer ....
(airport to suburbs):.....................................1300 856 444
Adelaide Metro Information Centre: ....(08) 8210 1000
....adelaidemetro.com.au
Skylink (airport to city): ....(08) 8332 0528
....skylinkadelaide.com

BUS - INTERSTATE
Bus SA: ....(08) 8303 0822, bussa.com.au
Firefly Express: ....1300 730 740, fireflyexpress.com.au
Greyhound Australia: ....13 14 39, greyhound.com.au
Premier Stateliner:..(08) 8415 5555
....premierstateliner.com.au
V/Line: ....13 61 96, vline.com.au

TRAIN - LOCAL
Adelaide Metro Information Centre: ....(08) 8210 1000
....adelaidemetro.com.au
TransAdelaide (trains/trams): ....(08) 8218 2462
....transadelaide.com.au

TRAIN - INTERSTATE
Great Southern Railway (Keswick): .13 21 47, gsr.com.au

TAXI
Adelaide Independent Taxis: 13 22 11
Suburban Taxis: 13 10 08
Yellow Cabs: 13 22 27
Adelaide Access Taxis (disabled): 1300 360 940

CAR HIRE
Acacia Car Rentals (Hilton):.......................(08) 8234 0911
....acaciacarrentals.com.au
Access Rent-A-Car:.....1800 812 580, accessrentacar.com
Action Rent-A-Car (Cowandilla): ....(08) 8352 7044
Avis (Adelaide Airport): ....(08) 8234 4558, avis.com.au
Budget (Adelaide Airport): ....(08) 8234 4111
....budget.com.au
Cut Price Rentals (Mile End South): ....(08) 8443 7788
....cutprice.com.au
Europcar (Adelaide Airport): ...13 13 90, europcar.com.au
Hawk Rent A Car: ....(08) 8211 6599
Hertz (Adelaide Airport): ......(08) 8234 4566, hertz.com.au
Koala Car Rentals (Mile End South): ....(08) 8352 7299
No Frills Car Rentals:...................................1800 999 978
....nofrillscarrent.com.au
Thrifty (Adelaide Airport):....1300 367 227, thrifty.com.au

MOTORCYCLE/SCOOTER HIRE
Show And Go Motorcycles (Somerton Park): ....
....(08) 8376 0444

BICYCLE HIRE
Beach Hire SA (Glenelg): ....(08) 8294 1477
Bicycle SA (first two hours free): ....(08) 8232 2644
Cannon St Backpackers: ....(08) 8410 1218
(first two hours free)...cannonst.com.au
Cycle Gallery (Findon): ....(08) 8356 8206
....cyclegallery.com.au
Glenelg Cycles (Glenelg):...........................(08) 8294 4741
Linear Park Bike Hire: 0400 596 065

THE WILDFLOWER STATE

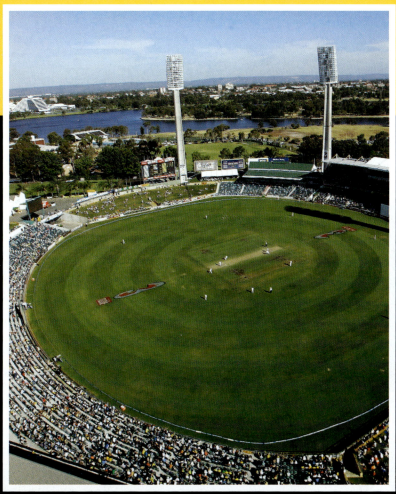

The WACA. Photo: Getty Images.

DECEMBER 14-18, 2006

3RD TEST
PERTH

PERTH CITY OVERVIEW

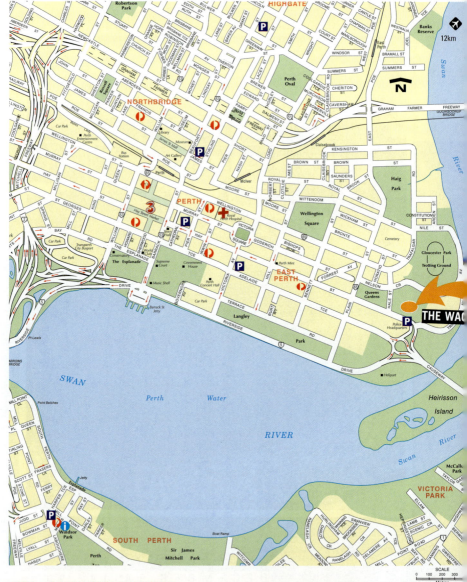

KEY... PERTH CITY OVERVIEW

- 3 store
- Hospital
- Police
- Post Office
- Tourist information
- Airport

Western Australia State Map

www.ashes06.com

WELCOME TO
-PERTH, WESTERN AUSTRALIA

Perth has more sunny days than any other Australian capital city, but even more remarkable is its isolation from the rest of the country. It is 2700km west of "neighbouring" Adelaide and over 4100km away from Sydney on the other side of the continent... that's London to Edinburgh six times!

Situated on the south-western tip of Australia and based on the Swan River, Perth is characterised by stunning sandy beaches, world-class golf courses, bustling markets, urban parklands and alfresco dining.

With 1.5 million residents, the city has steadily grown over the years and now includes the cosmopolitan port of Fremantle and the town of Rockingham. The CBD itself is easy for visitors to navigate thanks to its grid street system. City shopping is centred around Hay St Mall and Murray St Mall, while Forrest Place is a lively hub of street performers - just across from Wellington St Rail Station.

Perth has more sunny days than any other Australian capital city, but even more REMARKABLE is its isolation from the rest of the country

Home to cricketing champions Dennis Lillee, Rod Marsh and Justin Langer, Perth is a proud sporting city and thrives on Australian Rules football... tell the locals you barrack for the West Coast Eagles or Fremantle Dockers and you'll be immediately accepted!

There are plenty of great day-trip and short-stay options around Perth too. Swan Valley is a 30-minute drive east of the city and boasts an excellent selection of wineries, while Rottnest Island, 19km off the Fremantle coast, is famous for its snorkelling.

STATE FACTS... WESTERN AUSTRALIA
Founded: 1829 (originally as "Swan River Colony")
Population: 2.0 million (Perth = 1.5 million)
Colours: Black and yellow
Floral emblem: Red & Green Kangaroo Paw
Faunal emblems: Numbat & Black Swan
Domestic cricket team: Retravision Warriors
Average summer temperature: 29°C
Average winter temperature: 18°C
Time zone: GMT + 8 hours

While you're in Perth...

Eat: Pink snapper. With the Indian Ocean lapping at its shoreline, it's not surprising that WA is big on seafood. Pink snapper is a favourite among locals and regarded as a coastal delicacy. The Western Australian dhufish is another popular species, worth a try in one of Perth's multitude of seaside eateries.

Drink: Little Creatures Pale Ale. It's not as well known as other WA beers like Swan Lager or Emu Bitter, but Little Creatures Pale Ale has developed a cult following in WA. Gold and cloudy, the boutique style beer has won a swag of awards in recent years and should definitely be tried on tap.

See: Rottnest Island. A small island situated just off the coast of Perth, "Rotto" (as the locals call it) is renowned for its snorkelling, diving and surfing. A 90-minute ferry trip from the city will get you to this beautiful spot, which also has fantastic cycling and walking trails.

Do: "People watch" in Fremantle. Order an alfresco cappuccino along South Tce and indulge in a spot of "people watching" as the crowds wander past this trendy strip. Fremantle is a dynamic and multicultural port city, 30 minutes from the Perth CBD, and is known for its "alternative" nature and lively atmosphere.

The WACA.

THE WACA

The WACA scoreboard was built in 1954 after being donated by the North West Murchison Cricket Association, an association some 1800km north of Perth, but still in the state of Western Australia!

Operated by the Western Australian Cricket Association, the WACA is regarded as one of the fastest pitches in the world, with its traditionally high bounce tormenting batsmen over the years.

Located on Nelson Cres in East Perth, the WACA is home to the Retravision Warriors in the domestic cricket competition and in recent times has also played host to Australian Rules football, rugby league, rugby union and baseball.

While it was officially opened in 1893, the ground wasn't used for Test cricket until the 1970 Ashes series between Australia and England. And it was to celebrate this occasion that the Inverarity Stand (that still exists next to the main public entrance opposite the scoreboard) was built.

In 1984, the Prindiville Stand (next to the Inverarity Stand at the northern end) was established, before six 70-metre high light towers were erected in 1986 to accommodate night games.

Named after legendary Western Australian fast bowler Dennis Lillee and wicketkeeper Rod Marsh, the Lillee-Marsh Stand was built in 1988 for public seating, however a major redevelopment of the venue in 2002 saw the stand switch to a members only area.

The 2002 upheaval also saw the ground dimensions reduced to make the venue more suitable for cricket (as opposed to Aussie Rules footy), while a new Players Pavilion was established beside the Lillee-Marsh Stand. The old Players Pavilion and Farley Stand at the northern end were demolished as part of the revamp, and seats were replaced with grass hills on the eastern and western sides of the wicket.

In January 2005, the WACA hosted Australia's first Twenty20 match when the Retravision Warriors played the Victorian Bushrangers in front of a capacity crowd of 20,000.

www.ashes06.com

MATCH DAY INFORMATION

3RD TEST:
AUSTRALIA vs ENGLAND

The WACA, Dec 14-18, 2006

Gates:
Gates open at 8.30am on all five days of the Test. The main public entry gate is Gate 6 from Hale St on the western side of the ground. Spectators can also enter from Nelson Cres at the northern end of the venue through Gate 3.
Please refer to your ticket.

Match times:
FIRST SESSION:	11.00am - 1.00pm
Lunch:	1.00pm - 1.40pm
SECOND SESSION:	1.40pm - 3.40pm
Tea:	3.40pm - 4.00pm
THIRD SESSION:	4.00pm - 6.00pm

*Note: Times are subject to change.

[BE WARNED! It is a condition of entry to the WACA that you may be searched for prohibited items before you enter the venue. You may also be subject to monitoring by close circuit TV.]

Parking:
There are a number of permanent parking facilities around the WACA, with additional parking to be made available in the vicinity of the ground during the Test.

For up-to-date information, visit waca.com.au or phone (08) 9265 7222.

Prohibited items:
- Large eskies in seating areas
- Umbrellas
- Flag poles over 1m in length
- Chairs on grassed areas
- Weapons of any description or anything that can be potentially used as a weapon
- Alcohol
- Glass/cans or glass containers
- Any device that is capable of causing a public nuisance or injury
- Cameras, videos and recording devices

General information:
- The WACA box office is situated at Gate 6 on Hale St and opens an hour prior to gates opening (subject to change). Pre-paid tickets can be collected from the box office.
- EFTPOS facilities are available in the Inverarity Stand, in the ground floor bar.
- Disabled access is via Gate 6 from Hale St or Gate 3 from Nelson Cres. Limited Acrod parking is available in the Queens Gardens car park.
- Persons in possession of liquor will not be permitted to enter the WACA.
- Alcohol-free "dry areas" have been designated on the East Bank and Lower West Bank grassed areas. A small section of the Upper West Bank grassed area will serve light beer to patrons who are holders of tickets for the West Bank. A section of the Podium East Stand will also be alcohol-free.
- The WACA is a smoke-free venue. Smoking is not permitted except in designated smoking areas behind the stands. Patrons smoking outside designated areas will be asked to move immediately.
- Merchandise is available at the museum and other designated locations within the ground.
- Patrons holding concession tickets must take proof of concession status with them to the ground on match day.
- The members' entrance is via Gate 8 off Hay St at the southern end of the ground.

continued overpage...

MATCH DAY INFORMATION

...continued from page 87.

Food & beverage:
A wide range of food and beverage will be available throughout the stadium. Only mid-strength beer is available to the general public at the WACA.

TAB/Betting:
TAB facilities will be available in the bar area of the Inverarity Stand in the north-western corner of the stadium.

Smoking:
The WACA is a smoke-free venue. Smoking is not permitted within the venue except in designated smoking areas behind the stands. Patrons smoking outside designated areas will be asked to move immediately.

FESTIVAL OF CRICKET:

In the lead-up to the Third Ashes Test at the WACA from December 14-18, Perth has organised a "Festival of Cricket" to get the city in the swing.

Commencing on December 8 with the Lilac Hill exhibition match between a Cricket Australia Chairman's XI and an Invitational XI, the Festival then takes in the tour match between the Retravision Warriors and England on December 9-10 and a Legends Twenty20 game on December 11, both to be held at the WACA.

An interactive "Festival Village" will be set up in Forrest Place in the city centre between December 11-13, while the famous Ashes urn will be on rare display in the WA Museum from December 10-20.

For more information, visit cricketcityperth.com

The WACA.

WACA Ground
3 mobile Ashes Test
Australia v England

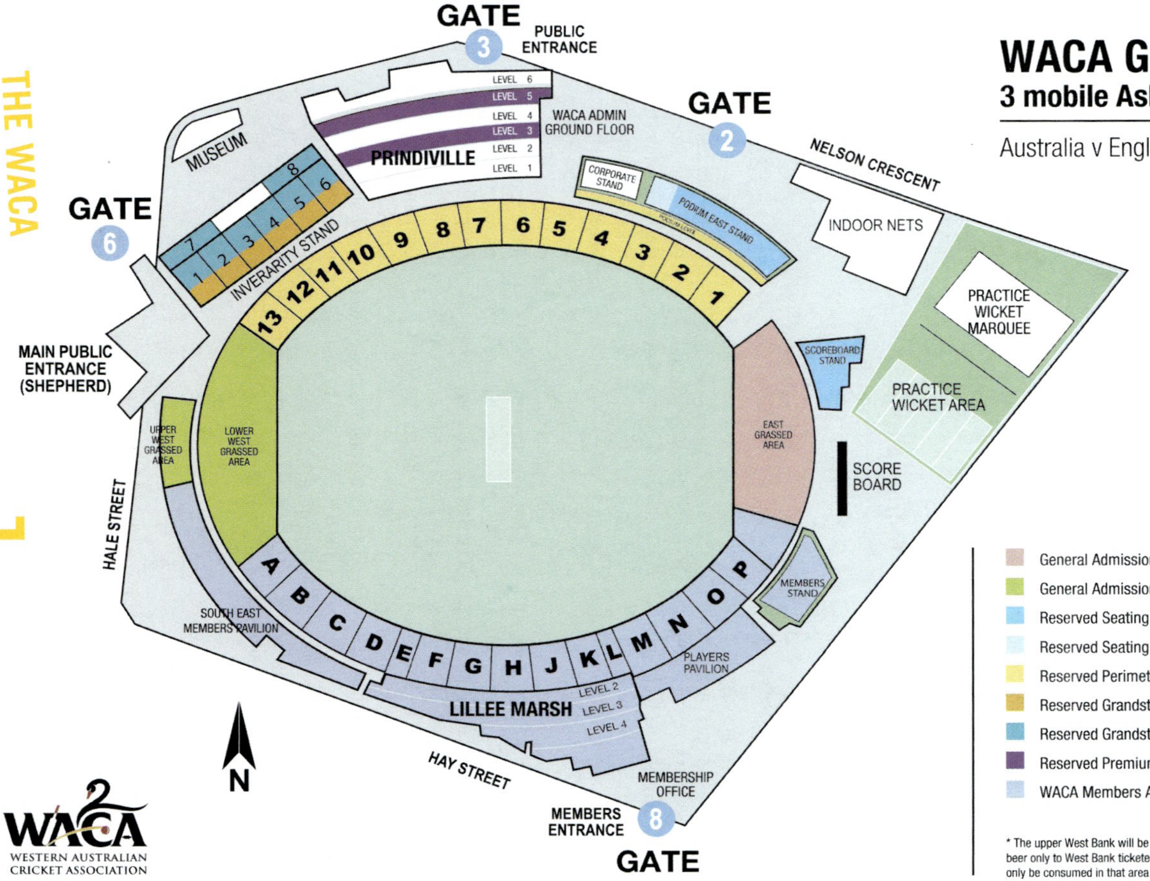

[SEATING PLAN]

- General Admission Grass - East (Alcohol Free)
- General Admission Grass - West* (Alcohol Free)
- Reserved Seating - Budget
- Reserved Seating - Budget (Alcohol Free)
- Reserved Perimeter & Podium Level 1 - Standard
- Reserved Grandstand - Budget (Front)
- Reserved Grandstand - Standard (Back)
- Reserved Premium (Prindiville, Level 3 & 5)
- WACA Members Area

* The upper West Bank will be a licenced area to sell light beer only to West Bank ticketed Patrons. The alcohol must only be consumed in that area.

THE WACA - SEATING PLAN

WESTERN AUSTRALIAN CRICKET ASSOCIATION

PERTH

[TRANSPORT

By Plane...

Perth's international (Terminal 1) and domestic (Terminals 2 and 3) airports are 15km and 11km north-east of the city respectively, equating to a 20-30-minute drive.

If you're travelling from Adelaide after the Second Test to Perth, **Qantas** (13 13 13, qantas.com.au) and **Virgin Blue** (13 67 89, virginblue.com.au) are your best options. A one-way ticket will set you back between $180-$240 (£75-£100), but be sure to check the respective airlines' websites for discounted fares and special deals.

Once you're in Perth, **Skywest** (1300 660 088, skywest.com.au) is a quality local carrier, and can fly you to many out-of-the-way Western Australian towns, including Albany, Esperance, Exmouth, Carnarvon and Kalgoorlie.

If you need to book your flight between Perth and Melbourne for the Fourth Test, a one-way fare with Qantas or Virgin Blue will cost between $210-$250 (£87-£105).

To/from Airport...

The privately operated **Airport-City Shuttle Bus** (08 9277 7015) meets every flight into the domestic and international terminals and provides transport to and from city hotels for $11-$13 (£4-£7) one way. The **Fremantle Airport Shuttle** (1300 668 687, fremantleairport shuttle.com.au) also operates seven days a week.

The city's public transport operator **Transperth** (13 62 13, transperth.wa.gov.au) runs a bus service (No. 37) every 30 minutes from the domestic airport to the Perth City Busport for $3 (£1.25).

Car hire is available through **Avis** (08 9325 7677, avis.com.au), **Budget** (08 9277 9277, budget.com.au), **Europcar** (08 9277 9144, europcar.com.au),

Hertz (08 9479 4788, hertz.com.au) and **Thrifty** (08 9464 7333, thrifty.com.au), or catch a taxi into the city which will cost you around $22 (£9) from the domestic terminal and $28 (£12) from the international.

By Train... (INTERSTATE)

The **Indian Pacific** train line is regarded as one of the world's great train journeys, running between Perth and Sydney via Adelaide. It travels twice weekly, each way, with fares between Adelaide and Perth starting from $340 (£142), while fares to and from Sydney start from $560 (£233).

Like all interstate buses and trains, the Indian Pacific arrives and departs from the East Perth Railway Terminal. Times are subject to change, but Wednesdays and Sundays are generally the days of departure. And if you're following the cricket from Perth to Melbourne, and prefer to travel by train, the Indian Pacific connects with the **Overland** in Adelaide. Contact **Great Southern Railways** (13 21 47, gsr.com.au) for ticket prices and timetables.

For intrastate travel, Western Australia has its **AvonLink**

www.ashes06.com

commuter service from Perth to Northam (via Midland and Toodyay) and the **Prospector** which runs to Kalgoorlie, both also using the East Perth Railway Terminal as their main base.

For all information on train travel, contact **Transwa** (1300 662 205, transwa.wa.gov.au).

By Bus... (INTERSTATE)

Due to its isolation from the rest of Australia, plane or train travel is a far better way of getting to and from Perth.

If you are desperate to take the bus though, and you've got plenty of time up your sleeve, the **Nullarbor Traveller** (1800 816 858, the-traveller.com.au) makes the journey in a leisurely manner using its fleet of minibuses.

continued overpage...

The **Indian Pacific** train line is regarded as one of the world's great train journeys, running between Perth and Sydney via Adelaide. It travels twice weekly, each way, with fares between Adelaide and Perth starting from $340 (£142), while fares to and from Sydney start from $560 (£233).

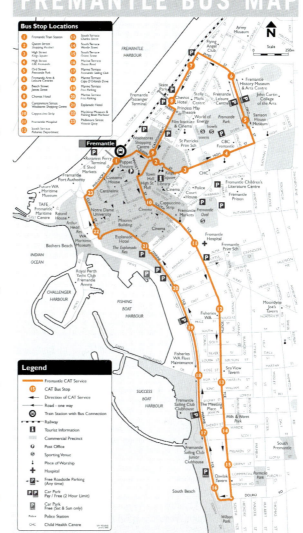

Perth Railway Station. Photo: Tourism Western Australia.

TRANSPORT
...continued from page 91.

For bus travel within Western Australia, check out **Transwa** (1300 662 205, transwa.wa.gov.au) for its multitude of services from the East Perth Railway Terminal to regional destinations such as Esperance, Kalbarri and Kalgoorlie.

The **Perth Goldfields Express** (1800 620 440, goldrushtours.com.au/express) travels to Laverton via Kalgoorlie, while **South West Coachlines** (08 9324 2333) runs daily services between the Perth City Busport and Margaret River. **Integrity Coachlines** (08 9226 1339, integritycoachlines.com.au) operates north-bound services from the Wellington St Bus Station as far up as Broome. **Easyrider Backpacker Tours** (08 9226 0307, easyridertours.com.au) also offers hop-on, hop-off services along the WA coast.

PUBLIC TRANSPORT...

Transperth (13 62 13, transperth.wa.gov.au) controls Perth's central public transport system, operating the city's buses, trains and ferries.

Fares are determined by nine zones, however most visitors will only need a 1-zone ticket which encompasses the main metropolitan area.

A **Free Transit Zone** (FTZ) also operates, allowing travellers to use any Transperth bus or train (including City West on the Fremantle line and Claisebrook on the Midland and Armidale lines) within the city boundary limits at no charge. FTZ signposts are displayed on the route limits.

For travel outside the "free zones", you can purchase a ticket upon boarding or from most newsagencies. A **DayRider** ticket entitles you to unlimited all day travel on all Transperth services after 9am on weekdays and all day on weekends and costs $7.60 (£3). Another option is a 10-trip **MultiRider** ticket which is about 15% cheaper.

By Public Bus...

You can get around the city centre free by taking a CAT bus, which run on three separate routes according to their colour (see map on opposite page). The **Blue CAT** travels in a north-south loop from the Barrack St Jetty to Northbridge, the **Red CAT** travels in an east-west loop from Queens Gardens in East Perth to Outram St in West Perth, while the **Yellow CAT** also operates in a loop from East Perth to West Perth. There is also a free **Fremantle CAT** established specifically for tourists.

www.ashes06.com

If you can't find a CAT bus, which is unlikely, the **Circle Route** is an inexpensive alternative, with city services (including Fremantle) operating every 15 minutes on weekdays and every 30 minutes on weeknights and weekends.

There are also late night buses (which will stop anywhere) every Friday and Saturday night, leaving from Wellington St Bus Station at midnight, 1am and 2am to Mirrabooka and Morley.

By Public Train...
The Perth Railway Station is located on Wellington St across the road from Forrest Place in the heart of the city, and is linked to the Wellington St Bus Station via a 200m walkway.

All suburban **Fasttrack** trains leave or pass through the Perth Railway Station, which has four main lines travelling to Fremantle, Midland, Armidale and Joondalup. Train services start at 5.30am and stop at 11.30pm on weekdays, with reduced services on the weekends - although late night services are available.

By Public Tram...
Trams also operate in Perth. Replicas of the 1899 trams that once serviced Perth are a great way of taking in the tourist sites, including Fremantle, Kings Park and the Burswood Casino. And the good news is, they offer full commentaries for passengers.

By Public Ferry...
The Transperth ferry runs between the city's main ferry terminal at Barrack St Jetty and Mends St Jetty in South Perth, crossing the river every half an hour during the day.

The ferry is a great way to visit some of Perth's best attractions, including the South Perth Esplanade, Perth Zoo, Old Mill and the Swan Bells at Barrack Square. You can also catch a ferry to and from Fremantle and Rottnest Island.

By Bicycle...
Cycling is a great way to explore Perth, and there are many bicycle routes around the city and its environs. One of the most popular routes is the circuit around the Swan River at the doorstep of the city.

To hire a bike, which will cost you around $9 (£4) an hour or $30 (£12.50) for a day, visit **About Bike Hire** (08 9221 2665, aboutbikehire.com.au) on the corner of Plain St and Riverside Dve near the Swan River foreshore.

By Taxi...
Designated taxi ranks are located throughout the city centre, including supervised ranks in party spot Northbridge on Friday and Saturday nights.

Taxis can also be hailed on the street or be booked by phoning:
Black & White Taxis 13 10 08
Swan Taxis 13 13 30

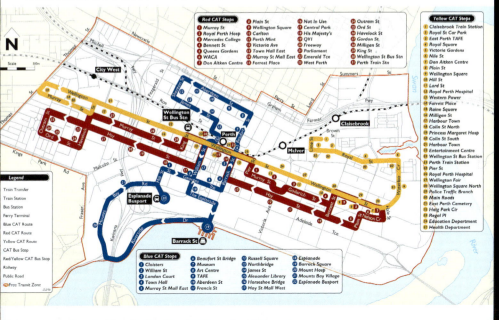

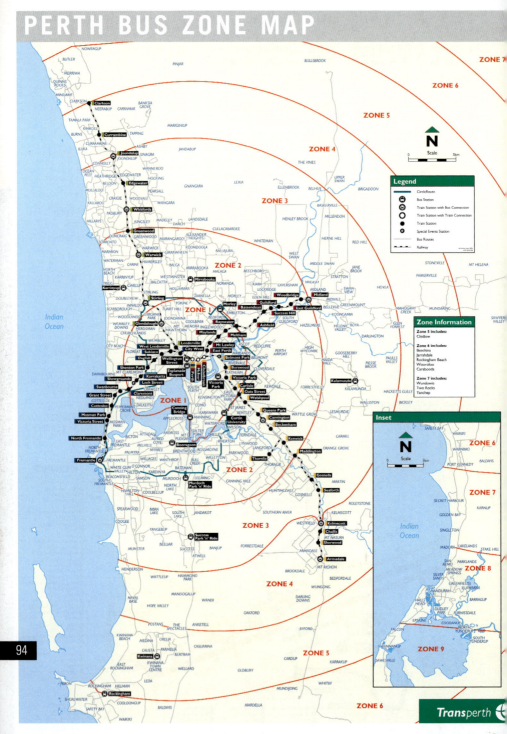

GETTING TO THE WACA

*Note: Please refer to waca.com.au for up-to-date event information.

Jumping on a bus **is the best way of reaching** the WACA from the city centre, **with a number OF FREE SERVICES** on offer during the Test match. **The Red and Yellow CAT buses** are good, and keep your eye **out for the additional free shuttles,** which the WACA will **ORGANISE TO AND FROM** the CBD for the **five days of cricket.**

On Foot...
Located in East Perth and bordered by Nelson Cres, Hale St and Hay St, the WACA can be reached on foot from the city centre, however expect a solid 30-40-minute trip.

On approaching the ground, the main public entrance is via Gate 6 from Hale St, however you can also enter through Gate 3 from Nelson Cres.
*Refer to your ticket for which gate to enter.

By Bus...
The WACA is serviced by the free **Red CAT** bus, which travels in an east-west loop from Queens Gardens in East Perth to Outram St in West Perth. From the city centre, board the Red CAT from Murray St or Wellington St, which will take you to Nelson Cres which runs adjacent to the WACA.

Overview of Perth featuring the WACA.
Photo: Tourism Western Australia.

The **Yellow CAT** is another option, which runs on an east-west loop also, but it does involve a short stroll to the ground from the corner of Waterloo Cres and Hale St.

Free shuttles will be organised by the WACA, which will operate from the Entertainment Centre car park on Wellington St, making pick-ups at the Wellington St Bus Station and Perth Railway Station.

By Train...
The Perth public train system should be kept as a means for sightseeing before or after the Test, as the **Fasttrack** trains won't get you too close to the WACA.

The nearest station is Claisebrook, which is a 20-minute hike from the ground or short ride on the Yellow CAT. If you have the choice, you're better off catching a free shuttle or the Red CAT bus service from the city centre.

By Taxi...
There are licensed ranks across Perth which will get you to the ground, as well as in Nelson Cres outside the WACA (opposite Gate 3), which will get you home - or to the pub - after a day's cricket. Otherwise call:
Black & White Taxis 13 10 08
Swan Taxis 13 13 90

By Car...
For the Third Test, the WACA will implement additional parking areas in the vicinity of the ground, on top of the permanent parking facilities available.

PERTH

[PERTH -ACCOMMODATION

View of the WACA from the Burswood Resort.

[NOTE: Hostels can be booked via www.hostelbookers.com or www.hostelworld.com. Hotels, motels and apartments can be booked via www.wotif.com]

HOSTELS

LOW-RANGE: < $100 (£42)

BILLABONG BACKPACKERS RESORT (pp108-109)
$19-$60 (£7-£25)
381 Beaufort St, Highgate
(08) 9328 7720
Reservations via email:
info@billabongresort.com.au
billabongresort.com.au

Billabong Backpackers Resort is located close to the trendy cafés and pubs of the Mt Lawley shopping district and is an easy walk to the city centre. You'll also find the WACA within close range too (3km). Billabong Backpackers Resort incorporates some great leisure facilities, including a swimming pool and gym, plus a beach volleyball court - all of which are free to use. The hostel also features 24-hour reception and a café. Rooms contain good standard amenities, private balcony, air-conditioning and ensuite bathroom. Prices are very reasonable and range from the eight-bed dorm rooms costing $19 (£7.50) per person to the single/double rooms costing $60 per night (£25).

COOLIBAH LODGE (pp108-109)
$21-$58 (£8-£24)
194 Brisbane St, Northbridge
1800 280 000 (free call within Australia) OR **(08) 9328 9958**
Reservations via email:
mail@coolibahlodge.com.au
coolibahlodge.com.au

Coolibah Lodge is housed in a renovated, heritage-listed colonial house just a few minutes walk from the great nightlife of Northbridge. And the WACA is only 3km away. Coolibah Lodge offers a variety of facilities, including two large screen televisions, laundry equipment, three fully fitted kitchens, wireless internet access, travel desk and licensed bar. The hostel also has various accommodation types, all of

www.ashes06.com

which are very affordable. Dorm beds start at $21 per night (£8.50) and contain air-conditioning and complimentary linen. If you're looking for comfort and privacy, the hostel also has singles, doubles and twins; a deluxe double starts at $58 per night (£24).

EXCLUSIVE BACKPACKERS
(pp108-109)
$19-$80 (£8-£33)
158 Adelaide Tce, Perth
(08) 9221 9991
Reservations via email: **exclusi vebackpackers@hotmail.com**
exclusivebackpackers.com

You'll find **Exclusive Backpackers** in a great location just a block from the scenic Swan River, and conveniently, only a 10-minute walk to the WACA (1km). Shopping and restaurants are also close by, with the city centre only a short stroll away. Exclusive Backpackers has very affordable rooms with good standard hostel facilities, including fully equipped kitchen, lounge area, internet access and laundry. The hostel also boasts a great café on site. Room rates range from comfortable dorm beds costing $19 per night (£8) to double rooms with ensuite and TV costing $80 per night (£33).

THE OLD SWAN BARRACKS
(pp108-109)
$19-$89 (£8-£37)
2-8 Francis St, Northbridge
(08) 9428 0000 Reservations via email: **enquiry@theoldswan barracks.com**
theoldswanbarracks.com

The **Old Swan Barracks**, constructed in 1896, is a significant historical landmark and one of the oldest buildings in Northbridge. While its regal facade makes it look like a medieval castle, its main function was to house enlisted Western Australian soldiers. The Barracks have been well maintained over time and now contain clean, good quality backpacker accommodation. The hostel offers excellent facilities including a kitchen, pool table, laundry, female-only wing, internet access, gym and a well-priced café. The hostel has a range of accommodation types on offer, with dorm beds starting at $19 per night (£8), standard doubles $59 per night (£25), and family rooms (including TV and bar fridge) $89 per night (£37).

UNDERGROUND BACKPACKERS (pp108-109)
$20-$65 (£8-£26)
268 Newcastle St, Northbridge
1800 033 089 (free call within Australia) OR **(08) 9228 3755**
Reservations via email: **info@undergroundbackpackers. com**
undergroundbackpackers. com.au

Underground Backpackers is a large hostel, custom-built in 2000 for backpackers. You know you've arrived when you see the large sign that looks like a London underground tube symbol. Underground Backpackers is located in the booming entertainment precinct of Northbridge and you'll find it only a short walk to the city centre. The WACA is also conveniently within close distance (3km). Underground Backpackers offers the latest facilities including air-conditioning, internet access, licensed bar and swimming pool; you'll also receive a complimentary continental breakfast. The hostel contains a variety of accommodation types to suit all budgets. Rates range from large dormitory beds costing $20 per night (£8) to the single/twin/double rooms with TV, DVD and fridge costing $65 per night (£26).

HOTELS, MOTELS & APARTMENTS

LOW-RANGE: < $100 (£42)

CITY WATERS PERTH (pp108-109)
$85-$140 (£35-£58)
118 Terrace Rd, Perth
1800 999 030 (free call within Australia) OR **(08) 9325 1566**
Reservations via email: **perth@citywaters.com.au**
citywaters.com.au

You'll find **City Waters Perth** in an excellent location opposite leafy Langley Park and just a block away from the scenic Swan River. Entertainment and city shops are also in close proximity, as is the WACA (1.5km). City Waters offers comfortable and inexpensive three-star suites and apartment-style accommodation. Rooms are serviced daily and feature good quality amenities. The apartments feature air-conditioning, separate kitchen

continued overpage...

ACCOMMODATION
...continued from page 97.

with microwave and fridge, dining area and TV. Room rates start from $85 per night (£35) for a single room, $90 (£38) for a double/twin room and $105 (£44) for a triple. One-bedroom studios are also available from $85 per night (£35), while two-bedroom apartments (five people) cost $140 (£58).

KINGS PERTH HOTEL (pp108-109)
$85-$100 (£35-£42)
517 Hay St, Perth
(08) 9325 6555 Reservations via email: info@kingshotel.com.au
kingshotel.com.au

Kings Perth Hotel is a well-priced hotel located in the heart of the city, just a few minutes walk from the Hay St shopping mall. Also close to the hotel is one of Perth's most well known monuments, the Swan Bell Tower, one of the largest musical instruments on earth and located on the picturesque Barrack St Jetty. The hotel's central location also makes it an easy walk to the WACA (1.5km). Kings Perth Hotel offers superb modern facilities including a restaurant, which has alfresco dining, a classy lounge bar, fitted with comfortable couches, and a separate bar for private functions. Standard rooms start at $85 per night (£35), superior rooms $95 (£40) and triple rooms $100 (£42). All rooms have air-conditioning and ensuite bathroom.

METRO HOTEL ON CANNING
(pp108-109)
$95-$130 (£40-£54)
61 Canning Hwy, South Perth

1800 004 321 (free call within Australia) OR **(08) 9367 6122**
Reservations via email:
southperth@metrohg.com
metrohotels.com.au

Metro Hotel on Canning is a three-and-a-half star, newly renovated hotel providing gorgeous views of the Swan River. Its prime location allows easy access to the entertainment and shopping of Perth's CBD, the Barrack St Jetty and Perth Zoo. The WACA isn't far away either (3km). The hotel complex offers great facilities including a licensed restaurant, bar, 24-hour reception, laundry and an outdoor swimming pool. Rooms have modern amenities such as air-conditioning, TV, fridge and ensuite bathroom. Metro Hotel on Canning has a variety of room types to suit different budgets. "Swan" and "Hillview" rooms start at $95 per night (£40), "Riverview" queen rooms $110 (£46) and "Club" rooms $130 per night (£54).

MURRAY ST LODGE (pp108-109)
$95-$120 (£40-£50)
718 Murray St, West Perth
1800 800 041 (free call within Australia) OR **(08) 9321 7441**
Reservations via email:
info@murraystlodge.com.au
murraystlodge.com.au

The **Murray St Lodge** is a well-priced hotel in a perfect location, within walking distance of inner city attractions such as Kings Park, the stunning Swan River, and of course its namesake, the Murray St Mall. It's also just minutes from the fashionable suburbs of Leederville and Subiaco. And the WACA is only 4km away. Though Murray St Lodge is a budget-priced hotel, you won't miss out on style and comfort. Rooms are fitted with good standard amenities including ensuite bathroom, air-conditioning, fridge and TV. Double/twin rooms start at $95 per night (£40), triple rooms $105 (£44) and family rooms $120 (£50).

ROYAL HOTEL (pp108-109)
$52-$96 (£22-£40)
531 Wellington St, Perth
(08) 9324 1510
Reservations via email:
wentpert@fchotels.com.au
royalhotelperth.com.au

The **Royal Hotel** is an extremely good value hotel in a fantastic location. Within minutes you'll find the Swan River and the shopping and entertainment precincts of Hay St Mall and Murray St Mall, and the WACA is only 2km away. Rooms at the Royal Hotel are clean and comfortable with good facilities such as air-conditioning, ensuite and TV. Single rooms with shared facilities start at $52 per night (£22), while single rooms with ensuite start at $65 per night (£27). Double rooms with shared facilities cost $65 (£27), double rooms with ensuite $79 (£33), while family apartments for four people start from $96 per night (£40).

HOTELS, MOTELS & APARTMENTS

MID-RANGE: $100-$200 (£42-£84)

AARONS HOTEL PERTH
(pp108-109)
$125-$165 (£52-£69)
70 Pier St, Perth

ACCOMMODATION

1800 998 133 (free call within Australia) OR **(08) 9325 2133**
Reservations via email: res@aaronsperth.com.au
aaronsperth.com.au

Aarons Hotel Perth is a newly refurbished hotel located right in the heart of Perth's CBD, just metres from the thriving shopping and entertainment precincts of the Murray and Hay St Malls. The WACA is also only a leisurely stroll away (1.5km). The hotel contains first-rate facilities, which include a tour desk, internet kiosk and a licensed bar and restaurant. Rooms feature well-appointed amenities such as air-conditioning, TV, ensuite bathroom and bar fridges. Room rates suit a variety of budgets, with standard double/twin rooms starting at $125 per night (£52), junior executive rooms $145 (£61) and corporate rooms $165 (£69).

COMFORT HOTEL PERTH CITY
(pp108-109)
$112-$145 (£47-£61)

200 Hay St, Perth
1800 888 678 (free call within Australia) OR **(08) 9220 7000**
Reservations via email: info@comforthotelperthcity.com.au
comforthotelperthcity.com.au

The **Comfort Hotel Perth City** offers high quality four-star accommodation at affordable prices. You'll find it in an excellent location just a block away from the shops and eateries of the Hay St Mall. Other major attractions also within close walking distance include the Western Australia Museum and the Art Gallery of Western Australia. The WACA is 2.5km away. The Comfort Hotel Perth City provides modern facilities and features 24-hour reception, luggage storage and a pleasant café. Rooms are comfortable and include air-conditioning, ensuite bathroom, fridge and TV with cable. Standard queen/twin rooms start at $112 per night (£47), while standard family rooms and studio king suites start at $145 per night (£61).

DURACK HOUSE BED & BREAKFAST
$150-$160 (£63-£67)
7 Almondbury Rd, Mount Lawley
(08) 9370 4305
Reservations via email: stay@durackhouse.com.au
durackhouse.com.au

If you're looking for a quiet retreat but still want to be close to the city centre, try **Durack House Bed & Breakfast**. Located in the lovely suburb of Mt Lawley, Durack House is conveniently close to the cafés, boutique shops and restaurants of fashionable Beaufort St. Durack House is also within close distance of the WACA (3km). Residing in an architecturally stunning Edwardian building, Durack House boasts lavish rooms, a cosy sitting room and gorgeous gardens. All rooms are fitted with large beds, air-conditioning, TV and ensuite. The "Courtyard" and "Veranda" rooms cost $150 per night (£63), while the "Camellia" room will set you back $160 (£67).

continued overpage…

Enjoy a swim while on holiday. Photo: Tourism Western Australia.

PERTH

ACCOMMODATION
...continued from page 99.

GOODEARTH HOTEL (pp108-109)
$100-$250 (£42-£104)
195 Adelaide Tce, Perth
1800 098 863 (free call within Australia) OR **(08) 9492 7777**
Reservations via email: **stay @goodearthhotel.com.au**
goodearthhotel.com.au

The **Goodearth Hotel** is a great value for money hotel in a wonderful location, adjacent to Langley Park, and overlooking the Swan River. You'll have easy access to entertainment at the Burswood Casino and the WACA is only a few minutes away (1km). The Goodearth contains both hotel and apartment style accommodation with high quality amenities including air-conditioning, TV and ensuite bathroom; the apartments feature self-contained kitchenettes with microwave. The Goodearth offers a variety of rooms to suit most budgets. Hotel rooms start from $100 per night (£42), studio apartments $165 (£69), executive apartments $190 (£79) and two-bedroom family apartments $250 (£104).

PERTH AMBASSADOR HOTEL
(pp108-109)
$140-$200 (£58-£83)
196 Adelaide Tce, Perth
1800 998 011 (free call within Australia) OR **(08) 9325 1455**
Reservations via email: **reserve @ambassadorhotel.com.au**
ambassadorhotel.com.au
Perth Ambassador Hotel is a centrally located hotel within minutes of many of the city's major attractions, including the Swan Bell Tower and Perth Mint. It's also just a stone's throw from the WACA (1km), so you won't have far to travel to catch all the action of the Third Test. You can expect great service and comfortable, affordable accommodation at the Perth Ambassador Hotel. Rooms feature contemporary fixtures including air-conditioning, TV with cable, and large bathrooms with separate bath and shower. The hotel itself features a café and modern bar lounge. Standard room rates start at $140 per night (£58), corporate rooms $170 (£71) and executive suites $200 (£83).

QUEST ON JAMES SERVICED APARTMENTS (pp108-109)
$174-$226 (£73-£94)
228 James St, Northbridge
(08) 9227 2888
Reservations via email: **questonja mes@questapartments.com.au**
onjames.property.questwa.com.au

Quest on James Serviced Apartments are situated in the lively suburb of Northbridge, minutes from great alfresco dining, markets, bars and the Perth Institute of Contemporary Arts. And the WACA is only 3km away. The apartment complex features superb facilities including a swimming pool, heated spa and barbecue area. Quest on James offers luxury one and two-bedroom apartments fitted with fully equipped kitchens, laundry, air-conditioning, fax/modem phone line and TV. Apartment rates are very affordable: one-bedroom apartments for two people cost $174 per night (£73), while two-bedroom apartments for four people cost $226 (£94).

HOTELS, MOTELS & APARTMENTS
HIGH-RANGE: $200+ (£84+)

DUXTON HOTEL PERTH (pp108-109)
$400-$1350 (£167-£563)
1 St Georges Tce, Perth
1800 681 118 (free call within Australia) OR **(08) 9261 8000**
Reservations via email: **res1@perth.duxton.com.au**
duxton.com

The **Duxton Hotel Perth** is one of the city's foremost luxury venues. Its prime location puts it only minutes away from most of the city's main attractions such as the Perth Concert Hall, the Playhouse, Barrack St Jetty and the beautiful Swan River. You'll find the WACA is also within walking distance (1.5km). The hotel provides outstanding facilities including 24-hour reception, room service, business centre, restaurant, bar, heated swimming pool, spa and sauna to name but a few. You can also expect high quality amenities inside each room, such as separate shower and bath, mini bar, full-length mirrors, TV with satellite and executive desk. The Duxton Hotel Perth offers a variety of room types, with deluxe king/twin rooms starting at $400 per night (£167), superior rooms $440 (£184), club rooms $490 (£204) and suites $520 (£217). Or if you really want to splash out, enquire about the Presidential Suite which costs a lazy $1350 a night (£563)!

CHIFLEY ON THE TERRACE
(pp108-109)
$286-$452 (£119-£188)
185 St Georges Tce, Perth
1300 650 464 (free call within Australia) OR **(08) 9226 3355**
Reservations via email:
reservations.theterrace@chifleyhotels.com
constellationhotels.com

The **Chifley on the Terrace** is an award-winning boutique hotel located in Perth's thriving West End. You'll find it situated only minutes from the restaurants and cafés of charming Barrack St Jetty and just a short stroll from the Convention Centre. The WACA is also only 2.5km away. The hotel offers exceptional facilities including restaurant, lounge bar, café, 24-hour reception, laundry, gym and room service. Rooms at the Chifley on the Terrace are high quality and fitted with air-conditioning, high-speed broadband, TV with satellite, mini bar and bathroom. Rates vary depending on room styles - standard deluxe rooms cost $286 per night (£119), executive suites $320 (£134) and spa suites $452 (£188).

INTERCONTINENTAL BURSWOOD RESORT PERTH
$208-$648 (£87-£270)
Burswood Entertainment Complex, Bolton Ave & Great Eastern Hwy, Perth
1800 000 867 (free call within Australia) OR **(08) 9362 7777**
Reservations via email:
reserve@burswood.com.au
ichotelsgroup.com

InterContinental Burswood Resort Perth is one of the city's premier five-star luxury hotels. Incorporated into the Burswood entertainment complex, you won't have far to go from your suite to experience the excitement of the casino, or if you want something a little lower key, enjoy a relaxing massage in the health spa. The complex also boasts nine restaurants and six bars, so if you're looking for a fantastic meal or just a quiet drink you'll be spoilt for choice. The hotel, which is also within walking distance of the WACA (1km), certainly lives up to its reputation, with guest rooms fitted with state-of-the-art amenities as well as air-conditioning, TV with satellite, broadband internet, safe, fridge, phone, private bathroom, mini bar, trouser press and valet service. Rooms range in price and style: "Classic Resort" king and twin rooms start from $208 per night (£87), "Contemporary Club" twin rooms $288 (£120) and "Panoramic River Suite" king spa rooms $648 (£270).

PACIFIC INTERNATIONAL SUITES PERTH (pp108-109)
$255-$295 (£106-£123)
305 Murray St, Perth
1800 224 584 (free call within Australia) OR **(08) 9347 7000**
www.pacificinthotels.com

Pacific International Suites Perth is one of Perth's newest hotel properties and is located right in the heart of the city centre, close to the shopping of Murray St Mall and the great nightlife of Northbridge. You'll also be able to easily make your way to the WACA, which is only 2.5km away. Pacific International Suites provides high quality hotel facilities and boasts an exceptional restaurant and wine bar called "BIN 305", which is open for breakfast, lunch and dinner. The hotel provides large, stylish suites featuring fully equipped kitchens, large bathrooms, air-conditioning and internet access. Studio queen suites start at $255 per night (£106), business studio suites $295 (£123) and studio executive queen suites $295 (£123).

SAVILLE PARK SUITES PERTH
(pp108-109)
$250-$310 (£104-£129)
201 Hay St, Perth
1800 150 464 (free call within Australia) OR **(08) 9267 4888**
Reservations via email:
perth.info@shg.com.au
savillesuites.com

Saville Park Suites Perth offers opulent hotel and apartment style accommodation and is situated in a fantastic location in downtown Perth. You'll find many rooms provide fantastic views of the Swan River and surrounding city area. Within walking distance are several of Perth's top attractions such as the Perth Cultural Centre, the Art Gallery of Western Australia and the WACA (2km). The hotel contains first-rate facilities including concierge, 24-hour reception, room service, gym, indoor heated pool, a restaurant and cocktail bar. Saville Park Suites' rooms and apartments feature high quality amenities including fully equipped kitchen, laundry, air-conditioning, private balcony, mini bar and TV with cable. Hotel rooms cost $250 per night (£104), one-bedroom suites $285 (£119), while two-bedroom suites cost $310 per night (£129).

Fishing Boat Harbour, Fremantle. Photo: Tourism Western Australia.

[PERTH -RESTAURANTS]

NORTH
OF THE WACA

The benchmark of fine dining in Perth is the divine Jackson's Restaurant, located in the stylish restaurant and pub mecca of Highgate. Chef Neal Jackson, who trained at London's illustrious Savoy Hotel, established the restaurant in 1998. With such an experienced and talented man at the helm, it's easy to see why Jackson's Restaurant has won multiple prestigious national awards. Indeed, Jackson's skills are evident when you sample the sublime dishes available on the exquisite a la carte menu, which combines rich European influences with fresh modern Australian imagination.

**483 Beaufort St, Highgate
(08) 9328 1177
Mains $30-$46 (£12.50-£19)**

Just around the corner from the WACA is Lamont's East Perth, the third link in a family chain of restaurants. Lamont's offers a first-rate seafood menu, which is appropriate given its location on the edge of the Claisebrook inlet. Lamont's signature dish is its Pemberton Marron, a type of crayfish found in the rivers and streams of the Western Australian town of Pemberton. This native delicacy comes fresh to the restaurant and is always a popular choice with patrons. Seafood isn't Lamont's only speciality, chefs also prepare exceptional beef and poultry dishes.

**11 Brown St, East Perth
(08) 9202 1566**
(pp108-109)
Mains $18-$39 (£7.50-£16)

For a fantastic Thai dining experience, head for the award-winning Saowanee's Place, voted "Best Thai in Perth" by the city's *Sunday Times Magazine*. Phuket-born owner Saowanee de Glanville has been creating tasty Thai dishes in Australia for over 30 years, so you can feel assured you will enjoy a truly authentic Thai meal. Saowanee's Place has an extensive menu ranging from hot curries to a paw paw salad with prawns and chilli.
348 Fitzgerald St, North Perth
(08) 9228 9307
Mains $11-$18 (£4.50-£7.50)

SOUTH
OF THE WACA

If you're looking for fine dining accompanied by stunning Swan River views, it's hard to go past Coco's Riverside Bar and Restaurant. Coco's is popular and it's easy to see why, with such a high quality and extensive seafood and beef menu. Try the delicious soya and sesame oysters with bonito, nori and coriander for entrée, followed by the tender Boyup Brook lamb cutlets served on Persian feta and potato mash. All dishes are made using fresh local produce. Coco's also features a vintage cellar so you can sample some wonderful wines direct from Perth's Margaret River and Swan Valley wine regions.
Southshore Centre, 85 The Esplanade, South Perth
(08) 9474 3030
Mains $20-$37 (£8-£15.50)

Frenchy's Cabaret Restaurant is located in the scenic suburb of Como, a great choice if you're tempted by authentic French cuisine. Frenchy's has all the traditional French favourites such as its soupe a l'oignon (French onion soup) and escargot de bourgogne (snails baked in their shells with garlic butter). Of course, the great alfresco dining and superb wine list aren't the only attractions for the clientele of this unique restaurant, many visit for Frenchy's terrific cabaret-style entertainment on the weekend.
125 Melville Pde,
Como Beach
(08) 9367 7411
Mains $15-$25 (£6-£10.50)

WEST
OF THE WACA

On Subiaco's lively dining strip, Rokeby Road, look for a bright neon sign and you'll find a wonderful Italian restaurant aptly named Funtastico. Most nights it's filled to the brim with happy locals who love the restaurant's wood-oven pizzas and tasty pasta. Try the inventive Funtastico pizza, named after the restaurant, which features "twin pizzas" - one half is a calzone filled with ricotta and salami, the other half is topped with tomato. Or if you feel like pasta, try the fagottini - a delicious homemade ravioli filled with chicken and spinach. And best of all, the yummy Mediterranean food is complemented by friendly staff.
12 Rokeby Rd, Subiaco
(08) 9381 2688
Mains $16-$34 (£6.50-£14)

The Witch's Cauldron Restaurant is one of Perth's veritable culinary institutions, still going strong after 30 years. It's best known for its excellent seafood dishes and finely cooked steaks. Ask most patrons and they'll tell you it's the garlic prawns - cooked in olive oil, garlic and chilli - that tempt them back time after time. The great thing about The Witch's Cauldron is its ample seating, catering for over 200 guests at a time. You can choose to sit and watch the Rokeby Road passers-by from the upstairs balcony or relax in the comfortable dining room.
89 Rokeby Rd, Subiaco
(08) 9381 2508
Mains $24-$40 (£10-£16.50)

FREMANTLE

Fremantle offers some of the best sidewalk cafés, restaurants and bistros in the state, trading off its rich maritime and cultural history. One of the stand-outs is the Bengal Indian Restaurant, housed in Freo's old heritage-listed fire station, which was constructed in 1909. Once threatened with demolition, the building was saved by locals who protested against its demise. Today, the restaurant maintains its historic appeal and serves up mouth-watering authentic Indian dishes to boot.
18 Phillimore St, Fremantle
(08) 9335 2400
Mains $15-$35 (£6-£14.50)

continued overpage...

RESTAURANTS
...continued from page 103.

> If you get a chance, pop into Gino's, one of Fremantle's most popular little cafés. No need to reserve a table, Gino's relaxed approach allows you to simply walk in and order. The cafe opens for coffee from 6am and serves delicious breakfasts from 7am, including its signature "uova strapazzate" consisting of scrambled eggs, prosciutto, tomato and cheese. And no visit would be complete without sampling Gino's unique special blend of coffee.
> 1 South Tce, Fremantle
> (08) 9336 1464
> Mains $12-$20 (£5-£15.50)

> The immensely popular Left Bank Café, Bar & Restaurant caters for everyone. You can enjoy drinks at the bar while watching all the Ashes highlights on the big screen TVs, or grab a light lunch in the café. If you're looking for something a little more formal, try the upstairs restaurant, which offers a wide range of dishes including a seafood platter and Thai duck curry. The restaurant is always busy as it provides spectacular views of the Swan River, so perhaps book in advance. The Left Bank also contains an innovative CineBar where you can sit back in comfort, with a beer or wine, and watch the latest films on selected nights.
> 15 Riverside Rd, East Fremantle
> (08) 9319 1315
> Mains $20-$58 (£8-£24)

Enjoy a drink on the Barrack St Jetty. Photo: Tourism Western Australia.

PERTH -PUBS & CLUBS

PUBS

NORTH
OF THE WACA

Combine French elegance with modern Australian flair and you get the award-winning Must Wine Bar. Over 500 wines from Australia and the world makes Must one of the premier wine bars in Perth. You can also check out Must's extensive selection of premium spirits, aperitifs and beers. The mouth-watering French cuisine, served up from the rotisserie in Must's bistro, is certainly worth trying - and you'll be assured of finding the right wine to accompany your meal!
519 Beaufort St, Highgate
(08) 9328 8255

The Queens Hotel is a heritage-listed hotel steeped in history. It was established in 1897 to meet the demands of the gold rush period. Today, recent renovations have returned the hotel to its former glory. You'll find the Queens Hotel in the fashionable suburb of Highgate, just minutes from the city, putting it close to many of Perth's main attractions and boutique shopping. Depending on your mood, the Queens Hotel has three distinct areas to choose from - the recently refurbished Lounge Bar & Restaurant provides a great selection of drinks and appetising dining options, the relaxed Melbourne Bar has 14 local and imported premium beers on tap, while the M Café offers alfresco and inside dining and is open from 6.30am for breakfast.
Beaufort St, Highgate
(08) 9328 7267

SOUTH
OF THE WACA

For a retro, quirky pub that has everything, try the eclectic Como Hotel. From its vivid purple exterior and original vespas to its lime green booths and leopard trim couches, when you enter the Como you'll think you've stepped back in time to the '60s. The Como offers a good

continued overpage...

[PUBS AND CLUBS
...continued from page 105.

selection of imported and local boutique beers, as well as a wide range of wines and a solid cocktail list. And if you choose to dine at the Como, you won't be disappointed either. The breakfast menu has a huge variety, as does the a la carte dinner menu, which, along with the great service, has won several awards over the years.
241 Canning Hwy, Como
(08) 9367 6666

WEST
OF THE WACA

The British-themed Moon & Sixpence features various British, international and local beers on tap and traditional British pub grub. Enjoy a quiet drink after a day's cricket in the beer garden that fronts the main street - the only beer garden of its type in Perth. If you visit on a Friday, Saturday or Sunday night, enjoy the pub's terrific live music or take part in the popular trivia nights.
300 Murray St, Perth
(pp108-109) (08) 9338 5000

Niche is a stylish lounge bar located in Leederville. It's a favourite with locals who go to unwind and listen to chilled beats. You can choose to relax on the comfy sofas inside or head outside to the large garden courtyard. While you indulge in the fantastic designer cocktails and premium imported and local beers, sample the "pide" - a delicious Middle Eastern toasted flat bread. Niche is open every Wednesday from 7pm-2am, Friday from 4pm-3am and Saturday from 7pm-3am.
Leederville Village, City End (off Oxford St), Leederville
(08) 9227 1007

The popular Oxford Hotel is a charming pub located in the fashionable suburb of Leederville. Most patrons come to sample the full range of imported and locally brewed beers, and the excellent wines produced in Perth's lush south-west wine regions. While you enjoy a quiet drink at the bar with the locals, you'll be able to catch all the Ashes highlights on the big screen television. At the Oxford you can also grab a nice meal as the hotel incorporates an excellent undercover garden bar and café (Perth's only), serving delicious Australian fare. Hang around and you can listen to the resident DJs playing house music on Friday and Saturday nights.
368 Oxford St, Leederville
(08) 9444 2193

Built in the late 1800s, the Subiaco Hotel is a great place for a drink, whether it be in the popular front bar complete with pool tables and big screen TVs, or the stylish cocktail bar, which offers tasty cocktails, premium beers and a vast selection of wines. The hotel also boasts an award-winning restaurant, which serves fantastic European style dishes and can hold up to 200 patrons.
465 Hay St, Subiaco
(08) 9381 3069

FREMANTLE

If you feel like venturing outside the city centre, take a trip to Fremantle where you'll find Little Creatures, a great local brewery that moonlights as a "cellar door" pub and restaurant. Little Creatures brewery is uniquely housed inside a converted boat shed located on Fishing Boat Harbour. The brewery is nationally and internationally recognised for its superb Little Creatures Pale Ale, Rogers' Beer and Pilsner. Little Creatures also sells merchandise, so you can remember your experience with a t-shirt, hat or beanie.
40 Mews Rd, Fremantle
(08) 9430 5555

Little Creatures brewery is uniquely housed inside a converted boat shed located on Fishing Boat Harbour

www.ashes06.com

The Ocean Beach Hotel in Cottesloe is a local favourite. Photo: Tourism Western Australia.

CLUBS
WEST
OF THE WACA

Black Betty's is one of Northbridge's most popular live venues playing host to some of the best local and interstate DJs and live bands. Open Wednesday through Sunday, Black Betty's offers different entertainment each night so you'll be able to choose the night that suits you. If you're on a tight budget, try Wednesdays, a popular night for students and backpackers because it includes free entry before 10pm, cheap drinks and prize giveaways. Entry is also free on Friday before 11pm and Saturday before 10pm, with a $5 (£2) cover charge thereafter, which includes a free drink.
133 Aberdeen St, Northbridge
(pp108-109) **(08) 9228 0077**

The Paramount Nightclub, opened in 1999, is everything you want in a pub and nightclub, all in the one happening venue. Listen to great live music downstairs or wander upstairs where local and interstate guest DJs play pulsating dance music. The Paramount offers five rooms catering for all tastes. In the busy "Ale Bar" sample top quality local and imported beers on tap, the "Garden Bar" is the place to be to catch all the 3 mobile Ashes highlights on the wide-screen TVs, the "Battleroom" is the hub of the Paramount where you can check out excellent live bands, or try the pumping disco with its huge dance floor and podiums.

And if you're still not satisfied, check out the relaxed "Tiger" lounge bar.
63 James St, Northbridge
(pp108-109) **(08) 9367 9111**

Established in 2002, Rise nightclub is the ultimate dance venue with just about the entire club space taken up with dance floor. Rise prides itself on catering for clubbers who like to dance by using a state-of-the-art sound system and innovative lighting. After a night (or morning) at Rise, it's easy to see why it was recently voted as having the "Best Club Night" in WA. Rise is located in the thriving entertainment district of Northbridge.
139 James St, Northbridge
(pp108-109) **(08) 9226 0322**

PERTH CITY MAP

PERTH CITY MAP (pp108-109)

ACCOMMODATION KEY

■ Denotes multiple venue

#	Ref	Name	Address	Phone	Website	$ Cost per night	RATE Star rating	OVAL Kilometres from the WACA
1	F5	1201 East Backpackers	195 Hay St, East Perth, 6004	08 9221 1666	www.1201east.com.au	15-24		0.68
2	D5	Aarons All Suite Hotel	12 Victoria Ave, Perth, 6000	08 9318 4444	www.aaronssuites.com.au	178-250	★★★★	1.95
3	D4	Aarons Hotel Perth	70 Pier St, Perth, 6000	08 9325 2133	www.aaronsperth.com.au	125-165	★★★★	2.80
4	D2	Acacia Hotel-Northbridge	15 Robinson Ave, Northbridge, 6003	08 9328 0000	www.acaciahotel.com.au	93-180	★★★★	3.17
5	F5	Alderney on Hay Apartment Hotel	193 Hay St, East Perth, 6004	08 9225 6600	www.starwest.com.au	123-250	★★★★	0.66
6	F4	Bailey's Parkside Motel/Hotel	150 Bennett St, East Perth, 6004	08 9325 3788	www.baileysmotel.com.au	79-160		1.25
7	A4	Best Western Emerald Hotel	24 Mount St, Perth, 6000	08 9481 0866	www.emeraldhotel.com.au	95-270	★★★★	3.72
8	E1	Billabong Backpackers Resort	381 Beaufort St, Highgate, 6003	08 9328 7720	www.billabongresort.com.au	19-60		3.48
9	A4	CBD Apartments	Suite 1/33 Malcolm St, West Perth, 6005	08 9324 2050	www.cbdapartments.com.au	75-130		4.55
10	B4	Chifley on the Terrace	185 St Georges Tce, Perth, 6000	08 9226 3355	www.chifleyhotels.com	149-452	★★★★	3.47
11	E5	City Waters Perth	118 Terrace Rd, Perth, 6000	08 9325 1566	www.citywaters.com.au	85-140	★★★	1.47
12	F5	Comfort Hotel Perth City	200 Hay St, Perth, 6000	08 9220 7000	www.comforthotelperthcity.com.au	112-145	★★★★	3.89
13	C4	Comfort Inn Wentworth Plaza	300 Murray St, Perth, 6000	08 9338 5000	www.wentworthplazahotel.com.au	72-145	★★★	3.45
14	D1	Coolibah Lodge	194 Brisbane St, Northbridge, 6003	08 9328 9958	www.coolibahlodge.com.au	21-58		3.67
15	D4	Criterion Hotel	560 Hay St, Perth, 6000	08 9325 5155	www.criterion-hotel-perth.com.au	75-145	★★★★	3.83
16	F6	Crowne Plaza	54 Terrace Rd, East Perth, 6004	08 9325 3811	www.crowneplaza.com.au	160-225	★★★★★	1.01
17	D5	Duxton Hotel Perth	1 St Georges Tce, Perth, 6000	08 9261 8000	www.duxton.com	400-1350	★★★★★★	3.09
18	D3	Emperor's Crown	85 Stirling St, Perth, 6000	08 9227 1400	www.emperorscrown.com	26-135		2.82
19	F5	Exclusive Backpackers	158 Adelaide Tce, Perth, 6000	08 9221 9991	www.exclusivebackpackers.com	19-80		0.87
20	C3	Globe Backpackers & City Oasis	561 Wellington St, Perth, 6000	08 9321 4080	www.globebackpackers.com.au	20-44		2.79
21	E5	Goodearth Hotel	195 Adelaide Tce, East Perth, 6004	08 9492 7777	www.goodearthhotel.com.au	100-250	★★★★	1.73
22	D2	Governor Robinsons	7 Robinson Ave, Northbridge, 6003	08 9328 3200	www.govrobinsons.com.au	22-35		3.13
23	F5	Hay St Backpackers	266-268 Hay St, Perth, 6000	08 9221 9880	www.haystbackpackers.com.au	20-30		3.88
24	B4	Holiday Inn City Centre Perth	778 Hay St, Perth, 6000	08 9261 7200	www.holiday-inn.com.au	240-270	★★★★	3.78
25	B3	Hotel Grand Chancellor	707 Wellington St, Perth, 6000	08 9327 7000	www.ghihotels.com	135-240	★★★★	4.46
26	B3	Hotel Ibis Perth	334 Murray St, Perth, 6000	08 9322 2844	www.accorhotels.com	89-99	★★★	3.51
27	D1	Hotel Northbridge	Cnr Lake & Brisbane St, Northbridge, 6003	08 9328 5254	www.hotelnorthbridge.com.au	110-600	★★★★	3.30
28	F6	Hyatt Regency Perth	99 Adelaide Tce, Perth, 6000	08 9225 1234	www.perth.regency.hyatt.com	150-610	★★★★★	1.15
29	B5	Medina Grand Perth	33 Mounts Bay Rd, Perth, 6000	08 9217 8000	www.medinaapartments.com.au	238-412	★★★★	3.33
30	D5	Mercure Hotel Perth	10 Irwin St, Perth, 6000	08 9326 7000	www.accorhotels.com.au	130-270	★★★★	2.54
31	H9	Metro Hotel on Canning	61 Canning Highway, South Perth, 6151	08 9367 6122	www.metrohotels.com.au	95-130	★★★★	3.45
32	D4	Miss Maud Sweedish Hotel	97 Murray St, Perth, 6000	08 9325 3900	www.missmaud.com.au	96-115	★★★	3.69
33	A4	Mounts Bay Waters Apartment	112 Mounts Bay Rd, Perth, 6000	08 9213 5333	www.mountsbay.com.au	122-450	★★★★	3.55
34	A4	Mountway Holiday Apartments	36 Mount St, Perth, 6000	08 9321 8307	www.mountwayapartments.com.au	59-79	★★★★	4.72
35	D2	North Lodge Accommodation	225 Beaufort St, Perth, 6000	08 9227 7588		25-60		3.11
36	E5	Novotel Langley Perth	221 Adelaide Tce, Perth, 6000	08 9221 1200	www.novotellangley.com.au	135-270	★★★★	0.65
37	B2	One World Backpackers	162 Aberdeen St, Northbridge, 6003	08 9228 8206	www.oneworldbackpackers.com.au	22-34		3.70

www.ashes06.com

#	Grid	Name	Address	Phone	Website	Price	Rating	Score
38	C4	Pacific International Suites-Perth	305 Murray St, Perth, 6000	08 9347 7000	www.pacificinthotels.com	165-295	★★★★★	3.71
39	B4	Parmelia Hilton Perth	14 Mill St, Perth, 6000	08 9215 2000	www.perth.hilton.com	245-315	★★★★★	3.41
40	E5	Perth Ambassador Hotel	196 Adelaide Tce, Perth, 6000	08 9325 1455	www.ambassadorhotel.com.au	140-250	★★★★	1.08
41	D4	Perth City YHA	300 Wellington St, Perth, 6000	08 9287 3333	www.yha.com.au	24-75		1.89
42	B2	Quest on James	228 James St, Northbridge, 6003	08 9227 2888	www.questonjames.com.au	174-314	★★★★★	3.66
43	B3	Quest West End Apartments	451 Murray St, Perth, 6000	08 9480 3888	www.questwestend.com.au	181-237	★★★★★	3.88
44	G4	Regal Apartments	11 Regal Pl, East Perth, 6004	08 9221 8614	www.regalapartments.com.au	117-250	★★★★	1.30
45	A4	Riverview on Mount St	42 Mount St, Perth, 6000	08 9321 8963	www.riverview.au.com	85-95		4.57
46	C3	Royal Hotel	531 Wellington St, Perth, 6000	08 9324 1510	www.royalhotelperth.com.au	52-114		4.48
47	F5	Saville Park Suites	201 Hay St, East Perth, 6004	08 9267 4888	www.savillesuites.com.au	140-330	★★★★	0.73
48	D4	Seasons of Perth	37 Pier St, Perth, 6000	08 9325 7655	www.seasonsofperth.com.au	150-320	★★★★★	2.73
49	E5	Sheraton Perth Hotel	207 Adelaide Tce, Perth, 6000	08 9224 7777	www.sheraton.com	199-566	★★★★★	0.64
50	D5	St George Boutique Apartments	2 St Georges Tce, Perth, 6000	08 6461 9100	www.stgeorgeboutiqueapartments.com.au	199-499		2.17
51	B3	Starwest Station CBD Apartments	418 Murray St, Perth, 6000	08 9211 0900	www.starwest.com.au	149-181	★★★★	3.76
52	D5	The Commodore Hotel	417 Hay St, Perth, 6000	08 9238 1888	www.thecommodorehotel.com.au	110-260	★★★★	3.86
53	D4	The Kings Hotel	517 Hay St, Perth, 6000	08 9325 6555	www.kingshotel.com.au	85-129	★★★★	2.67
54	C5	The New Esplanade Hotel	18 The Esplanade, Perth, 6000	08 9325 2000	www.newesplanade.com.au	85-135	★★★★	2.75
55	D3	The Old Swan Barracks	2-8 Francis St, Northbridge, 6003	08 9428 0000	www.theoldswanbarracks.com	19-89		3.00
56	B3	The Quality Hotel Melbourne	Cnr Hay & Milligan Sts, Perth, 6000	08 9320 3333	www.melbournehotel.com.au	130-300	★★★★	3.93
57	G4	The Sebel Residence East Perth	60 Royal St, East Perth, 6004	08 9223 2500	www.mirvachotels.com.au	165-325	★★★★	1.29
58	D1	The Shiralee Hostel	107 Brisbane St, Northbridge, 6003	08 9227 7448	www.shiralee.com.au	21-44		3.54
59	E5	Townsend Lodge	240 Adelaide Tce, Perth, 6000	08 9325 4143	www.townsend.wa.edu.au	28-62		1.33
60	C2	Underground Backpackers	268 Newcastle St, Northbridge, 6003	08 9228 3755	www.undergroundbackpackers.com.au	20-65		3.28
61	E4	YMCA Jewell House	180 Goderich St, Perth, 6000	08 9325 8488	www.ymcajewellhouse.com	36-40		1.48

continued overpage...

PERTH CITY MAP (pp108-109)

RESTAURANTS KEY

■ Denotes multiple venue
$ Cost of main meal

#	Ref	Name	Address	Phone	Website	Cuisine	$	BYO
27	D1	210 Rest. & Cocktail Bar	210 Lake St, Northbridge, 6003	08 9328 5254	www.hotelnorthbridge.com.au	Modern Australian	25	N
63	B4	44 King St	44 King St, Perth, 6000	08 9321 4476		Modern Australian	18-33	N
64	G4	A Little Moorish	10 Eastbrook Tce, East Perth, 6004	08 9225 7880		Mediterranean	18-30	N
65	G4	Antico Caffe	81 Royal St, East Perth, 6004	08 9221 8222		Italian	14-34	N
57	G4	Ba Ba Black	60 Royal St, East Perth, 6004	08 9421 1206	www.babablack.com.au	Café	8-16	Y wine-$1pp corkage
67	C4	Balthazar	6 The Esplanade, Perth, 6000	08 9421 1206		Modern Australian	20-34	N
68	D2	Barocco	318 William St, Northbridge, 6003	08 9228 3888	www.barocco.com.au	Italian	13-29	Y wine-$5 corkage
69	G4	Basil Leaves	82 Royal St, East Perth, 6004	08 9221 8999		Asian/Thai	11-21	Y wine-$1.50 corkage
70	B3	Belgian Beer Café	347 Murray St, Perth, 6000	08 9321 4094	www.belgianbeer.com.au	European	14-30	N
47	F5	Bensons	201 Hay St, Perth, 6004	08 9267 4991		Modern Australian	18-26	N
72	C3	Brassgrill-Chargrill	209 William St, Northbridge, 6003	08 9227 9596	www.thebrassmonkey.com.au	Modern Australian	13-37	N
73	E1	Brisbane Hotel	292 Beaufort St, Highgate, 6003	08 9227 2300	www.thebrisbanehotel.com.au	Modern Australian	13-26	N
74	C4	C Lounge	44 St Georges Tce, Perth, 6000	08 9220 8333	www.crestaurant.com.au	Modern Australian	28-37	N
28	F6	Café at the Hyatt	99 Adelaide Tce, Perth, 6000	08 9225 1257	www.perth.hyatt.com	International	45-49	N
76	B3	Carnegies	356 Murray St, Perth, 6000	08 9481 3222	www.carnegies.net	Modern Australian	15-25	N
77	B4	CBD	Cnr Hay & King St, Perth, 6000	08 9263 1859	www.rydges.com	Modern Australian	18-33	N
28	F6	Chanterelle at Jessica's	Hyatt Centre, Terrace Rd, East Perth, 6004	08 9325 2511		Modern Australian	30	N
79	9B	Charthouse	112 Mill Point Rd, South Perth, 6151	08 9474 2229	www.windsorhotel.com.au	Modern Australian	22-30	N
80	9B	Coco's Riverside	85 Esplanade, South Perth, 6151	08 9474 3030	www.cocosperth.com	Modern Australian	20-37	N
81	D3	Court Wine	84 Beaufort St, Perth, 6000	08 9227 1200		European	25	N
44	G4	Cream	11 Regal Place, East Perth, 6004	08 9221 0404		Modern Australian	25-33	N
15	D4	Criterion Hotel	560 Hay St, Perth, 6000	08 9325 5155	www.criterion-hotel-perth.com	Modern Australian	16-30	N
84	B2	Dusit Thai	249 James St, Northbridge, 6003	08 9328 7647	www.dusitthai.com.au	Thai	13-30	N
85	B4	E Cucina	777 Hay St, Perth, 6000	08 9481 1020		Italian	22	N
86	C4	Emporio Bar & Café	77 St Georges Tce, Perth, 6000	08 9325 7077		Modern Australian	17	N
87	C3	Francine's Café	206 William St, Northbridge, 6003	08 9227 5082		Café	9-24	Y wine-no corkage
88	F6	Friends	20 Terrace Rd, East Perth, 6004	08 9221 0885	www.friendsrestaurant.com.au	International	30-35	N
28	F6	Gershwin's at Hyatt	99 Adelaide Tce, Perth, 6000	08 9215 2421	www.perth.hyatt.com	Fine dining	30	N
39	B4	Globe Wine Bar	Mill St, Perth, 6000	08 9215 2421	www.perth.hilton.com	International	30	N
91	C5	Grand Palace	3 The Esplanade, Perth, 6000	08 9221 6333		Chinese	15-60	N
72	C3	Grapeskin	209 William St, Northbridge, 6003	08 9227 9596	www.thebrassmonkey.com.au	Modern Australian	13-33	N
93	E5	Grosvenor Hotel	339 Hay St, Perth, 6000	08 9325 3799		Modern Australian	16-30	N
94	C5	Halo	2 Barrack Square, Perth, 6000	08 9335 4575	www.halocafe.com.au	Modern Australian	28	N
30	D5	Hydrant on Hay	10 Irwin St, Perth, 6000	08 9326 7000	www.accorhotels.com.au	International	8-13	N
26	B3	I Bistro	334 Murray St, Perth, 6000	08 9322 2844		International	13-20	N

112

www.ashes06.com

97	C3	Il Padrino Caffe	198 William St, Northbridge, 6003	08 9227 9065	www.ilpadrinocaffe.com	Italian	13-29	Y wine-$3.50 corkage
28	F6	Joes Oriental Diner	99 Adelaide Tce, Perth, 6000	08 9225 1268	www.perth.hyatt.com	Asian	19	Y wine-$5pp corkage
12	F5	K Café	200 Hay St, Perth, 6004	08 9220 7000	www.comforthotelperthcity.com	Modern Australian	16-28	N
100	G4	Korean Shilla BBQ	20 Royal St, East Perth, 6004	08 9221 7171		Korean	23	Y wine-$7 corkage
101	G3	Lamonts East Perth	11 Brown St, East Perth, 6004	08 9202 1566	www.lamonts.com.au	Modern Australian	18-39	N
102	G4	Le Croissant on the Cove	Shop 24, 108 Royal St, East Perth, 6004	08 9325 9424		Café	6-10	N
103	C2	Maya Masala Indian	49 Lake St, Northbridge, 6003	08 9328 5655		Indian	15	Y wine-$1.50p corkage
104	F9	Roxby Thai	298 Mill Point Rd, South Perth, 6151	08 9368 2292		Thai	12-28	Y wine-$2pp corkage
57	G4	Royal Bar & Brasserie	60 Royal St, East Perth, 6004	08 9221 0466	www.royalbarandbrasserie.com.au	International	16-39	N
106	G1	Spirit of the West	East Perth Rail Terminal, Summer St, 6004	08 9328 8460	www.spiritofthewest.com.au	Modern Australian	85-200	N
107	E2	The Coolgardie Safe	101 Edward St (Off Lord St), Perth, 6004	08 9328 1143	www.accoladewa.com.au	Australian	16-30	Y wine-$3 corkage
17	D5	The Duxton Grill	1 St Georges Tce, Perth, 6000	08 9261 8025	www.duxton.com	Modern Australian	16-32	N
109	C2	The Greek Taverna	124 James St, Perth, 6000	08 9227 7346		Greek	15-30	N
110	D2	The Moon Café	323 William St, Northbridge, 6003	08 9328 7474		Modern Aust/Pizza	10-22	Y wine-$2.50pp corkage
80	9B	The Oyster Bar	85 South Perth Esp, South Perth, 6151	08 9368 4999	www.meads.com.au	Seafood	22-33	N
112	C2	The Shed	69-71 Aberdeen St, Northbridge, 6003	08 9228 2200	www.the-shed.com.au	Steak	10-30	N
113	F4	Vivace	71 Bennett St, East Perth, 6004	08 9325 1788		Italian	15-29	Y wine-$5 corkage
114	C3	Vulture's	Francis St, Northbridge, 6003	08 9227 9087	www.vultures.com.au	International	19-32	Y wine-$7 corkage

continued overpage....

PERTH CITY MAP (pp108-109)

PUBS & CLUBS KEY

- FOX Sports Bar
- B/R Bistro/Restaurant
- TAB Betting facilities
- OVAL Kilometres from the WACA
- ■ Denotes multiple venue

# Ref	Name	Address	Phone	Website	Closing Time	FOX	B/R	TAB	OVAL
115 D4	Ambar Nightclub	104 Murray St, Perth, 6000	08 9325 6677	www.ambar.net.au	Thurs-Sat: 6am	No	No	No	2.40
67 C4	Balthazar	6 The Esplanade, Perth, 6000	08 9421 1206		Mon-Sat: Midnight	No	Yes	No	2.89
117 C2	Base	139 James St, Northbridge, 6003	08 9226 0322	www.base.net.au	Wed-Sat: 5am	No	No	No	3.24
70 B3	Belgian Beer Cafe	347 Murray St, Perth, 6000	08 9321 4094	www.belgianbeer.com.au	Mon-Sun: Midnight	No	Yes	No	3.26
119 C2	Black Betty's	133 Aberdeen St, Northbridge, 6003	08 9228 0077	www.blackbettys.com.au	Wed & Sat: 4am	No	No	No	3.60
13 C4	Bobby Dazzlers	300 Murray St, Perth, 6000	08 9481 0728	www.bobbydazzlers.com.au	Mon-Thurs & Sun: 11pm, Fri-Sat: Midnight	Yes	Yes	No	3.05
72 C3	Brass Monkey	209 William St, Northbridge, 6003	08 9227 9596	www.thebrassmonkey.com.au	Mon-Thurs: Midnight, Fri-Sat: 2am, Sun: 10pm	No	Yes	No	3.19
73 E1	Brisbane Hotel	292 Beaufort St, Highgate, 6003	08 9227 2300		Mon-Tues: 11pm, Wed-Sat: Midnight, Sun: 10pm	No	Yes	No	3.30
76 B3	Carnegie's Bar	356 Murray St, Perth, 6000	08 9481 3222	www.carnegies.net	Mon-Thurs: 1am, Fri-Sat: 3am, Sun: Midnight	Yes	Yes	No	3.16
124 C2	Church Nightclub	69 Lake St, Northbridge, 6003	08 9328 1065		Fri-Sat: 6am	No	No	No	3.46
79 B9	Courtyard Bar	112 Mill Point Rd, South Perth, 6151	08 9474 2229	www.windsorhotel.com.au	Mon-Sat: Midnight, Sun: 10pm	No	Yes	No	5.63
15 D4	Criterion Hotel	560 Hay St, Perth, 6000	08 9325 5155	www.criterion-hotel-perth.com.au	Mon-Fri: Midnight, Sat-Sun: 2am	No	Yes	No	3.92
127 C2	Deen Nightclub	84 Aberdeen St, Northbridge, 6003	08 9227 9361	www.thedeen.com	Mon, Thurs & Sat: 2am	No	No	No	3.40
128 B3	Durty Nelly's	397 Murray St, Perth, 6000	08 9226 0233	www.durtynellys.com.au	Daily: Midnight	Yes	Yes	Yes	3.26
17 D5	Duxton Hotel Bar	1 St Georges Tce, Perth, 6000	08 9261 8000	www.duxton.com	Daily: 6am	No	Yes	Yes	2.46
130 C2	Elephant & Wheelbarrow	53 Lake St, Northbridge, 6003	08 9228 4433		Mon-Wed: Midnight, Thurs-Sat: 1am, Sun: 10pm	Yes	Yes	Yes	3.36
36 E5	Fenian's Pub	221 Adelaide Tce, Perth, 6000	08 9221 1200	www.novotellangley.com.au	Mon-Thu: Midnight, Fri-Sat: 1am, Sun: 10pm	Yes	Yes	No	0.85
132 C3	Geisha Bar	135a James St, Northbridge, 6003	08 9328 9808	www.geishabar.com.au	Fri-Sat 2am, Sun: Midnight	No	No	No	3.30
93 E5	Grosvenor Hotel	339 Hay St, Perth, 6000	08 9325 3799		Mon-Sat: Midnight, Sun: 10pm	No	Yes	Yes	3.87
134 E2	Heat Nightclub	187 Stirling St, Perth, 6000	08 9228 9622	www.heatclub.com.au	Mon-Thurs: 3am, Fri-Sat: 6am	No	No	No	2.95
80 B9	Incontro	South Perth Esp, South Perth, 6151	08 9474 5566	www.incontro.com.au	Tues-Sun: til late	No	Yes	No	5.80
12 F5	K Bar	200 Hay St, East Perth, 6004	08 9220 7000	www.comforthotelperthcity.com.au	Mon-Sun: Midnight	No	Yes	No	0.95
56 B3	Melbourne Hotel	942 Hay St, Perth, 6000	08 9320 3333	www.melbournehotel.com.au	Mon-Sun: Midnight	Yes	Yes	No	4.08
79 B9	Mends St Bar	112 Mill Point Rd, South Perth, 6151	08 9474 2229	www.windsorhotel.com.au	Mon-Wed: 11pm, Thurs-Sun: Midnight	Yes	Yes	No	5.63
139 B2	Metro City	146 Roe St, Northbridge, 6003	08 9228 0500	www.metrocity.com.au	Sat: 6am	No	No	No	3.80
13 C4	Moon & Sixpence	300 Murray St, Perth, 6000	08 9481 0727		Mon-Thurs: Midnight, Fri-Sat: 1am, Sun: 10pm	Yes	Yes	Yes	3.05

www.ashes06.com

141 C2	Mustang Bar	46 Lake St, Northbridge, 6003	08 9328 2350		Mon-Tues: 11pm, Wed-Sat: 2am, Sun:10pm	Yes	Yes	No	3.24
142 B2	Paramount Nightclub	163 James St, Northbridge, 6003	08 9228 1344	www.paramountnightclub.com.au	Mon-Thurs: 11pm, Fri-Sat: 6am	No	No	No	3.32
28 F6	Plain St Bar	99 Adelaide Tce, Perth, 6000	08 9225 1292		Mon-Thurs: 11pm, Fri-Sun: 2am	Yes	Yes	No	0.84
117 C2	Rise	139 James St, Northbridge, 6003	08 9328 7447	www.rise.net.au	Fri-Sat: 6am	No	No	No	3.24
145 B2	Rosie O'Grady's	205 James St, Northbridge, 6003	08 9328 1488		Mon-Wed: Midnight, Thurs: 1am, Fri-Sat: 2am	Yes	Yes	No	3.43
57 G4	Royal Bar & Brasserie	60 Royal St, East Perth, 6004	08 9221 0466	www.royalbarandbrasserie.com.au	Daily: 11pm	Yes	Yes	No	1.50
147 C4	The Bar on Barracks	43 Barrack St, Perth, 6000	08 9421 1333	www.functionjunction.com.au	Mon-Wed: 9pm, Thurs-Fri: Midnight	Yes	Yes	No	3.11
148 C5	The Lucky Shag	Barrack Sq, Perth, 6000	08 9221 6011		Mon-Thurs: Midnight, Fri-Sat: 1am, Sun: 10pm	Yes	Yes	No	2.80
80 B9	The Oyster Bar	85 South Perth Esp, South Perth, 6151	08 9368 4999	www.meads.com.au	Daily: 10pm	No	Yes	No	5.73
112 C2	The Shed	69-71 Aberdeen St, Northbridge, 6003	08 9228 2200	www.the-shed.com.au	Wed-Thurs & Sun: Midnight, Fri-Sat: 2am	Yes	Yes	No	3.34
79 B9	The Windsor Bar & Café	112 Mill Point Rd, South Perth, 6151	08 9474 2229	www.windsorhotel.com.au	Mon-Wed: Midnight, Thurs-Sat: 1am, Sun: 10pm	No	Yes	No	5.63
152 B2	Varga Lounge	161 James St, Northbridge, 6003	08 9328 7200	www.vargalounge.com.au	Fri-Sat: 2am	No	No	No	3.32

Rottnest Island. Photo: Tourism Western Australia.

PERTH -ATTRACTIONS

Rottnest Island

Rottnest Island is an ideal day trip, with its superb beaches and pristine waters full of tropical fish and magnificent coral.

Located 19km off the coast of Fremantle (a 90-minute ferry trip from Perth), the sandy island has a relaxed holiday atmosphere with a pleasant seaside village charm and is renowned for its snorkelling, diving and surfing.

Home to the "quokka", a small indigenous marsupial resembling a rat, "Rotto" has virtually no motorised traffic, with walking and cycling the preferred means of getting around. There are restaurants to cater for all tastes, as well as budget and luxury accommodation for those wanting to stay on.

Fremantle

Lively and multicultural, popular Fremantle is just 30 minutes south-west of the CBD.

Known as "Freo" to the locals, the dynamic port city has its own unique style full of outdoor cafes, humming markets and an arty atmosphere in which buskers flourish.

Enjoy the international spread of restaurants, fashion boutiques and bars, or for something different, check out the Old Fremantle Prison where former guards conduct guided tours. Built in 1859 and only ceasing as a working jail in 1991, the prison is worth a visit after dark for a fantastic, yet unnerving night tour through the gallows.

Northbridge

Northbridge is the pulse of Perth and is the place to be when night falls. Weekends are particularly busy as restaurants, pubs and clubs fill to capacity to

www.ashes06.com

Organised tours... The open-top, red double-decker buses of City Sightseeing Perth (08 9203 8882, citysightseeing.com.au) are a terrific way of exploring the city, while Captain Cook Cruises (08 9325 3341, captaincookcruises.com.au) can take you to the Swan Valley or Fremantle via the magnificent Swan River. The Western Australian Tourist Centre on the corner of Forrest Pl and Wellington St (1300 361 351, westernaustralia.com/en) can give you further information on touring Perth, or visit the comprehensive experienceperth.com website.

create a cosmopolitan party atmosphere.

Northbridge is also a great place to get your cultural taste, with the Art Gallery of Western Australia, the Perth Institute of Contemporary Art, the State Library and the Western Australia Museum all located there.

Kings Park
For amazing panoramic views of Perth and the Swan River, head up to tranquil Kings Park, just a short stroll to the city's west.

The park incorporates a massive area of beautiful Botanic Garden and a section of natural bushland for visitors to admire.

The Kings Park walk and cycle trails are a great way of taking in the natural flora, serene lakes and scenic lookouts. There are also some great picnic spots, as well as an elevated Federation Walkway, which guides you through the lofty treetops.

Swan Valley
The Swan Valley is Western Australia's oldest wine growing region and is home to award-winning wineries such as Houghton and Sandalford Estate, as well as hip cafes and cosy restaurants.

Located 30 minutes from Perth, the Swan Valley also boasts olive groves, chocolate, cheese,

nougat and fresh produce stalls, plus a vibrant arts scene adding to the region's cultural vibe.

Margaret River
One of Australia's most popular surfing spots, Margaret River is a popular haunt for big wave riders and is worth the five-hour drive south from Perth if you've got a few days to kill.

Margaret River also serves up some of the country's finest wines, with local vineyards particularly adept in producing sauvignon blanc.

Lancelin
A hot spot for windsurfers and sandboarders, Lancelin is situated 130km north of Perth and features kilometres of brilliant white beach and soaring sand dunes.

The seaside fishing village is an ideal day trip or short stay for adventure sport enthusiasts, particularly scuba divers who can descend into the Indian Ocean and explore the 15 wrecks just off shore. Dolphins and sea lions are also a hit with visitors.

Rockingham
Located a 45-minute drive south of Perth, coastal Rockingham is another Western Australian paradise for water and nature lovers, attracting sailors, windsurfers, divers and kiteboarders.

Visitors can also swim with dolphins before a tantalising seafood meal of crabs, mussels and crayfish, which are abundant in the region.

Sandboarding is big in Lancelin.
Photo: Tourism Western Australia.

SUGGESTED -ITINERARIES

If you're after some cool ideas to spend a day or a week before or after the Third Test in Perth, here are a few tips to help you plan your stay:

A day...

Start your day with a **City Sightseeing Perth (08 9203 8882, citysightseeing.com.au)** tour to get yourself better acquainted with the Western Australian capital, then make your way to Fremantle by train, bus, ferry or hire a scooter.

Enjoy an alfresco cappuccino in Fremantle's trendy South Tce as hordes of day-trippers wander by, before sitting down to lunch in the port city's colourful Fishing Boat Harbour.

In the afternoon, refresh yourself with a swim further up the coast in popular Cottesloe beach, before heading back into town to Northbridge for a big night of partying in one of the many pubs and clubs.

A few days...

After a day of sightseeing in and around Perth and Fremantle, jump on a ferry and spend a day on peaceful Rottnest Island.

"Rotto" is great for walking, cycling and swimming, and at just 11km long and 4.5km wide, is easy to circumnavigate. Cafes and restaurants cater for visitors, and while you're there, keep an eye out for the native quokka - a small nocturnal marsupial of the wallaby family.

Cap off your stay in Perth with a visit to the Swan Valley for a wine tasting session. The 32km Swan Valley Food and Wine Trail takes in 80 wineries, restaurants and breweries and more than 50 fresh produce stalls, as well art galleries and heritage buildings. A classic day trip!

A week...

Western Australia is a big place, so don't expect to see everything even if you do have a week or two to wander. Outside of Perth, seaside Rockingham and Mandurah are easily accessible places to visit to the south, as is Lancelin to the north and Northam to the east.

Margaret River is perhaps the most recommended spot though, particularly if you like the beach and especially if you enjoy surfing. A five-hour drive south of Perth, Margaret River is an ideal place to chill out for a few days before or after the cricket.

And while you're in this part of the world, continue down the coast and check out the Valley of the Giants near Albany - a unique expanse of tingle trees that can live up to 400 years and grow to 60m tall and 16m wide around their base!

Margaret River is a favourite spot for surfers.
Photo: Tourism Western Australia.

PERTH

PERTH
DIRECTORY

CRICKET
Cricket Australia:..............(03) 9653 9999, cricket.com.au
WACA:...............................(08) 9265 7222, waca.com.au

EMERGENCY
Ambulance: 000
Fire:..000
Police:...000
Police (non-emergency):..13 14 44
RACWA Roadside Assistance:.........13 11 11, rac.com.au
Lifeline (crisis counselling): 13 11 14
Sexual Assault Resource Centre: ....(08) 9340 1828

HEALTH
Royal Perth Hospital: ....(08) 9224 2244
Fremantle Public Hospital:.........................(08) 9431 3333
Princess Margaret Children's Hospital (Subiaco):.............
....(08) 9340 8222
East Perth Medical Centre:........................(08) 9221 4242
Sir Charles Gairdner Hospital (Nedlands): (08) 9346 3333
Perth Women's Centre:...............................(08) 9227 9032
Lifecare - Dentist (Perth):..........................(08) 9221 2777
Travel Medicine Centre (Perth):.................(08) 9321 7888

INTERNET ACCESS
Backpackers Travel Centre:..........William St, Northbridge
Outback Travel Centre:................William St, Northbridge
Traveller's Club:..................................Wellington St, Perth
Cybercorner Café: ....Willmott Ave, Margaret River

MONEY
American Express:1300 139 030, americanexpress.com.au
Travelex: ....1800 637 642, travelex.com.au

PHONE/MOBILE
3 mobile: ....131 681, three.com.au
International code to UK:..
............0011 (or 0018) + 44 + Area Code + Local Number
Country Direct (reverse charge/credit to UK): ....
....................1800 881 440, 1800 881 441, 1800 881 417
Directory Assistance: ....12455 (local/international)

POST
Perth GPO (Forrest Pl):...(08) 9237 5000, austpost.com.au

TOURISM
Western Australian Visitor Centre (cnr Forrest
Pl/Wellington St): 1300 361 351,westernaustralia.com
i-City Information Kiosk (cnr Forrest Pl/Murray St Mall): ..
....1300 361 351
Experience Perth: ....experienceperth.com
Fremantle Tourist Bureau:.......................(08) 9431 7878,
....fremantlewa.com.au
City Sightseeing Perth: ....(08) 9203 8882,
....citysightseeing.com.au
Super Roo Eco Fun Tours: ....(08) 9335 4214,
....superrootours.com.au
Captain Cook Cruises (WA):.....................(08) 9325 3341,
....captaincookcruises.com.au
Backpackers Travel Centre (Northbridge): (08) 9228 1877,
....backpackerstravel.net.au
Outback Travel Centre (Northbridge):.......(08) 9228 3812,
....goworknetwork.com.au
Traveller's Club (Perth): ....(08) 9226 0660,
....travellersclub.com.au
Swan Valley & Eastern Region Visitor Centre: ....
....(08) 9379 9400
Out & About Wine Tours: ....(08) 9377 3376,
....outandabouttours.com.au
Rottnest Island Visitor Centre: ....(08) 9372 9732,
....rottnestisland.com
Rottnest Express cruises:.........................(08) 9421 5888,
....boattorque.com.au
Oceanic Cruises Rottnest:........................(08) 9325 1191,
....oceaniccruises.com.au
Malibu Dive (Rottnest Island): ....(08) 9292 5111,
....rottnestdiving.com.au
Dr Marion Hercock's Explorer Tours: ....(08) 9361 0940,
....explorertours.com.au
H2 Overland Surf Adventures:....................0438 658 059,
....h2osurfadventure.com
Travelabout Outback Adventures:............(08) 9244 1200,
....travelabout.com.au
Margaret River Visitor Information Centre:(08) 9757 2911

TRANSPORT
PLANE
Qantas: ....13 13 13, qantas.com.au
Virgin Blue:.............................13 67 89, virginblue.com.au
Skywest (regional): ....1300 660 088, skywest.com.au

Golden Eagle Airlines (regional): ....(08) 9172 1777,
........................goldeneagleairlines.com/regional
Skippers (regional): ....1300 729 924, skippers.com.au
Rottnest Air Taxi: 1800 500 006

BUS - LOCAL
Transperth: ....13 62 13, transperth.wa.gov.au
Airport-City Shuttle Bus: ....(08) 9277 7015
Fremantle Airport Shuttle: 1300 668 687,
....fremantleairportshuttle.com.au

BUS - REGIONAL/INTERSTATE
Greyhound Australia: ....13 14 99, greyhound.com.au
Transwa: ....1300 662 205, transwa.wa.gov.au
South West Coachlines: ....(08) 9324 2333
Perth Goldfields Express: 1800 620 440,
....goldrushtours.com.au/express
Integrity Coachlines: ....(08) 9226 1339,
....integritycoachlines.com.au
Nullarbor Traveller: .....1800 816 858, the-traveller.com.au
Easyrider Backpacker Tours: ....(08) 9226 0307,
....easyridertours.com.au

TRAIN - LOCAL
Transperth: ....13 62 13, transperth.wa.gov.au
Perth Tram: ....(08) 9322 2006, perthtram.com.au

TRAIN - REGIONAL/INTERSTATE
Transwa: ....1300 662 205, transwa.wa.gov.au
Great Southern Railways (Indian Pacific): 13 21 47,
....gsr.com.au

Kangaroos on the golf course at Swan Valley.
Photo: Tourism Western Australia.

FERRY
Transperth: ....13 62 13, transperth.wa.gov.au

TAXI
Black & White Taxis: 13 10 08
Swan Taxis: 13 13 30

CAR HIRE
Avis: ....(08) 9325 7677, avis.com.au
Budget (Perth Airport): .....(08) 9277 9277, budget.com.au
Europcar (Perth Airport):(08) 9277 9144, europcar.com.au
Hertz (Perth Airport): ....(08) 9479 4788, hertz.com.au
Thrifty (Perth Airport): ....(08) 9464 7333, thrifty.com.au
Bayswater Car Rental: ....(08) 9325 1000,
....bayswatercarrental.com.au
Action Hire Cars (Redcliffe): ....(08) 9277 4522,
....actionhirecars.com.au
Hawk Rent A Car (Redcliffe): ....(08) 9478 6999,
....hawkrentacar.com
Aussie Drive - 4WD (Welshpool): ....(08) 9333 4333,
....aussiedrive.com.au

MOTORCYCLE/SCOOTER HIRE
Lancelin Off Road Motorbike Hire: 0417 919 550,
....dirtbikehire.com.au

BICYCLE HIRE
Bicycle Transportation Alliance: ....(08) 9420 7210,
....multiline.com.au/~bta
About Bike Hire (Perth): ....(08) 9221 2665,
....aboutbikehire.com.au
Koala Bike Hire (Kings Park): ....(08) 9321 3061
Cycle Centre (Perth): ....(08) 9325 1176
Rottnest Bike Hire: ....(08) 9292 5105

Come join us!

For access to tickets, exclusive team news, player events and money can't buy experiences

ESCC Membership includes:

- Entry into ESCC ballots for England international tickets
- Regular e-news and interviews straight from the team dressing room
- Access to member events and match day bars when available
- An exclusive membership pack including:
  a baseball cap, mouse mat, car sticker and pin badge
- 10 free copies of All Out Cricket magazine - worth £35
- A discount at the ECB online store
- Plus many more 'money can't buy' benefits...

For more information or to join instantly visit
ecb.co.uk/escc or call **+44 (0)870 444 3722**

THE GARDEN STATE

Melbourne Cricket Ground. Photo: Getty Images.

DECEMBER 26-30, 2006

4TH TEST
MELBOURNE

MELBOURNE CITY OVERVIEW

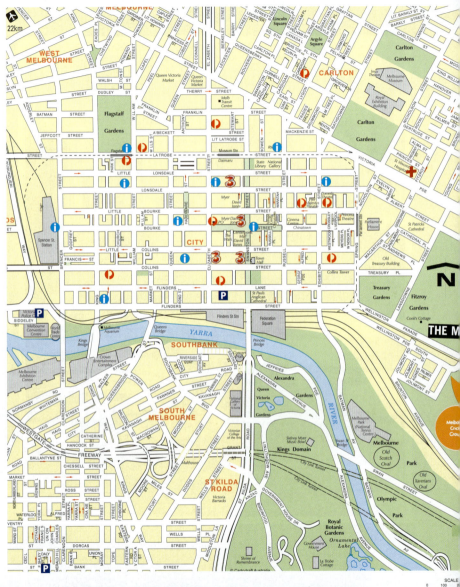

KEY... MELBOURNE CITY OVERVIEW

- 3 store
- Hospital
- Police
- Post Office
- Tourist information
- Airport

Victoria State Map

www.ashes06.com

WELCOME TO
-MELBOURNE, VICTORIA

If your passion for sport extends beyond your love of cricket then you'll definitely enjoy Melbourne.

In 1837, the south-eastern Australian city was named after Lord Melbourne, the Prime Minister of Britain at the time, and since then it has become the unofficial sporting capital of the country.

It's the home of Aussie Rules football, the Australian Open tennis and the Australian Grand Prix, and of course Test and one-day cricket. Melburnians will throw their support behind any event of note, rugby union and soccer internationals among the fixtures warmly embraced by the sporting public.

But there is so much more to Melbourne, which should make your stay in Victoria memorable. Locals love its vibrant energy, overwhelming choice of restaurants, cafes and funky bars, boutique shopping strips and art galleries. The diversity is not just confined to the city, with most nearby suburbs maintaining their own identity and charm.

Melbourne has an average summer temperature of 26°C but often has inconsistent weather - it's often ribbed for having "four seasons in one day".

With a population of 3.7 million, Melbourne is the second biggest city in Australia. But, only hours away from the hustle and bustle of the sophisticated CBD, tourists can enjoy some of the nation's most spectacular coastlines and rural settings. The Great Ocean Road provides the perfect route to some gorgeous and character-filled towns, while the vineyards of the Yarra Valley also provide a tranquil alternative to the urban lifestyle.

STATE FACTS... VICTORIA
Founded: 1837
Population: 5.0 million (Melbourne = 3.7 million)
Colours: Blue and white
Floral emblem: Common Heath
Faunal emblems: Landbeater's Possum & Helmeted Honeyeater
Domestic cricket team: Victorian Bushrangers
Average summer temperature: 26°C
Average winter temperature: 16°C
Time zone: GMT + 11 hours

While you're in Melbourne...

Eat: Souvlaki. There are countless restaurant and café strips across Melbourne with a strong multicultural feel, so it's tough to identify a dish that's quintessentially Victorian. Melbourne has the third biggest Greek population in the world so if you've had a big night out, an early-morning souvlaki (otherwise known as a "kebab", "yiros" or "gyros") is a must.

Drink: VB. Melbourne's most popular beer is Victoria Bitter. "VB" has captured the imagination of the beer-drinking public through its catchy advertising theme song and its sponsorship of major sports across the nation, and remains one of the highest-selling lagers in Australia. VB has a full flavour with a clean, hop bitterness.

See: The Yarra Valley. It's Victoria's most famous vineyard district with more than 20 wineries available for you to visit and sample their produce. Located about 90 minutes from Melbourne, the region is perfect for a day trip. Other activities include the Yarra Valley Regional Food Trail (featuring 14 farm-gate taste and buy stop-points) or a picnic among Australian wildlife at the Yarra Valley farm.

Do: St Kilda's café strip and Esplanade. Jump on the number 96 tram from Bourke St and relax during the 25-minute ride to Melbourne's playground. Enjoy some "people watching" from the abundance of cafés and pubs on Fitzroy St or Acland St. Or if you're a little more energetic, join the rollerbladers and cyclists on the Esplanade. For the young at heart, Melbourne's Luna Park also beckons with 18 thrill rides.

Boxing Day at the MCG.

MELBOURNE CRICKET GROUND

What's in a name?
It's called the Melbourne Cricket Ground, but the stadium actually hosts far more Australian Rules football every year than cricket. Considered the "home of footy" by most Aussies, the MCG - or the "G" as it is affectionately called - is where the AFL Grand Final is played every September.

It's a five-minute walk from the CBD but some believe the Melbourne Cricket Ground is the heart of the city.

The MCG in Jolimont is home to the Victorian Bushrangers in the Australian domestic competition and is considered the most outstanding sporting ground in the country and one of the best in the world.

Established in 1853, the MCG has changed dramatically over the years, with the $150 million (£63 million) Great Southern Stand, built 15 years ago, the major feature of the stadium.

The landscape of the site has changed even more this year for the Commonwealth Games, which were held in March. A multi-million dollar upgrade of more than half the ground has now returned the seating capacity to around 100,000 people.

The ground has a strong link with the Ashes, hosting the first Test between Australia and England. And there have been plenty of memorable cricket moments since. The late David Hookes smashed five boundaries off a Tony Greig over in the 1977 Centenary Test against England, and who could forget the infamous Trevor Chappell underarm incident in an Australia v New Zealand one-day match in 1981.

The MCG is a busy place. There are more than 90 days of cricket and Australian Rules footy played on the surface each year, with total attendances reaching more than 3.5 million annually.

There have also been several international rugby union and soccer matches held at the venue, and in 1956, the "G" was the home of the Olympics.

www.ashes06.com

MATCH DAY INFORMATION

4TH TEST:
AUSTRALIA vs ENGLAND

Melbourne Cricket Ground, December 26-30, 2006

Gates:
MCC members reserve gates open at 8.30am. Public and AFL members gates open at 9.00am. Public access is via the Great Southern Stand (Gates 4 and 5), the Ponsford Stand (Gate 1) and the Olympic Stand (Gate 3).

Match times:
FIRST SESSION:	10.30am - 12.30pm
Lunch:	12.30pm - 1.10pm
SECOND SESSION:	1.10pm - 3.10pm
Tea:	3.10pm - 3.30pm
THIRD SESSION:	3.30pm - 5.30pm

*Note: Times are subject to change.

[BE WARNED! Gate staff may conduct bag searches on entry to the MCG to check for prohibited items. In the event prohibited items are found, patrons will be asked to dispose of items prior to entering the ground. Security cameras operate within the MCG.]

Tickets:
The Ticketmaster Box Office opens at 8.00am and closes one hour after the lunch break on each day of the Test. Phone Ticketmaster on 1300 136 122 or visit ticketmaster.com.au

Car parking:
Car parking is usually available at the MCG in Yarra Park and costs about $6 (£2.50), however space is limited. Drivers are encouraged to use the high-rise parking buildings in the CBD and then walk to the ground.

Prohibited items:
- Alcohol
- Opened soft drink containers
- Cans/glass
- Torn-up paper
- Musical instruments
- Whistles
- Flags with handles exceeding 1.8m
- Fireworks, flares, laser lights
- Chairs/stools
- Rollerblades, skateboards, scooters
- Animals (guide & hearing dogs may enter)
- Video cameras
- Audio recording equipment
- Any large article that cannot be placed under a seat
- Any device that, in the opinion of the Melbourne Cricket Club management, has potential to cause injury or public nuisance.

continued overpage...

For up-to-date information, visit cricketvictoria.com.au or phone (03) 9653 1100.

MATCH DAY INFORMATION
...continued from page 127.

General information:
- Access to Gate 1 (Ponsford Stand) is via the Rod Laver Arena footbridge or ramp on the corner of Jolimont St and Jolimont Tce.
- The Ticketmaster Box Office is located at Gate 3, however account pick-ups can also be made at Gate 1 outside the Ponsford Stand.
- Disability parks are available at any of the entrances to Yarra Park and outside Gates 5 and 6 for those sitting in the Great Southern Stand and AFL Members Reserve.
- Disability access to the ground is through Gates 4 or 5 (Great Southern Stand) or via Gate 7 (AFL Members Reserve).
- Umbrellas can be taken inside the MCG but cannot be raised in seating areas while cricket is playing.
- St John's Ambulance staff will have first-aid offices throughout the stadium during the Test. To locate the nearest first-aid provider, ask one of the events staff or security guards at the ground.

Food & beverage:
Food and drink outlets can be found behind general public seating areas throughout the stadium. These facilities, marked by red and white signage, serve traditional fast food such as hot chips, meat pies and hotdogs, as well as sandwiches and salads.

There are also four Red Rooster stores, six Piazza Espresso coffee outlets and two licensed cafes, which help make up the 150 different food and beverage products offered around the ground.

If you need to quench your thirst, Carlton Mid (mid-strength) and Carlton Sterling (light) are the beers on offer at the MCG on Boxing Day, with Carlton Draught (full-strength) added to the selection on days 2-5 of the Test.

Smoking:
Smoking is banned within the MCG and within designated smoke-free areas outside the stadium. Patrons may be asked to leave the ground if they ignore the ban.

TAB/Betting:
TAB betting facilities are available on Level B1 of the Ponsford Stand and on Level B1 of the Great Southern Stand, and open from 9.30am on each day of the Test. A TAB outlet is also located on Level 4 of the MCC Members Pavilion.

The MCG can hold 100,000 people. Photo: Tourism Victoria.

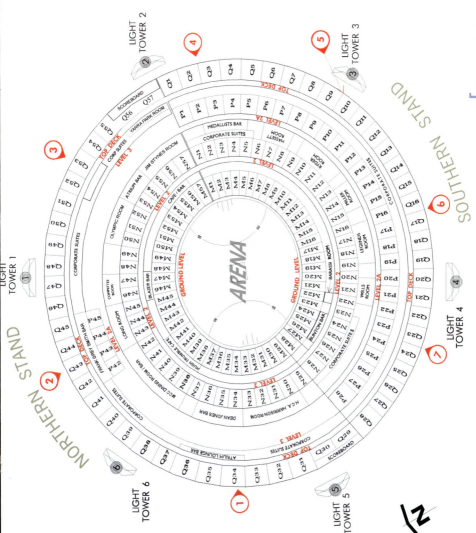

*Reproduced with the kind permission of the Melbourne Cricket Club.

MELBOURNE CRICKET GROUND
-SEATING PLAN

[TRANSPORT

By Plane...

Melbourne Airport (03 9297 1600, melair.com.au) is located 22km from the city centre and is the city's main entry point by plane, while **Avalon Airport** (avalonairport.com.au), located further out near Geelong, is used by discount airline **Jetstar** (131 538, jetstar.com.au).

More than 20 airlines operate scheduled international flights through Melbourne Airport, including Qantas, Singapore Airlines, Malaysia Airlines, Cathay Pacific and Garuda Indonesia. British Airways also provides international access to Melbourne through code-shared services with Qantas.

Qantas (13 13 13, qantas.com.au) and **Virgin Blue** (13 67 89, virginblue.com.au) are the two key airlines within Australia and operate interstate routes to Test cities Brisbane, Perth, Adelaide and Sydney. If you're following the cricket from Perth to Melbourne, a one-way ticket will set you back between $210-$250 (£87-£105), and if you're continuing on to Sydney for the Fifth Test, expect to pay around $130-$190 (£54-£79) for a one-way fare.

To/from Airport...

The **Skybus** airport shuttle (03 9335 2811, skybus.com.au) operates a 24-hour, seven days a week shuttle bus between Melbourne Airport and the city centre. The two major city stops are the Southern Cross Station on Spencer St and the Melbourne Transit Centre on Franklin St, however it does make stops at city hotels for travellers. Shuttles run every 10-15 minutes during the day and every 30-60 minutes overnight and cost $15 (£6.25) for a one-way airport-city trip.

Public buses also operate from the terminal to various areas in and around Melbourne. Information on destinations and schedules can be obtained from the information desks within the airport.

Car hire is also available at Melbourne Airport through **Avis** (13 63 33, avis.com.au), **Budget** (13 27 27, budget.com.au), **Europcar** (1300 131 390, europcar.com.au), **Hertz** (13 30 39, hertz.com.au) and **Thrifty** (1300 367 227, thrifty.com.au), or hail a taxi which will cost around $40 (£17) for the airport-city trip.

By Train... (INTERSTATE)

Great Southern Railways (13 21 47, gsr.com.au) operates several interstate train services from its Southern Cross Station (Spencer St) in the heart of Melbourne.

The **Overland** travels between Melbourne and Adelaide three times a week, with the 11-hour, 828km journey costing $68 (£28). If you're travelling to Melbourne from the Third Test in Perth, you will need to board the **Indian Pacific** in the first instance, however since it doesn't go through Melbourne en route to Sydney, you will need to switch to the Overland in Adelaide.

CountryLink's (13 22 32, countrylink.info) XPT train runs twice daily between Melbourne and Sydney and is an ideal choice for those following the cricket. The journey takes 11 hours, with a one-way fare costing around $125 (£52).

For regional travel within Victoria, **V/Line** (13 61 96, vline.com.au) is the state's largest passenger transport operator, offering rail and coach services.

www.ashes06.com

By Bus... (INTERSTATE)

Melbourne's central bus station, the Melbourne Transit Centre, is on Franklin St, near Swanston St in the city. It has ticket offices for all major statewide and interstate bus companies, including **Firefly Express** (1300 730 740, fireflyexpress.com.au), **Greyhound Australia** (13 14 99, greyhound.com.au), **V/Line** (13 61 96, vline.com.au) and **Premier Motor Service** (13 34 10, premierms.com.au).

The respective bus companies have fare and timetable information on their websites. As a guide, a one-way fare from Melbourne to Adelaide (11 hours) will cost between $50-$65 (£22-£28), while the Melbourne to Sydney journey (12-15 hours) will cost between $65-$72 (£27-£30).

PUBLIC TRANSPORT...

Melbourne's automated public transport ticketing system, **Metlink** (13 16 38, metlinkmelbourne.com.au), operates on all train, tram and bus services in the metropolitan area, with electronically-coded tickets called Metcards.

One ticket can give you flexible travel between trains, trams and buses. You can purchase your Metcard from the MetShop, at shops and newsagents displaying the blue Metcard sign, and at train stations, ticket machines on board trams (coin only) or from bus drivers.

Most fares are based on three zones, however most visitors to Melbourne will most likely only travel within Zone 1, which covers the city and inner suburban area, including St Kilda.

Full fare **City Saver** tickets cost $2.30 (95p), which is a single journey only fare. Full fare **2 Hour Zone 1** tickets cost $3.20 (£1.30) and allow unlimited train, tram and bus travel for at least two hours, while full fare **Daily Zone 1** tickets cost $6.10 (£2.50) and allow unlimited travel on trains, trams and buses for a whole day.

Public bus...

Melbourne's bus services provide more flexibility than trains, travelling to many more inner suburbs than their rail counterparts.

If you're out on the town at night, keep the **NightRider** bus service in mind for public transport after midnight on Fridays and Saturdays. You can jump on a NightRider on Swanston St (between Collins St and Flinders St), at Crown

continued overpage...

A tram outside Flinders St Station. Photo: Tourism Victoria.

[TRANSPORT
...continued from page 131.

Cycling along Melbourne's Yarra River. Photo: Tourism Victoria.

Entertainment Centre or at any NightRider stop along one of its nine routes. NightRider tickets are available from the driver when you board the bus, with most fares costing $6 (£2.50). Metcards are not valid on any of the NightRider services.

Public train...

The Melbourne train system is quick and easy to use. Flinders St Station is the main terminal from which trains operate, with frequent services running between 5am and midnight every day (except Sundays where operating hours are between 8am and 11pm).

The city service includes an underground **City Loop**, travelling between Parliament, Melbourne Central, Flagstaff, Southern Cross and Flinders St stations.

Public tram...

Melbourne has one of the largest tram networks in the world,
covering the city and inner suburbs. Services run along most routes every 6-8 minutes during peak times and 10-15 minutes during off-peak periods. Services are less frequent on weekends and late at night.

A popular choice for tourists is the **City Circle Tram** which provides a free service around central Melbourne and links with other tram and train services. This "hop on, hop off" tram will take you past all the city's major shopping malls and major attractions, including the Princess Theatre. To catch the free service, wait at any of the specially marked stops along the route.

They operate seven days a week between 10am and 6pm (except Christmas Day), with extended services to 9pm on Thursdays, Fridays and Saturdays.

By Bicycle...

With its wide streets and abundance of parks and gardens,
Melbourne is a great city for a bike ride... and it's relatively flat too!

Hire a Bike (0417 339 203, byohouse.com.au/bikehire) is located riverside at Federation Square in the city and loans bicycles for $15 (£6.25) an hour or $35 (£15) all day. **St Kilda Cycles** (03 9534 3074, stkildacycles.com.au) on the corner of Carlisle St and Albert St in St Kilda is another creditable bike hire outlet with its coastal location ideal for those wanting a beachside ride.

By Taxi...

There are licensed ranks across the city, with an average trip from Melbourne Airport to the CBD costing about $40 (£17). If you can't find a taxi rank, contact:

Embassy Taxis 13 17 55
Taxis Australia 13 22 27
Arrow 13 22 11
Silver Top Taxis..........13 10 08
North Suburban..........13 11 19

Melbourne Tram Network

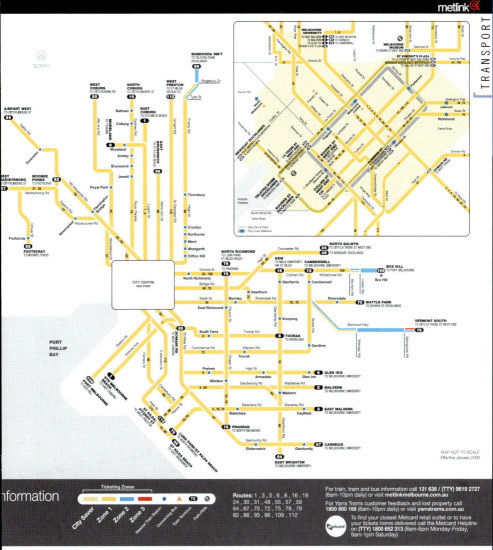

FREE CITY CIRCLE TRAM: A popular choice for tourists is the City Circle Tram which provides a free service around central Melbourne and links with other tram and train services. This "hop on, hop off" tram will take you past all the city's major shopping malls and major attractions. To catch the free service, wait at any of the specially marked stops along the route.

continued overpage…

City Saver Area

Trams showing Route number and Terminus or major stopping place

Buses showing Route number and Terminus or major stopping place
Bus routes are depicted in different colours when travelling along common roads and streets

Trains showing Station name

SKYBUS
Skybus arrival/departure point

NIGHTRIDER
NightRider services departure points

© Copyright Metlink Victoria Pty Ltd.

GETTING TO
THE MELBOURNE CRICKET GROUND

Obviously it depends on where you're staying during the Fourth Test, but THE TRAIN IS PROBABLY THE BEST WAY OF GETTING to and from the MCG for the cricket. That's unless of course you're staying in the CBD, in which case a 15-minute walk will get you to the Jolimont-based arena.

BUSES AND TRAMS also service the stadium from inner and outer suburban Melbourne.

On Foot...
The MCG is a leisurely 15-minute stroll from the city centre and is a wise method of getting to the ground if you're staying in the CBD.

On approaching the stadium, public entrances are located at Gates 4 and 5 for the Great Southern Stand, Gate 1 for the Ponsford Stand and Gate 3 for the Olympic Stand.

By Bus...
Spectators coming from the northern or southern suburbs of Melbourne can use route 246 of the National Bus Company. It links La Trobe University with Elsternwick Station and stops at Punt Rd which is within easy walking distance of the ground.

By Train...
The two closest train stations to the MCG are Jolimont (better known as MCG Station) and Richmond.

Jolimont is north of the ground and about a five-minute walk through Yarra Park from the stadium. If you're coming from the city, take the Hurstbridge or Epping lines.

Commuters wanting to access the south-eastern side of the MCG can catch the train to Richmond. It's a slightly longer walk to the ground, but does take you past Punt Rd Oval to the Great Southern Stand side. Take any train from the city on the Lilydale, Belgrave, Alamein, Glen Waverley, Dandenong, Pakenham, Cranbourne, Frankston or Sandringham lines to get to Richmond Station.

By Tram...
There is a choice of two trams to catch from the Flinders St Station in the city to the MCG. Both the number 48 (City-North Balwyn) and the number 75 (City-Vermont South) will stop just outside the oval. Alight the tram at the Hilton Hotel, which is at the corner of Wellington Pde and Clarendon St, and walk through Yarra Park.

The number 70 (City-Wattle Park) is not as direct, as it heads along Swan St, but it's only a short walk over the footbridge from the tennis courts of Melbourne Park.

By Taxi...
There are licensed taxi ranks across the city. Fares to the MCG from locations within the CBD should cost about $10-$15 (£4-£7). If you're struggling to hail a cab, phone:
Taxis Australia 13 22 27
Arrow 13 22 11
Embassy Taxis 13 17 55
Silver Top Taxis 13 10 08
North Suburban 13 11 19

By Car...
Car parking is usually available at the MCG in Yarra Park and costs about $6 (£2.50), however space is limited. Drivers are encouraged to use the high-rise parking buildings in the CBD and walk to the ground.

The MCG.

[MELBOURNE -ACCOMMODATION

Melbourne has a great selection of accommodation. Photo: Tourism Victoria.

HOSTELS

LOW-RANGE: < $100 (£42)

CENTRAL MELBOURNE ACCOMMODATION
$25 (£10)
21 Bromham Pl, Richmond
(03) 9427 9826 Reservations via email: info@centralaccommodation.net
centralaccommodation.net

Central Melbourne Accommodation (CMA) has 30 beds and guests can choose from dorms, single or double rooms. The hostel has a laundry, TV, video, internet, free barbecue and off-street parking. There is also a free pick-up from hostels or bus and train stations. CMA is 10 minutes from the MCG and is in the heart of Melbourne's café, restaurant and discount shopping district. If you're looking to spread your leisure activities beyond the cricket and attend a musical, hostel staff have great contacts for entertainment tickets. CMA specialises in long-term stays so ask about weekly rates if you'll be in Melbourne for the duration of the Fourth Test.

CLAREMONT GUEST HOUSE
$25-$80 (£10-£33)
189 Toorak Rd, South Yarra
(03) 9826 8000
Reservations via email:
info@hotelclaremont.com
hotelclaremont.com

The **Claremont Guest House** is an ideal base for tourists. South Yarra has countless pubs, nightclubs, cinemas and restaurants and is in walking distance or a short tram ride away from Melbourne's major attractions. The Claremont offers 77 rooms, tour booking desk, gifts and pharmacy, internet access, guest lounge, meals room, laundry, 24-hour reception, TVs in all rooms, individual heating and cooling fans, free tea, coffee and breakfast.

[NOTE: Hostels can be booked via www.hostelbookers.com or www.hostelworld.com. Hotels, motels and apartments can be booked via www.wotif.com]

Keep in mind that twin rooms contain a bunk bed, not separate beds. There are ample shared bathrooms, linen is provided for every bed and clean towels are supplied daily. If you need to change over some money there is also an exchange centre nearby.

URBAN CENTRAL (pp148-149)
$21-$28 (£9-£12)
334 City Rd, Southbank
1800 631 288 (free call within Australia) Reservations via email:
stayplay@urbancentral.com.au
urbancentral.com.au

Urban Central is one of the newer hostels in Melbourne and is secure and affordable. Guests receive individual security swipe cards on arrival and the presence of staff 24 hours a day makes the building ultra-safe. The hostel has the latest computers and high-speed internet, a television room with a plasma screen, games area, library, bar with big screen projector and a daily program of events to get involved in. Guests can also enjoy free breakfast, tea, coffee, rice and pasta. Each room has a maximum of four beds and ensuite bathrooms are available if you want to pay a little extra. There's a tour desk if you need help finding fun activities but Urban Central's fantastic location lends itself to exploring Melbourne by yourself.

THE NUNNERY
$26-$75 (£11-£31)
116 Nicholson St, Fitzroy

1800 032 635 (free call within Australia) Reservations via email:
info@nunnery.com.au
nunnery.com.au

The Nunnery has a wide range of accommodation spread over two Victorian-style buildings and caters for a diverse group of travellers. It has dormitory-style accommodation for those on a small budget or private rooms for those with a little extra money to spend. All room styles are provided with bedding, towels, heating and have a shared bathroom, laundry and kitchen facility. Homemade soup or ice-cream and the occasional barbecue are among the free goodies you'll get when you check in. Other services include phone, fax, internet, message and mail service and free newspapers. The Nunnery is only a short stroll from the MCG and other sporting venues, the city's Museum, Fitzroy Gardens and Brunswick St.

ELIZABETH HOSTEL (pp148-149)
$17-$50 (£7-£21)
490-494 Elizabeth St, Melbourne
1800 611 897 (free call within Australia) Reservations via email:
elizabethhostel@hotmail.com
elizabethhostel.com.au

You'll never be stranded or hungry at the **Elizabeth Hostel** - it's next to the Melbourne Transit Centre, while the Queen Victoria Market is across the road. All the city's attractions are within walking distance and the tram is in close proximity too. The hostel

was recently renovated and each floor has a kitchen, lounge room, laundry and shower facilities. Other features include a mini theatre, free internet, luggage storage areas and a convenience store. Reception hours are from 8am-10pm.

HOTELS, MOTELS & APARTMENTS

LOW-RANGE: < $100 (£42)

KINGSGATE HOTEL (pp148-149)
$77-$96 (£32-£40)
131 King St, Melbourne
1300 734 171 (free call within Australia) Reservations via email:
info@kingsgatehotel.com.au
kingsgatehotel.com.au

The **Kingsgate Hotel** is located at the western end of the CBD and is near the Telstra Dome, Crown Casino, Victoria Markets and the Melbourne Aquarium. Public transport ensures all other Melbourne attractions are only a short ride away. Rooms at the Kingsgate are comfortable and basic but have all the facilities you'll need for a relaxing stay in Victoria's capital. Other features at the hotel include internet access and a cocktail bar and lounge. The Kingsgate has a French restaurant which is open for breakfast and in the evening.

QUEST ON REDAN
$95 (£40)
25 Redan St, St Kilda
(03) 9529 7595

If you enjoy the beach and a quiet atmosphere, the **Quest on Redan** may be the

continued overpage...

ACCOMMODATION
...continued from page 137.

accommodation lodging for you! This East St Kilda hotel is a tram ride away from the Esplanade and the suburb's shopping and café district. The 40 apartments on Redan St are adequately furnished and come with a small kitchenette. There's no in-house restaurant but the choice of nearby eateries means you'll probably want to eat out anyway. Catch a tram to get to the MCG.

ENTERPRIZE HOTEL (pp148-149)
$96-$146 (£40-£61)
44 Spencer St, Melbourne
(03) 9629 6991
Reservations via email:
info@hotelenterprize.com.au
hotelenterprize.com.au

The Enterprize Hotel is a short stroll from the Spencer St bus and train terminal and a short drive from Melbourne Airport. The Crown Casino, Federation Square and other attractions can also be accessed easily from this site. Well-furnished guestrooms have all the basic amenities. Enjoy Melbourne's finest restaurants and cafés or dine in at the Jarrah Room that serves Asian food in the evening and a buffet breakfast in the morning.

EXPLORERS HOTEL MELBOURNE (pp148-149)
$100 (£42)
16 Spencer St, Melbourne
(03) 9621 3333
Reservations via email:
admin@explorersinn.com.au
explorershotel.com.au

Tourists shouldn't have a problem finding a place to rest at the **Explorers Hotel Melbourne**, which offers 113 air-conditioned rooms. The hotel has a bar and cafe which serves breakfast and light snacks. Internet access and laundry facilities are the other main features of this basic but presentable accommodation site. The hotel is within walking distance of local attractions, and for slightly longer journeys, the City Circle trams and standard trams are close by.

HOTELS, MOTELS & APARTMENTS
MID-RANGE: $100-$200 (£42-£84)

THE ALBANY
$139-$164 (£58-£68)
Cnr Toorak Rd & Millswyn St, South Yarra **1800 338 877** (free call within Australia)
Reservations via email:
enquiries@thealbany.com.au
thealbany.com.au

Get away from the hustle and bustle of Melbourne's CBD but not too far away to miss out on the action at **The Albany** in South Yarra. The hotel is a five-minute walk from the Botanical Gardens, and a slightly longer stroll will see you back into the heart of the city. The hotel has spacious rooms with modern amenities. The Albany has a garden restaurant which is open for breakfast and other meals, a lounge area for relaxing, while the building's function rooms are another key feature. These rooms can cater for a variety of events.

THE VICTORIA HOTEL (pp148-149)
$135 (£56)
215 Little Collins St, Melbourne
(03) 9669 0000
Reservations via email:
stay@victoriahotel.com.au
victoriahotel.com.au

The Victoria Hotel was built in the late 1800s but there's nothing tired about this old gal. Guests are just a hop, skip and a jump away from the Melbourne Town Hall, the Princess Theatre, the Art Gallery and the city's major shopping precinct. The MCG and other sporting grounds are also very accessible. Rooms are comfortable and well-equipped, and if you're on a tight budget, you can book an economy room which has shared bathroom facilities. There's all-day dining, including a buffet at Alice's Restaurant, while a bar and pool room is on offer for those looking to unwind after a day at the cricket. Other features include a sauna and spa, internet access and currency exchange.

SAVILLE CITY SUITES (pp150)
$141+ (£59+)
133 Jolimont Rd,
East Melbourne **1300 734 782** (free call within Australia)
Reservations via email:
eastmelbourne.info@shg.com.au   savillesuites.com

The **Saville City Suites** is one of Melbourne's most stylish and fresh apartment hotels. It's located on the CBD's outer and is opposite the MCG. The complex is near other attractions including the Botanic Gardens and the Victorian Arts Centre, which makes it a perfect base to explore Melbourne. There are more than 130 rooms available which can be booked by phone or on the internet. There's an on-site restaurant, 24-hour reception, parking, laundry, swimming pool and gymnasium. Currency exchange facilities are also available.

TRAVELODGE HOTEL SOUTHBANK (pp148-149)
$149-$175 (£62-£73)
Cnr Southgate Ave & Riverside Quay, Southbank **(03) 8696 9600**
travelodge.com.au

Want to enjoy the morning session of the Test but enjoy a sleep-in too? The Travelodge Hotel is just minutes from the MCG. The Melbourne Aquarium, Rod Laver Arena (home of the Australian Open tennis), the Botanic Gardens and a variety of restaurants, cafes and shopping are also just a stroll away. The hotel has 275 air-conditioned guestrooms featuring kitchenettes and other modern facilities. Breakfast is available while a variety of local restaurants can deliver directly into your room.

RENDEZVOUS HOTEL (pp148-149)
$195-$315 (£81-£131)
328 Flinders St, Melbourne
(03) 9250 1888 Reservations via email: **res@melbourne.rendezvous.com.au**
rendezvoushotels.com

Formerly the Commercial Travellers Club, the **Rendezvous Hotel** is a heritage-listed building built in 1913. It has been restored to reflect its rich history and is now one of the higher profile hotels in Melbourne. It's across the road from the Flinders St Railway Station and is only a quick walk from Crown Casino. There are 338 rooms available with five room categories ensuring the hotel can cater for a range of visitors. The Rendezvous has an impressive but moderately priced restaurant that caters for 96 people and is open seven days a week. A club lounge, bar and room service are the other major drawcards of the hotel.

RAMADA MELBOURNE HOTEL (pp148-149)
$165-$225 (£69-£94)
270 Flinders St, Melbourne
(03) 9654 6888
ramadamelbourne.com.au

The **Ramada Melbourne Hotel** is located directly opposite the Flinders St Railway Station and is in walking distance to most of Melbourne's popular sites. It features 182 rooms which have data ports for high-speed internet access, complimentary Foxtel, air-conditioning and mini-bar. If you don't have your own computer you can visit the hotel's business centre which has all the facilities you need to contact loved ones

continued overpage...

Travelodge Hotel Southbank. Photo: Tourism Victoria.

[ACCOMMODATION
...continued from page 139.

interstate or overseas. Rooms are divided into standard, deluxe or waterview deluxe. Waterview deluxe rooms feature some of the best views in Melbourne. Other notable features include 24-hour room service, a limousine service and babysitting.

HOTELS, MOTELS & APARTMENTS

HIGH-RANGE: $200+ (£84+)

QUEST ON BOURKE (pp148-149)
$213-$233 (£89-£97)
155 Bourke St, Melbourne
(03) 9631 0400
Reservations via email:
questonbourke@
questapartments.com.au
questonbourke.com

Families on tour are sure to be attracted to the **Quest on Bourke** serviced apartments. The complex has a babysitting service, gymnasium, meeting rooms and room service. It's located in the business, theatre and government district of the city and is adjacent to Chinatown. The apartments are big enough to relax in and there's plenty for the family to see and do just outside the front door.

HOTEL LINDRUM (pp148-149)
$225+ (£94)
26 Flinders St, Melbourne
(03) 9668 1111 Reservations via email: reservations@
hotel lindrum.com.au
hotellindrum.com.au

Hotel Lindrum is located in the heart of Melbourne and is only minutes away from entertainment venues, countless restaurants, and more importantly, the MCG. There are 59 rooms available aimed at visitors looking to relax and spoil themselves in luxury for a few days. Standard rooms feature air-conditioning, phone and fax line and stereo. Superior rooms offer a bigger bed and more cupboard space, while deluxe rooms and junior suites offer amazing views of Melbourne Park and more room to feel at home. The hotel has a dining room and lounge for a quiet drink or game of billiards. If you prefer to stay in a place that prides itself on its classy design and stylish furniture, then this is the place for you.

QUAY WEST SUITES (pp148-149)
$269 (£112)
26 Southgate Ave, Southbank
(03) 9693 6000
mirvachotels.com.au

Quay West features 95 spacious suites that have a sitting room, kitchen, washing machine and up to three bedrooms. Guests are reluctant to leave the complex for their dining experience because the hotel's terrace-style restaurant and bar overlook the Yarra River and city - the scenery is spectacular! The menu features contemporary Australian cuisine, with Mediterranean and Asian influences. Quay West also features a library and business centre.

LANGHAM HOTEL
$288+ (£120)
1 Southgate Ave, Southbank
(03) 8696 8888
langhamhotels.com.au

Make your stay in Melbourne a luxurious one by staying at the **Langham Hotel**. Located in Southbank on the Yarra River, the hotel is within easy reach of all the major tourist attractions and popular café precincts. There are amazing views from many of the 387 rooms. Enjoy the fine international cuisine at the Melba Brasserie Restaurant - it's open for breakfast, lunch and dinner and features a la carte or buffet service. The Tisane Lounge and bar serves cocktails and hot drinks too. Other features include a babysitting service, business centre (featuring PC terminals), gymnasium, health club, spa and sauna.

COMO HOTEL
$308-$394 (£128-£164)
630 Chapel St, South Yarra
(03) 9825 2222
mirvachotels.com.au

The **Como Hotel** has 105 one and two-bed rooms, penthouses and studios. Other features of this luxurious building are the business centre, cocktail bar, currency exchange, gymnasium, sauna and swimming pool. Located in South Yarra, the Como is in close proximity to the CBD, the MCG and other major tourist facilities.

[MELBOURNE -RESTAURANTS

Scusami Ristorante in Southbank. Photo: Tourism Victoria.

CENTRAL

The Transport Hotel's Taxi Dining Room is fast becoming one of Melbourne's most popular restaurants. The Taxi Dining Room has a modern Australian menu that uses the best flavours and techniques from Asian cooking to get mouths watering. The entrée section also has a strong Asian focus with a selection of sushi and sashimi proving popular. And importantly, the menu focuses on fresh, seasonal produce, ensuring you have a truly Melburnian eating experience. The atmosphere at this restaurant cannot be rivalled thanks to its ultra-modern design and its location at Federation Square.

Cnr Flinders St & Swanston St, Melbourne
(pp148-149) **(03) 9654 8808**
Mains $26.50-$45 (£11-£19)

Yak is a modern city restaurant and bar with old-style values. The fresh interior, which combines a red colour scheme with dark wood, is an attractive look and could suggest a certain degree of exclusivity. But in reality, Yak's accommodating business hours, welcoming staff and kitchen ensure this Flinders Lane haven attracts a wide range of people. The popular eatery has a good selection of tapas while the Mediterranean main meals include roast duck, chicken breast and risottos.

There is a small range of traditional but delicious desserts too. Lunch and breakfast are also available. And once you've enjoyed your dinner, relax in the lounge and kick-start your night with some drinks at the bar.
150 Flinders Lane, Melbourne
(pp148-149) **(03) 9654 6699**
Mains $9.50-$28.50 (£4-£12)

SOUTH YARRA

The Botanical is a trendy favourite on Melbourne's thriving restaurant scene, open for breakfast (from 8am), lunch and dinner, seven days a week. Featuring an eclectic menu with a range of international

continued overpage...

RESTAURANTS
...continued from page 141.

influences, the wine-focused Botanical is particularly adept in preparing quality seafood (try the sashimi of yellow fin tuna or the roasted snapper), while its grazing menu (including everything from dips, chips and cheeses to oysters and calamari) is also popular. Characterised by knowledgeable staff and first-rate service, the venue is a great place to have a drink too, with its intimate Bubble Bar providing a relaxed yet classy atmosphere.
**169 Domain Rd, South Yarra
(03) 9820 7888
Mains $32-$46 (£13-£19)**

> **Souk Restaurant** predominantly features a modern, Middle Eastern menu although many dishes have a Greek Islands influence. Locals enjoy this venue as it is perfect for business lunches, afternoon snacks or private functions. The dining room is a conversation starter - the heritage building has new ornate plaster ceilings, a stainless steel chandelier that has to be seen and simple but classy table and chair settings that enable visitors to feel relaxed but special at the same time. Staff are friendly and main meals don't take forever to arrive. Tapas are also available if you're looking for a lighter meal.
**267 Chapel St, South Yarra
(03) 9533 7022
Mains $29-$34 (£12-£14)**

> The **France-Soir** is a popular restaurant that runs hot seven days a week. Opened in 1986, the restaurant was a Melbourne leader in French cuisine and since then has grown in stature and reputation. The staff at France-Soir know when they are onto a good thing - their friendly service and menu hasn't changed over the years which appeals to regulars who like what they see, smell and taste. The line-up features traditional French dishes including garlic snails, frites and crème brulee. Accompanying the great food is an amazing wine list that features more than 1500 different European and Australian wines. The restaurant's energy and long, narrow layout make it a memorable place to eat.
**11 Toorak Rd, South Yarra
(03) 9866 8569
Mains $29.50-$34.50 (£12-£15)**

SOUTHBANK

> All aboard! The **Blue Train Café** can get busy! Open seven days a week from 7am-1am, the cafe is a popular spot that can cater for more than 200 people both inside and out. Its specialties include hot rock pizzas and pastas but there is a large number of other affordable meals to choose from. The menu is just as impressive for those wanting breakfast and lunch. Be mindful that there can sometimes be a small wait for meals (up to 20 minutes) but the place has such a great atmosphere that most people don't mind the delay. There's a large central bar in the café, couches to relax on and plenty of "people watching" to do in this busy part of the city.
Mid Level Southgate Landing, Southbank
(pp148-149) **(03) 9696 0111
Mains $11-$23 (£5-£10)**

> Visitors are sure to be impressed by the **Red Emperor's** endless menu and modern and spacious eating area. There is a long list of delicious meals on offer, and like most Asian restaurants, the Emperor breaks its food list into sections. Seafood and poultry dishes are a popular choice while overseas tourists enjoy the meat and "Dundee" section. Dundee dishes incorporate kangaroo and crocodile into the line-up of otherwise traditional ingredients. The "beggars chicken" is another favourite. The restaurant is split level, tables are tastefully set and plenty of large windows ensure there is a light and bright atmosphere inside.
Level 3, Southgate, Southbank
(pp148-149) **(03) 9699 4170
Mains $22-$36 (£9-£15)**

FITZROY

Part of the busy Brunswick St restaurant strip, De Los Santos has been serving quality Spanish cuisine since the mid-1990s. The feature feed is tapas and paella - there's a huge range of appetisers that range in price between $6 and $12 (£2.50 and £5). And the Spanish donuts provide a fitting end to a frenetic banquet! If you're on your own or you prefer your meal all in one go, there's a range of seafood, chicken and vegetarian meals to meet all tastes. Complete the experience with a drink - De Los Santos has a wine list that features choices from Spain and Chile. It's a busy establishment but there's a relaxed mood and friendly service. The restaurant is open from 6pm until late every evening. A Sunday lunch is also on offer from midday.
175 Brunswick St, Fitzroy
(03) 9417 1567
Tapas $6-$12 (£2.50-£5)
Mains $17.50-$20.50 (£7-£9)

RICHMOND

The Fenix Restaurant's location and presentation sets it apart from other Melbourne venues. The restaurant overlooks the Yarra River, while surrounding bush land makes guests feel as if they are in a secluded area of Victoria. This is especially apparent when sitting in the outdoor eating area. The Fenix has white linen adorning its tables, floor to ceiling mirrors and comfy suede furniture that is sure to make any visitor feel like they are living the high life! Management hires chefs with overseas experience so the quality of food is of international standard. The Victoria Rd business is open for lunch seven days a week and for dinner Monday to Saturday. It has an a la carte menu.
680 Victoria Rd, Richmond
(03) 9427 8500
Mains $32-$34 (£13-£14)

Churchers on Richmond Hill uses beautiful architecture of the past to create a pleasant atmosphere for eating - the restaurant site was formerly an 1870s Victorian-style house. The bluestone building hosts weddings, parties and corporate functions, but it's the regular menu that sees visitors coming back for more. There is a long list of dishes to choose from and they are divided into lighter and larger meal sections. Chefs prefer to use local produce for their creations but there's a distinctive French or Asian influence to most dishes. Enjoy the wine list which features predominantly Australian boutique labels. Dim lighting and white linen are a must in this restaurant, making it ideal for a smart casual gathering of friends or a more intimate occasion. Churchers is open for dinner Tuesday to Saturday while lunch is served Wednesday to Saturday.
364 Church St, Richmond
(03) 9429 1777
Mains $17-$29 (£7-£12)

ST KILDA

There is nothing traditional about funky Japanese restaurant Mikoshi. The owners of this Tokyo-style business are not Asian, the kitchen has created several Australian/Japanese taste sensations and there's not an over emphasis on decorating the place in Japanese knick-knacks. If you make the effort to visit this thriving business, its owners suggest trying the Cali-dogs, rice burgers and ramens. For those who like their Japanese food (authentic Japanese, that is), familiar dishes such as California rolls, sushi and sashimi can be ordered too. And if you don't feel like eating out you can always tap into Mikoshi's takeaway menu.
155 Fitzroy St, St Kilda
(03) 9534 9559
Mains $16-$20 (£7-£8.50)

Mash describes many of the meals on its Australian cuisine menu as "gutsy". Dishes such as corn beef hash with fried eggs, salmon fishcake and spinach and, of course, bangers and mash are favourites among regulars. Mash has a relaxed staff and a friendly atmosphere and is ideal if you're looking for a wholesome feed or just a light snack and a drink. There is seating outside, but if you're checking out the Fitzroy St crowd you might just miss the funky music being played inside the modern café.
Shop 2/12 Fitzroy St, St Kilda
(03) 9537 1777
Mains $16-$28.50 (£7-£12)

MELBOURNE

Photo: Tourism Victoria.

MELBOURNE - PUBS & CLUBS

PUBS & CLUBS

CENTRAL

Young & Jackson is perhaps Australia's most famous pub. It's nearly 140-years-old but has a fresh appearance after a $6 million (£2.5 million) revamp in 2001. The well-worn interior now has a classier feel - upstairs is a plush lounge area, downstairs has polished wooden floorboards, while a café-style area complements the bar and ensures the much-loved building is used by a variety of patrons. For all the improvements, the original charm of Young & Jackson remains. Chloe, a 19th century French academic nude painting by Jules Lefebvre, is a feature piece of the pub. Young & Jackson has a good selection of beers and is accessible by car, tram, train or water taxi. It's opposite the Flinders St Railway Station, near Federation Square, and is sure to catch the eye of visitors enjoying the hustle and bustle of Melbourne by night.

Cnr Swanston St & Flinders St, Melbourne
(pp148-149) **(03) 9650 3884**

The **Transport Hotel** is located at Federation Square and features the Transport Public Bar on the ground floor, the Taxi Dining Room on Level 1 and the Transit Lounge on Level 2. The Transport Public Bar caters for 700 people, with up to 4000 revellers passing through its doors each night. This hub of activity has more than 130 beers on offer, regular DJs and live performances and is open from midday until 3am. The design has to be seen to be believed - it fits in with the funky theme of Federation Square with a zinc-clad interior, polished concrete bars and angular structures. The Transit Lounge was opened in 2005 and provides views towards the MCG, the Yarra River and the Botanic Gardens. The roof-top area was designed to provide people with a more relaxed and sophisticated place to congregate. There are

www.ashes06.com

countless bottles of wine to choose from and live music makes it popular during summer.
Cnr Flinders St & Swanston St, Melbourne
(pp148-149) **(03) 9654 8808**

The Hairy Canary opened on Little Collins St in 1997, with its bar/restaurant combination attracting a diverse range of clients. The tiny upstairs bar has a simple and modern design and is definitely a place to be seen, particularly if you can get a seat near the window overlooking the street. The Hairy Canary has a menu available until 3am, which is popular with people who like to party hard, while an early morning opening sees people converge as they wind down from an eventful night. It's a classy place that often attracts professionals, shoppers and local celebrities. It's not every sporting fan's cup of tea, but most appreciate the different atmosphere.
212 Little Collins St, Melbourne
(pp148-149) **(03) 9654 2471**

The Bearbrass has great food and novelty value for visitors. For under $30 you can have a two-course meal, a couple of drinks and a water taxi trip down the Yarra. Other food and drink specials are also on offer during the week. A diverse crowd enjoys this bar thanks to its easy-going atmosphere and open plan design. Friday sees a buzzing work crowd winding down after a hard week, and after a few hours, evening revellers of all walks of life make their way to this impressive establishment. The place doesn't slow down on Sunday with people coming in for a recovery breakfast or to enjoy the scenery during a lunchtime stay.
3 Southgate Ave, Southbank
(pp148-149) **(03) 9682 3799**

3 Below is for visitors who appreciate boutique wines, imported beers and simple and hearty meals. The place has a café feel by day but has a more social feel as the sun sets. It's not a huge place but it's set up so you can easily find small, intimate areas to talk and drink with mates. It's a perfect place to celebrate - or commiserate - after a big day's cricket. 3 Below's location ensures it attracts a work crowd but it's not long before revellers emerge and the fun begins. It has a modern look featuring wooden panels, stone walls and funky bar stools. Food on the menu includes rogan josh, steak and lasagne.
3 City Square, Melbourne
(pp148-149) **(03) 9662 9555**

Lounge bars don't get much smoother than the stylish Melbourne Supper Club Bar, a favourite with its young and savvy regulars. It's hidden above the popular European café-restaurant on Spring St, but you'll find it absolutely worth the hunt when you see the stunning views its divine bay windows provide of Parliament House and Treasury Gardens. While you're admiring the view, order a wine from the club's extensive list and recline in one of the ultra-comfy leather couches.
161 Spring St, Melbourne
(pp148-149) **(03) 9654 6300**

Honkytonks is one of the swankiest clubs in Melbourne, attracting both celebrities and the cream of Melbourne's hip and fashionable. You'll find it's worth dressing to impress: not only for the benefit of the gorgeous young things inside, but also the door security, who can be a little choosy about who they let in. Once inside you'll see why it's such a sought-after venue. It's a luscious blend of ritzy cabaret bar, steamy tropical-style hideaway and pumping dance music den. While you're deciding which floor space suits you, order one of the divine cocktails or premium wines.
96 Flinders St, Melbourne
(pp148-149) **(03) 9662 4555**

continued overpage...

Melbourne skyline at night. Photo: Tourism Victoria.

PUBS AND CLUBS
...continued from page 145.

RICHMOND

Conveniently within 10 minutes walking distance of the MCG is the London Tavern Hotel, the pub of choice for locals after any sporting event at the famous ground. Whether it's cricket or Aussie Rules football, the hordes converge on the London Tavern in droves. Most come for its lively atmosphere and a chance to revisit the day's play with friends. The hotel's certainly well-equipped for the masses: it contains a huge beer garden where you can order tasty bar meals, and also features a lovely restaurant area where you can dine more formally as the friendly staff serve quality a la carte fare. Of course, if you're simply after a cold pint, the hotel has a great selection of local beers on tap.
238 Lennox St, Richmond
(pp145) (03) 9428 6894

The Swan Hotel is another post-match favourite with locals looking to celebrate their team's victory or commiserate their team's loss with a few cold beers. You'll find the hotel is always busy, drawing crowds in with great live bands and DJs, while still being big enough if you want to find a quiet little spot. If you're heading to the hotel for a meal, the Swan offers well-priced pub fare. On a sunny day, most patrons enjoy their meals in the beer garden, which resembles a tropical oasis with its palms and hanging baskets.
425 Church St, Richmond
(03) 9428 2112

Next to the Swan Hotel is Public House, which is best described as a "grown-up local". Patrons thrive on its casual atmosphere, which is certain to be appreciated during the Fourth Test as the MCG is within easy reach (just off Swan St near the East Richmond Railway Station). A funky drinking hole with upstairs, downstairs and terrace areas, Public House is stacked with top notch wines, beers and cocktails, and offers a delicious selection of Mediterranean and Middle Eastern-inspired tapas to graze on. Recently ranked among Melbourne's top five beer gardens by *The Age*, Public House is open seven days from midday until late (last kitchen orders at 11pm). Keep in mind the hotel doesn't accept dinner bookings, so just wander in and enjoy!
433-435 Church St, Richmond
(03) 9421 0187

The Corner Hotel is another popular Swan St pub (on the corner of Stewart St next to the railway bridge) within close proximity of the MCG. Big on live music, the Corner welcomes punk, rock, salsa, reggae and folk bands among others, so it's not surprising that it draws a diverse crowd. The front bar is characterised by its grungy feel, while the recently renovated upstairs beer garden is proving a hit with its fantastic views of the city. You can have dinner at the Corner every night except Monday, while lunch is available on weekends – the mountainous "Burger de Corner" is a favourite!
57 Swan St, Richmond
(pp150) (03) 9427 9198

Holliava has three bars and premium beers - a perfect combination for a thirsty sports-lover looking to mix with a cool Melbourne crowd. The place is always busy and its beer garden is a real drawcard. During summer, the garden's retractable roof is opened so you can enjoy a drink or two in the open air. Some have likened the Holliava's wood-dominated interior to a ship's galley or a sauna - venture there yourself to make up your own mind. It's a great bar for drinking and socialising - there's no dance floor so the younger crowd often moves on to other pubs and clubs as the night progresses.
36 Swan St, Richmond
(pp150) (03) 9421 5155

Photo: Tourism Victoria.

Photo: Tourism Victoria.

The Mountain View Hotel on flourishing Bridge Rd is perfect for a beer after the cricket as it's just a stone's throw from the MCG. In fact, you can marvel at the great stadium from the pub's new beer garden deck on the fourth floor! Formally owned by Aussie Rules legend Ron Barassi, the Mountain View offers 10 beers on tap, including Bonningtons and Becks, plus Fosters in stubby form. Renowned for its pub meals, the Mountain View has six big-screen TVs with surround sound to keep sports fans happy.
70 Bridge Rd, Richmond
(pp150) **(03) 9428 3973**

The Retreat Hotel offers something different depending on when you decide to pull up a stool and enjoy a beer. For most of the week the front bar has a grunge feel to it and people can be seen chatting or reading a book with their favourite drink. The same people are in awe of the kitchen staff who produce some of the best value meals in town - nothing too fancy but definitely a drawcard for people with an empty stomach! On the weekend, the hotel pulls a different bunch of revellers. Out the back is a beer garden, which generates a great atmosphere, with regular DJ appearances and band performances making this pub a worthy option.
280 Sydney Rd, Brunswick
(03) 9380 4090

FITZROY

If you fancy a pint after spending the day shopping on fashionable Brunswick St, head to the Napier Hotel, a cosy little pub in Fitzroy. Constructed in 1891, the hotel has preserved much of its original historic charm: be sure to take a look at the wonderful Fitzroy Football Club memorabilia that adorns the pub's walls. The Napier is popular with locals who come to enjoy the reasonably priced pub fare and a quiet drink in the small but pleasant beer garden.
210 Napier St, Fitzroy
(03) 9419 4240

For female fans looking to enjoy a more glamorous night out, Ginger might be for you. Located on Brunswick St in Fitzroy, Ginger is about a five-minute tram ride from Melbourne's CBD. It has around 70 cocktails to choose from and attracts "the beautiful people" of Victoria. There's a modern atmosphere at Ginger but it's actually set in an 1890s heritage-listed building. A marble fireplace, polished floorboards and 15-foot ceilings make it a special place to visit.
272 Brunswick St, Fitzroy
(03) 9419 8058

ST KILDA

Live bands, no dress code and a great atmosphere seven days a week makes The Esplanade - or "The Espy" - a popular drinking destination for tourists. The hotel was built in 1880 and is now a combination of architecture from the past with modern improvements from today. The building has three main drinking areas and its popular new Espy Kitchen. The eatery has two levels which can seat 85 people, serving a variety of pub meal favourites along with some dishes for the more adventurous. There's a grunge feel to this place, so if you're after somewhere casual that promotes local music talent, then this is the place for you. The Esplanade is only a 15-20-minute train ride out of Melbourne.
11 The Esplanade, St Kilda
(03) 9534 0211

MELBOURNE CITY MAP

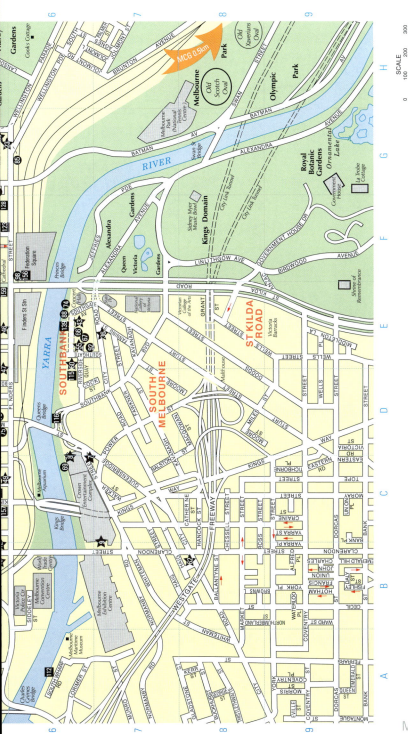

MCG MAP

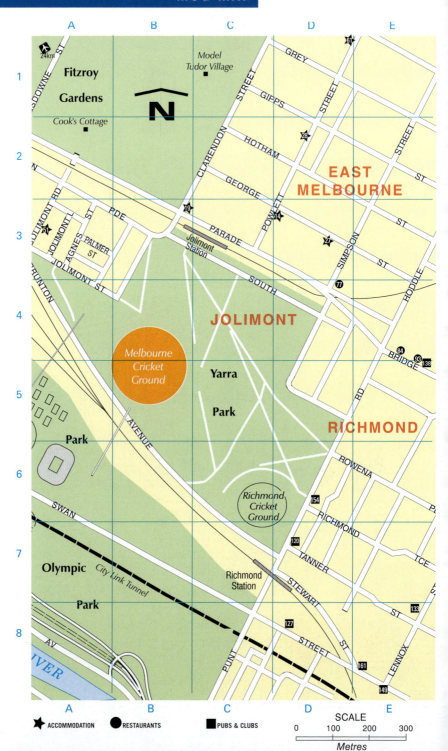

MELBOURNE CITY MAP (pp148-150)

■ Denotes multiple venue

ACCOMMODATION KEY

$ Cost per night **RATE** Star rating **OVAL** Kilometres from MCG

#	Map	Ref	Name	Address	Phone	Website	$	RATE	OVAL
1	148-149	F5	Adelphi Hotel	187 Flinders Lane, Melbourne, 3000	03 9650 7555	www.adelphi.com.au	206-625	****	2.33
2	148-149	G4	All Seasons Crossley Hotel	51 Little Bourke St, Melbourne, 3000	03 9639 1639	www.allseasonscrossley.com	118-320	****	1.69
3	148-149	E4	Causeway Inn on the Mall	327 Bourke St Mall, Melbourne, 3000	03 9650 0688	www.causewayinn.com.au	148-215	****	2.40
4	148-149	G4	City Centre Budget Hotel	22-30 Little Collins St, Melbourne, 3000	03 9654 5401	www.citycentrebudgethotel.com.au	40-65		1.65
6	148-149	G4	City Limits Hotel	20 Little Bourke St, Melbourne, 3000	03 9662 2544	www.citylimits.com.au	125-165	****	1.77
7	148-149	C6	Crown Promenade Hotel	9 Whiteman St, Southbank, 3006	03 9292 6688	www.crownpromenade.com.au	269-1350	*****	3.03
8	148-149	C6	Crown Towers	8 Whiteman St, Southbank, 3006	03 9292 6666	www.crowntowers.com.au	336-2750	*****	3.03
9	148-149	B7	Crowne Plaza Melbourne	1-5 Spencer St, Melbourne, 3000	03 9648 2777	www.ichotelsgroup.com	170-500	*****	2.80
10	148-149	E2	Elizabeth Hostel	1/490-494 Elizabeth St, Melbourne, 3000	03 9663 1685	www.elizabethhostel.com.au	17-50		3.06
11	148-149	B5	Enterprise Hotel	44 Spencer St, Melbourne, 3000	03 9629 6991	www.hotelenterprize.com.au	96-146		2.91
12	148-149	B5	Explorers Inn	16 Spencer St, Melbourne, 3000	03 9621 3333	www.explorersinn.com.au	99-150	****	2.84
13	148-149	C2	Flagstaff Motel Melbourne	45 Dudley St, Melbourne, 3000	03 9329 5788	www.flagstaffinn.com.au	105-325	****	4.05
14	150	D3	George Powlett Apartments	30 Powlett St, East Melbourne, 3002	03 9419 9488	www.georgepowlett.com.au	145	***	0.65
15	148-149	D5	Golden Tulip Melbourne	60 Market St, Melbourne, 3000	03 9602 3476	www.goldentulipmelbourne.com	320-460	****	2.40
16	148-149	B5	Grand Hotel	33 Spencer St, Melbourne, 3000	03 9611 4567	www.grandhotelsofitel.com.au	205-510	*****	2.90
17	148-149	F5	Grand Hyatt-Melbourne	123 Collins St, Melbourne, 3000	03 9657 1234	www.melbourne.hyatt.com	195-1500	*****	1.66
18	148-149	B3	Harbourview Apartment Hotel	585 LaTrobe St, Melbourne, 3000	03 9321 0900	www.hview.com.au	139-329	****	3.72
19	150	B3	Hilton on the Park Melbourne	192 Wellington Pde, East Melbourne, 3002	03 9419 2000	www.melbourne.hilton.com	155-450	*****	0.50
20	148-149	B5	Holiday Inn on Flinders	575 Flinders Lane, Melbourne, 3000	03 9629 4111	www.holiday-inn.com	160-400	****	2.93
21	148-149	E5	Hotel Causeway	275 Little Collins St, Melbourne, 3000	03 9660 8888	www.hotelcauseway.com.au	176-330	****	2.36
22	148-149	F4	Hotel Grand Chancellor	131 Lonsdale St, Melbourne, 3000	03 9656 4000	www.ghihotels.com	135-350	****	2.19
23	148-149	G5	Hotel Lindrum	26 Flinders St, Melbourne, 3000	03 9668 1111	www.hotellindrum.com.au	215-475	*****	1.06
24	148-149	E2	Hotel Y	489 Elizabeth St, Melbourne, 3000	03 8327 2777	www.hotely.com.au	94-179	***	3.19
25	148-149	C4	Ibis Little Bourke St	600 Little Bourke St, Melbourne, 3000	03 9672 0000	www.accorhotels.com.au	99-119	***	3.52
26	148-149	C4	Kingsgate Hotel	131 King St, Melbourne, 3000	03 9629 4171	www.kingsgatehotel.com.au	77-96	***	3.17
27	150	D3	Knightsbridge Apartments	101 George St, East Melbourne, 3002	03 9419 1333	www.knightsbridgeapartments.com.au	129-198	****	0.80
28	150	D2	Magnolia Court	101 Powlett St, East Melbourne, 3002	03 9419 4222	www.magnolia-court.com.au	160-300		0.95
29	148-149	G4	Melbourne Marriott Hotel	Lonsdale St, Melbourne, 3000	03 9622 3900	www.marriott.com	225-775	*****	1.90
30	148-149	G5	Mercure Hotel Melbourne	13 Spring St, Melbourne, 3000	03 9205 9999	www.accorhotels.com	130-220	****	1.36
31	148-149	E4	Mercure Hotel Welcome	265-281 Little Bourke St, Melbourne, 3000	03 9639 0555	www.mercurewelcome.com.au	109-134	***	2.63
32	148-149	E2	Nova StarGate Apartment	118 Franklin St, Melbourne, 3000	03 9321 0300	www.novastargate.com.au	215-295	*****	3.10
33	148-149	E5	Novotel Melbourne on Collins	270 Collins St, Melbourne, 3000	03 9667 5800	www.novotelmelbourne.com.au	167-741	*****	2.00

continued overpage...

MELBOURNE CITY MAP (pp148-150)

ACCOMMODATION KEY

■ Denotes multiple venue

#	Map	Ref	Name	Address	Phone	Website	$ Cost per night	RATE Star rating	OVAL Kilometres from MCG
34	148-149	G5	Pacific International Apart	100 Exhibition St, Melbourne, 3000	03 9361 4444	www.pacificinthotels.com	158-380	★★★★	1.48
35	148-149	E4	Pacific International Apart	318 Little Bourke St, Melbourne, 3000	03 9664 2000	www.pacificinthotels.com	154-450	★★★★♦	2.52
36	148-149	E7	Pacific International Suites	31 City Rd, Southbank, 3006	03 8696 7222	www.pacificinthotels.com	165-390	★★★★♦	3.11
37	148-149	D4	Park Hyatt Melbourne	1 Parliament Sq, Melbourne, 3002	03 9607 3000	www.melbourne.park.hyatt.com	180-560	★★★★★	3.01
38	148-149	H5	Punt Hill Flinders Lane	267 Flinders Lane, Melbourne, 3000	03 9224 1234	www.melbourne.park.hyatt.com	260-695	★★★★★	1.46
39	148-149	E5	Punt Hill Little Bourke	11-17 Cohen Place, Melbourne, 3000	1300 731 299	www.punthill.com.au	181-319	★★★★♦	2.08
40	148-149	F4	Punt Hill Manhattan	57 Flinders Lane, Melbourne, 3000	1302 731 299	www.punthill.com.au	181-372	★★★★♦	2.16
41	148-149	G5	Quality Hotel Batman's Hill	623 Collins St, Melbourne, 3000	1301 731 299	www.punthill.com.au	181-372	★★★★	1.31
42	148-149	B5	Quay West Suites	26 Southgate Ave, Southbank, 3006	03 3614 6344	www.batmanshill.com.au	155-273	★★★★	3.02
43	148-149	E6	Quest on Bourke Aparts	155 Bourke St, Melbourne, 3000	03 9693 6000	www.mirvachotels.com.au	269	★★★★★	2.97
44	148-149	F4	Radisson - Flagstaff Gardens	380 William St, Melbourne, 3000	03 9631 0400	www.questonbourke.com	213-233	★★★★♦	1.92
45	148-149	D3	Ramada Melbourne	270 Flinders St, Melbourne, 3000	03 3322 8000	www.radisson.com	169-299	★★★★♦	3.47
46	148-149	E5	Rendezvous Hotel	328 Flinders St, Melbourne, 3000	03 9654 6888	www.ramadamelbourne.com.au	165-225	★★★★♦	1.82
47	148-149	D5	Rialto Hotel on Collins	495 Collins St, Melbourne, 3000	03 9250 1888	www.rendezvoushotels.com	195-315	★★★★♦	2.00
48	148-149	C5	Riverside Apartments	474 Flinders St, Melbourne, 3000	03 9620 9111	www.riatohotel.com.au	195-1075	★★★★★	2.87
49	148-149	C5	Rydges Melbourne	186 Exhibition St, Melbourne, 3000	03 9619 9199	www.riversideaparts.com.au	1785-295	★★★★	2.50
50	148-149	G4	Saville City Suites	133 Jolimont Rd, East Melbourne, 3002	03 9662 0511	www.rydges.com	150-215	★★★★	1.85
51	150	A3	Sofitel Melbourne	25 Collins St, Melbourne, 3000	03 9663 4321	www.savillesuites.com	135-210	★★★★	0.67
52	148-149	G5	Somerset Gordon Place	24 Little Bourke St, Melbourne, 3000	03 9653 0000	www.sofitelmelbourne.com.au	476-626	★★★★★	1.55
53	148-149	G4	Stamford Plaza Melbourne	111 Little Collins St, Melbourne, 3000	03 9663 2888	www.the-ascott.com	170-410	★★★★♦	1.75
54	148-149	F5	The Langham Hotel	1 Southgate Av, Southbank, 3006	03 9659 1000	www.stamford.com	280-600	★★★★♦	1.73
55	148-149	E6	The Victoria Hotel	215 Little Collins St, Melbourne, 3000	03 8696 8888	www.langhamhotels.com.au	288-745	★★★★♦	3.19
56	148-149	F5	The Westin Melbourne	205 Collins St, Melbourne, 3000	03 9669 0000	www.victoriahotel.com.au	99-220	★★★♦	2.23
57	148-149	F5	The Windsor	103-115 Spring St, Melbourne, 3000	03 9635 2222	www.westin.com	248-789	★★★★♦	2.32
58	148-149	G4	Toad Hall Hotel Backpackers	441 Elizabeth St, Melbourne, 3000	03 9633 6000	www.thewindsor.com.au	299-2400	★★★★★	1.52
59	148-149	E3	Travelodge Southbank	Riverside Quay, Southbank, 3006	03 9600 9010	www.toadhallhotel.com.au	23-85		3.04
60	148-149	E6	Treasury Apartment Hotel	Powlett St, East Melbourne, 3002	03 8696 9600	www.travelodgehotels.com.au	149-175	★★★★	3.13
61	150	D1	Urban Central	334 City Rd, Southbank, 3006	03 9417 5281	www.treasurymotorlodge.com.au	115-170	★★★♦	1.18
62	148-149	B8			03 9693 3700	www.urbancentral.com	28-90		3.53

www.ashes06.com

RESTAURANTS KEY

■ Denotes multiple venue
■ Cost of main meal

#	Map	Ref	Name	Address	Phone	Website	Cuisine	$	BYO
63	148-149	G5	111 Spring St Restaurant	111 Spring St, Melbourne, 3000	03 9633 6004	www.thewindsor.com.au	International	27	N
64	148-149	G4	Bamboo House	47 Little Bourke St, Melbourne, 3000	03 9662 1565	www.bamboohouse.com.au	Chinese	15-21	N
65	148-149	F4	Banana Palm Curry House	195 Little Bourke St, Melbourne, 3000	03 9639 2680	www.bananapalm.com.au	Malaysian	10-29	Y
66	148-149	E6	Bearbrass	Southgate Arts & Leisure, Southbank, 3006	03 9682 3799	www.bearbrass.com.au	Modern Australian	15-25	N
67	148-149	E6	Blue Train Café	Southgate Landing, Southbank, 3006	03 9696 0111	www.bluetrain.com.au	Modern Australian	11-23	N
68	148-149	E6	Bottega	74 Bourke St, Melbourne, 3000	03 9654 2252	www.bottega.com.au	Italian	23-34	N
69	148-149	C6	Cecconi's Restaurant	Shop 1/8 Whiteman St, Southbank, 3006	03 9686 8648	www.cecconis.com	Modern Italian	17-43	N
70	148-149	E4	De Lacy	29 Niagara La, Melbourne, 3000	03 9670 9099		Modern Australian	21	N
71	148-149	F4	Empress of China	120 Little Bourke St, Melbourne, 3000	03 9663 1883	www.empressofchina.com.au	Chinese	20-38	Y wine-$3pp corkage
72	148-149	F5	Ezard	187 Flinders La, Melbourne, 3000	03 9639 6811	www.ezard.com.au	Modern Australian	38-48	N
73	148-149	G5	Felt - Hotel Lindrum	26 Flinders St, Melbourne, 3000	03 9668 1111	www.hotellindrum.com.au	Modern Australian	26-30	N
74	148-149	E6	Florence on the Yarra	Southbank Prm, Melbourne, 3000	03 9876 9688	www.florence.com.au	Modern Australian	20-32	N
75	148-149	D5	Flower Drum	17 Market La, Melbourne, 3000	03 9662 3655		Chinese	35-49	N
76	148-149	F4	Gaylord Indian	4 Tattersalls La, Melbourne, 3000	03 9663 3980	www.gaylordindianrestaurant.com.au	Indian	12-17	Y wine-$1pp corkage
77	150	D4	Glaze	62 Wellington Pde, East Melbourne, 3002	03 9415 8639	www.glaze.com.au	Modern Australian	19-33	N
78	148-149	G4	Grossi Florentino	80 Bourke St, Melbourne, 3000	03 9662 1811	www.grossiflorentino.com.au	Traditional Italian	28-58	N
79	148-149	D5	Hofbrauhaus	18-24 Market La, Melbourne, 3000	03 9663 3361	www.hofbrauhaus.com.au	German	20-29	N
80	148-149	F5	Italy1	27 George Pde, Melbourne, 3000	03 9654 4430	www.italy1.com.au	Italian	19-32	N
81	148-149	F4	James Squire Brewhouse	Little Collins St, Melbourne, 3000	03 9654 5000	www.portlandhotel.com.au	Modern Australian	16-25	N
82	148-149	G4	Kappo Okita	17 Liverpool St, Melbourne, 3000	03 9662 2206		Japanese	10-20	Y wine-no corkage
83	148-149	G5	Kenzan	45 Collins St, Melbourne, 3000	03 9654 8933	www.kenzan.com	Japanese	22-35	N
84	150	E4	Krua Thai 2	37 Bridge Rd, Richmond, 3121	03 9428 6128		Thai	7-11	N
85	148-149	G6	Langton's Rest. & Wine Bar	61 Flinders La, Melbourne, 3000	03 9663 0222	www.langtonsrestaurant.com.au	Modern European	35-38	N
86	148-149	F4	Lebanese House	268 Russell St, Melbourne, 3000	03 9662 2230		Lebanese	10-22	Y wine-no corkage
87	148-149	F4	Max Brenner Chocolate Bar	210 Lonsdale St, Melbourne, 3000	03 9663 6000	www.maxbrenner.com.au	Desserts	4-13	N
88	148-149	E6	Melbourne River Cruises	Vault 11 Banana Alley, Melbourne, 3000	03 8610 2600	www.melbcruises.com.au	Various	128	N
89	148-149	G4	Oyster	35 Little Bourke St, Melbourne, 3000	03 9650 0988	www.oysterlittlebourke.com.au	European	20-32	N

continued overpage...

MELBOURNE CITY MAP (pp148-150)

RESTAURANTS KEY

■ Denotes multiple venue
$ Cost of main meal

#	Map	Ref	Name	Address	Phone	Website	Cuisine	$	
90	148-149	G4	Punch Lane	43 Little Bourke St, Melbourne, 3000	03 9639 4944	www.punchlane.com.au	Modern Australian	25-34	N
38	148-149	H5	Radii	1 Parliament Sq, East Melbourne, 3002	03 9224 1211	www.melbourne.park.hyatt.com	Mediterranean	32-39	N
92	148-149	E6	Red Emporer's	3 Southgate Ave, Southbank, 3006	03 9699 4170	www.redemperor.com	Chinese	22-36	N
93	150	E4	Richmond Hill Café	48-50 Bridge Rd, Richmond, 3121	03 9421 2808	www.rhcl.com.au	Medit/Modern Aust	16-26	Y wine-$10 corkage
94	148-149	F4	Shark Fin House	131 Little Bourke St, Melbourne, 3000	03 9663 1555		Chinese	18	N
52	148-149	G5	Sofitel Melbourne-Café La Level 35, 25 Collins St, Melbourne, 3000		03 9653 7744	www.sofitelmelbourne.com.au	Modern Australian	16-41	N
96	148-149	C5	St Arnou Beef Café	582-584 Lt Collins St, Melbourne, 3000	03 9620 9720	www.stamou.melbourneaustralia.com.au	Modern Australian	15-25	N
97	148-149	F4	Stalactites	177-183 Lonsdale St, Melbourne, 3000	03 9663 3316	www.stalactites.com.au	Greek	7-22	Y wine-no corkage
98	148-149	F6	Taxi Dining Room	Federation Sq, Melbourne, 3000	03 9654 8808	www.transporthotel.com.au	Modern Australian	27-45	N
100	148-149	D3	The Bureau Melbourne	299 Queen St, Melbourne, 3000	03 9606 0055	www.bureaumelbourne.com	Modern Australian	19-31	N
101	148-149	H5	The Commune	2 Parliament Pl, East Melbourne, 3002	03 9654 5477	www.thecommune.com.au	Italian	6-25	N
102	148-149	G4	Elephant & Wheelbarrow 94-96 Bourke St, Melbourne, 3000		03 9639 8444		Modern Australian	11-22	N
103	148-149	G4	The European	161 Spring St, Melbourne, 3000	03 9654 0811		European	20-34	N
104	148-149	G5	The Italian	2 Malthouse La, Melbourne, 3000	03 9654 9499	www.theitalian.com.au	Italian	23-28	N
105	148-149	D5	The Trust	405-411 Flinders La, Melbourne, 3000	03 9629 9300	www.thetrust.com.au	Modern Italian	28-38	N
106	148-149	E5	Tony Starr's Kitten Club	267 Little Collins St, Melbourne, 3000	03 9650 2448	www.kittenclub.com.au	Modern Australian	24-27	N
107	148-149	D5	Treasury	394 Collins St, Melbourne, 3000	03 9211 6699	www.treasuryrestaurant.com.au	International	27-34	Y wine-no corkage
108	148-149	G5	Verge	1 Flinders La, Melbourne, 3000	03 9639 9500		Mod. Oz & Japanese	24	N
109	148-149	G4	Water and Grass	32 Bourke St, Melbourne, 3000	03 9650 7020	www.waterandgrass.com	Modern Australian	22-34	N
110	148-149	F5	Yak Bar & Food	150 Flinders Lane, Melbourne, 3000	03 9654 6699	www.yakbarfood.com.au	Mediterranean	10-29	N

www.ashes06.com

PUBS & CLUBS KEY

■ Denotes multiple venue

FOX Sports Bar   B/R Bistro/Restaurant   TAB Betting facilities   OVAL Kilometres from the MCG

#	Map	Ref	Name	Address	Phone	Website	Closing Time	FOX	B/R	TAB	OVAL
111	148-149	F5	3 Below	44-86 Swanston St, Melbourne, 3000	03 9662 9555	www.threebelow.com.au	Daily: til late	No	Yes	No	1.68
112	148-149	A6	Alumbra	6B South Wharf Rd, Southbank, 3006	03 8606 4466	www.alumbra.com.au	Wed-Thurs & Sun: 1am, Fri-Sat: 5am	Yes	No	No	3.94
113	148-149	G4	Aura the Lounge	12 Bourke St, Melbourne, 3000	03 9654 3533	www.aurathelounge.com.au	Wed-Sat: Midnight	No	Yes	No	1.54
■ 66	148-149	E6	Bearbrass	3 Southgate Ave, Southbank, 3006	03 9682 3799	www.bearbrass.com.au	Mon-Sun: 2am	No	Yes	Yes	3.19
115	148-149	D6	Belgian Beer Café Eureka	5 Riverside Quay, Southbank, 3006	03 9690 5777	www.belgianbeercafemelbourne.com	Daily: 1am	No	Yes	No	3.06
116	148-149	D6	BLVD Bar	6 Queensbridge Sq, Southbank, 3006	03 9686 6610		Daily: til late	No	Yes	No	2.40
117	148-149	D5	Bull and Bear Tavern	347 Flinders Ln, Melbourne, 3000	03 9629 4116	www.offthecuffcatering.com.au	Mon-Fri: Midnight	Yes	Yes	No	2.08
118	148-149	F4	Cookie	252 Swanston St, Melbourne, 3000	03 9663 7660		Daily: til 3am	No	Yes	No	2.52
119	148-149	G3	Coopers Inn	282 Exhibition St, Melbourne, 3000	03 9639 2111	www.coopersinn.com.au	Mon-Wed: Midnight, Thurs-Sat: 1am	Yes	Yes	No	2.00
120	150	D7	Cricketer's Arms	327 Punt Rd, Richmond, 3121	03 9428 7471	www.cricketersarms.com.au	Daily: til 1am	No	No	No	1.59
121	148-149	G5	Cricketers Club Bar	103 Spring St, Melbourne, 3000	03 9633 6170		Mon-Sat: 10pm	Yes	Yes	No	1.34
122	148-149	E5	De Biers Bar and Club	279 Flinders Lane, Melbourne, 3000	03 9654 0444	www.debiers.com.au	Wed-Thurs: 11pm, Fri-Sat: 5am	Yes	Yes	No	1.85
123	148-149	F5	Duke of Wellington	146 Flinders St, Melbourne, 3000	03 9650 4984		Mon-Sat: Midnight, Sun: 8pm	Yes	Yes	Yes	1.36
■ 102	148-149	G4	Elephant & Wheelbarrow	94-96 Bourke St, Melbourne, 3000	03 9639 8444		Mon-Wed: 10pm, Thurs: 1am, Fri-Sat: 3am	Yes	Yes	No	1.64
125	148-149	C5	Fourth Watch Sportsbar	26-32 King St, Melbourne, 3000	03 9614 0722	www.thefourthwatch.com.au	Mon-Sat: 8pm, Fri-Sat: 1am	Yes	No	Yes	2.63
126	148-149	F4	Hairy Canary	212 Little Collins St, Melbourne, 3000	03 9654 2471		Mon-Sat: 3am, Sun: 1am	No	Yes	No	1.80
127	150	D8	Holliava	36 Swan St, Richmond, 3121	03 9421 5155	www.holliava.com.au	Tues-Sun: 1am	Yes	Yes	No	1.65
128	148-149	F5	Honkytonks	Level 2/96 Flinders St, Melbourne, 3000	03 9662 4555	www.honkytonks.com.au	Wed-Thurs: 3am, Fri-Sun: 5am	No	No	No	1.51
129	148-149	G4	Imperial	2-8 Bourke St, Melbourne, 3000	03 9662 1007	www.bourkestimperial.com	Mon-Sat: Midnight, Sun: 9pm	Yes	Yes	No	1.56
■ 81	148-149	F4	James Squire Brewhouse	Russell St, Melbourne, 3000	03 9654 5000	www.portlandhotel.com.au	Daily: Midnight	Yes	Yes	No	2.15
131	148-149	F3	Jwow Bar	243 Little Lonsdale St, Melbourne, 3000	03 9663 5986	www.jwowbar.com	Mon-Thurs: 8pm, Fri-Sat: 1am	No	No	No	2.40
132	148-149	D3	La La Land	391 Little Lonsdale St, Melbourne, 3000	03 9670 5011	www.lalaland.com.au	Daily: til late	No	No	No	2.81
133	150	E8	London Tavern Hotel	238 Lennox St, Richmond, 3121	03 9428 6894		Mon-Thurs: 11pm, Fri-Sat: Midnight	Yes	Yes	No	1.87
134	148-149	E3	Melbourne Central Lion	211 La Trobe St, Melbourne, 3000	03 9663 5977		Mon-Sun: 3am	Yes	Yes	No	2.55
135	148-149	G4	Melbourne Supper Club	161 Spring St, Melbourne, 3000	03 9654 6300		Daily: til late	No	No	No	1.49
136	148-149	D2	Mercat Cross Hotel	456 Queen St, Melbourne, 3000	03 9326 5187	www.mercatcross.com.au	Wed-Thurs: 11pm, Fri-Sat: 7am	No	Yes	No	3.24
137	148-149	C3	Metropolitan	Lonsdale St, Melbourne, 3000	03 9670 1385	www.themetropolitanhotel.com.au	Daily: til late	No	Yes	No	3.40
138	150	E5	Mountain View Hotel	70 Bridge Rd, Richmond, 3121	03 9428 6654		Sun-Thurs: 10pm, Fri-Sat: 1am	Yes	Yes	No	1.20
139	148-149	E6	P.J.O'Brien's Irish Pub	Southbank, 3006	03 9686 5011	www.pjobriens.com.au	Mon-Thurs: 1.30am, Fri-Sun: 3am	Yes	Yes	Yes	3.13
140	148-149	D4	Pugg Mahones	106 Hardware St, Melbourne, 3000	03 9670 6155	www.puggs.com.au	Mon-Fri: 1am, Sat, Sun: 11.30pm	Yes	Yes	No	2.75
142	148-149	C4	Royal Melbourne Hotel	629 Bourke St, Melbourne, 3000	03 9629 2400	www.royalmelbournehotel.com.au	Mon-Fri: Midnight, Sat: 4am	Yes	Yes	No	3.02

continued overpage...

MELBOURNE MAPS

MELBOURNE CITY MAP (pp148-150)

■ Denotes multiple venue

PUBS & CLUBS KEY

FOX Sports Bar   B/R Bistro/Restaurant   TAB Betting facilities   OVAL Kilometres from the MCG

#	Map	Ref	Name	Address	Phone	Website	Closing Time	FOX	B/R	TAB	OVAL
143	148-149	E5	Six Links	Flinders La, Melbourne, 3000	03 9650 2977	www.6links.com.au	Tues-Sat: til late	Yes	No	No	1.71
52	148-149	G5	Sofitel	25 Collins St, Melbourne, 3000	03 9653 7767	www.sofitelmelbourne.com.au	Mon-Sun: til late	Yes	Yes	No	1.22
145	148-149	F4	Stellar Bar	98 Bourke St, Melbourne, 3000	03 9663 8600		Mon-Thurs & Sun: Midnight, Fri-Sat: 3am	No	Yes	No	1.64
146	148-149	E2	Stork Hotel	504 Elizabeth St, Melbourne, 3000	03 9663 6237	www.storkhotel.com	Daily: til late	Yes	Yes	No	2.97
147	148-149	G5	The Courtyard Tavern	86A Collins St, Melbourne, 3000	03 9650 8500	www.courtyardtavern.com.au	Mon-Sat: 3am	Yes	Yes	No	1.48
148	148-149	E1	The Arthouse	616 Elizabeth St, Melbourne, 3000	03 9347 3917	www.thearthouse.com	Mon-Sun: 3am	No	No	No	3.44
149	150	E8	The Depot	60 Swan St, Richmond, 3121	03 9427 0500		Sun-Wed: Midnight, Thurs-Sat: 3am				1.76
150	148-149	G5	The European Bier Café	120 Exhibition St, Melbourne, 3000	03 9663 1222	www.europeanbiercafe.com.au	Sun-Thurs: 1am; Fri-Sat: 3am	Yes	Yes	No	1.72
151	148-149	D5	The Irish Times	427 Lt Collins St, Melbourne, 3000	03 9642 1699		Mon-Sat: til late	Yes	Yes	No	2.43
152	148-149	D3	The Mint	William St, Melbourne, 3000	03 9602 5622	www.themint.com.au	Mon-Fri: til late	Yes	Yes	No	3.33
153	148-149	E2	The Public Bar	238 Victoria St, Melbourne, 3000	03 9329 6522		Mon-Thurs: 2am, Fri-Sat 6am, Sun: 11pm	No	Yes	No	3.46
154	150	D6	The Royal Hotel	287 Punt Rd, Richmond, 3121	03 9428 2015		Daily: til late	Yes	Yes	No	1.40
155	148-149	F4	Three Degrees Bar	Lonsdale St, Melbourne, 3000	03 9639 6766	www.3degrees.com.au	Mon-Sat: til late	Yes	Yes	No	2.30
156	148-149	F6	Transport Hotel	Federation Sq, Melbourne, 3000	03 9654 8808	www.transporthotel.com.au	Mon-Sun: 2am	Yes	Yes	No	1.69
157	148-149	C5	Waterside Hotel	508 Flinders St, Melbourne, 3000	03 9629 1350	www.watersidehotel.com.au	Sun-Thurs: 3am; Fri-Sat: 5am	Yes	Yes	No	2.90
158	148-149	F4	Welcome Stranger	128 Bourke St, Melbourne, 3000	03 9639 4555		Daily: 24 hours	Yes	Yes	No	1.95
159	148-149	E5	Young & Jackson Hotel	1 Swanston St, Melbourne, 3000	03 9650 3884	www.youngandjackson.com.au	Mon-Sun: til late	Yes	Yes	No	1.82
161	150	E8	Corner Hotel	57 Swan St, Richmond, 3121	03 9427 9198	www.cornerhotel.com	Mon-Sat: 3am; Sun: 1am	No	Yes	No	1.74

www.ashes06.com

Flemington Racecourse is home of the prestigious Melbourne Cup. Photo: Tourism Victoria.

MELBOURNE
-ATTRACTIONS

Federation Square
Conveniently located in the centre of Melbourne, Federation Square (03 9655 1900, federationsquare.com.au) is a lively hub of attractions and a focal point for locals and visitors alike.

Boasting some of the world's most amazing architecture, Federation Square incorporates The Ian Potter Centre: NGV Australia (dedicated to Australian art), the Australian Centre for the Moving Image and the Australian Horse Racing Museum and Hall of Fame.

Federation Square also boasts a range of restaurants, cafes and bars, as well as open public spaces which host up to 2000 events every year.

Melbourne Docklands
Located just minutes from Melbourne's CBD on the Victoria Harbour and stretching 3km along the Yarra River, the Docklands (1300 663 008, docklands.com) is an impressive combination of residential, commercial, retail and leisure activities.

A range of restaurants, bars and cafés make it a popular place during the evening, while 40 hectares of deep sheltered waters are perfect for fishing and water sports. And if you want to combine both, book a dinner cruise for a night to remember.

Official Neighbours Tour
For fans of internationally-renowned TV programme Neighbours, the Official Neighbours Tour (03 9534 4755, neighbourstour.com) is a must-do while in Melbourne.

Pin Oak Crt in Vermont South is better known as Ramsay St in

continued overpage...

ATTRACTIONS
...continued from page 157.

GET YOUR DISCOUNT CARD!

The Smartvisit Card (1300 661 711, online.smartvisitcard.com/melbourne) allows you free entry to over 50 Melbourne attractions for one all-inclusive price.

Experience arts and cultural centres, wildlife reserves, zoos, galleries, museums, sporting tours, river cruises, train tours and historic sites all for the one price.

There are two, three and seven-day Smartvisit Cards available, with prices starting from $99 (£41). Every card comes with a free, full colour 128-page Melbourne Smartvisit Guide.

Erinsborough, which tour guests can see first-hand, as well as Erinsborough High and the show's studio complex.

A professional tour guide, on-board entertainment and complimentary refreshments are included in the three-hour bus tour, which departs twice daily from various city pick-ups and St Kilda for $30 (£12.50).

Flemington Racecourse

There's nothing like a day at the races and Melbourne's Flemington Racecourse (1300 727 575, melbournecup.com) is arguably Australia's premier venue.

Visitors flock to Federation Square
Photo: Tourism Victoria.

Established in 1840 (and originally called Melbourne Racecourse), Flemington is the oldest continuing metropolitan track in Australia and is the home of the famous Melbourne Cup.

Flemington is the place to be in early November for the annual Spring Racing Carnival and is a popular venue to start the new year with its annual New Year's Day program.

Organised tours... There are a host of organised tours to help you take in Melbourne's best sights, including Walk 'n' Talk Melbourne City Tours (03 9699 1850, walkntalktours.com.au), Sole Tours (0425 705 679, melbournesoletours.com.au) and **Melbourne Sports Tours** (03 8802 4547, melbournesportstours.com.au). For more information or tour options, contact the **Melbourne Visitor Centre** in Federation Square (03 9658 9658, thatsmelbourne.com.au) or see the **Melbourne Visitor Booth** in the Bourke St Mall.

Crown Entertainment Complex
Located in Southgate by the Yarra River, the Crown Entertainment Complex (03 9292 8888, crowncasino.com.au) is a relatively new addition to the city's nightlife.

Spearheaded by a glamorous casino, the complex features more than 40 restaurants, bars and cafés, and includes cinemas, game arcades, designer shopping outlets and nightclubs. Something for everyone!

Melbourne Observation Deck
Take in breathtaking 360-degree panoramic views of the city from the Melbourne Observation Deck (03 9629 8222, melbournedeck.com.au) on the 55th floor of the Rialto Towers building.

Situated high up on Collins St, the Melbourne Observation Deck also features a 20-minute sight and sound show for visitors, as well as gift shops and a licensed café.

Queen Victoria Market
Located on the corner of Victoria St and Elizabeth St in the city, the Queen Victoria Market (03 9320 5822, qvm.com.au) is the largest of its kind in the state, showcasing more than 1000 stalls selling produce and merchandise.

Visitors can take a "Foodies Dream Tour" or "Heritage Tour" of the 120-year-old venue, or simply stroll around at their leisure.

The Queen Victoria Market is open every Tuesday and Thursday from 6am-2pm, Friday from 6am-6pm, Saturday from 6am-3pm and Sunday from 9am-4pm.

Puffing Billy Steam Railway
Board the century-old Puffing Billy Steam Train at Belgrave, one hour east of Melbourne, and enjoy the scenery as you travel along its original mountain track to Gembrook in the picturesque Dandenong Ranges.

Puffing Billy operates every day, except Christmas Day, and offers lunch and dinner specials for passengers. Phone (03) 9754 6800 or visit puffingbilly.com.au.

Sovereign Hill, Ballarat
Ballarat has recreated a goldrush town with amazing detail at Sovereign Hill, a 90-minute drive from Melbourne.

An interactive experience for people of all ages, Sovereign Hill is set over 25 hectares and includes working Clydesdales, craftsmen at work in traditional 1850s trades, street performers and a creek where you can pan for real gold.

Sovereign Hill comes alive at night with a sound and light show that depicts Australia's only armed civil rebellion. Phone (03) 5337 1100 or visit sovereignhill.com.au.

SUGGESTED ITINERARIES

[Looking for something to do before or after the Fourth Test in Melbourne? Here are some ideas to help you plan your stay:]

A day...

If you're in need of some retail therapy, take a trip down to the vibrant Queen Victoria Market, where you'll find fresh produce, souvenirs, cheap fashion clothing and plenty of local characters.

A quick trip on public transport will see you back in the heart of the city, with a short stroll to the Yarra River a perfect place for lunch.

Walk off your lunch with a brief amble to Federation Square. The cultural and entertainment precinct features art galleries, museums and live events in what is a uniquely designed pocket of Melbourne's city centre.

After a day of sightseeing, take a tram to St Kilda and enjoy a drink or an ice cream down at the Esplanade. There are plenty of restaurants and cafes to choose from for dinner, and a good selection of bars and clubs to keep you rocking into the wee hours.

A week...

The Great Ocean Road is arguably Australia's most popular drive-by holiday. Hire a car and take a leisurely cruise along the route which features some of the nation's most spectacular coastlines.

The road, which was built in the 1930s as a memorial to the servicemen of World War I, is about 250km in length and starts at Torquay - about 90 minutes from Melbourne.

There are many stops along the way, including beautiful Lorne on the Erskine River, Otway National Park and Shipwreck Coast at Princetown where you'll find the famous rock formations "The Twelve Apostles".

The beautiful coastal scenery keeps coming until the end of the road at Port Fairy. It's a memorable drive with plenty of beach activities, hang-gliding and golf to enjoy along the way.

A few days...

So you've immersed yourself in culture in Federation Square, checked out the stunning views from the Melbourne Observation Deck in Rialto Towers and had some fun in the Crown Entertainment Complex. It's time for an excursion to the coast!

Get up close and personal with some of Australia's cutest wildlife on Phillip Island, an easy 90-minute drive from Melbourne. Take to the beach at sunset and watch the penguin colony waddle their way ashore after a stint out in the ocean.

If you prefer fur to feathers, Phillip Island is also home to the Koala Conservation Centre. Boardwalks built at tree-top height ensure tourists have a face-to-face encounter with the marsupials.

The Twelve Apostles along the Great Ocean Road.
Photo: Tourism Victoria.

www.ashes06.com

MELBOURNE DIRECTORY

CRICKET
Cricket Australia:..............(03) 9653 9999, cricket.com.au
Cricket Victoria:.....(03) 9653 1100, cricketvictoria.com.au

EMERGENCY
Ambulance:...000
Fire:..000
Police:...000
Police (non-emergency):..11 400
RACV (Emergency Roadside Service):................13 11 11,
....racv.com.au
Lifeline Counselling:...13 11 14
Royal Women's Hospital Centre Against Sexual Assault
(Carlton):..(03) 9344 2201
Travellers' Aid Society of Victoria (Swanston St):............
....(03) 9654 2600

HEALTH
Royal Melbourne Hospital (Parkville):........(03) 9342 7000
Royal Children's Hospital (Parkville):.........(03) 9345 5522
Royal Women's Hospital (Carlton):............(03) 9344 2000
St Vincent's Hospital (Fitzroy):...................(03) 9288 2211
The Alfred Hospital (Prahran):....................(03) 9276 2000
Dental Emergency Service (Carlton):.........(03) 9341 1040

INTERNET ACCESS
Central Internet Café:............279 La Trobe St, Melbourne
Austra Servita Internet Café:....227 Collins St, Melbourne
Globalchat Internet Café:........22 Elizabeth St, Melbourne
E:fiftyfive:...............................55 Elizabeth St, Melbourne
Dotcom Internet Café:..........349 Elizabeth St, Melbourne
Villete Internet Café:.............115 Lonsdale St, Melbourne
Maru Internet Café:..............100 Harbour Esp, Docklands
Internet M & H Café:............789 Glenferrie Rd, Hawthorn
Internet Cybernet Café:........812 Glenferrie Rd, Hawthorn
Net City:..63 Fitzroy St, St Kilda
World Wide Wash:..........................Brunswick St, Fitzroy
Hns Internet Café:...................182 Sydney Rd, Brunswick
A White Monkey Internet Café:55 Sydney Rd, Brunswick
Cyberage Internet Café:...............587 Station St, Box Hill
BT's Internet & Gaming Café: 78 O'Shanassy St, Sunbury
Gus's Internet Café Services: ...50 Geelong Rd, Footscray
Letzong Internet Café:425 Burwood Hwy,Wantirna South

MONEY
American Express:......................................1300 139 060,
....americanexpress.com.au
Travelex:............................1800 637 642, travelex.com.au

continued overpage...

Melbourne skyline. Photo: Tourism Victoria.

[DIRECTORY
...continued from page 161.

PHONE/MOBILE
3 mobile: ....131 681, three.com.au
International code to UK: ....
............0011 (or 0018) + 44 + Area Code + Local Number
Country Direct (reverse charge/credit to UK):...................
...................1800 881 440, 1800 881 441, 1800 881 417
Directory Assistance:....................1223 (local/national) or
....1225 (international)

POST
Melbourne GPO (cnr Little Bourke/Elizabeth Sts):.............
....13 13 18, austpost.com.au

TOURISM
Melbourne Visitor Centre (Federation Sq):
.........................(03) 9658 9658, thatsmelbourne.com.au
Melbourne Visitor Booth:.........................Bourke St Mall
Information Victoria (356 Collins St):..........1300 366 356,
....information.vic.gov.au
See Melbourne & Beyond (Smartvisit Card):....................
.......1300 661 711, online.smartvisitcard.com/Melbourne
Walk 'n' Talk Melbourne City Tours (Southbank):.............
.......................(03) 9699 1850, walkntalktours.com.au
Sole Tours (Melbourne): 0425 705 679,
....melbournesoletours.com.au
Melbourne Sports Tours (Federation Sq): ....
...............(03) 8802 4547, melbournesportstours.com.au
Official Neighbours Tour: ....(03) 9534 4755,
....neighbourstour.com
Shopping Spree Tours (Brighton): ....(03) 9596 6600,
....shoppingspree.com.au
Global Ballooning (Richmond): 1800 627 661,
....globalballooning.com.au

TRANSPORT
PLANE
Melbourne Airport:............(03) 9297 1600, melair.com.au
Qantas:..13 13 13, qantas.com.au
Virgin Blue: ....13 67 89, virginblue.com.au
Jetstar: ....131 538, jetstar.com.au

BUS - LOCAL
Metlink: ....131 638, metlinkmelbourne.com.au
MetShop (cnr Swanston/Little Collins Sts): 131 638
Skybus (Melbourne Airport): ....(03) 9335 2811,
....skybus.com.au

Sunbus Airport Transfers (Melbourne & Avalon Airports
...........................(03) 9689 6888, sunbusaustralia.com.au

BUS - INTERSTATE
Greyhound Australia:............13 14 99, greyhound.com.au
Firefly Express: ....1300 730 740, fireflyexpress.com.au
V/Line:..13 61 96, vline.com.au
Premier Motor Service: ....13 34 10, premierms.com.au

TRAIN - LOCAL
Metlink: ....131 638, metlinkmelbourne.com.au
MetShop (cnr Swanston/Little Collins Sts): 131 638

TRAIN - REGIONAL/INTERSTATE
Great Southern Railway: ....13 21 47, gsr.com.au
CountryLink:............................13 22 32, countrylink.info

TAXI
Arrow:...13 22 1
Taxis Australia:..13 22 2
Embassy Taxis: 13 17 5
Silver Top Taxis:..13 10 0
North Suburban: 13 11 1

CAR HIRE
Avis:..13 63 33, avis.com.au
Budget: ....13 27 27, budget.com.au
Europcar:.........................1300 131 390, europcar.com.au
Hertz:..13 30 39, hertz.com.au
Thrifty: ....1300 367 227, thrifty.com.au
Rent-A-Bomb (Richmond):......................(03) 9428 0088
....rentabomb.com.au

MOTORCYCLE/SCOOTER HIRE
Garner's Hire Bikes (North Melbourne): ...(03) 9326 8676
....garnersmotorcycles.com.au
Harley Rides (North Blackburn):..................1800 182 282
....harleyrides.com.au

BICYCLE HIRE
Hire a Bike (Federation Sq, Melbourne): 0417 339 203
....byohouse.com.au/bikehire
St Kilda Cycles:........(03) 9534 3074, stkildacycles.com.au
Borsari Cycles (Carlton):...........................(03) 9347 4100
....borsaricycles.com.au
Fitzroy Cycles: ....(03) 9419 4357, fitzroycycles.com.au
Mascot Cycles (Richmond):......................(03) 9428 412

Sydney Cricket Ground.

THE HARBOUR CITY

JANUARY 2-6, 2007

5TH TEST
SYDNEY

SYDNEY CITY OVERVIEW

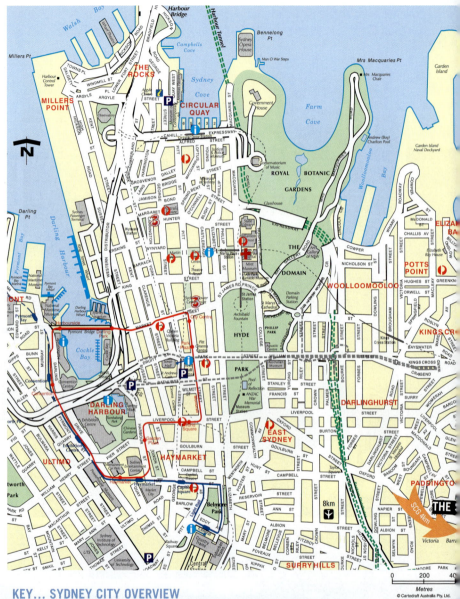

KEY... SYDNEY CITY OVERVIEW

- 3   3 store
- Hospital
- P   Police
- Post Office
- Tourist information
- Airport

New South Wales State Map

www.ashes06.com

WELCOME TO
-SYDNEY, NEW SOUTH WALES

While you're in Sydney...

As the gateway to Australia, Sydney has so much to offer visitors. Scaling the famous Sydney Harbour Bridge, swimming in trendy Bondi Beach or being wowed at the world-class Sydney Aquarium are just a few of the many attractions.

Home to a host of cricket legends, including Sir Donald Bradman and Richie Benaud, as well as modern day marvels Steve and Mark Waugh, Glenn McGrath and Mark Taylor, Sydney has cultivated

Sydney is one of the world's great cities; sexy and sophisticated, with a vibrant atmosphere where cultures combine and style reigns supreme.

With 4.6 million residents, Sydney is the country's oldest and largest city - and indeed one of the biggest in the world - and has a plethora of great restaurants, hip bars and a nightlife as good as any on the planet.

The capital of New South Wales is characterised by its spectacular harbour, which divides the city into north and south, with the bridge and Harbour Tunnel joining the two shores. The city centre includes Circular Quay and Central Station, with Darling Harbour to the west and Kings Cross, Paddington and Darlinghurst to the east.

many sporting champions and has hosted numerous international sporting events over the years, including the highly praised 2000 Olympics.

With so much to see and do in Sydney, you may find yourself hard pressed to wander further afield, but you'll be very impressed if you do. The gorgeous Blue Mountains, the idyllic Hunter Valley wineries and super cool Byron Bay are classic NSW hotspots in their own right and are definitely worth the effort.

Eat: Anything from the Sydney Fish Market. For over 100 species of exquisite seafood, check out the Sydney Fish Market in Blackwattle Bay on the foreshore of Sydney Harbour. It's the largest market of its kind in the Southern Hemisphere and the world's second largest seafood market outside of Japan.

Drink: James Squire beer. The website of the Malt Shovel Brewery, which produces the glorious range of James Squire beers, honours a Benjamin Franklin quote that "beer is living proof that God loves us and wants to see us happy". A glass or two of James Squire will have you proclaiming these words yourself! Try the Original Amber Ale or the Golden Ale.

See: Sydney Aquarium. The Sydney Aquarium draws over 1.3 million visitors every year and stands as one of Australia's most popular tourist attractions. Home to over 11,500 aquatic animals, including platypus, sharks, seals, fairy penguins and crocodiles, the Sydney Aquarium is an exciting and educational marine experience not to be missed.

Do: Climb Sydney Harbour Bridge. Take a walk on the wild side and climb the iconic Sydney Harbour Bridge. BridgeClimb (5 Cumberland St, The Rocks) offers three-and-a-half-hour adventures departing every 15 minutes daily, with your reward for reaching the top being one of the most breathtaking views you will ever see!

STATE FACTS... NEW SOUTH WALES
Founded: 1788
Population: 6.8 million (Sydney = 4.6 million)
Colours: Light blue & dark blue
Floral emblem: Waratah
Faunal emblems: Platypus & Kookaburra
Domestic cricket team: New South Wales Blues
Average summer temperature: 26°C
Average winter temperature: 17°C
Time zone: GMT + 11 hours

Sydney Cricket Ground. Photo: SCG Trust.

SYDNEY CRICKET GROUND

The SCG is one of Australia's premier sporting venues and is steeped in history.

Located 4km from the CBD at the corner of Moore Park and Driver Ave in Paddington, the Sydney Cricket Ground is one of Australia's premier sporting venues and is steeped in history.

Next door to rugby-dominated Aussie Stadium, the SCG hosts international and domestic cricket in summer and is the home ground of the New South Wales Blues, while in winter, the Sydney Swans take over as Australian Rules football moves in.

A much more intimate venue than Victoria's MCG, the SCG's origins date back to 1810, however it only officially became known as the Sydney Cricket Ground in 1894 - 12 years after hosting its first Test match in which Australia defeated England by five wickets.

The ground has seen scores of amazing achievements, including Don Bradman's unbeaten 452 for NSW against Queensland in 1930, which remains the highest individual innings in Australian cricket. English fans will also remember fast bowler Darren Gough's hat-trick in 1999, which was England's first and only Ashes hat-trick in the 20th century.

The stadium has continued to develop over the years, particularly since the Bradman Stand in the north-eastern corner of the venue was completed in 1973. Light towers were added in 1978 to allow the first official night match to be played (Australia v West Indies), with the Brewongle Stand opening in 1980 ahead of the first electronic video scoreboard in 1983.

In 1984, the Pat Hill Stand (later re-named the O'Reilly Stand) was built, while the Doug Walters Stand was constructed on "the Hill" in conjunction with the Clive Churchill Stand a year later.

Noted as a spinner's paradise, the SCG's playing surface was dramatically overhauled in 2000 at a cost of $2 million (£833,000), with its 157m long and 154m wide dimensions making it one of the smaller fields in Australia.

The biggest ever crowd recorded at the SCG is 78,056 for a domestic rugby league match between St George and South Sydney in 1965, with the largest cricket attendance remaining the 58,446 people who watched Australia play England in the 1928 Ashes series. Today, the venue has a capacity of 44,002.

www.ashes06.com

MATCH DAY INFORMATION

5TH TEST:
AUSTRALIA vs ENGLAND

Sydney Cricket Ground,
January 2-6, 2007

Gates:
Gates open at 8.30am.

Match times:

FIRST SESSION:	10.30am - 12.30pm
Lunch:	12.30pm - 1.10pm
SECOND SESSION:	1.10pm - 3.10pm
Tea:	3.10pm - 3.30pm
THIRD SESSION:	3.30pm - 5.30pm

*Note: Times are subject to change.

[BE WARNED! The SCG reserves the right to refuse entry to people who are intoxicated and/or disorderly. All persons' movements upon entering the SCG are subject to monitoring by closed circuit television.]

Parking:
Public car parking is available in Fox Studios Car Park on Lang Rd, with limited parking also available in the Moore Park Car Park on Driver Ave and in the grounds of Sydney High Schools from Cleveland St.
Note: Parking in the Gold Members Car Park on Driver Ave is restricted to members throughout the Test.

For up-to-date information, visit cricketnsw.com.au or phone (02) 9339 0999.

Prohibited items:
- Alcoholic refreshments
- Illicit drugs
- Glass bottles or breakable containers
- Offensive weapons, including potential missiles
- Metal containers and cans
- Skateboards, scooters, rollerblades and bicycles
- Dogs and other pets
- Large eskies that cannot fit under a grandstand seat
- Flags over 1m x 1m in size
- Any item which, as deemed by the Sydney Cricket & Sports Ground Trust, could cause public nuisance or offence to other users of the venue.

General information:
- All patrons may be subject to bag searches before entering the venue.
- Spectators who enter the playing arena without authorisation will be prosecuted.
- ATMs are located around the stadium, including in the Churchill Stand in the south-western corner (next to the main video scoreboard), the O'Reilly Stand on the eastern side (next to the Walters Stand and the main video scoreboard) and in the Noble Stand (members) at the northern end (directly opposite the main video scoreboard).
- Wheelchair viewing bays are located in front of the Messenger Stand on the eastern side, between the O'Reilly and Walters stands in the south-eastern corner (next to the scoreboard) and in front of the Brewongle Stand on the western side.
- A medical room for patrons is situated in front of the Churchill Stand in the south-western corner of the stadium (next to main scoreboard).

continued overpage...

MATCH DAY INFORMATION
...continued from page 167.

- A police base can be found behind the Walters Stand next to the main scoreboard in the south-eastern corner of the stadium.
- No alcohol can be taken from the SCG premises.
- Pass-outs will not be issued.

Food & beverage:
Every food group is catered for at the SCG. There is a Burger Bar in the public O'Reilly Stand where patrons can also buy pizzas, pies, hotdogs, fish and chips, as well as chicken wings and a number of other culinary delights.

Similar fare is available in plentiful supply in grandstands around the ground and near the main scoreboard.

And to wash it down, the SCG offers an assortment of soft drinks, juices, coffees and water, plus Carlton Mid (mid-strength) and Carlton Sterling (light) beers. Full-strength beer is only available in the members.

Smoking:
Smoking is prohibited in all seating areas, bars and restaurants within the SCG. However, smoking is permitted in designated areas behind the grandstands.

TAB/Betting:
If you fancy a punt on the cricket, TAB facilities are available between the O'Reilly and Walters Stands on Yabba's Hill in the south-eastern corner of the venue (just around from the main video scoreboard), and in the Noble Stand (members) at the northern end (directly opposite the main video scoreboard).

SCALPING
It is an offence to re-sell any tickets to any Test match in Australia at a premium or to use any of them for advertising, promotional or other commercial purposes without the prior written consent of Cricket Australia or the relevant state cricket association.

If the ticket is sold or used in contravention of this condition, the bearer of the ticket will be denied admission to the venue.

The SCG. Photo: SCG Trust.

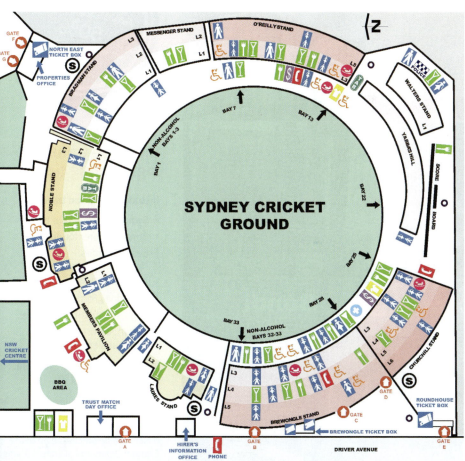

SYDNEY CRICKET GROUND
-SEATING PLAN

See it all with a
Sydney pass

"A 3 day SydneyPass saves you up to 50% on individual ticket purchases"

Sydney *explorer*
HOP ON - HOP OFF BUS
- 26 Stops
- 20 min service frequency
- 2 hours round trip

The ultimate all inclusive transport sightseeing ticket!

Includes unlimited travel on:
- Sydney Explorer tour bus
- Bondi Explorer tour bus
- Sydney Ferries Harboursights cruises
- All Sydney Buses services
- All Sydney Ferries services
- Regular CityRail (CBD) trains
+ Return Airport Link train transfers

Bondi *explorer*
HOP ON - HOP OFF BUS
- 19 Stops
- 30 min service frequency
- 2 hours round trip

3, 5 and 7 day tickets available. Adult 3 day pass $110.

Your 3, 5 or 7 day SydneyPass can be used over an 8 day calendar period. SydneyPass and individual Explorer tickets can be purchased on board Explorer Buses and at Transit Shops (Circular Quay, Wynyard and QVB).

SydneyPass and individual Explorer tickets include discounts at Sydney based attractions and venues.

www.sydneypass.info

TRANSPORT

By Plane...
Located 8km south of the city centre, **Sydney Airport** (02 9667 9111, sydneyairport.com.au) is the city's main airport, incorporating an international and domestic terminal spread 4km apart. Free shuttle buses link these terminals.

If you're travelling to Sydney from Melbourne after the Fourth Test, check out **Qantas** (13 13 13, qantas.com.au), **Virgin Blue** (13 67 89, virginblue.com.au) and **Jetstar** (131 538, jetstar.com.au), which have numerous flights servicing the popular route. A one-way ticket will set you back around $200 (£83), but check the respective airlines' websites for special deals.

To/from Airport...
Airport Link (02 8337 8417, airportlink.com.au) is connected to Sydney's principal CityRail train network and has services leaving every 15 minutes between 5am and midnight. The 13-minute journey from the airport into the city costs $11 (£4.50).

There are also a number of shuttle bus companies which will take you from the airport to your city hotel for between $10-$15 (£4-£6). Try Kingsford Smith Transport's **Sydney Airporter** (02 9666 9988, kst.com.au) or **Sydney Super Shuttles** (02 9311 3789, supershuttle.com.au).

Taxis from the airport to the city centre cost about $27 (£11), while car hire is available through **Avis** (13 63 33, avis.com.au), **Budget** (13 27 27, budget.com.au), **Europcar** (1300 131 390, europcar.com.au), **Hertz** (13 30 39, hertz.com.au) and **Thrifty** (1300 367 227, thrifty.com.au).

By Train... (INTERSTATE)
Central Station, located at the top of George St in downtown Sydney, is the main city and interstate train station. All interstate trains depart from here and it's a major CityRail hub for local services too.

The main regional rail carrier is **Countrylink** (13 22 32, countrylink.info), which operates lines from the city to outer suburbs and beyond. Of its interstate services, fares for the 11-hour Sydney to Melbourne and 15-hour Sydney to Brisbane routes cost around $75-$125 (£31-£52).

If you've got time on your side, consider a journey on the famous **Indian Pacific**, which runs between Sydney and Perth via Adelaide. It travels twice weekly each way, with fares from one side of the country to the other starting from $560 (£233). Contact **Great Southern Railways** (13 21 47, gsr.com.au) for timetable information.

By Bus... (INTERSTATE)
The **Sydney Coach Terminal** (02 9281 9366) on the corner of Eddy Ave and Pitt St (adjacent Central Station) is the base for all long distance bus services.

Greyhound Australia (13 14 99, greyhound.com.au) is the country's biggest coach line, with smaller regional operators including **Firefly Express** (1300 730 740, fireflyexpress.com.au), **Premier Motor Service** (13 34 10, premierms.com.au), **Fearnes Coaches** (02 6921 2316, fearnes.com.au) and **Murrays Coaches** (13 22 51, murrays.com.au).

As a guide, Greyhound Australia charges $65-$72 (£27-£30) for a one-way ride between Sydney and Melbourne (12-14 hours), $110-$130 (£46-£54) between Sydney and Brisbane (16-18 hours), and $158 (£66) between Sydney and Adelaide (24 hours).

PUBLIC TRANSPORT...
The **State Transit Authority** (sta.nsw.gov.au) operates **Sydney Buses** (13 15 00, sydneybuses.info), **CityRail** (13 15 00, cityrail.info) runs the urban and suburban trains, while **Sydney Ferries** (02 9207 3166, sydneyferries.info) operates the public passenger ferry network.

continued overpage...

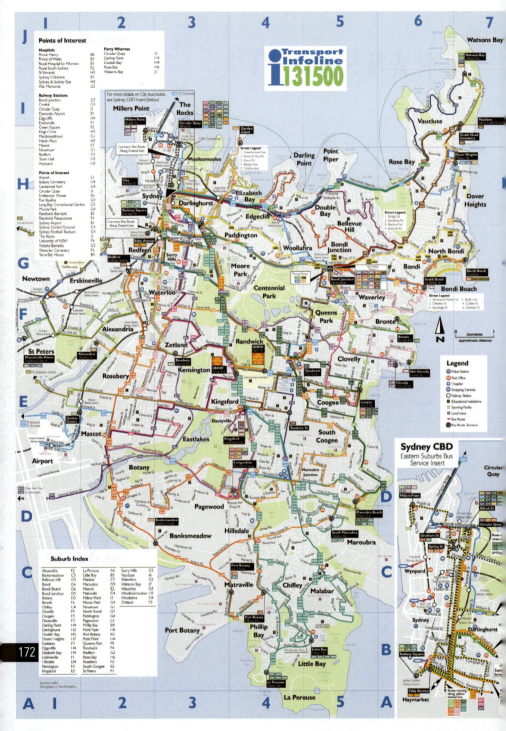

TRANSPORT

...continued from page 171.

The **Sydney Monorail** (02 9285 5600, metromonorail.com.au) connects the city centre to Darling Harbour, while the **Metro Light Rail** (02 9285 5600, metrolightrail.com.au) runs between Central Station and Wentworth Park in Pyrmont.

For fare and timetable information on buses, ferries and trains, contact the **Transport Infoline** (13 15 00, 131500.com.au).

If you're planning on using public transport extensively while you're in Sydney, it's cheaper to buy a special pass rather than individual tickets each time. There are several passes available, however the **SydneyPass** (13 15 00, sydneypass.info) is easily the most popular, giving users unlimited travel on the city's entire metropolitan transport network via three, five and seven-day tickets. The SydneyPass includes regular train, bus and ferry networks, return transfers on **Airport Link** trains, three **Harboursights Cruises**, as well as unlimited travel on **Sydney Explorer** and **Bondi Explorer** hop-on, hop-off tourist buses. A three-day SydneyPass (which can be used over an eight-day period) costs $110 (£46), a five-day pass costs $145 (£60), while a seven-day pass costs $165 (£69).

A week-long **TravelPass** allows unlimited travel on buses, trains and ferries, with five ticket variations depending on the distance you intend to travel. The **RedPass** and **GreenPass** are the most common. The RedPass costs $32 (£13) and covers all transportation within the city centre and neighbouring areas, while the GreenPass costs $40 (£17) and includes more distant destinations such as Manly.

A **DayTripper** ticket gives you unlimited bus, train and ferry travel for one day and costs $15 (£6), while a **CityHopper** ticket allows unlimited all-day travel on CityRail trains bounded by Kings Cross, North Sydney and Redfern, and costs between $4.80-$6.80 (£2-£3) depending on whether you travel in off-peak or peak times.

If you're sticking to bus transport only, a **TravelTen** ticket gives you 10 bus rides for a discounted price, with the Blue and Brown variations among the most popular. Prices start at $13.60 (£5.70) for a Blue TravelTen,

continued overpage...

Darling Harbour. Photo: Tourism New South Wales.

[TRANSPORT
...continued from page 173.

SYDNEY BUSES - NIGHTRIDE

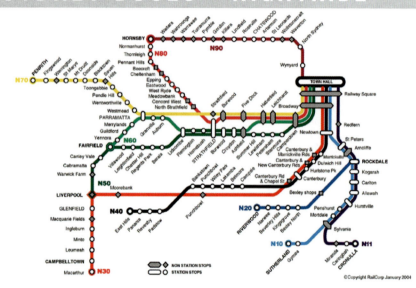

which covers two sections on the route. **FerryTen** tickets are also available from $32.50 (£13.50), giving you 10 trips within the inner harbour.

Public Bus...
There are plenty of **Sydney Buses** (13 15 00, sydneybuses.info) servicing the metropolitan area, which you will find clean and reliable. They generally operate between 5am and midnight every day.

The minimum fare, which covers most short hops in the city, is $1.60 (70p) for a 4km "section". Sections are marked on bus stand signs, but can still be confusing. If in doubt, ask the bus driver.

Most buses bound for the northern suburbs, including night buses to Manly and the bus to Taronga Zoo, leave from Wynyard Park on Carrington St (behind the Wynyard train station on George St). Buses to the southern beaches, including Bondi and Bronte, and the western and eastern suburbs, leave from Circular Quay.

The bright red **Sydney Explorer** (13 15 00, sydneypass.info) buses operate every day and are geared especially for tourists with on-board commentaries. Travelling in a 28km circuit, the Sydney Explorer stops at 26 places of interest, including the Sydney Opera House, the Art Gallery of New South Wales,

Kings Cross and The Rocks. Buses depart from Circular Quay at 18-minute intervals starting at 8.40am, with the last round-trip service departing at 5.20pm. Tickets cost $39 (£16) and are available on board the bus, with a complete circuit taking around an hour and 40 minutes.

The bright blue **Bondi Explorer** (13 15 00, sydneypass.info) bus operates every day also (with an on-board commentary too), travelling a 30km circuit around the eastern harbourside bays and coastal beaches. Stops along the way include Kings Cross, Double Bay, Bondi Beach, Oxford St and Martin Place. The bus departs from Circular Quay at 30-minute intervals starting at 8.45am, with

SYDNEY MONORAILS

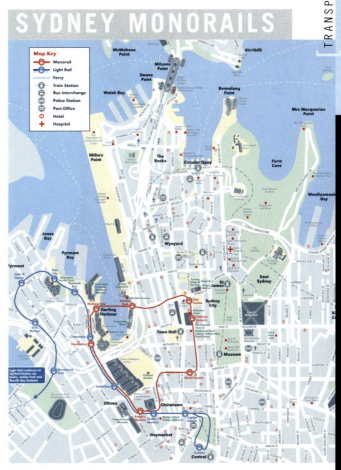

the last round-trip service departing at 4.15pm. Tickets cost $39 (£16) and can be bought on board the bus.

You can also buy a **Combined Explorer** two-day ticket for both the Sydney and Bondi Explorer buses, which costs $68 (£28).

And for all you party animals, keep in mind the **NightRide** (13 15 00, cityrail.info/nightride) bus service, which covers Sydney's city and suburban areas between midnight and 4.30am. Ticket prices depend on distance travelled, however most visitors will only need a three-section ticket which costs $3.70 (£1.50).

Public Train...

Sydney's **CityRail** (13 15 00, cityrail.info) train system is a quick and cheap way of getting around town, with single tickets for city centre travel costing $3 (£1.25). Unfortunately for tourists, popular destinations such as Manly, Bondi Beach and Darling Harbour are not serviced by the train network, which operates from 5am to midnight.

It is worth remembering that all city-bound trains stop at Central Station, which has a good information kiosk near platforms 4 and 5.

Public Monorail...

The **Metro Monorail** (02 9285 5600, metromonorail.com.au), with its single overhead line, connects the CBD to Darling Harbour, taking about 12 minutes. There's a monorail every 3-5 minutes, with the system operating every day from 7am-10pm (and until midnight on Friday and Saturday). Single trip tickets cost $4.50 (£1.90).

Public Ferry...

What better way to see Sydney Harbour and marvel at the city views than by taking a ferry (02 9207 3166, sydneyferries.info)

continued overpage...

Sydney's best views are just the beginning...

SPECIAL 15% OFF
Adult & Child

Sydney Tower takes you to the highest point above Sydney for breathtaking 360-degree views of our beautiful harbour city. You'll be amazed by Sydney's best views! Plus your ticket to the Observation Deck includes **OzTrek**, an amazing virtual adventure across Australia with 3D holograms, 180-degree cinema screens, surround sound and heart-stopping real-motion seating.

SYDNEY TOWER + OzTREK
1st stop at the top!

**Centrepoint Podium Level,
100 Market Street Sydney
Open daily: 9.00am to 10.30pm
(Saturdays to 11.30pm)
Tel: (02) 9333 9222
www.sydneytoweroztrek.com.au**

* Not valid with family, groups or concession tickets, nor with any other offer or promotion.
Valid to 31/01/07

[**TRANSPORT**
...continued from page 175.

from the main terminal at Circular Quay. Tickets, which are available from machines at each wharf, cost $5 (£2.10) for one-way journeys within the inner harbour.

The Manly ferry from Wharf 3 is slightly more expensive at $6.20 (£2.60) and takes 30 minutes, or if you're in a hurry, catch the **JetCat** service which will get you there in half the time for $7.90 (£3.30). Ferries run from approximately 6am to midnight.

There are also **Harboursights Cruises** available which include an on-board commentary. A one-hour morning cruise departs at 10.30am daily and costs $18 (£7.50), a two-and-a-half-hour afternoon cruise departs at 1pm (12.30pm on weekends) and costs $24 (£10), while a 90-minute evening cruise departs at 8pm from Monday to Saturday and costs $22 (£9).

DAY TRIPPERS!

A **DayTripper** ticket gives you unlimited bus, train and ferry travel for one day and costs $15 (£6), while a **CityHopper** ticket allows unlimited all-day travel on CityRail trains bounded by Kings Cross, North Sydney and Redfern, and costs between $4.80-$6.80 (£2-£3) depending on whether you travel in off-peak or peak times.

Public Tram...

The **Metro Light Rail** (02 9285 5600, metrolightrail.com.au) is a system of trams operating 24 hours a day on a route that traverses a 3.6km track between Central Station and Wentworth Park in Pyrmont via Chinatown, Darling Harbour, Star City Casino and the Sydney Fish Markets.

Trams run every 10-15 minutes, with one-way fares costing between $3-$4 (£1.25-£1.70) depending on distance travelled.

By Bicycle...

Centennial Park is widely regarded as the best place to cycle in Sydney, with bikes for hire from **Centennial Park Cycles** in Randwick (02 9398 5027, cyclehire.com.au) for $12 (£5) an hour or $32 (£13) for the day.

Bicycles in the City on George St near Central Station (02 9280 2229) also rents bikes (and in-line skates) or try **Sydney**

Olympic Park (02 9714 7888, sydneyolympicpark.com.au).

By Taxi...

There are plenty of metered taxis in Sydney, which line up at stands throughout the city, including Circular Quay and Central Station. Cabs are licensed to carry four people, with companies including:

ABC:	13 25 22
Legion Cabs:	13 14 51
Premier:	13 10 17
RSL Taxis:	13 22 11
St George:	13 21 66
Manly:	13 16 68
Combined:	13 33 00

TOLLS ON THE HARBOUR BRIDGE & HARBOUR TUNNEL

Remember that tolls are in place at the Harbour Bridge and Harbour Tunnel, so if you cross either in a cab, it will cost you an extra $3 (£1.25).

Water taxis, or "Harbour Taxis" as they are called, are also available, operating 24 hours a day and providing quick and easy access across the water and to waterfront restaurants and harbour attractions. The main operator is **Water Taxis Combined** (1300 666 484).

AUSTRALIA'S UNIQUE WILDLIFE IN THE HEART OF THE CITY

Opening in September 2006, Sydney Wildlife World will showcase the best of Australia's unique wildlife right in the heart of Darling Harbour. Visitors will see koalas, wallabies, reptiles, birds and more, all living within natural ecosystems and environments. Open 9am to 10pm. Call +61 2 9333 9288 or visit www.sydneywildlifeworld.com.au

Sydney WildlifeWorld
DARLING HARBOUR

GETTING TO THE SCG

Getting to the SCG, in **Moore Park** near Paddington, is FAIRLY STRAIGHTFORWARD, WITH A NUMBER OF PUBLIC trains and buses servicing the ground if you're not in the mood to walk from the CBD.

On Foot...

The SCG is only 4km from Sydney's CBD so walking to the cricket is an option if you're staying in the city... and if you're reasonably fit!

From Central Station, proceed along Foveaux St and Fitzroy St, while from Bondi Junction Station west of the ground, proceed along Oxford St.

By Bus...

From Central Station: Express buses will operate between Central Station and the SCG throughout the Test. Otherwise, from Stand A in Eddy Ave, take the 378 via Oxford St to Greens Rd, which is just a short stroll to the stadium.

And don't worry if the first bus is full - services run every 10 minutes every day!
You can also take the 339, 374, 376 or 391 from Stand C in Eddy Ave, which gets you to the ground via Anzac Pde, or from Railway Square at Central Station board the 372, 393 or 395 from Stand A, which travels via Cleveland St.

From Circular Quay: Take a 371-377 or 392-399 bus from Alfred St via Philips St, Elizabeth St and Anzac Pde, or jump on the 380, 383 or L82 which travels via Oxford St to Greens Rd and a short walk to the SCG. Services generally run every five minutes.

From Martin Place: Take a 371-377 or 392-399 bus from Alfred St via Philip St, Elizabeth St and Anzac Pde to Moore Park and the SCG. Or catch bus number 378, 380, 383 or L82 via Oxford St to Greens Rd.

www.ashes06.com

GETTING TO THE SCG

From the Museum: Catch a 371-377 or 392-399 bus from Alfred St via Philip St, Elizabeth St and Anzac Pde, or take a 378, 380, 383 or L82 bus which runs down Oxford St to Greens Rd and a stone's throw from the SCG.

From Bondi Junction: Jump on the 352 or 355 from Stand H. The 352 travels down Oxford St to Oatley Rd within walking distance of the stadium, while the 355 goes via Cook Rd and Lang Rd to Moore Park. Otherwise, from Stand N take the 378, 380 or L82 along Oxford St to Oatley Rd.

By Train...
If you're staying outside the city centre, make your way to Central Station where it's just a short walk - or an even shorter bus ride - to the SCG.

And if you want to be really clever, purchase a **Moore Park Link** ticket (available at CityRail stations) which combines public train and bus transportation to and from the SCG on a single ticket.

By Taxi...
There is a permanent taxi rank in Fox Studios (adjacent the SCG) in Errol Flynn Blvd near the Horden Pavilion, south of the stadium. Otherwise call:
ABC 13 25 22
Legion Cabs 13 14 51
Premier 13 10 17
St George 13 21 66
Manly 13 16 68
RSL Taxis 13 22 11
Combined 13 33 00

PARKING...
Public car parking is available in Fox Studios Car Park on Lang Rd, with limited parking also available during the cricket in the Moore Park Car Park on Driver Ave and in the grounds of Sydney High Schools from Cleveland St.

Parking in the Gold Members Car Park on Driver Ave is restricted to members throughout the Test.

Disabled parking is available in the Moore Park Car Park, Fox Studios Car Park and Gold Members Car Park.

Express shuttle buses will run regularly from Chalmers St at **Central Station to the SCG** throughout the Test. **For bus and train timetable** information, contact 13 15 00 OR VISIT 131500.com.au

The SCG. Photo: SCG Trust.

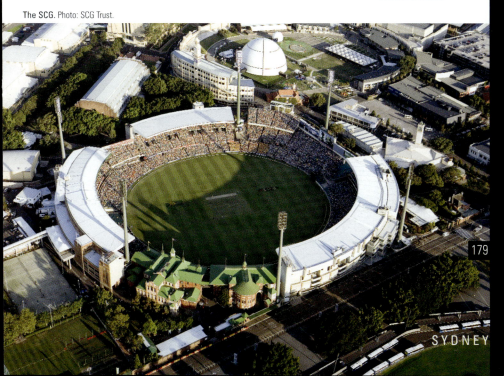

SYDNEY

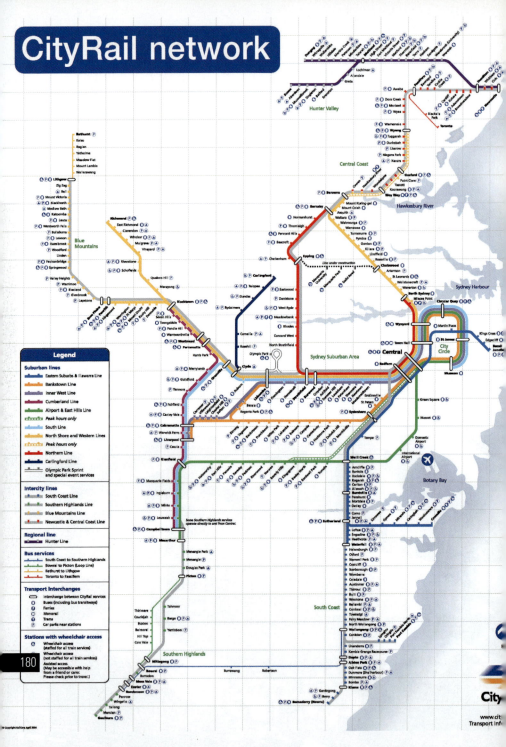

SYDNEY -ACCOMMODATION

InterContinental Sydney.

[NOTE: Hostels can be booked via www.hostelbookers.com or www.hostelworld.com. Hotels, motels and apartments can be booked via www.wotif.com]

HOSTELS

LOW-RANGE: < $100 (£42)

AUSTRALIAN BACKPACKERS
(pp198-199)
$22-$27 (£9-£11)
132 Bourke St, Woolloomooloo
1800 350 211 (free call within Australia) OR **(02) 9331 0822**
Reservations via email:
ausbak@hotmail.com
australianbackpackers.com.au

You'll find **Australian Backpackers** in famous Woolloomooloo - the inner-city Aussie suburb immortalised in the Monty Python skit "Bruce's Philosophers' Song". Woolloomooloo is close to many recognisable landmarks such as Hyde Park and the Opera House. Fortunately, you'll find the SCG conveniently within range too (3km). Australian Backpackers has great hostel facilities including a roof-top with awesome city views, internet, 24-hour building access, laundry, kitchen and newly refurbished bathrooms. The hostel also offers complimentary breakfast and free daily shuttle buses to the beach. Dorm beds cost $22 per night (£9), while twin/double rooms (with fridge and TV) cost $27 per night (£11).

BASE BACKPACKERS (pp198-199)
$28-$95 (£11-£39)
477 Kent St, Sydney
1800 242 273 (free call within Australia) OR **(02) 9267 7718**
Reservations via email: sydney
@basebackpackers.com
basebackpackers.com

continued overpage...

[**ACCOMMODATION**
...continued from page 181.

Base Backpackers, also known as the Base Wanderers on Kent, is one of Sydney's most popular hostels. Base's great location in the heart of the city puts it within minutes of Sydney Tower and Paddy's Markets. And the SCG is only 3km away. The hostel has friendly staff and offers good facilities, including internet access, laundry, kitchen, restaurant, 24-hour reception, travel desk, air-conditioning and a nightclub. The hostel offers a range of room types for all budgets: dorm beds start at $38 per night (£11), a bed in the girls only Sanctuary room costs $34 per night (£14), while double/twin/single rooms cost $95 per night (£39).

BIG HOSTEL (pp198-199)
$27-$102 (£11-£42)
212 Elizabeth St, Surry Hills
1800 212 244 (free call within Australia) OR **(02) 9281 6030**
Reservations via email:
reception@bighostel.com
bighostel.com

Big Hostel is a recent inclusion to Sydney's backpacker accommodation scene - and it's a most welcome addition! It has hotel standard amenities and room to sleep 155 guests, plus it's in a great location just minutes from factory outlet stores, noodle bars and grocers of lively China Town. It's also only a short walk to picturesque Darling Harbour, and the SCG is only 2km away. Facilities include 24-hour reception, kitchen, laundry, travel desk, roof-top barbecue area, restaurant and free linen and breakfast. Dorm beds start at $27 per night (£11), twin rooms with ensuite $89 (£37) and triple rooms with ensuite $102 (£42).

THE GLOBE BACKPACKERS
(pp198-199)
$22-$32 (£11-£13)
40 Darlinghurst Rd, Kings Cross
1800 806 384 (free call within Australia) Reservations via email:
info@globebackpackers.com
globebackpackers.com

The **Globe Backpackers** is located in the inner-city suburb of Kings Cross: a buzzing entertainment hub! You'll find it close to cool bars, clubs and restaurants. The SCG is also just 2.5km away. The hostel itself boasts a lively social atmosphere, with colourful on-site facilities. Unwind in the Blue Room or catch a film in the Lava Lounge. Other features include internet access, laundry, kitchen, travel desk, free breakfast and linen, and there's a courtyard with a barbecue. Room types range from dorm beds for $22 per night (£9) to double/twin rooms with TV and fridge from $32 per night (£13).

KANGAROO BAKPAK (pp200)
$23-$30 (£9-£12)
665 South Dowling St, Surry Hills
(02) 9319 5915 Reservations via email: reservations@kangaroo bakpak.com.au
kangaroobakpak.com.au

If you want to roll out of bed and be right outside the SCG gates, head for **Kangaroo Bakpak**, a friendly little hostel in the trendy inner-city suburb of Surry Hills. The hostel's also just minutes from happening Crown St pubs and the impressive Fox Studios. Facilities at Kangaroo Bakpak include a fully-equipped kitchen, outdoor barbecue area, lounge with TV and video, internet access and tour desk, all within walking distance of the SCG. Prices start from $23 per night (£9) for space in an eight-bed dorm room to $30 per night (£12) for a double/twin room.

SYDNEY BACKPACKERS
(pp198-199)
$28-$55 (£11-£23)
7 Wilmot St, Sydney
1800 887 766 (free call within Australia) OR **(02) 9267 7772**
Reservations via email:
info@sydneybackpackers.com
sydneybackpackers.com

Sydney Backpackers is a custom-built hostel that provides hotel quality services rather than standard backpacker accommodation. Its great location in the centre of the Sydney CBD makes it all the more appealing - the Sydney Harbour Bridge and Pitt St Mall are within close proximity, and the SCG is only 3km away.
The hostel offers guests excellent facilities including a games room with pool table, karaoke, TV, DVD player, fully-equipped kitchen, 24-hour reception, laundry and a large roof-top terrace with barbecue. Rooms also contain climate-controlled air-conditioning, fridge and TV with DVD. A variety of accommodation types are available to suit all budgets: a night in an eight-bed dorm room costs $28 (£11), twin rooms cost $39 per person per night (£16) and single rooms cost $55 per night (£23).

HOTELS, MOTELS & APARTMENTS

LOW-RANGE: < $100 (£42)

HOTEL FORMULE 1 KING CROSS (pp198-199)
$79 (£33)
191-201 Williams St, Kings Cross
(02) 9326 0300 Reservations via email:
H5675-RE@accor.com formule1.com.au

Hotel Formule 1 Kings Cross is a well-priced hotel within walking distance of many of Sydney's top attractions like the Opera House, Royal Botanic Gardens and Pitt St Mall - the SCG is also accessible on foot (2km). Rooms at Hotel Formule 1 are clean and comfortable and feature good standard facilities such as ensuite bathroom and TV. All rooms start at $79 per person per night (£33).

MACQUARIE BOUTIQUE HOTEL SYDNEY (pp198-199)
$88-$155 (£36-£64)
42 Wentworth Ave, Sydney **1800 998 962**
(free call within Australia) OR **(02) 8262 8344**
Reservations via email: stay@macquariehotel.com
macquariehotel.com

The heritage-listed **Macquarie Boutique Hotel Sydney** provides exceptional budget accommodation in a prime location just minutes from Hyde Park, Sydney Tower and the SCG (2km). The Macquarie offers an extensive range of services and is a popular local pub containing two bars and a restaurant. The Macquarie's charming rooms have air-conditioning, ensuite, fridge, TV and internet access. Single rooms cost $88 per night (£36), doubles/twins $110 (£46) and triple rooms $155 (£64).

PARK LODGE HOTEL (pp200)
$82-$198 (£34-£82)
747 South Dowling St, Moore Park
(02) 9318 2393 Reservations via email:
reservations@parklodgehotel.com
parklodgehotel.com

The **Park Lodge** is a quaint boutique hotel in close walking distance to the SGC (1km), with Fox Studios, China Town and the Paddington Markets also nearby. Constructed in 1880, the Park Lodge recently underwent a major refurbishment, which has revived its beautiful

continued overpage...

ACCOMMODATION
...continued from page 183.

Victorian architecture. Facilities reflect the upgrade, including 24-hour reception, laundry, a dry cleaning service, internet and an attractive courtyard to relax in. Economy rooms start at $82 per night (£34), queen ensuites $121 (£50), king superior ensuites $154 (£64), while studio suites start at $198 per night (£82).

SYDNEY CENTRAL ON WENTWORTH (pp198-199)
$59-$159 (£24-£66)
75 Wentworth Ave, Sydney
(02) 9212 1005 Reservations via email: info@sydneycentralonwentworth.com.au
sydneycentralonwentworth.com.au

Sydney Central on Wentworth offers affordable budget accommodation in a fantastic location. It's within comfortable walking distance of most of Sydney's main attractions like Darling Harbour, Pitt St Mall and the Harbour Bridge. The hotel's central location also makes it within easy reach of the SCG, which is only 2.5km away. The complex offers good quality facilities including 24-hour reception, kitchen, free internet and coin-operated laundry. Standard budget rooms contain a fridge and shared bathroom facilities, with single rooms starting at $59 per night (£24). Deluxe rooms contain ensuite, air-conditioning, TV and fridge, with family rooms starting at $159 a night (£66).

THE WOOL BROKERS HOTEL AT DARLING HARBOUR (pp198-199)
$66-$160 (£27-£66)
22 Allen St, Pyrmont
(02) 9552 4773 Reservations via email: woolbrokers@ozemail.com.au
members.ozemail.com.au/~woolbrokers/intro.htm

The Wool Brokers at Darling Harbour is a bed-and-breakfast hotel housed in a heritage-listed building that dates back to 1886. The Wool Brokers is just minutes from the restaurants of Cockle Bay, while the SCG is 4km away. It provides comfortable and clean budget accommodation. Single rooms cost $66 per night (£27), double/twin rooms $89 (£37), triple rooms $125 (£50) and quad rooms $160 (£66).

Y HOTEL SYDNEY (pp198-199)
$35-$175 (£14-£73)
5-11 Wentworth Ave, Sydney
1800 994 994 (free call within Australia) OR **(02) 9264 2451** Reservations via email: enquiry@yhotel.com.au
yhotel.com.au

Part of the YMCA chain of hotels, **Y Hotel Sydney** is a centrally located budget hotel adjacent beautiful Hyde Park, close to many of the city's main attractions such as Sydney Tower and Pitt St Mall. The SCG is also within walking distance (2km). Y Hotel Sydney has good hotel amenities including a reception, lounge, café and laundry. Rooms at the Y also contain internet access, ensuite, fridge, TV and phone. Traditional rooms come in a variety of sizes - singles cost $75 per night (£31), doubles $90 (£37), twin/kings $99 (£41) and

triples $110 (£46). Deluxe, studio and corporate style rooms are also available.

HOTELS, MOTELS & APARTMENTS

MID-RANGE: $100-$200 (£42-£84)

BONDI SERVICED APARTMENTS (pp201)
$105-$120 (£43-£79)
212 Bondi Rd, Bondi **1300 364 200** (free call within Australia) OR **(02) 8837 8000** Reservations via email: bondi@waldorf.com.au
bondi-servicedapartments.com.au

Bondi Serviced Apartments are within easy reach of Bondi Beach, while the SCG is located just 4km away (a five-minute taxi ride). The apartments feature a fully-equipped kitchen, separate dining area, air-conditioning, fridge, electric stove and TV. The apartments are also serviced weekly and have 24-hour reception, roof-top pool, and a caretaker. Budget studios start from $105 per day (£43) while standard studios start at $120 per day (£50).

DIVE HOTEL (pp198-199)
$180 (£75)
234 Arden St, Coogee
(02) 9665 5538
divehotel.com.au

Dive Hotel is a charming boutique hotel in the popular seaside suburb of Coogee. If you fancy walking into the city, you can take a leisurely stroll through the lovely Centennial Parklands. The SCG is only 5km away - just a five-minute taxi ride. Dive contains lavish rooms (some with superb ocean views) with contemporary fittings, each with a modern bathroom, self-contained kitchenette, fridge, microwave, TV and DVD player. Dive is great value given its fantastic location, with standard rooms costing $180 per night (£75).

THE MACLEAY SERVICED APARTMENT HOTEL (pp198-199)
$160-$180 (£66-£75)
28 Macleay St, Potts Point
1800 357 775 (free call within Australia) OR (02) 9357 7755
Reservations via email:
reservations@macleay-hotel.com.au
themacleay.com

The **Macleay Serviced Apartment Hotel** offers excellent hotel and apartment-style accommodation in scenic Potts Point. It's just a short walk to the Royal Botanic Gardens, the Opera House and the shops of Pitt St Mall. The SCG is also easily accessible (3km). The hotel provides first-rate facilities, including 24-hour reception, tour desk, pool, barbecue, internet and guest laundry. It also supplies room service on request. Rooms are well-equipped with kitchenette, fridge, air-conditioning, TV and ensuite. Standard studio rooms cost $160 per night (£66), while harbour/city view apartments cost $180 (£75).

THE RUSSELL HOTEL (pp196-197)
$140-$280 (£58-£116)
143a George St, The Rocks
(02) 9241 3543
Reservations via email:
info@therussell.com.au
therussell.com.au

In Sydney's oldest precinct you'll find **The Russell Hotel** - an elegant reminder of the 19th century. Its fantastic location puts all harbour attractions within easy reach, such as the Opera House and the Sydney Harbour Bridge. The SCG is also only 4.5km away. The Russell is home to one of the city's oldest licensed pubs, the Fortune of War Hotel, and Acacia restaurant which offers a great modern Australian menu. There's also a roof-top garden overlooking Circular Quay. Rooms at the Russell feature antique-style furnishings and are well-priced given their location. Standard rooms with shared bathroom cost $140 per night (£58), standard rooms with ensuite $235 (£98), deluxe rooms with ensuite $270 (£112) and suites $280 (£116).

SULLIVANS HOTEL SYDNEY (pp198-199)
$145-$225 (£60-£93)
21 Oxford St, Paddington
(02) 9361 0211
Reservations via email:
sydney@sullivans.com.au
sullivans.com.au

Sullivans Hotel Sydney is located in the lovely inner-city suburb of Paddington, close to many premier tourist attractions. From the hotel, you can walk to beautiful Centennial Park for a spot of rollerblading or horse riding, while the SCG is only 1km away. The hotel contains excellent facilities, including gym, pool, laundry, 24-hour reception, internet access, travel desk, luggage store and a quiet garden courtyard. Rooms are air-conditioned and contain ensuite bathroom and TV. Standard

single/queen/twin rooms cost $145 per night (£60), while garden single/queen/twin rooms cost $160 (£66). Interconnecting family rooms are also available for $225 (£93).

TRAVELODGE MANLY WARRINGAH
$159-$186 (£66-£79)
4-10 Victor Rd, Brookvale
1300 886 886 (free call within Australia) OR (02) 8978 1200
travelodge.com.au

Travelodge Manly Warringah is situated in sun-drenched Manly, just a 30-minute ferry ride from Circular Quay and the Sydney CBD. The hotel is close to the restaurants and cafés of The Corso, which links harbourside Manly with the beach. Expect good quality amenities at the Travelodge Manly Warringah. Each room has ensuite bathroom, kitchenette with microwave, satellite TV and air-conditioning. Rates are reasonable too: standard queen/twins cost $159 per night (£66) - or $186 (£79) if you want breakfast.

HOTELS, MOTELS & APARTMENTS

HIGH-RANGE: $200+ (£84+)

CROWNE PLAZA COOGEE BEACH
$255-$315 (£106-£131)
242 Arden St, Coogee
1800 000 867 (free call within Australia) OR (02) 9315 7600
crowneplaza.com.au

The **Crowne Plaza Coogee Beach** is located in an idyllic

continued overpage...

ACCOMMODATION
...continued from page 185.

seaside setting, just minutes from Sydney's CBD and about 5km from the SCG. The Crowne Plaza provides lavish resort-style accommodation, offering 24-hour reception, seven restaurants, a bar, internet access, pool and travel desk. Guest rooms and suites feature high quality amenities, including fully-equipped kitchen, laundry, air-conditioning, fridge, mini bar and TV with satellite. Village view rooms cost $255 per night (£106), ocean and beach view rooms with balcony cost $295 (£123), while ocean and beach view suites with balcony cost $315 (£131).

INTERCONTINENTAL SYDNEY
(pp196-197)
$465-$990 (£194-£412)
117 Macquarie St, Sydney
(02) 9253 9000
Reservations via email:
sydney@interconti.com
sydney.intercontinental.com

Inhabiting Sydney's heritage-listed Treasury Building, the luxurious **InterContinental Sydney** is in a prime location adjacent to the Royal Botanic Gardens, with the Harbour Bridge and Opera House nearby. You'll also find the SCG within close range (3.5km). The InterContinental has first-class hotel facilities, including 24-hour reception, restaurant, lounge bar, internet access, gym, sauna, pool and a laundry. Internet access, a personal safe, air-conditioning, separate bathroom with shower and bathtub, bathrobes, mini bar

and complimentary newspaper are provided for each room. City view rooms cost $465 per night (£194), bridge view rooms $535 (£223) and executive suites $990 (£412).

MEDINA ON CROWN EXECUTIVE (pp198-199)
$350-$490 (£146-£204)
359 Crown St, Surry Hills
1300 633 462 (free call within Australia) OR **(02) 8302 1000**
Reservations via email:
moce@medina.com.au
medinaapartments.com.au

The **Medina on Crown** offers high quality one and two-bedroom apartments. Located on busy Crown St, an emerging restaurant and pub hotspot, the Medina on Crown is within easy walking distance to the SCG (1km). It contains top-class facilities including 24-hour reception, pool, spa, sauna, gym and three restaurants. The apartments are fitted with modern fixtures and contain air-conditioning, fully-equipped kitchen, laundry, lounge and dining areas, a safe, TV, video and stereo system. A one-bedroom apartment with a view of Crown St (1-2 people) costs $350 per night (£146), while a two-bedroom variant (2-4 people) costs $450 (£187). One-bedroom apartments with a city view (1-2 people) are $390 per night (£162), while two-bedroom city view apartments (2-4 people) cost $490 (£204).

RADISSON HOTEL & SUITES SYDNEY (pp198-199)
$309-$459 (£129-£191)
72 Liverpool St, Darling Harbour
1800 333 333 (free call within Australia) OR **(02) 8268 8888**

The Russell Hotel in The Rocks.

Reservations via email:
reservations@radisson-sydney.com.au
radisson.com

Radisson Hotel & Suites Sydney offers all the luxury of a premier hotel with the charm of boutique-style accommodation. Located in the heart of the city, you'll find it only minutes from gorgeous Darling Harbour and the restaurants of Cockle Bay, Haymarket and China Town. It's also just a short journey to the SCG (3km). The Radisson provides excellent facilities such as a gym, indoor pool, spa, sauna, 24-hour reception, restaurant and cocktail bar. Rooms and suites are fitted with air-conditioning, safe, TV with satellite, broadband internet access and bathroom. Studio guest rooms start at $309 per night (£129), one-bedroom suites $329 (£137) and two-bedroom suites $459 (£191).

SHANGRI-LA HOTEL (pp196-197)
$550-$1250 (£229-£521)
176 Cumberland St, The Rocks
(02) 9250 6000
Reservations via email:
slsn@shangri-la.com
shangri-la.com

The **Shangri-La Hotel** is one of Sydney's finest luxury hotels and is located in The Rocks district - only minutes from the Opera House and Sydney Harbour Bridge. The SCG can also be reached on foot for the energetic (4km). The hotel offers 24-hour reception, express check-in/check-out, beauty salon, florist, gift shop, travel desk, laundry, valet and several award-winning restaurants and bars. All guest rooms possess amazing harbour views and incorporate the finest amenities, including private bathroom, air-conditioning, broadband internet access, fridge, mini bar, safe and satellite TV. King/twin rooms cost $550 a night (£229) for views of Darling Harbour or $600 (£250) for views of the Opera House. Or really splash out and book the opulent Grand Harbour Suite for $1250 a night (£521).

SWISS-GRAND RESORT & SPA BONDI BEACH (pp201)
$350-$1800 (£145-£750)
Cnr Campbell Pde/Beach Rd, Bondi Beach **1800 655 252** (free call within Australia) OR
(02) 9365 5666
swissgrand.com.au

Swiss-Grand Resort & Spa Bondi Beach overlooks the water and is close to the many cafés, restaurants and bars on the seafront. It is also only 5km from the SCG. The complex features superb facilities including 24-hour reception, laundry, heated swimming pool, sauna, spa, gym, bar and restaurants. Suites contain high quality amenities including air-conditioning, bathroom, safe, mini bar and internet access. Deluxe suites cost $350 per night (£145), executive suites $500 (£208) and executive ocean view spa suites $550 (£229), while the grand suite costs $1800 a night (£750).

SIR STAMFORD AT CIRCULAR QUAY (pp196-197)
$300-$1350 (£125-£562)
93 Macquarie St, Sydney
(02) 9252 4600
Reservations via email:
sales@sscq.stamford.com.au
stamford.com.au

Sir Stamford at Circular Quay is an award-winning luxury hotel that provides spectacular views of the harbour and the city skyline. Located next to the Royal Botanic Gardens and only metres from the Opera House, it is also within close proximity (3.5km) of the SCG. The hotel occupies a heritage-listed building and boasts 18th century antique furnishings and an impressive private collection of artwork. Amenities are excellent, including 24-hour reception, restaurant, four function rooms, lounge bar, gym, heated pool, sundeck and sauna. Rooms are elegant and contain balcony, bathroom, broadband internet access, TV with satellite, mini bar and safe. Superior city view rooms start at $300 per night (£125), deluxe harbour view rooms from $580 (£242) and executive suites from $1350 (£562).

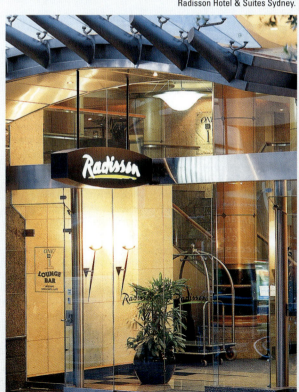

Radisson Hotel & Suites Sydney.

Alfresco dining at The Australian Hotel. Photo: Tourism New South Wales.

SYDNEY -RESTAURANTS

EAST
OF THE SCG

> Overlooking stunning Bondi Beach is the stylish and sophisticated Iceberg's Dining Room & Bar. To accompany the breathtaking view is the equally superb Mediterranean and Italian-inspired cuisine, served fresh by friendly staff in the dining room. If you're limited for time, enjoy oysters with friends in Iceberg's chic bar area, or if you're looking for the perfect wine to complement your meal, you'll be overwhelmed by choice from a list that features selections from premier wine regions across Australia and indeed the world.
1 Notts Ave, Bondi Beach
(pp201) **(02) 9365 2000**
Mains $38-$42 (£15-£17)

NORTH
OF THE SCG

> If you get a chance to visit lovely Balmoral Beach for the day, drop into The Bathers' Pavilion for a divine meal with an ocean view. What was once a beach changing shed for Balmoral bathers in the 1920s is now an award-winning restaurant. This place is certainly deserving of the accolades it has received with such a high quality menu on offer. All dishes are original - like the roast venison with sautéed mushroom and baby parsnip, pomme purée and porcini sauce - with Quebec-born chef Serge Dansereau making a name for himself with his European-inspired cuisine.
4 The Esplanade, Balmoral
(02) 9969 5050
Mains $60 (£25)

> Combine spectacular views of Sydney Harbour with an outstanding a la carte menu and you have Café Sydney. The modern Australian cuisine, with an emphasis on seafood, is a delight to the palate. The restaurant also includes a wood-fired grill, and for those craving Asian or Indian flavours, the kitchen features an authentic wok and Indian tandoor oven. If you're with friends and have enough room after the ample mains, the desserts platter will certainly tempt you. Excellent wines and cocktails are also available.
Fifth Floor, Customs House, 31 Alfred St, Circular Quay
(pp196-197) **(02) 9251 8683**
Mains $24-$135 (£10-£56)

So the Ashes action has finished for the day and you're not sure where to go for some quality food with a great backdrop? Try the Longrain Asian restaurant, only 2km from the SCG. The Longrain is housed in a converted warehouse, giving it a smart, modern feel and providing ample room for diners. The Thai-inspired menu is inventive and extensive so you'll have plenty of delicious dishes to choose from. Enjoy a drink in the stylish lounge bar before hopping into a fantastic main like the salt and pepper baby barramundi or the caramelised pork hock with chilli vinegar and deep fried eschalots.
85 Commonwealth St, Surry Hills
(pp198-199) **(02) 9280 2888**
Mains $18-$40 (£7-£16)

Spanish Terrazas Restaurant is the place to dine if you crave excellent Spanish and Mediterranean-inspired food. You'll find this gem in Sydney's lively Spanish Quarter. At Terrazas, enjoy a sublime assortment of well-priced Tapas including calamari, meatballs and Terrazas chicken (a specialty), followed by tantalising mains like the traditional seafood paella. If you visit on a Thursday night you'll be treated to a flamenco show, live on stage, while on Friday and Saturday nights, groove away to hot Latin American beats.
541 Kent St, Sydney
(pp198-199) **(02) 9283 3046**
Mains $20-$60 (£8-£25)

If you're spending time in The Rocks, the oldest district in Sydney, and fancy stopping off for some excellent Japanese cuisine, head into The Rocks Teppanyaki. Located next to the luxurious Shangri-La Hotel, The Rocks Teppanyaki exudes the same style and sophistication. Enjoy a pre-dinner drink in the restaurant's comfortable lounge, and then indulge in the great range of dishes available on the a la carte or set menu. You'll find everything from sashimi to beef sirloin cooked fresh on the teppanyaki grill!
176 Cumberland St, The Rocks
(pp196-197) **(02) 9250 6020**
Mains $26-$120 (£10-£50)

continued overpage...

Café on Bondi Beach. Photo: Tourism New South Wales.

[RESTAURANTS
...continued from page 189.

Want to escape to exotic Africa for the evening? Catch the ferry to Manly where you can experience a slice of spicy Morocco at Out of Africa. Out of Africa is a hit with locals and visitors alike, who come for the ever-popular Moroccan meatballs tajine. Of course, the fantastic atmosphere is also a major drawcard, with patrons spilling in from the bustling Manly Esplanade. And if you visit on a Thursday or Sunday night, you will be treated to some traditional African beats from live bands.
43-45 East Esplanade, Manly
(pp202) **(02) 9977 0055**
Mains $20-$30 (£8-£12)

Sydney's most well-know Italian restaurant is Machiavelli, an institution that continues to attract politicians, celebrities and devoted locals. As soon as you sample the superb traditional cuisine from the extensive menu, you'll see why it has earned such iconic status. Patrons warmly appreciate the exquisite antipasto selection, fresh salads and large range of pasta dishes. And the service by the experienced and friendly waiters is second-to-none.
123 Clarence St, Sydney
(pp198-199) **(02) 9299 3748**
Mains $24-$40 (£10-£16)

[Groove away to hot Latin American beats at the Spanish Terrazas Restaurant.]

Pre-dinner cocktails in Darling Harbour. Photo: Tourism New South Wales.

www.ashes06.com

Lunch at The Rocks. Photo: Tourism New South Wales.

WEST
OF THE SCG

One of Sydney's favourite dining and entertainment precincts is pretty Cockle Bay on the water's edge of beautiful Darling Harbour. On the Roof Terrace of Cockle Bay Wharf is what looks like a Malaysian temple, but it is in fact the superb Chinta Ria restaurant. The venue's trademark grinning Buddha is on hand to welcome you as you arrive, and you'll find yourself smiling too when you taste the mouth-watering Malaysian cuisine. To keep the atmosphere lively, the restaurant also features DJs every night.
Cockle Bay Wharf, Darling Harbour
(pp198-199) **(02) 9264 3211**
Mains $12-$30 (£5-£12)

Just a few minutes walk from scenic Cockle Bay is the restaurant haven of King St Wharf. Here you'll find Sydney's premier steakhouse, Kingsleys. This excellent eatery has a reputation for high quality food and service, and you'll see why when you sample the perfectly cooked steaks. The restaurant also caters for non-beef-eaters with worthy alternatives like oysters and barramundi. Boasting an extensive wine list from some of Australia's favourite regions, Kingsleys also has an impressive selection of local and imported beers to choose from. There is also a lovely terrace for diners to enjoy their meals while overlooking picturesque Darling Harbour.
17 Lime St, King St Wharf
(pp196-199) **(02) 9279 2225**
Mains $29-$40 (£12-£16)

[One of Sydney's favourite dining and entertainment precincts is pretty Cockle Bay on the water's edge of beautiful Darling Harbour.]

SYDNEY PUBS & CLUBS

The Australian Hotel. Photo: Tourism New South Wales.

PUBS

EAST
OF THE SCG

The massive Hotel Bondi is located in Sydney's most popular and famous beach destination. This sprawling hotel features five different bar areas, a nightclub, restaurant, café and good quality budget accommodation. If you're after a relaxed drink with gorgeous views of the beach, pop in during the day, but if you want to party into the wee hours with a huge crowd of young revellers, wait until after dark and you won't be disappointed.
**178 Campbell Pde,
Bondi Beach**
(pp143) **(02) 9130 3271**

The next best thing to seeing the Ashes live at the SCG is heading into the Light Brigade Hotel on bustling Oxford St, just a few minutes walk from the ground. Recently renovated, the Light Brigade has a range of separate bar areas, including a relaxed front bar, a more refined rear bar area, a plush upstairs lounge bar with comfy lounges and a fantastic brasserie: you'll have no problem finding everything you want and need in a top quality Aussie pub! Of course, if you simply want to watch all the great Ashes action with a cold beer in hand, grab a stool in front of the huge plasma screens.
2a Oxford St, Woollahra
(pp200) **(02) 9331 2930**

NORTH
OF THE SCG

In the historic Rocks district, you'll find a grand Edwardian building which houses one of Sydney's favourite pubs, The Australian Hotel. The Australian certainly lives up to its reputation with its delicious Mediterranean-inspired modern Australian cuisine (the gourmet pizzas are a must!) served fresh in the hotel's brasserie. The Australian also offers inexpensive boutique bed-and-breakfast style accommodation. Rooms are comfortable and you'll receive a complimentary continental breakfast. Be sure to visit the hotel's roof terrace so you can enjoy stunning views of the harbour. Rooms start at $125 per night (£52).
**100 Cumberland St,
The Rocks**
(pp196-197) **(02) 9247 2229**

If you'd like to see some breathtaking views of Sydney Harbour followed by a genuine Bavarian brew, board the Manly ferry from Circular Quay, disembark at Manly Wharf and drop into the popular Bavarian Bier Café. This excellent establishment offers the finest traditional Bavarian favourites such as Spaten Munchen and

the Lowenbrau range - you can even get a non-alcoholic beer! The Bavarian's beer garden is ideal for a session in the afternoon sun.
Shops 2-5 Manly Wharf, Manly
(pp202) **(02) 9977 8088**

Stunning Darling Harbour is a must-see while you're in Sydney, with its great variety of restaurants, cafés, pubs and bars overlooking the water sure to impress. One of the best drinking holes in the area is the ultra-modern Cargo Bar, a fantastic addition to the local scene. When you arrive be sure to head upstairs for some of the most spectacular views of the harbour. Cargo offers excellent local and imported beer and top-shelf spirits, but if wine is your pleasure, the venue has an extensive range from some of the best vineyards in Australia. Cargo also offers a wonderful array of meals from its a la carte menu, with the gourmet pizzas a favourite with regulars.
52-60 The Promenade, King St Wharf, Darling Harbour
(pp198-199) **(02) 9262 1777**

Recent refurbishments have made Cruise Bar & Lounge one of the most stylish and popular venues in Sydney. On the first floor, you'll find the sleek Cruise Bar where you can sample luscious cocktails mixed by welcoming bar staff or select a meal from the excellent European-inspired menu. On the second floor is the Cruise Lounge overlooking Circular Quay, the perfect spot to unwind with friends over a glass of wine, while the top floor houses the well-priced Cru Restaurant where you can indulge in high quality French cuisine. Cruise offers fantastic entertainment every night of the week and features great DJs on the weekend.
Overseas Passenger Terminal, West Circular Quay, The Rocks
(pp196-197) **(02) 9251 1188**

While you're visiting The Rocks - Sydney's historic birthplace - pop into the Lord Nelson, one of the city's oldest licensed hotels.

continued overpage...

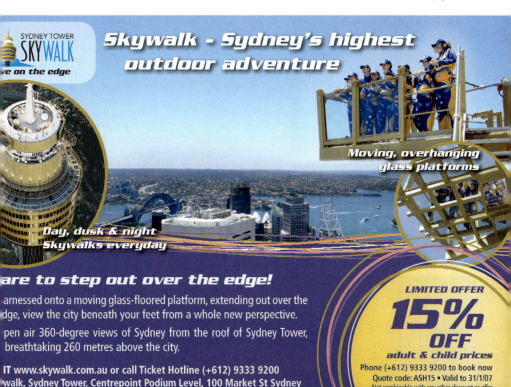

[PUBS AND CLUBS

...continued from page 193.

Arguably Sydney's best British-style pub, the Lord Nelson delights patrons with its rich history and impressive architecture. Along with an extensive range of local and imported beers, the hotel offers a fine range of ales brewed on-site in the hotel's microbrewery. On the first floor, you'll find the brasserie where you can enjoy some lovely French-inspired dishes. The Lord Nelson also offers accommodation with modern and comfortable suites. Rooms with shared bathroom start at $120 per night (£50), while rooms with ensuite cost $180 per night (£75).
19 Kent St, The Rocks
(pp196-197) **(02) 9251 4044**

Australia has embraced the Irish pub theme and there is none more popular in Sydney than the Mercantile in The Rocks, which boasts views of the Sydney Harbour Bridge. The Mercantile has a distinctly authentic Irish feel, with a cosy little bar where you can chat away with friends for hours. Pop into the main bar any night of the week and you'll see the place buzzing with the rapturous sounds of happy local and global revellers, singing, chatting and enjoying pints of Guinness.
25 George St, The Rocks
(pp196-197) **(02) 9247 3570**

The Oaks Hotel is one of North Shore's hottest pubs - a favourite with both locals and visitors alike. Inside, the hotel features four bars and two restaurants, so you're assured to find the right atmosphere to suit you.
In summer, most patrons relax under the hotel's famous oak tree in the impressive beer garden, where you can not only indulge in a pint or two, but where you can also cook your own meat or seafood on the char-grill.
118 Military Rd, Neutral Bay
(02) 9953 5515

The Olympic Hotel in Paddington is just a few minutes walk from the SCG and is a favourite spot with locals who go to enjoy a post-match beverage. Once inside you'll see why it's so popular - the hotel boasts an award-winning bistro that serves up fantastic Italian cuisine and an excellent, recently renovated lounge and cocktail bar where you can catch the Ashes on an enormous wide-screen. The Olympic also provides good quality budget accommodation, with guest rooms starting at $75 per night (£31).
308 Moore Park Rd, Paddington
(pp200) **(02) 9361 6515**

No visit to Sydney is complete without doing the mandatory pub crawl down thriving Oxford St - Sydney's foremost pub, restaurant and shopping strip! Be sure to pop into the Paddington Inn Hotel along the way, an award-winning pub offering two distinct bar areas and a nice little bistro. The front bar is the place to enjoy a pint while you play a game of pool or watch the Oxford St pedestrian traffic, while the rear bar is a cosy place to unwind with friends, doubling as an inviting dining area.
338 Oxford St, Paddington
(pp200) **(02) 9380 5913**

If you visit Sydney Opera House, Australia's most famous landmark, consider dropping into the popular Opera Bar located on the lower concourse level. Featuring a fantastic beer garden and amazing views of the harbour, the Opera Bar offers 40 wines by the glass, an excellent cocktail menu and a great range of local and imported beers.
You can also sample delicious Italian-inspired cuisine from the bistro. The Opera Bar has live jazz and funk music throughout the week.
Lower Concourse Level,
Sydney Opera House
(pp196-197) **(02) 9247 1666**

Photo: Tourism New South Wales.

www.ashes06.com

SOUTH
OF THE SCG

One of Sydney's most popular tourist areas is the tranquil beachside suburb of Coogee. You'll find it only a few kilometres from the city centre, so it's perfect for a day trip. While you're there, it's worth checking out the Coogee Bay Hotel - a sprawling entertainment complex that contains six bars (the sports bar has one of the largest TV screens in the world!), a great beer garden and huge nightclub.

There's also a brasserie for lunch and dinner (try the seafood platter!), as well as luxury boutique rooms for overnighters, with prices starting from $155 per night (£64).
**Coogee Bay Rd, Coogee
(02) 9665 0000**

CLUBS

NORTH
OF THE SCG

Want to escape the usual hot, sweaty and overcrowded nightclub scene? Then Sydney's Minus5 bar is a very cool alternative. True to its name, this little gem is kept at a constant temperature of -5°C to ensure the hand-crafted ice interiors don't become a raging torrent! Sounds a bit too chilly for you? Don't worry, all guests are provided with warm, fluffy coats, gloves and boots. Once inside, management give you 30 minutes to admire the sculptures and marvel at the friendly bar staff smashing your glass when you've finished your vodka. It seems a bit quick, but any longer and hypothermia could set in. $30 (£12.50) covers entry into this sub-zero wonderland and a drink from the icy bar.
2 Opera Quays, Circular Quay
(pp196-197) **(02) 9251 0311**

If you've finished your pub crawl along buzzing Oxford St but are still looking to party into the early hours, head for DMC, voted the best club in the Southern Hemisphere by *Harper's Bazaar*. DMC offers three bars, two chill-out rooms and plenty of dance space, with resident and interstate guest DJs playing pulsating house music late into the night.
**33 Oxford St, Darlinghurst
(Map ?) (02) 9267 7036**

The Slip Inn is a huge multi-purpose entertainment complex overlooking stunning Darling Harbour. Boasting two stylish bars, two nightclubs and a delightful courtyard, you'll be able to find the right atmosphere to suit your mood. Try the sultry Sand Bar if you want intimate surroundings and a chilled-out atmosphere, or if you fancy a game of pool or a pint with some mates, grab a stool in the Slip Bar. You'll find a great party atmosphere in the Garden Bar (a huge courtyard that seats over 400 patrons), the Chinese Laundry is a cool club, while the Cave Nightclub has a distinctive sandstone interior that will have you second-guessing whether you're actually underground! Locals say this is where Prince Frederick of Denmark met his Tasmanian wife Mary Donaldson.
111 Sussex St, Sydney
(pp198-199) **(02) 8295 9911**

Kings Cross is Sydney's red-light district but don't let its seedy reputation put you off visiting. "The Cross" is home to some of the city's best clubs and they don't come much better that Sugareef. Not only does Sugareef attract a young, trendy crowd and a plethora of celebrities, you'll also find it welcomes a swag of high calibre local and international DJs. Sugareef pumps Thursdays to Saturdays from 9pm until late; admission costs around $10 (£4).
**20 Bayswater Rd,
Kings Cross**
(pp198-199) **(02) 9380 9326**

Cave Nightclub. Photo: Tourism New South Wales.

SYDNEY CITY MAP

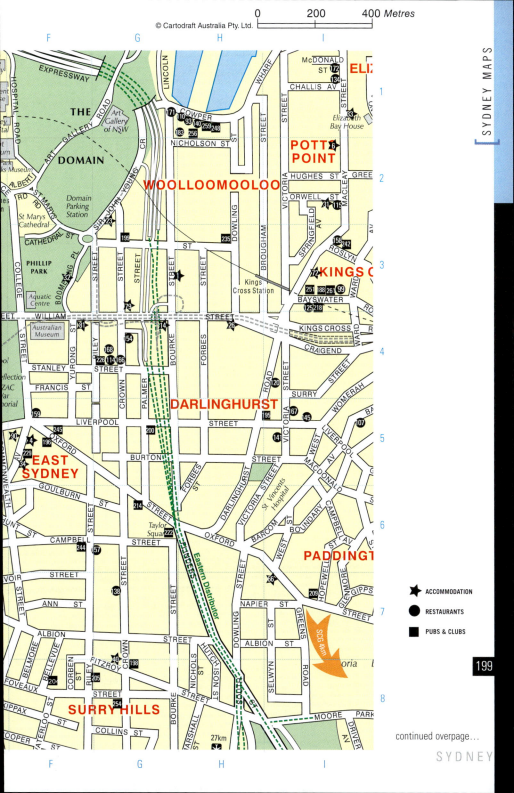

SCG MAP

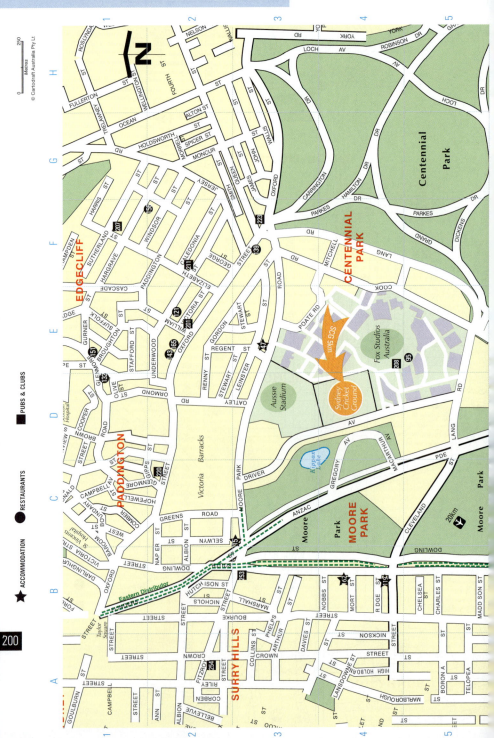

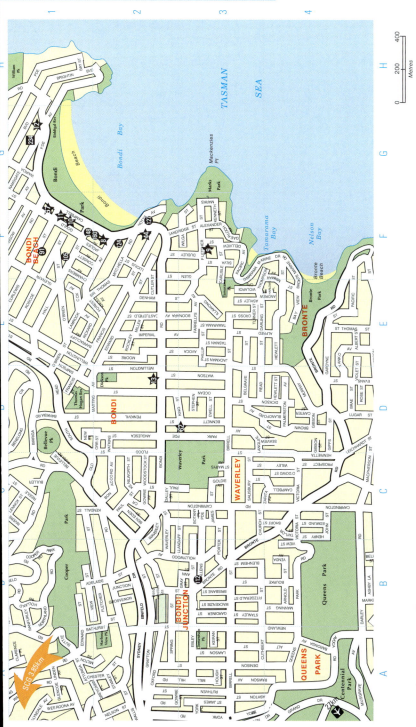

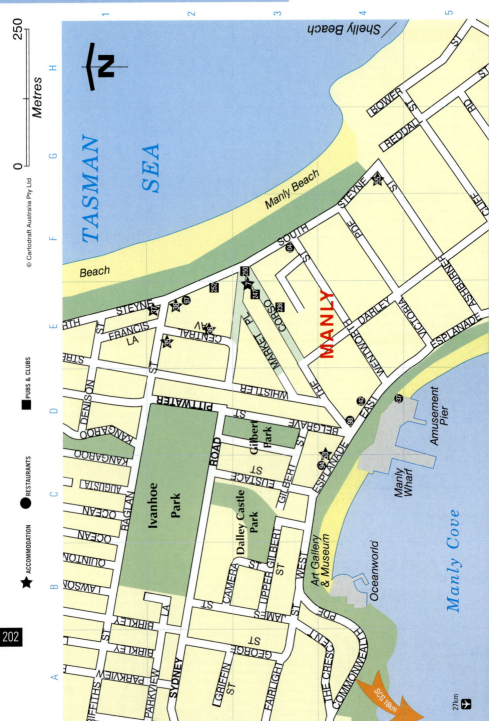

SYDNEY CITY MAP (pp196-202)

ACCOMMODATION KEY

■ Denotes multiple venue
★ Denotes multiple venue

#	Map	Ref	Name	Address	Phone	Website	$ Cost per night	RATE Star rating	OVAL Kilometres from SCG
1	198-199	G3	Australian Backpackers	132 Bourke St, Woolloomooloo, 2011	02 9331 0822	www.australianbackpackers.com.au	21-70		2.93
2	198-199	D5	Avillion Hotel Sydney	389 Pitt St, Sydney, 2000	02 8268 1888	www.avillion.com.au	440-1000	*****	4.09
3	198-199	C4	Base Backpackers	477 Kent St, Sydney, 2000	02 9267 7718	www.basebackpackers.com	28-95		4.48
4	198-199	F5	Best Western Hotel Stellar	4 Wentworth Ave, Surry Hills, 2010	02 9264 9754	www.hotelstellar.com	140-265	****	3.30
5	198-199	E6	Big Hostel	212 Elizabeth St, Surry Hills, 2010	02 9281 6030	www.bighostel.com	27-102		2.84
6	198-199	I2	Blue Parrot	87 Macleay St, Potts Point, 2011	02 3356 4888	www.blueparrot.com.au	25-40		3.87
7	202	E3	Board Rider Backpacker	63 The Corso, Manly, 2095	02 9977 7077	www.boardrider.com.au	24-85	*****	18.26
8	201	F2	Bondi Backpackers	110 Campbell Pde, Bondi Beach, 2026	02 9130 4660	www.bondibackpackers.com.au	22-72		6.51
9	201	F3	Bondi Beachouse YHA	63 Fletcher St, Bondi Beach, 2026	02 9365 2088	www.yha.com.au	28-80		6.24
10	201	F1	Bondi Beachside inn	152 Campbell Pde, Bondi Beach, 2026	02 9130 5311	www.bondiinn.com.au	80-130	***	6.23
11	201	F1	Bondi Hotel	178 Campbell Pde, Bondi Beach, 2026	02 9130 3271	www.hotelbondi.com.au	50-300	***	6.72
12	201	G1	Bondi Sands	252 Campbell Pde, Bondi Beach, 2026	02 9365 3703	www.bondisands.com	25-90		7.90
13	201	D2	Bondi Serviced Apartments	212 201 Rd, Bondi Beach, 2026	02 8837 8000	www.bondi-serviced-apartments.com.au	105-120	***	5.01
14	198-199	G4	Boomerang Backpackers	141 William St, KingsCross, 2010	1800 266 636	www.boomerangbackpackers.com.au	20-55		2.99
15	200	C6	Captain Cook Hotel	162 Flinders St, Paddington, 2021	02 9360 4327	www.thecaptaincookhotel.com.au	18-25		1.93
16	198-199	E7	Citigate Sebel Sydney	28 Albion St, Surry Hills, 2010	02 9213 3820	www.mirvachotels.com.au	175-280	****	2.77
17	198-199	C4	Crowne Plaza	150 Day St, Darling Harbour, 2000	02 9261 1188	www.ichotelsgroup.com	205-825	*****	4.80
18	198-199	D6	Footprints Westend	412 Pitt St, Sydney, 2000	02 9211 4588	www.footprintswestend.com.au	28-85		3.59
19	198-199	C3	Four Points by Sheraton	161 Sussex St, Sydney, 2000	02 9290 4000	www.starwoodhotels.com	495-690	*****	4.62
20	198-199	C5	Four Seasons Hotel Sydney	199 George St, Sydney, 2000	02 9238 0000	www.fourseasonshotel.com	395-4300	*****	5.13
21	198-199	D6	George St Private Hotel	700A George St, Sydney, 2000	02 9211 1800	www.thegeorge.com.au	25-69	***	3.96
22	198-199	A3	Grand Mercure	50 Murray St, Sydney, 2000	02 9563 6666	www.accorhotels.com.au	111-600	*****	6.11
23	198-199	G2	Harbour City Hotel	50 Sir John Young Cr, Woolloomooloo, 2011	02 9380 2922	www.harbourcityhotel.com.au	23-70	***	3.57
24	196-197	C4	Harbour Rocks Hotel	34-52 Harrington St, The Rocks, 2000	02 8220 9999	www.harbourrocks.com.au	240-620	****	5.42
102	198-199	D3	Hilton Sydney	488 George St, Sydney, 2000	02 9266 2000	www.hiltonsydney.com.au	270-500	*****	3.07
25	198-199	E7	HomeBase Backpackers	238 Elizabeth St, Sydney, 2000	1800 444 527	www.hbase.com.au	20-60		3.17
26	198-199	H4	Hotel Formule 1 Kings Cross	191-201 Williams St, Kings Cross, 2010	02 9326 0300	www.formule1.com.au	79		3.15
27	198-199	A3	Hotel Ibis Darling Harbour	70 Murray St, Darling Harbour, 2000	02 9563 0888	www.ibishotels.com.au	149-179	***	5.80
28	198-199	D5	Hotel Ibis World Square	384 Pitt St, Sydney, 2000	02 8267 3111	www.ibishotels.com.au	130-199	****	4.09
29	198-199	E5	Hyde Park Inn	271 Elizabeth St, Sydney, 2000	02 9264 6001	www.hydeparkinn.com.au	140-324	****	3.52
30	196-197	E5	InterContinental Sydney	117 Macquarie St, Sydney, 2000	02 9253 9000	www.sydneyhotels.intercontinental.com	485-4400	*****	4.41
31	198-199	I2	Jolly Swagman Backpackers	27 Orwell St, Kings Cross, 2010	02 9358 6400	www.jollyswagman.com.au	21-60		3.80

continued overpage...

SYDNEY CITY MAP (pp196-202)

■ Denotes multiple venue
★ ACCOMMODATION KEY

#	Map	Ref	Name	Address	Phone	Website	$ Cost per night	RATE Star rating	OVAL Kilometres from SCG
32	198-199	F3	Kia-Ora Sydney Apartments	1 Boomerang Plc, Sydney, 2000	02 9331 5857	www.casinclair.com.au	165-200	★★★★	3.20
33	198-199	I1	Macleay Serviced Apart.	28 Macleay St, Potts Point, 2011	02 9357 7755	www.themacleay.com	160-180	★★★★	4.00
34	198-199	F5	Macquarie Boutique Hotel	42 Wentworth Ave, Sydney, 2000	02 8262 8844	www.macquariehotel.com	88-155	★★★	2.89
35	202	E2	Manly Backpackers	28 Raglan St, Manly, 2095	02 9977 3411	www.manlybackpackers.com.au	22-27	★★★✫	17.92
36	202	E2	Manly Beach Holiday Apart.	22 Central Ave, Manly, 2095	02 9977 2444	www.manlyapartments.com	85-540	★★★✫	17.99
37	202	E2	Manly Pacific Sydney	55 North Steyne, Manly, 2095	02 9977 7666	www.accorhotels.com	209-609	★★★★★	18.17
38	202	E2	Manly Paradise Motel	54 North Steyne, Manly, 2095	02 9977 5799	www.manlyparadise.com	160-400	★★★★	18.17
39	198-199	C4	Medina Grand Sydney	511 Kent St, Sydney, 2000	02 9274 0000	www.medina.com	199-385	★★★★	4.11
40	198-199	G7	Medina on Crown Executive	359 Crown St, Surry Hills, 2010	02 8302 1000	www.medina.com.au	145-345	★★★★	2.20
41	198-199	D4	Meriton Rialto Apartments	329 Pitt St, Sydney, 2000	02 8263 7400	www.meritonapartments.com.au	178-399	★★★★★	4.15
42	198-199	D5	Meriton World Tower	91 Liverpool St, Sydney, 2000	02 8263 7500	www.meritonapartments.com.au	500-700	★★★★★	4.20
43	198-199	D4	Metro Hotel on Pitt	300 Pitt St, Sydney, 2000	02 9283 8088	www.metrohotels.com.au	155-400	★★★★	3.89
44	201	F2	Noah's Bondi Beach	2 Campbell Pde, Bondi Beach, 2026	02 9365 7100	www.noahsbondibeach.com	22-65		6.69
45	198-199	A4	Novotel Sydney	100 Murray St, Sydney, 2000	02 9934 0000	www.accorhotels.com	385-913	★★★★	6.00
46	196-197	C4	Old Sydney Holiday Inn	55 George St, The Rocks, 2000	02 9252 0524	www.ichotelsgroup.com	210-299	★★★★★	6.27
47	200	E3	Olympic Hotel	308 Moore Park Rd, Paddington, 2021	02 9361 6315	www.olympichotel.com.au	75-100		1.74
48	198-199	D7	Pacific International Apart.	653 George St, Sydney, 2000	02 9284 4500	www.pacificinthotels.com	165-415	★★★★	4.18
49	198-199	D7	Pacific International Hotel	717 George St, Sydney, 2000	02 9289 4400	www.pacificinthotels.com	120-155	★★★★	3.63
50	198-199	C3	Pacific International Suites	433 Kent St, Sydney, 2000	02 9289 4422	www.pacificinthotels.com	195-370	★★★★★	4.69
51	196-197	E4	Quay Grand Suites Sydney	61 Macquarie St, Sydney, 2000	02 9256 4000	www.mirvachotels.com.au	470-1500	★★★★★	4.61
52	196-197	C5	Quay West Suites Sydney	98 Gloucester St, The Rocks, 2000	02 9240 6000	www.mirvachotels.com.au	520-1900	★★★★★	5.28
53	202	C4	Quest Grande Esplanade	54A West Esp, Manly, 2095	02 9976 4600	www.questapartments.com.au	209-365	★★★★	17.97
54	198-199	C5	Radisson Hotel & Suites	72 Liverpool St, Darling Harbour, 2000	02 8268 8888	www.radisson.com	309-900	★★★★★	4.85
55	202	G4	Radisson Kestrel Hotel	8 South Steyne, Manly, 2095	02 9977 8866	www.radisson.com	245-495	★★★★	18.86
56	196-197	D7	Radisson Plaza Hotel	27 O'Connell St, Sydney, 2000	02 8214 0000	www.radisson.com	300-395	★★★★★	4.57
57	196-197	C4	Rendezvous Stafford Hotel	75 Harrington St, The Rocks, 2000	02 9251 6711	www.rendezvoushotels.com.au	215-275	★★★★	5.36
58	198-199	C6	Rydges Jamison Sydney	11 Jamison St, Sydney, 2000	02 9696 2500	www.rydges.com	450	★★★★★	5.19
59	198-199	C6	Saville 2 Bond St	Cnr George & Bond St, Sydney, 2000	02 9250 9555	www.savillesuites.com	360	★★★★✫	5.00
60	196-197	B5	Shangri-La Hotel	176 Cumberland St, The Rocks, 2000	02 9250 6000	www.shangri-la.com	550-4900	★★★★★	2.20
61	198-199	E3	Sheraton on the Park	161 Elizabeth St, Sydney, 2000	02 9286 6000	www.starwoodhotels.com	525-3605	★★★★★	4.05
62	201	D3	Sinclairs of Bondi	11 Bennett St, Bondi, 2026	02 9388 9911	www.sinclairsbondi.com	24-88		4.89
63	196-197	E5	Sir Stamford	93 Macquarie St, Sydney, 2000	02 9252 4600	www.stamford.com.au	540-4000	★★★★★	4.50
64	196-197	D7	Sofitel Wentworth Sydney	61 Phillip St, Sydney, 2000	02 9230 0700	www.accorhotels.com	390-546	★★★★★	4.30
65	198-199	C4	Somerset	252 Sussex St, Sydney, 2000	02 8280 5000	www.somersetdarlingharbour.com	320-820	★★★★★	4.36

www.ashes06.com

■ Denotes multiple venue

ACCOMMODATION KEY

$ Cost per night   RATE Star rating   OVAL Kilometres from SCG

#	Map	Ref	Name	Address	Phone	Website	$	RATE	OVAL
66	198-199	I7	Sullivans Hotel Sydney	21 Oxford St, Paddington, 2021	02 9361 0211	www.sullivans.com.au	145-225	****	2.67
67	201	F1	Swiss-Grand Resort & Spa ■	Beach Rd, Bondi Beach, 2026	02 9365 5666	www.swissgrand.com.au	350-1800	*****	5.25
68	198-199	D4	Sydney Backpackers	7 Wilmot St, Sydney, 2000	02 9267 7772	www.sydneybackpackers.com	28-55		4.01
69	198-199	E6	Sydney Central	75 Wentworth Ave, Sydney, 2000	02 9212 0067	www.sydneycentralonwentworth.com.au	59-250	**	3.35
70	196-197	D5	Sydney Harbour Marriott	30 Pitt St, Sydney, 2000	02 9259 7000	www.marriott.com	550-750	*****	4.86
71	198-199	D3	The Castlereagh Boutique	169 Castlereagh St, Sydney, 2000	02 9284 1000	www.thecastlereagh.com.au	153-238	****	3.97
72	198-199	I3	The Globe Backpackers	40 Darlinghurst Rd, Kings Cross, 2010	02 9326 9675	www.globebackpackers.com	22-33		3.13
73	198-199	D2	The Grace Hotel	77 York St, Sydney, 2000	02 9272 6888	www.gracehotel.com.au	300-440	*****	5.00
74	198-199	D6	The Maze Backpackers	417 Pitt St, Sydney, 2000	02 9211 5115	www.mazebackpackers.com	19-60		4.04
75	196-197	C7	The Menzies Sydney	14 Carrington St, Sydney, 2000	02 9299 1000	www.sydneymenzieshotel.com.au	300-450	****	5.19
76	196-197	A5	The Observatory Hotel	89 Kent St, Sydney, 2000	02 9256 2222	www.observatoryhotel.com.au	795-2995	*****	5.87
77	198-199	C5	The Russell Hotel	143a George St, The Rocks, 2000	02 9241 3543	www.therussell.com.au	140-280	***	2.74
78	196-197	C2	The Sebel Pier One Sydney	11 Hickson Rd, Sydney, 2000	02 8298 9999	www.mirvachotels.com.au	290-780	*****	5.68
79	198-199	G3	The Sydney Boulevard	90 William St, Woolloomooloo, 2011	02 9383 7222	www.boulevard.com.au	170	****	3.00
80	198-199	D1	The Westin Sydney	1 Martin Pl, Sydney, 2000	02 8223 1111	www.westin.com.au	325-3500	*****	4.80
81	198-199	F4	The Wood Duck Inn	49 William St, East Sydney, 2010	1800 110 025	www.woodduckinn.com.au	22		3.39
82	198-199	A4	The Wool Brokers Hotel	22 Allen St, Pyrmont, 2009	02 9552 4773	www.members.ozemail.com.au	66-160	*****	4.50
83	196-197	B6	The York Apartment Hotel	5 York St, Sydney, 2000	02 9210 5000	www.theyorkapartments.com.au	220-450		5.26
84	198-199	E2	Travelodge Phillip St	165 Phillip St, Sydney, 2000	02 8224 9400	www.travelodge.com.au	165-225	****	4.43
85	198-199	E5	Travelodge Wentworth	Goulburn St, Sydney, 2000	02 8267 1700	www.travelodge.com.au	169-225	****	3.45
86	196-197	B6	Travelodge Wynyard Sydney	7 York St, Sydney, 2000	02 9274 1222	www.travelodge.com.au	168-298	****	5.26
87	198-199	E6	Trendwest Suites Sydney	33-45 Wentworth Ave, Sydney, 2000	02 9277 3388	www.trendwestsuites.com.au	245-380	****	3.49
88	198-199	E6	Vibe Hotel Goulburn St	111 Goulburn St, Sydney, 2000	02 9282 0987	www.vibehotel.com.au	320-450		3.50
89	198-199	D7	Wake Up! Sydney Central	509 Pitt St, Sydney, 2000	02 9288 7888	www.wakeup.com.au	24-98		3.52
90	198-199	F5	Y Sydney Hotel	5-11 Wentworth Ave, Sydney, 2000	02 9264 2451	www.yhotel.com.au	35-175	****	5.73

continued overpage....

SYDNEY MAPS

SYDNEY CITY MAP (pp196-202)

■ Denotes multiple venue
$ Cost of main meal

RESTAURANTS KEY

#	Map	Ref	Name	Address	Phone	Website	Cuisine	$	BYO
91	201	F1	3 Fat Fish	141 Curlewis St, Bondi Beach, 2026	02 9365 0088		Seafood	9-20	N
92	198-199	D2	360 Bar & Dining Room	100 Market St, Sydney, 2000	02 9235 2188	www.trufflegroup.com.au	European	42	N
93	198-199	H1	Aki's	6 Cowper Wharf Rd, Woolloomooloo, 2011	02 9332 4600	www.akisindian.com.au	Indian	19-33	N
94	200	C4	Alhambra	Shop 1, 54 West Esp, Manly, 2095	02 9976 2975	www.alhambra.citysearch.com.au	Spanish	19-25	Y wine-$3pp corkage
95	200	E5	Arena	Fox Studios, Driver Ave, Moore Park, 2021	02 9361 3930	www.arenabistro.com.au	Modern Australian	25-29	Y wine-$15 corkage
96	196-197	E4	Aria	1 Macquarie St, East Circular Quay, 2000	02 9252 2555	www.ariarestaurant.com	Modern Australian	42-49	N
97	202	E2	Barking Frog	48 North Steyne, Manly, 2095	02 9977 6307		Modern Australian	25	Y wine-$3 corkage
98	202	D4	Bavarian Bier Café Manly	Manly Wharf, East Esp, Manly, 2095	02 9977 8088	www.bavarianbiercafe.com.au	European	20-27	N
99	198-199	I3	Bayswater Brasserie	32 Bayswater Rd, Kings Cross, 2011	02 9357 2177	www.bayswaterbrasserie.com.au	Modern Australian	22-31	N
100	198-199	C5	BBQ King	18 Goulburn St, Sydney, 2000	02 9267 2586		Chinese	15	Y wine-$2pp corkage
101	196-197	B6	Bistro Lilly	168 Kent St, Sydney, 2000	02 9252 1116	www.bistrolilly.com.au	Modern Australian	23-30	Y wine-$5pp corkage
47	200	E3	Bistro Moore	308 Moore Park Rd, Paddington, 2022	02 9361 6315	www.olympichotel.com.au	Italian	20-28	N
103	198-199	B3	Blackbird Café	Harbour St, Darling Harbour, 2000	02 9283 7385	www.blackbirdcafe.com.au	Café	8-19	N
104	202	F3	Blue Water Café	28 South Steyne, Manly, 2095	02 9976 2051		Modern Australian	20	Y wine-$2.20pp corkage
105	201	F1	Bungabar	77 Hall St, Bondi Beach, 2026	02 9300 6766		Varied	9-16	N
106	198-199	B1	Bungalow 8	3 Lime St, Darling Harbour, 2000	02 9299 4770	www.bungalow8sydney.com	Modern/Seafood	18-22	N
107	198-199	I5	Buon Ricordo	108 Boundary St, Paddington, 2022	02 9360 6729	www.buonricordo.com.au	Italian	37-49	N
108	196-197	D5	Café Sydney	31 Alfred St, Sydney, 2000	02 9251 8683	www.cafesydney.com.au	Modern Australian	24-135	N
109	198-199	B2	Cargo Bar	52-60 The Prm, Darling Harbour, 2000	02 9262 1777	www.cargobar.com.au	Pizza	17	N
110	198-199	H1	China Doll	6 Cowper Wharf Rd, Woolloomooloo, 2011	02 9380 6744	www.chinadoll.com.au	Chinese	25-38	N
111	198-199	C3	Chinta Ria	201 Sussex St, Darling Harbour, 2000	02 9264 3211		Malaysian	12-30	Y wine-$6 corkage
112	201	B3	Circa Lounge Bar	2-4 Bronte Rd, Bondi Junction, 2022	02 9389 3288	www.teagardenshotel.com.au	Modern Australian	5-11	N
113	198-199	B3	Coast	Harbour St, Darling Harbour, 2000	02 9267 6700	www.coastrestaurant.com.au	Modern Australian	29-38	N
114	198-199	G4	Divino Restaurant	70 Stanley St, Darlinghurst, 2010	02 9360 9911	www.divino.com.au	Italian	18-26	Y wine-$3pp corkage
115	198-199	I2	Doma Bohemian Café	29 Orwell St, Potts Point, 2011	02 9331 0022		European	12-16	Y wine-$4 corkage
116	196-197	D4	Doyles at the Quay	Circular Quay, Sydney, 2000	02 9252 3400	www.doyles.com.au	Seafood	30	N
117	196-197	C6	est	252 George St, Sydney, 2000	02 9240 3010	www.merivale.com	Modern Australian	42-45	N
118	198-199	B2	Genghis Khan Mongolian King St Wharf, 30a Lime St, Sydney, 2000		02 9290 1818		Asian	17-26	N
102	198-199	D3	Glass Brasserie	488 George St, Sydney, 2000	02 9265 6068	www.glassbrasserie.com.au	French	30-40	N
120	198-199	I4	Govinda's	112 Darlinghurst Rd, Darlinghurst, 2010	02 9380 5155	www.govindas.com.au	Vegetarian	16	Y wine-$1.50pp corkage
121	200	E2	Grand National	161 Underwood St, Paddington, 2022	02 9363 3096		Modern Australian	25-30	N
122	198-199	E6	Harry's Singapore Chilli Crab	Level 1, 198 Elizabeth St, Sydney, 2000	02 9281 5565	www.harryschillicrab.com.au	Asian	12-72	Y wine-$5 corkage
123	196-197	C6	Heritage Belgian Café	129-135 Harrington St, Sydney, 2000	02 9241 1775	www.belgian-beer-cafe.com.au	International	20-27	N
124	201	F2	Hugo's	70 Campbell Pde, Bondi Beach, 2026	02 9300 0900	www.hugos.com.au	Modern Australian	34-38	N

206

www.ashes06.com

RESTAURANTS KEY

● Denotes multiple venue
$ Cost of main meal

#	Map	Ref	Name	Address	Phone	Website	Cuisine	$	BYO
125	198-199	I3	Hugo's Bar Pizza	19 Bayswater Rd, Kings Cross, 2011	02 9332 1227		Italian	20	N
126	198-199	B4	I'm Angus Steak House	The Prm, Darling Harbour, 2000	02 9264 5822	www.nicks-seafood.com.au	Steak/Seafood	25	N
127	201	F2	Icebergs	1 Notts Ave, Bondi Beach, 2026	02 9365 9000		Mediterranean	38-42	N
128	198-199	B2	James Squire Brewhouse	The Prm, Darling Harbour, 2000	02 8270 7999	www.malt-shovel.com.au	Modern Australian	24	N
129	198-199	B1	Kingsley's Prime Steakhouse	17 Lime St, Darling Harbour, 2000	02 9279 2225	www.kingsleyssteak.com.au	Steak	29-40	N
130	196-197	C6	Kingsley's Prime Steakhouse	7 Bridge St, Sydney, 2000	02 9252 7777	www.kingsleysprime.com.au	Steak	32	N
131	198-199	E6	La Sala	23 Foster St, Surry Hills, 2010	02 9281 3352	www.lasala.com.au	Italian	21-39	N
132	200	D1	Local Wine Bar & Rest.	211 Glenmore Rd, Paddington, 2022	02 9332 1577		Varied	22-29	N
133	198-199	E8	Longrain	85 Commonwealth St, Surry Hills, 2010	02 9280 2888	www.longrain.com.au	Asian	18-40	N
134	198-199	I1	Lotus	22 Challis Ave, Potts Point, 2011	02 9326 9000	www.merivale.com	Modern Australian	26	N
135	196-1973	C4	Lowenbrau Keller	12-18 Argyle St, The Rocks, 2000	02 9247 7785	www.lowenbrau.com.au	German	15-28	N
136	198-199	C1	Machiavelli	123 Clarence St, Sydney, 2000	02 9299 3748	www.machiavelli.com.au	Italian	24-40	N
137	202	D4	Manly Wharf Hotel	Manly Wharf, East Esp, Manly, 2095	02 9977 1266	www.manlywharfhotel.com.au	Modern Australian	28-32	N
138	198-199	G7	Marque	355 Crown St, Surry Hills, 2010	02 9332 2225		French	38	Y
139	200	F3	Max Brenner's Chocolate Bar	447 Oxford St, Paddington, 2022	02 9357 5055		Dessert	4-13	N
140	198-199	H1	Nove Cucina	6 Cowper Wharf Rd, Woolloomooloo, 2011	02 9368 7599	www.otto.net.au	Italian	20	N
141	198-199	I5	Oh Calcutta	251 Victoria St, Darlinghurst, 2010	02 9360 3650	www.ohcalcutta.com.au	Indian	17-27	Y wine-$5pp corkage
142	202	D4	Out of Africa	43-45 East Esplanade, Manly, 2095	02 9977 0055	www.outofafrica.com.au	African	20-30	Y wine-$5pp corkage
143	200	E2	Paddington Inn	338 Oxford St, Paddington, 2022	02 9380 5277		Modern Australian	16	N
144	196-197	C3	Pancakes on the Rocks	4 Hickson Rd, The Rocks, 2000	02 9247 6371	www.pancakesontherocks.com.au	Varied	14-15	N
145	198-199	I5	Phamish	354 Liverpool St, Darlinghurst, 2010	02 9357 2688		Vietnamese	12	Y wine-$1pp corkage
146	196-197	C4	Philip's Foote	101 George St, The Rocks, 2000	02 9241 1485	www.phillipsfoote.com.au	Steak	17-25	N
147	196-197	C4	Quay	Circular Quay, The Rocks, 2000	02 9251 5600	www.quay.com.au	Modern Australian	48	N
148	201	F1	Ravesi's	118 Campbell Pde, Bondi Beach, 2026	02 9365 4422	www.ravesis.com.au	Varied	23-30	N
149	198-199	C2	Redoak Boutique Café	201 Clarence St, Sydney, 2000	02 9262 3303	www.redoak.com	Modern Australian	17-29	N
150	196-197	C4	Rockpool	107 George St, The Rocks, 2000	02 9252 1888	www.rockpool.com	Varied	150	N
151	200	E1	Royal Hotel Restaruant	237 Glenmore Rd, Paddington, 2022	02 9331 5055	www.royalhotel.com.au	Modern Australian	24	N
152	198-199	D5	Saap Thai	378 Pitt St, Sydney, 2000	02 9267 9604		Thai	7-13	Y wine-$1.50 corkage

continued overpage...

SYDNEY MAPS

SYDNEY CITY MAP (pp196-202)

RESTAURANTS KEY

● Denotes multiple venue
■ Cost of main meal

#	Map	Ref	Name	Address	Phone	Website	Cuisine	$	BYO
153	198-199	C5	Spanish Terrazas Rest.	541 Kent St, Sydney, 2000	02 9283 3046		Spanish	20-60	N
154	198-199	G4	Tasman's	118 Crown St, East Sydney, 2010	02 9368 0002	www.tasmans.com.au	Steak/Seafood	23-90	Y wine-$2 corkage
155	196-197	C4	The Australian Hotel	100 Cumberland St, The Rocks, 2000	02 9247 2229	www.australianheritagehotel.com.au	Modern Australian	17	N
156	200	F2	The Bellevue	159 Hargrave St, Paddington, 2022	02 9363 2293	www.bellevuehotel.com.au	Modern Australian	18-35	N
157	198-199	G6	The Bentley	320 Crown St, Surry Hills, 2010	02 9332 2344	www.thebentley.com.au	European	27-29	N
158	198-199	I3	The Bourbon	24 Darlinghurst Rd, Darlinghurst, 2011	02 9358 1144	www.thebourbon.com.au	Modern Australian	27	N
159	198-199	F5	The Dark Side of Hyde Park	38 College St, Sydney, 2000	02 9361 5987	www.thedarkside.com.au	Modern Australian	19-30	N
160	201		The Italian Job	112-116 Campbell Pde, Bondi Beach, 2026	02 9130 8292		Italian	8-22	Y wine-$2.50pp corkage
161	198-199	B2	The Malaya	39 Lime St, Darling Harbour, 2000	02 9279 1170	www.themalaya.com.au	Asian	15-27	N
60	196-197	B5	The Rocks Teppanyaki	176 Cumberland St, The Rocks, 2000	02 9250 6020	www.shangri-la.com	Japanese	26-120	Y wine-$30 corkage
78	196-197	C2	The Sebel Pier One	11 Hickson Rd, The Rocks, 2000	02 8298 9999	www.mirvachotels.com.au	Modern Australian	9-30	N
164	196-197	B3	The Wharf Restaurant	Pier 4, Hickson Rd, The Rocks, 2000	02 9250 1761	www.newharfrestaurant.com.au	Modern Australian	27-35	N
165	200	E2	Toko	362 Oxford St, Paddington, 2022	02 9380 7001	www.toko.com.au	Japanese	8-14	Y wine-no corkage
166	198-199	G4	Travota Mediterranean	76 Stanley St, East Sydney, 2010	02 9361 4437		Mediterranean	19	Y wine-no corkage
167	198-199	I5	Una's	338-340 Victoria St, Darlinghurst, 2010	02 9360 6885	www.unas.com.au	European	12-19	Y wine-$1.50 corkage
168	198-199	G4	Voiaj Restaurant	66 Stanley St, East Sydney, 2010	02 9380 4252	www.voiaj.com.au	Modern Australian	19-29	Y wine-$8 corkage
169	198-199	B2	Wagamama	49 Lime St, Darling Harbour, 2000	02 9299 6944	www.wagamama.com.au	Asian	13	N
170	196-197	C3	Wolfies Grill	27 Circular Quay, The Rocks, 2000	02 9241 5577		Modern Aust/Steak	28-40	N
171	198-199	G1	Woolloomooloo Steak & Ale	2 Bourke St, Woolloomooloo, 2011	02 9357 1177		Steak	15-43	N
172	198-199	I1	Yellow Bistro & Food Store	57 Macleay St, Potts Point, 2011	02 9357 3400		Modern Australian	8-26	N
108	196-197	D5	Young Alfred	31 Alfred St, Sydney, 2000	02 9251 5192		Italian	16-20	N

www.ashes06.com

PUBS & CLUBS KEY

FOX Sports Bar **B/R** Bistro/Restaurant **TAB** Betting facilities **OVAL** Kilometres from the SCG

▮ Denotes multiple venue

#	Map	Ref	Name	Address	Phone	Website	Closing Time	FOX	B/R	TAB	OVAL
174	198-199	D2	Angel Hotel	125 Pitt St, Sydney, 2001	02 9233 3131	www.merivale.com	Daily: til late	No	No	No	4.76
95	200	E5	Arena Bar	Fox Studios, Bent St, Moore Park, 2021	02 9361 3930		Mon-Thurs: 12.30am, Fri-Sun: 2am	No	Yes	No	0.25
176	198-199	D2	Arthouse Hotel	275 Pitt St, Sydney, 2000	02 9284 1200	www.thearthousehotel.com.au	Mon-Wed: Midnight, Thurs: 3am, Fri-Sat: 4am	Yes	Yes	No	3.76
177	198-199	E8	Aurora Hotel	324 Elizabeth St, Surry Hills, 2010	02 9211 3462		24 hours	Yes	Yes	Yes	2.56
179	198-199	C1	Bar 333	333 George St, Sydney, 2000	02 9299 8333	www.bar333.com	Mon-Sat: 2am	Yes	Yes	No	4.43
180	198-199	C2	Bavarian Bier Cafe	Level 2, 24 York St, Sydney, 2000	02 8297 4111	www.bavarianbiercafe.com	Mon-Thurs: Midnight, Fri-Sat: 1am	Yes	Yes	No	4.55
98	202	D4	Bavarian Bier Cafe	Manly Wharf, East Esp, Manly, 2095	02 9977 8088	www.bavarianbiercafe.com.au	Daily: Midnight	Yes	Yes	No	18.52
156	200	F2	Bellevue Hotel	159 Hargrave St, Paddington, 2021	02 9363 2293	www.bellevuehotel.com.au	Mon-Sat: Midnight, Sun: 10pm	Yes	Yes	Yes	2.89
183	198-199	G1	Bells Hotel	1 Bourke St, Woolloomooloo, 2011	02 9357 1656		Mon-Sat: 1am, Sun: Midnight	Yes	No	No	3.59
184	198-199	B2	Bistro Arms Retro Bar	81 Sussex St, Sydney, 2000	02 9262 5491	www.theretro.com.au	Mon-Thurs: 9pm, Fri-Sat: 5am	No	No	No	5.40
60	196-197	B5	Blu Horizon Bar	176 Cumberland St, The Rocks, 2000	02 9250 6123	www.altitudesydney.com.au	Mon-Thurs: 1am, Fri-Sat: 2am, Sun: Midnight	No	Yes	No	5.25
105	201	F1	Bungabar	77 Hall St, Bondi Beach, 2026	02 9300 6766		Mon-Sat: Midnight, Sun: 11pm	Yes	Yes	No	5.92
106	198-199	B1	Bungalow 8	Lime St, Darling Harbour, 2000	02 9299 4770	www.bungalow8sydney.com	Mon-Wed: Midnight, Thurs-Sat: 2am	No	Yes	No	5.20
188	198-199	I3	Candys Apartment	22 Bayswater Rd, Kings Cross, 2011	02 9380 5600	www.candys.com.au	Wed-Sat: 6am, Sun: Midnight	No	No	No	3.05
109	198-199	B2	Cargo Bar	King St Wharf, 52-60 The Prm, 2000	02 9262 1777	www.cargobar.com.au	Daily: til late	No	Yes	No	4.90
190	198-199	C2	CBD Hotel	52 King St, Sydney, 2000	02 8297 7000	www.merivale.com	Mon-Sat: til late	Yes	Yes	No	4.41
37	202	E2	Charlton Bar	55 North Steyne, Manly, 2095	02 8966 7172		Mon-Thurs: Midnight, Fri-Sun: til late	No	Yes	No	18.36
192	198-199	C2	City Hotel	347 Kent St, Sydney, 2000	02 9299 4877		Wed: Midnight, Thurs: 1am, Fri: 3am, Sat: late	Yes	Yes	No	4.40
193	198-199	D5	Civic Hotel	388 Pitt St, Sydney, 2000	02 8080 7000	www.civichotel.com.au	Tues-Sun & Sun: Midnight, Fri-Sat: 3am	No	Yes	No	3.12
194	196-197	C4	Cruise Bar	O/S Pass Term, The Rocks, 2000	02 9251 1188	www.cruiserestaurant.com.au	Mon-Thurs: Midnight, Fri-Sat: 1am, Sun: 10pm	No	Yes	No	5.00
195	198-199	I5	Darlo Bar	306 Liverpool St, Darlinghurst, 2010	02 9331 3672	www.darlobar.com.au	Daily: Midnight	No	No	No	2.53
196	198-199	F5	DCM	33 Oxford St, Darlinghurst, 2010	02 9267 7036		Fri-Sat: 8am	No	No	No	2.59
197	198-199	A4	Docks Hotel	Darling Dve, Darling Harbour, 2000	02 9280 2270	www.dockshotel.com.au	Sun-Thu: Midnight, Fri-Sat: 3am	Yes	Yes	No	5.58

continued overpage...

SYDNEY CITY MAP (pp196-202)

PUBS & CLUBS KEY

■ Denotes multiple venue

FOX Sports Bar B/R Bistro/Restaurant TAB Betting facilities OVAL Kilometres from the SCG

#	Map	Ref	Name	Address	Phone	Website	Closing Time	FOX	B/R	TAB	OVAL
198	198-199	G8	Dolphin Hotel	412 Crown St, Surry Hills, 2010	02 9331 4800	www.dolphinhotel.com.au	Mon-Sun: 2am	Yes	Yes	No	2.00
199	198-199	G3	East Sydney Hotel	Crown St, Woolloomooloo, 2011	02 9358 1975		Mon-Sat: 1am, Sun: Midnight	Yes	No	No	3.03
200	198-199	G5	East Village	234 Palmer St, Darlinghurst, 2010	02 9331 5457	www.eastvillage.com.au	Mon-Sat: Midnight, Sun: 10pm	Yes	Yes	No	2.61
201	200	E2	Elephant & Wheelbarrow	384 Oxford St, Paddington, 2021	02 9360 9668		Mon-Thurs: 11pm, Fri-Sat: Midnight, Sun: 10pm	Yes	Yes	No	2.16
202	198-199	D5	Equilibrium Hotel	World Sq, 680 George St, Sydney, 2000	02 8272 2400		Daily: 2am		Yes	No	3.29
117	196-197	C6	Establishment	248-252 George St, Sydney, 2000	02 9240 3000	www.merivale.com	Mon,Tues,Sun: 1am, Wed: 2am, Thurs-Sat: 3am	Yes	Yes	No	4.90
204	198-199	F8	Excelsior Hotel	64 Foveaux St, Surry Hills, 2010	02 9211 4945	www.excelsiorhotel.com.au	Daily til late	No	Yes	No	2.20
205	198-199	G8	Forresters Hotel	336 Riley St, Surry Hills, 2010	02 9211 2095	www.forresters.com.au	Mon-Thurs: Midnight, Fri-Sat: 1am, Sun: 10pm	Yes	Yes	No	2.05
206	196-197	C4	Fortune of War Hotel	137 George St, The Rocks, 2000	02 9247 2714		Mon-Thurs: 11pm, Fri-Sat: 1am, Sun: 10pm	Yes	No	No	5.27
207	200	F1	Four In Hand Hotel	105 Sutherland St, Paddington, 2021	02 9362 1999	www.fourinhand.com.au	Mon-Sun: 11pm, Sun: 10pm		Yes	No	2.93
208	200	E4	Fox & Lion Hotel	Fox Studios, Bent St, Moore Park, 2021	02 9380 7020	www.foxandlion.com	Mon-Thurs: 12.30am, Fri-Sun: 2am	Yes	Yes	No	0.25
209	198-199	I7	Fringe	106 Oxford St, Paddington, 2021	02 9360 5443	www.thefringe.com.au	Sun-Wed: Midnight, Thurs-Sat: 3am	Yes	Yes	No	1.99
210	196-197	C4	Glenmore Hotel	96 Cumberland St, The Rocks, 2000	02 9247 4794	www.glenmorehotel.com.au	Mon-Thurs: Midnight, Fri-Sat: 1am, Sun: 10pm	Yes	Yes	Yes	5.54
211	200	F2	Grand National	161 Underwood St, Paddington, 2021	02 9363 3096	www.grandnationalhotel.com.au	Daily: Midnight		Yes	No	2.69
212	196-197	C3	Harbour Kitchen & Bar	7 Hickson Rd, The Rocks, 2000	02 9256 1660	www.harbourkitchen.com.au	Daily: 11pm	No	Yes	No	5.75
213	196-197	B3	Harbour View Hotel	18 Lower Fort St, The Rocks, 2000	02 9252 4111	www.harbourview.com.au	Mon-Sat: Midnight, Sun: 10pm	Yes	Yes	No	5.90
214	198-199	G6	Havana Club Deluxe	L2, 169 Oxford St, Darlinghurst, 2010	02 9331 7729		Mon-Thurs & Sun: 2am, Fri-Sat: 6am	No	No	No	2.20
123	196-197	C6	Heritage Belgian Café	129-135 Harrington St, The Rocks, 2000	02 9241 1775	www.belgian-beer-cafe.com.au	Daily: 12.30am	Yes	Yes	No	5.17
11	201	F1	Hotel Bondi	178 Campbell Pde, Bondi Beach, 2026	02 9130 3271	www.hotelbondi.com.au	Mon-Sat: 4am, Sun: Midnight	Yes	Yes	No	6.67
217	198-199	E7	Hotel Hollywood	2 Foster St, Surry Hills, 2010	02 9281 2765	www.hotelhollywood.com.au	Mon-Wed: Midnight, Thurs-Sat: 3am	No	No	No	2.84
218	198-199	I3	Hugo's Lounge	L1, 33 Bayswater Rd, Kings Cross, 2011	02 9357 4411	www.hugos.com.au	Tues-Sat & Sun: Midnight, Fri-Sat: 3am	No	Yes	No	3.18
127	201	F2	Icebergs Dining Room	1 Notts Ave, Bondi Beach, 2026	02 9365 9000	www.idrb.com	Mon-Thurs & Sun: Midnight, Fri-Sat: 2am	No	Yes	No	6.12
220	200	C6	Imperial Hotel Pty Ltd	252 Oxford St, Paddington, 2021	02 9331 2023		Mon-Sat: Midnight, Sun: 10pm	Yes	Yes	No	1.79

www.ashes06.com

PUBS & CLUBS KEY

FOX Sports Bar B/R Bistro/Restaurant TAB Betting facilities OVAL Kilometres from the SCG

■ Denotes multiple venue

#	Map	Ref	Name	Address	Phone	Website	Closing Time	FOX	B/R	TAB	OVAL
128	198-199	B2	James Squire Brewhouse	22 The Prm, Sydney, 2000	02 8270 7999	www.malt-shovel.com.au	Daily: til late	Yes	Yes	No	4.80
222	198-199	G6	Kinsela's	383 Bourke St, Darlinghurst, 2010	02 9331 3100	www.kinselas.com	Daily: Midnight	No	Yes	No	2.09
223	200	F3	Light Brigade Hotel	2a Oxford St, Woollahra, 2025	02 9331 2930		Mon,Sun: 10pm, Tues,Thurs: Midnight, Fri-Sat: 1am	No	Yes	No	2.21
133	198-199	E8	Longrain	85 Commonwealth St, Surry Hills, 2010	02 9280 2888	www.longrain.com.au	Mon-Sat: Midnight	No	Yes	No	3.06
225	196-197	A4	Lord Nelson	19 Kent St, The Rocks, 2000	02 9251 4044	www.lordnelson.com.au	Mon-Sat: 11pm, Sun: 10pm	Yes	Yes	No	4.70
226	198-199	G4	Lord Roberts Hotel	64 Stanley St, East Sydney, 2010	02 9331 1326	www.lordrobertshotel.com.au	Daily: 3pm	No	Yes	No	3.15
135	196-197	C4	Lowenbrau Keller	12-18 Argyle St, The Rocks, 2000	02 9247 7785	www.lowenbrau.com.au	Daily: 3am	Yes	Yes	No	5.50
137	202	D4	Manly Wharf Hotel	Manly Wharf, East Esp, Manly, 2095	02 9977 1266	www.manlywharfhotel.com.au	Mon-Sat: Midnight, Sun: 10pm	Yes	Yes	No	18.50
229	198-199	F5	Mars Lounge	16 Wentworth Ave, Surry Hills, 2010	02 9267 6440	www.marslounge.com.au	Wed: Midnight, Thurs & Sun: 1am, Fri-Sat: 3am	No	Yes	No	2.81
230	198-199	D1	Martin Place Bar	51 Martin Pl, Sydney, 2000	02 9231 5575	www.mpb.net.au	Mon-Fri: 2am, Sat: 4.30am	Yes	Yes	No	4.11
231	196-197	C3	Mercantile Hotel	25 George St, The Rocks, 2000	02 9247 3570		Sun-Wed: Midnight, Thurs-Sat: 1am	Yes	Yes	No	6.13
232	196-197	C6	Metropolitan Hotel	244 George St, Sydney, 2000	02 9247 5744		Daily: Midnight	Yes	Yes	No	4.87
233	196-197	E5	Minus5	2 Opera Quays, Circular Quay, 2000	02 9251 0311	www.minus5experience.com	Mon-Sat: Midnight, Sun: 8pm	No	No	No	4.72
234	201	G1	North Bondi RSL Club	120 Ramsgate Ave, Bondi Beach, 2026	02 9130 3152		Daily: Midnight	Yes	Yes	Yes	7.43
235	198-199	H3	Old Fitzroy Hotel	129 Dowling St, Woolloomooloo, 2011	02 9356 3848	www.oldfitzroy.com.au	Mon-Sat: Midnight, Sun: 10pm	No	Yes	No	3.33
236	202	E3	Old Manly Boatshed	40 The Corso, Manly, 2095	02 9977 4443	www.manlyboatshed.com.au	Mon-Sun: 2am	No	Yes	No	18.61
47	200	E3	Olympic Hotel	308 Moore Park Rd, Paddington, 2021	02 9361 6315	www.olympichotel.com.au	Mon-Sat: Midnight, Sun: 10pm	Yes	Yes	Yes	1.61
238	196-197	E3	Opera Bar	Lwr Conc, Opera House, Sydney, 2000	02 9247 1666	www.operabar.com.au	Sun-Thurs: Midnight, Fri-Sat: 1am	Yes	Yes	No	4.90
239	196-197	C4	Orient Hotel	89 George St, The Rocks, 2000	02 9251 1255	www.orienthotel.com.au	Daily: 2am	Yes	Yes	Yes	5.41
143	200	E2	Paddington Inn Hotel	338 Oxford St, Paddington, 2021	02 9380 5913	www.paddingtoninn.com.au	Sun-Wed: Midnight, Thurs-Sat: 1am	No	Yes	No	2.02
241	198-199	B3	Pier 26	Aquarium Wharf, Weat Rd, 2000	02 8270 5126	www.pier26.com.au	Daily: til late	Yes	Yes	No	4.70
242	198-199	I3	Plantation Bar	2 Roslyn St, Kings Cross, 2011	02 9360 7531	www.plantationbar.com.au	Fri-Sat: 6.30am	Yes	No	No	3.19
243	198-199	C3	Pontoon Bar	201 Sussex St, 2000	02 9267 7099		Mon-Sun: 2am	Yes	Yes	No	4.55
244	198-199	F6	Porterhouse Hotel	233 Riley St, Surry Hills, 2010	02 9211 4454	www.hotelhollywood.com.au	Mon-Sun: Midnight	Yes	Yes	No	2.52
245	198-199	F5	Q Bar	L2, 34-44 Oxford St, Darlinghurst, 2010	02 9331 1936	www.qbar.com.au	Mon-Thurs & Sun: 4am, Fri-Sat: 9am	Yes	No	No	2.92

continued overpage...

SYDNEY MAPS

SYDNEY CITY MAP (pp196-202)

PUBS & CLUBS KEY

■ Denotes multiple venue

FOX Sports Bar **B/R** Bistro/Restaurant **TAB** Betting facilities **OVAL** Kilometres from the SCG

#	Map	Ref	Name	Address	Phone	Website	Closing Time	FOX	B/R	TAB	OVAL
196	198-199	F5	Rose Shamrock & Thistle	27-33 Oxford St, Paddington, 2021	02 9360 4662		Sun-Thurs: 1am, Fri-Sat: 3am	Yes	Yes	No	1.93
247	202	E3	Shark Bar	L2, 71 The Corso, Manly, 2095	02 9977 3722	www.sharkbar.com.au	Mon-Sat: 5am, Sun: Midnight	No	Yes	No	18.47
248	198-199	H1	Sienna Marina	7-41 Cowper Wharf Rd, Woolloomooloo, 2011	02 9358 6299	www.siennamarina.com.au	Daily: Midnight	No	Yes	No	3.58
249	198-199	B2	Slip Inn	111 Sussex St, Sydney, 2000	02 8295 9911	www.merivale.com	Mon-Wed: Midnight, Thurs-Fri: 2am, Sat: 3am	Yes	Yes	No	5.44
250	202	F3	Steyne Hotel	75 The Corso, Manly, 2095	02 9977 4977		Thurs: 3am, Fri-Sat: 4.30am, Sun: Midnight	Yes	Yes	No	18.47
251	198-199	I3	Sugareef	20 Bayswater Rd, Kings Cross, 2011	02 9380 9326		Thurs-Sat: til late	No	No	No	3.07
155	196-197	C4	The Australian Hotel	100 Cumberland St, The Rocks, 2000	02 9247 2229		Mon-Sat: Midnight, Sun: 10pm	Yes	Yes	No	5.51
252	202	E2	The Barking Frog	48 North Steyne, Manly, 2095	02 9977 6307		Mon-Tues: 3am, Wed-Sat: Midnight, Sun: 10pm	No	Yes	No	18.39
253	200	B3	The Cricketers Arms	106 Fitzroy St, Surry Hills, 2010	02 9331 3301		Mon-Sat: Midnight, Sun: 10pm	No	Yes	No	1.60
254	200	A2	The White Horse	381-385 Crown St, Surry Hills, 2010	02 8333 9900	www.thewhitehorse.com.au	Mon-Thurs: 11pm, Fri-Sat: 2am	Yes	Yes	No	1.92
255	198-199	D5	Three Wise Monkeys	555 George St, Sydney, 2000	02 9283 5855		Mon-Thurs: 3am, Fri-Sat: 4am, Sun: 10pm	Yes	Yes	No	3.27
256	198-199	H1	Tilbury Hotel	12-18 Nicholson St, Woolloomooloo, 2011	02 9368 1955	www.tilburyhotel.com.au	Mon-Sat: 11.30pm, Sun: 9.30pm	Yes	Yes	No	3.60
196	198-199	F5	UN Nightclub	33 Oxford St, Darlinghurst, 2010	02 9267 7380		Fri-Sun: 6am	No	No	No	2.90
258	198-199	C3	Wallaby Bar	201 Sussex St, Sydney, 2000	02 9267 4118	www.wallabybar.com.au	Tues-Thurs: Midnight, Fri-Sat: 3am	Yes	Yes	No	4.55
259	198-199	H1	Water Bar	6 Cowper Wharf Rd, Woolloomooloo, 2011	02 9331 9000	www.whotels.com	Tues-Sat: Midnight, Sun-Mon: 10pm	No	Yes	No	3.55
260	198-199	A4	Watershed Hotel	Darling Dve, Darling Harbour, 2000	02 9282 9444		Daily: til late	Yes	Yes	No	5.70
261	198-199	I3	World Bar	24 Bayswater Rd, Kings Cross, 2011	02 9357 7700	www.theworldbar.com	Sun-Thurs: 3am, Fri-Sat: 7am	No	No	No	3.07
11	201	F1	Zinc Nightclub	178 Campbell Pde, Bondi Beach, 2026	02 9130 3271		Tue-Sat: 3.30am	No	No	No	6.67

www.ashes06.com

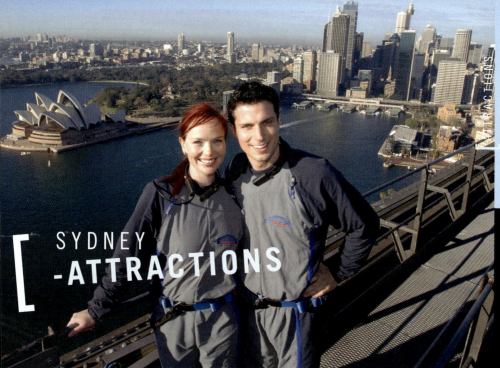

The BridgeClimb offers spectacular views of Sydney. Photo: BridgeClimb.

SYDNEY -ATTRACTIONS

Sydney Harbour Bridge

The quintessential image of Sydney is its Harbour Bridge, built in 1932 and spanning the 503m from the harbour's south shore to the north. It accommodates two railway lines, an eight-lane road and pedestrian walkways which take about 30 minutes to cross.

But for a real buzz, the **BridgeClimb** (02 9240 1100, bridgeclimb.com) is an absolute must! The experience takes about three hours from the time you check in at the BridgeClimb base on Cumberland St in The Rocks to completion.

Climbers wear special suits and are harnessed to a line. Unfortunately, you're not allowed to carry anything up with you, not even your camera, and be advised that it's not the best activity for those hungover after a big night - participants are breath-tested for alcohol! Climbs cost $160 (£67) or $225 (£94) for a twilight climb.

Bondi Beach

Visiting Sydney during the Australian summer from December to February is truly something to cherish, with its awesome beaches rated as good as any in the world.

Without question, the most famous is Bondi Beach, which is located south of Sydney Harbour (30-45 minutes on public transport from the CBD) and swarms with people when the sun's out. Lifeguards are on patrol to ensure swimmers' safety, while nearby restaurants and cafes add to the trendy vibe.

Other great Sydney beaches include Bronte (20-minute walk from Bondi), Tamarama, Clovelly and Coogee to the south of the city, and Manly, Shelly, Curl Curl, Dee Why, Narrabeen, Avalon and Palm Beach to the north.

continued overpage...

ATTRACTIONS
...continued from page 213.

Organised tours... Sydney offers a multitude of organised tours, including popular on-foot excursions such as **The Rocks Walking Tour** (02 9247 6578) and **Sydney Guided Tours** (02 9660 7157), which both give a fantastic history of the city. Not surprisingly, harbour cruises are extremely popular with tourists, with **Sydney Ferries' Evening Harbour Lights tour** (13 15 00, sta.nsw.gov.au) rated one of the best. **Captain Cook Cruises** (02 9206 1111, captaincook.com.au) offers several harbour excursions too, including its **Coffee Cruise** (two hours), **Harbour Highlights Cruise** (one hour) and its hop-on, hop-off **Sydney Harbour Explorer** cruise.

Kings Cross
If you want to party, head to "The Cross" for an eye-opening night on the go!

Full of restaurants, cafes, pubs and clubs, Sydney's red-light district attracts an intriguing cross-section of revellers from high society types to backpackers. This place certainly lives up to its "sex, drugs and rock'n roll" reputation.

Sydney Opera House
Perhaps Australia's most recognisable icon, the Sydney Opera House is perched over the harbour and is a truly memorable place to see a concert or simply enjoy a cappuccino in an adjacent outdoor café.

Opened in 1973, the Opera House hosts theatre, classical music, ballet and film, as well as the odd free outdoor rock concert.

Sydney Wildlife World
It's Australia's wildest new flora and fauna attraction and it's located right in the heart of the city at Darling Harbour... it's Sydney Wildlife World!

A world-class exhibit where koalas, wallabies, birds, insects and reptiles live within their natural habitats and ecosystems, Sydney Wildlife World (adjacent Sydney Aquarium) opened in September 2006 at a cost of $50 million (£21 million) and is the city's newest large-scale attraction.

Sydney Aquarium
When you consider there are over 11,500 Australian aquatic animals on display at Sydney Aquarium (02 8251 7800, sydneyaquarium.com.au), it's

Bondi is Australia's most famous beach. Photo: Tourism New South Wales.

easy to see why it attracts over 1.3 million visitors every year. Located on the city side of Darling Harbour near the Pyrmont Bridge, Sydney Aquarium boasts 160m of underwater tunnels, the largest Great Barrier Reef display in the world, plus an amazing all natural seal sanctuary.

Sydney Tower Skywalk

Since opening in October 2005, Sydney Tower Skywalk (02 9333 9222, skywalk.com.au) has proven a hit with thrill-seeking sightseers who have made the 260m high journey to the top of Sydney Tower for exquisite views of the city.

Dressed in protective clothing and harnessed to safety rails by sliding cables, Skywalkers can marvel at Sydney from a glass-floored viewing platform, twice the height of the Harbour Bridge! Day, dusk and night walks are available.

Blue Mountains

Spend a day or three exploring caves and hiking among gumtree forests in the spectacular Blue Mountains (1300 653 408, bluemountainsaustralia.com) which start just 74km west of Sydney.

The Blue Mountains National Park is a particular favourite among visitors, offering superb natural scenery, fantastic bushwalks and a heap of canyons and cliffs to marvel.

A World Heritage region covering 1436km^2, the Blue Mountains are easily accessible by car, fast electric train from the city or on one of the many coach tours that visit the area daily.

SIGHTSEEING DISCOUNT CARDS...

See Sydney & Beyond Card (02 9247 6611, seesydneycard.com): A cashless smart card packaging more than 40 of Sydney's main attractions and tours. The See Sydney & Beyond Card can be purchased for one, two, three or seven-day periods, with prices starting at $65 (£27) for the single day card.

Privileges Card (02 6161 1999, privilegescard.com): Save money on major Sydney tourist attractions with the Privileges Card, which offers two-for-one admissions, reduced price tickets and buy-one-get-one-free deals. The card costs $35 (£15) and is valid for one month. It is also available in Melbourne, Canberra and on the Gold Coast.

Manly beach. Photo: Tourism New South Wales.

[SUGGESTED -ITINERARIES

A day...

If you're only in Sydney for a short time, make sure you check out the big three visitor hot spots - the Sydney Harbour Bridge, Sydney Opera House and Bondi Beach.

A ride on the hop-on, hop-off Sydney Explorer or Bondi Explorer tourist buses are a fantastic way of seeing the major sights all in one day, or for a truly memorable experience, take a harbour cruise and breathe in the thriving beauty of this buzzing city from the water.

As evening falls, take your pick from an abundance of cool pubs to enjoy a drink, including the Australian Hotel and Lord Nelson Brewery Hotel in The Rocks, and to really party the night away, continue on in brash Kings Cross.

Beach cricket. Photo: Tourism New South Wales.

There's always something fishy going on.
Open 9am-10pm every day at Darling Harbour. www.sydneyaquarium.com.au Ph.+61 2 8251 7800

A few days...

After a full day of sightseeing in inner Sydney, take some time to visit a few of the world-class attractions on offer.

The popular Sydney Aquarium in Darling Harbour is just a short monorail ride from the city centre, and is located next to Sydney Wildlife World, the city's newest large-scale attraction. Animal lovers will also enjoy a trip to Taronga Zoo, which is a short ferry ride from Circular Quay to Mosman.

Thrill seekers are in for a treat as well, with a BridgeClimb on Sydney Harbour or a Skywalk on Sydney Tower certain to get the adrenalin pumping!

And who could pass up a lazy day on the beach? Bondi is the obvious choice, but keep in mind Bronte and Coogee Beach to the south, and Manly and Curl Curl to the north.

A week...

If you've got time to venture further afield, there are some great day trips to be had from Sydney.

With its rugged scenery, invigorating bushwalks and stunning gardens, the World Heritage-listed Blue Mountains National Park is a particular favourite among visitors, offering superb natural scenery, fantastic bushwalks and a heap of canyons and cliffs to marvel. It comes highly recommended, as does the Hunter Valley, one of Australia's premier wine regions.

Head north along the coast to laidback Byron Bay and you won't be disappointed, or head south until you get to the Snowy Mountains and Kosciuszko National Park. Throw in Newcastle, Port Macquarie or a trip to magnificent Lord Howe Island and you've got a smorgasbord of sightseeing options.

[Visitors to Sydney are spoilt for choice with so much to see and do.]

Cruising on Sydney Harbour. Photo: Tourism New South Wales.

SYDNEY DIRECTORY

CRICKET
Cricket Australia: .... (03) 9653 9999, cricket.com.au
Cricket NSW: .... (02) 9339 0999, cricketnsw.com.au

EMERGENCY
Ambulance: 000
Fire: 000
Police: 000
Police (non-emergency): 13 14 44
National Roads & Motorists' Association
(roadside service): .... 13 21 32, nrma.com.au
Emergency Prescription Service: .... (02) 9235 0333
Lifeline (crisis counselling): 13 11 14
Rape Crisis Centre: 1800 424 017

HEALTH
Sydney Hospital (Macquarie St): .... (02) 9382 7111
Royal North Shore Hospital (St Leonards): (02) 9926 7111
St Vincent's Hospital (Darlinghurst): .... (02) 8382 7111
Park Medical Centre (Sydney): .... (02) 9264 4488
Kings Cross Travellers Clinic: .... (02) 9358 3066
Travellers Medical & Vaccination Centre (Sydney): ....
.... (02) 9221 7133
City Dental Practice (Macquarie St): .... (02) 9221 3300
Dental Emergency Information: .... (02) 9369 7050

INTERNET ACCESS
City Hunter: .... 374 Sussex St, Sydney
Travellers Contact Point: .... 428 George St, Sydney
Everywhere Internet: .... Cnr Liverpool/
.... Castlereagh St, Sydney
Global Gossip: .... 415 Pitt St, Sydney
Global Gossip: .... 790 George St, Sydney
Global Gossip: .... 14 Wentworth Ave, Sydney
Global Gossip: .... 61 Darlinghurst Rd, Kings Cross
Global Gossip: .... 37 Hall St, Bondi Beach
The MousePad Internet Cafe: ....
.... 52 Spring St, Bondi Junction
Come Clean & Chat: .... 39 East Esplanade, Manly
The Ch@t Site: .... 65 Belmore Rd, Randwick
The Ch@t Site: .... 192 Coogee Bay Rd, Coogee

BeachBumz Internet Cafe: ...... 1056 Pittwater Rd, Collaroy
B Game Internet Cafe: .... 168 Best Rd, Seven Hills
Kings Net Cafe: .... 47 Beecroft Rd, Epping

MONEY
American Express: 1300 139 060,
.... americanexpress.com.au
Travelex: .... 1800 637 642, travelex.com.au
Western Union Money Transfer: 1800 501 500,
.... westernunion.com

PHONE/MOBILE
3 mobile: .... 131 681, three.com.au
International code to UK: ....
.... 0011 (or 0018) + 44 + Area Code + Local Number
Country Direct (reverse charge/credit to UK): ....
.... 1800 881 440, 1800 881 441, 1800 881 417
Directory Assistance: .... 12455 (local/international)

POST
General Post Office (130 Pitt St): 13 13 18,
.... austpost.com.au

TOURISM
NSW Visitor Centre (Sydney Airport): ...... (02) 9667 6053,
.... visitnsw.com.au
Sydney Visitor Centre (The Rocks): 1800 067 676,
.... sydneyvisitorcentre.com
Sydney Visitor Centre (Darling Harbour): . (02) 9240 8788,
.... sydneyvisitorcentre.com
City Host Information Kiosks: .... Town Hall/Circular
.... Quay/Martin Place
Manly Visitor Information Centre: .... (02) 9976 1430,
.... manlyweb.com.au
Travellers Aid Society (Central Station): ... (02) 9211 2469
Captain Cook Cruises (Circular Quay): ...... (02) 9206 1111
.... captaincook.com.au
City Sightseeing (Darling Harbour/The Rocks): ....
.... (02) 9567 8400, city-sightseeing.com
BridgeClimb (The Rocks): .... (02) 8274 7777
.... bridgeclimb.com

The Cargo Bar. Photo: Tourism New South Wales.

Sydney Aquarium: ....(02) 8251 7800, ...sydneyaquarium.com.au
Sydney Tower Skywalk: .(02) 9333 9222, skywalk.com.au
Blue Mountains Visitor Information Centre: ....1300 653 408, bluemountainsaustralia.com
SydneyPass: ....13 15 00, sydneypass.info
See Sydney & Beyond Card:.....................(02) 9247 6611, ...seesydneycard.com
Privileges Card: ....(02) 6161 1999, privilegescard.com

TRANSPORT

PLANE
Sydney Airport: .....(02) 9667 9111, sydneyairport.com.au
Qantas: ....13 13 13, qantas.com.au
Virgin Blue:............................13 67 89, virginblue.com.au
Jetstar:..131 538, jetstar.com.au

BUS - LOCAL
State Transit Authority: ....13 15 00, sta.nsw.gov.au
Sydney Buses:.......................13 15 00, sydneybuses.info
Transport Infoline: 13 15 00, 131500.com.au
Sydney Explorer (Circular Quay): ....13 15 00, ...sydneypass.info
Bondi Explorer (Circular Quay): 13 15 00, sydneypass.info

NightRide:........................13 15 00, cityrail.info/nightride
Sydney Airporter: ....(02) 9666 9988, kst.com.au
Sydney Super Shuttle (Sydney Airport): ...(02) 9311 3789, ...supershuttle.com.au

BUS - REGIONAL/INTERSTATE
Sydney Coach Terminal:...........................(02) 9281 9366
Greyhound Australia: ....13 14 99, greyhound.com.au
Firefly Express: ....1300 730 740, fireflyexpress.com.au
Premier Motor Service:.........13 34 10, premierms.com.au
Fearnes Coaches:.............(02) 6921 2316, fearnes.com.au
Murrays Coaches: ....13 22 51, murrays.com.au

TRAIN - LOCAL
CityRail:...13 15 00, cityrail.info
Transport Infoline: 13 15 00, 131500.com.au
Airport Link: ....(02) 8337 8417, airportlink.com.au
Metro Light Rail: ...(02) 9285 5600, metrolightrail.com.au
Sydney Monorail: (02) 9285 5600, metromonorail.com.au

TRAIN - INTERSTATE
Countrylink: ....13 22 32, countrylink.info
Great Southern Railways: ....13 21 47, gsr.com.au

continued overpage…

[SYDNEY DIRECTORY
...continued from page 219.

FERRY
Sydney Ferries: ....(02) 9207 3166, sydneyferries.info
Transport Infoline: 13 15 00, 131500.com.au

TAXI
ABC: 13 25 22
Legion Cabs: 13 14 51
Premier: 13 10 17
St George: 13 21 66
Manly: 13 16 68
RSL Taxis: 13 22 11
Combined: 13 33 00
Water Taxis Combined: 1300 666 484

CAR HIRE
Avis: ....13 63 33, avis.com.au
Budget: ....13 27 27, budget.com.au
Europcar: ....1300 131 390, europcar.com.au
Hertz: ....13 30 39, hertz.com.au

Thrifty: ....1300 367 227, thrifty.com.au
Bayswater Car Rentals (Kings Cross): ......(02) 9360 3622,
....bayswatercarrental.com.au
Exel Car Rental (Sydney): ....(02) 9283 3311,
....exelcarrental.com
Network Car & Truck Rentals (Sydney): 1800 736 825,
....networkrentals.com.au

MOTORCYCLE/SCOOTER HIRE
Blue Thunder Motorcycle Tours: ....(02) 9977 7721,
....bluethunderdownunder.com.au
Bikescape (Annandale): 1300 736 869, bikescape.com.au

BICYCLE HIRE
Bicycles in the City (722 George St): ....(02) 9280 2229
Centennial Park Cycles (Randwick): ....(02) 9398 5027,
....cyclehire.com
Sydney Olympic Park: ....(02) 9714 7888,
....sydneyolympicpark.com.au

Bondi Beach. Photo: Tourism New South Wales.

www.ashes06.com

Cricket fans at the MCG.

THE ASHES DOWN UNDER 06/07

EXTRAS

[2006/2007 CRICKET CALENDAR]

November 10	Australian Prime Minister's XI vs England (Canberra)
November 12-14	New South Wales vs England (Sydney)
November 17-19	South Australia vs England (Adelaide)
November 23-27	**FIRST TEST: Australia vs England (Brisbane)**
December 1-5	**SECOND TEST: Australia vs England (Adelaide)**
December 8	CA Chairman's XI vs Invitational XI (Lilac Hill, WA)
December 9-10	Western Australia vs England (Perth)
December 14-18	**THIRD TEST: Australia vs England (Perth)**
December 26-30	**FOURTH TEST: Australia vs England (Melbourne)**
January 2-6	**FIFTH TEST: Australia vs England (Sydney)**
January 9	Twenty20: Australia vs England (Sydney)
January 12	One-Day: Australia vs England (Melbourne)
January 14	One-Day: Australia vs New Zealand (Hobart)
January 16	One-Day: England vs New Zealand (Hobart)
January 19	One-Day: Australia vs England (Brisbane)
January 21	One-Day: Australia vs New Zealand (Sydney)
January 23	One-Day: England vs New Zealand (Adelaide)
January 26	One-Day: Australia vs England (Adelaide)
January 28	One-Day: Australia vs New Zealand (Perth)
January 30	One-Day: England vs New Zealand (Perth)
February 2	One-Day: Australia vs England (Sydney)
February 4	One-Day: Australia vs New Zealand (Melbourne)
February 6	One-Day: England vs New Zealand (Brisbane)
February 9	One-Day: FIRST FINAL (Melbourne)
February 11	One-Day: SECOND FINAL (Sydney)
February 13	One-Day: THIRD FINAL (if needed, Adelaide)

www.ashes06.com

[SCORECARD]
AUSTRALIA vs ENGLAND 06/07

1ST TEST - BRISBANE
November 23-27, 2006 @ the Gabba

..................................won the toss and elected to ....

	First Innings	Second Innings
AUSTRALIA	....	....
Highest scorers	....	....
	....	....
	....	....
Wicket takers	....	....
	....	....
	....	....
ENGLAND	....	....
Highest scorers	....	....
	....	....
	....	....
Wicket takers	....	....
	....	....
	....	....
RESULT	....	
Man of the Match	....	
SERIES SCORE	....	

notes: ....

....

....

....

EXTRAS

[SCORECARD]
AUSTRALIA vs ENGLAND 06/07

2ND TEST - ADELAIDE
December 1-5, 2006 @ Adelaide Oval

....won the toss and elected to ....

	First Innings	Second Innings
AUSTRALIA	....	....
Highest scorers	....	....
	....	....
	....	....
Wicket takers	....	....
	....	....
	....	....
ENGLAND	....	....
Highest scorers	....	....
	....	....
	....	....
Wicket takers	....	....
	....	....
	....	....

RESULT ....

Man of the Match ....

SERIES SCORE ....

notes: ....

....

....

....

www.ashes06.com

THE ASHES DOWN UNDER
[SCORECARD]
AUSTRALIA vs ENGLAND 06/07

3RD TEST - PERTH
December 14-18, 2006 @ the WACA

....won the toss and elected to ....

	First Innings	Second Innings
AUSTRALIA		
Highest scorers		
Wicket takers		
ENGLAND		
Highest scorers		
Wicket takers		

RESULT ....

Man of the Match ....

SERIES SCORE ....

notes: ....

EXTRAS

[SCORECARD]
AUSTRALIA vs ENGLAND 06/07

4TH TEST - MELBOURNE
December 26-30, 2006 @ the MCG

................................won the toss and elected to....................

	First Innings	Second Innings
AUSTRALIA		
Highest scorers		
Wicket takers		
ENGLAND		
Highest scorers		
Wicket takers		

RESULT ....

Man of the Match ....

SERIES SCORE ....

notes: ....

www.ashes06.com

THE ASHES DOWNUNDER
[SCORECARD]
AUSTRALIA vs ENGLAND 06/07

5TH TEST - SYDNEY
January 2-6, 2007 @ the SCG

.....................................won the toss and elected to.....................

	First Innings	Second Innings
AUSTRALIA		
Highest scorers		
Wicket takers		
ENGLAND		
Highest scorers		
Wicket takers		

RESULT ....

Man of the Match ....

SERIES SCORE ....

notes: ....

....

....

....

EXTRAS

CRICKET TICKET REFUNDS

Cricket Australia has developed a National Refund Policy for the 2006-07 international season, which applies to all Test matches, one-day games and Twenty20 fixtures.

When are you eligible for a refund?

In summary, you may be eligible for a refund of 100% of the value printed on your ticket for the relevant match, less a $2.50 administration fee, if:

TEST - DAY TICKET…
Less than 10 overs are played during that day and neither side won the match (and the match did not end in a tie). If between 10-25 overs are played during that day, you may be eligible for a refund of 50% of the ticket value.

ONE-DAY INTERNATIONAL…
Less than 10 overs are played during the whole match and there is no result recorded. If between 10-25 overs are played in total, and there is no result recorded, you may be eligible for a refund of 50% of the ticket value.

TWENTY20…
Less than 15 overs are played during the whole match and there is no result recorded.

When can I apply to exchange my ticket?

If you qualify for a refund in accordance with Cricket Australia's National Refund Policy, instead of obtaining a refund you may apply to exchange your ticket.

Tickets will be exchanged for a ticket of the same value (not necessarily the same seat) at another match (or day's play in the case of a Test) during the same cricket season, subject to availability, and only for the same venue at which the original match was scheduled to be played.

If an exchange is not possible, you may apply for a refund instead, or if tickets of a higher value are available, you may pay the difference between the value of your original ticket and the value of a ticket of that higher class.

How do I apply for a refund or exchange?

If you wish to obtain a refund, you must present the original ticket to the ticket agency where it was purchased (or as otherwise instructed by Cricket Australia or the ticket agency) within 30 days of the end of the match in respect of which the refund is sought. In all states, refunds will be subject to a $2.50 administration charge.

To exchange a ticket, you must present the original ticket to the ticket agency where it was purchased (or as otherwise instructed by Cricket Australia or the ticket agency). You should liaise directly with the ticket agency to determine whether an exchange is possible in the circumstances.

cricket.com.au
For a full copy of the Cricket Australia National Refund Policy, visit cricket.com.au

www.ashes06.com

ASHES URN
RETURNS TO AUSTRALIA

The prized Ashes urn returns to Australia this summer for just the second time in history.

The Marylebone Cricket Club (MCC) in England, the protector of the sacred little trophy, has organised an exhibition to coincide with the highly anticipated 2006/07 Ashes series.

The urn will visit all five Test cities - Sydney, Brisbane, Adelaide, Perth and Melbourne - commencing its tour in Sydney on October 21.

The Ashes urn last visited Australia in 1988 to commemorate the country's bicentennary. An exhibition had been planned for the 2002/03 season, but had to be cancelled when x-rays revealed serious cracks in the urn's stem. Repair works since mean it is now in a suitable condition to be flown between England and Australia.

The MCC has been the guardian of the Ashes since 1927, when they were presented to the club by the wife of former England captain Ivo Bligh. In 2005 alone, more than 35,000 people visited the MCC Museum at Lord's to see the tiny urn.

ASHES URN TOUR 2006/07

Sydney: October 21-November 8 (Museum of Sydney)

Brisbane: November 12-November 22 (Queensland Museum)

Adelaide: November 26-December 6 (South Australian Museum)

Perth: December 10-December 20 (Western Australian Museum)

Melbourne: December 26-January 7 (Melbourne Museum) & January 9-January 14 (Melbourne Cricket Club Museum, MCG)

2007 ONE-DAY SCHEDULE
AUSTRALIA/ENGLAND/NEW ZEALAND

New Zealand will join host Australia and England for this summer's One-Day International Series, which commences in January.

Pitting the world champion Aussies against the Kiwis (ranked three in the world) and Poms (ranked seventh), the 2007 One-Day International Series will visit Melbourne, Hobart, Brisbane, Sydney, Adelaide and Perth.

Melbourne and Sydney will stage the first two finals on February 9 and February 11, with Adelaide to host the third and deciding final, if required, on February 13.

January 12	One-Day: Australia vs England	(Melbourne)
January 14	One-Day: Australia vs New Zealand	(Hobart)
January 16	One-Day: England vs New Zealand	(Hobart)
January 19	One-Day: Australia vs England	(Brisbane)
January 21	One-Day: Australia vs New Zealand	(Sydney)
January 23	One-Day: England vs New Zealand	(Adelaide)
January 26	One-Day: Australia vs England	(Adelaide)
January 28	One-Day: Australia vs New Zealand	(Perth)
January 30	One-Day: England vs New Zealand	(Perth)
February 2	One-Day: Australia vs England	(Sydney)
February 4	One-Day: Australia vs New Zealand	(Melbourne)
February 6	One-Day: England vs New Zealand	(Brisbane)
February 9	One-Day: FIRST FINAL	(Melbourne)
February 11	One-Day: SECOND FINAL	(Sydney)
February 13	One-Day: THIRD FINAL (if needed)	(Adelaide)

One-Day history Down Under

World Series Cricket heralded the introduction of the one-day concept in Australia in 1977, however the first official tri-series Down Under remains the 1979/80 tournament when the West Indies and England visited.

Bellerive Oval in Hobart will host two One-Day Internationals on January 14 and January 16, 2007.

ONE-DAY SERIES RESULTS IN AUSTRALIA

Australia has hosted a one-day series every summer since, having won 18 of the 27 tournaments contested. This year's visitors England and New Zealand have had little success in that time - the Poms' win in 1986/87 remains their only triumph, while the Kiwis have never won a one-day series on Australian soil.

Twenty20 is back!
Following the success of last year's inaugural Twenty20 international in Australia (in which the Aussies defeated South Africa at the Gabba), the bash and crash concept is back for another one-off battle this summer.

AUSTRALIA VS ENGLAND
Where: Sydney Cricket Ground
When: January 9, 2007
Time: 7.30pm

SEASON	1st	2nd	3rd
1979-80	West Indies	England	Australia
1980-81	Australia	New Zealand	India
1981-82	West Indies	Australia	Pakistan
1982-83	Australia	New Zealand	England
1983-84	West Indies	Australia	Pakistan
1984-85	West Indies	Australia	Sri Lanka
1985-86	Australia	India	New Zealand
1986-87	England	Australia	West Indies
1987-88	Australia	New Zealand	Sri Lanka
1988-89	West Indies	Australia	Pakistan
1989-90	Australia	Pakistan	Sri Lanka
1990-91	Australia	New Zealand	England
1991-92	Australia	New Zealand	England
1992-93	West Indies	Australia	Pakistan
1993-94	Australia	South Africa	New Zealand
1994-95	Australia	Australia A	England/Zimbabwe
1995-96	Australia	Sri Lanka	West Indies
1996-97	Pakistan	West Indies	Australia
1997-98	Australia	South Africa	New Zealand
1998-99	Australia	England	Sri Lanka
1999-00	Australia	Pakistan	India
2000-01	Australia	West Indies	Zimbabwe
2001-02	South Africa	New Zealand	Australia
2002-03	Australia	England	Sri Lanka
2003-04	Australia	India	Zimbabwe
2004-05	Australia	Pakistan	West Indies
2005-06	Australia	Sri Lanka	South Africa

The WACA in Perth will stage one-dayers on January 28 and January 30, 2007.

EXTRAS

Callum Ferguson in one-day mode for the West End Redbacks. Photo: South Australian Cricket Association.

DOMESTIC CRICKET
DOWN UNDER

The Australian domestic cricket scene is arguably the toughest on the planet, with world-class players representing their respective states in the four-day Pura Cup, One-Day Domestic Series and Twenty20 competition.

Queensland, South Australia, Western Australia, Victoria, New South Wales and Tasmania are the six competing teams in all three forms of the game.

In the Pura Cup (previously known as the Sheffield Shield) and One-Day Domestic Series (previously known as the ING Cup and Mercantile Mutual Cup), each state plays every other state on a home-and-away basis, with the two leading teams at the end of the season meeting in the final at the home ground of the number one ranked side.

The recently introduced Twenty20 format is still in its early development so doesn't yet command the same level of importance as the Pura Cup and One-Day Domestic Series, with the 2007 "Big Bash" to be held over a two-week period in early January.

2007 TWENTY20

DATE	GAME	VENUE
Jan 1	QLD vs TAS	*TBC
Jan 1	SA vs VIC	Adelaide
Jan 1	WA vs NSW	WACA
Jan 4	WA vs SA	WACA
Jan 5	QLD vs NSW	Gabba
Jan 5	TAS vs VIC	Bellerive
Jan 7	NSW vs SA	*TBC
Jan 7	VIC vs QLD	*TBC
Jan 7	TAS vs WA	Bellerive
Jan 10	NSW vs TAS	*TBC
Jan 10	SA vs QLD	Adelaide
Jan 10	VIC vs WA	*TBC
Jan 13	FINAL	*TBA

www.ashes06.com

2006/07 PURA CUP

DATE	GAME	VENUE
Oct 13-16	QLD vs TAS	Gabba
Oct 15-18	WA vs VIC	WACA
Oct 17-20	NSW vs SA	SCG
Oct 22-25	WA vs TAS	WACA
Oct 27-30	QLD vs NSW	Gabba
Oct 27-30	SA vs VIC	Adelaide
Nov 3-6	SA vs NSW	Adelaide
Nov 12-15	WA vs QLD	WACA
Nov 14-17	VIC vs TAS	MCG
Nov 24-27	NSW vs WA	SCG
Nov 24-27	VIC vs QLD	MCG
Dec 6-9	TAS vs SA	Bellerive
Dec 15-18	VIC vs NSW	MCG
Dec 15-18	SA vs QLD	Adelaide
Dec 19-22	TAS vs WA	Bellerive
Jan 16-19	NSW vs VIC	SCG
Jan 19-22	TAS vs QLD	Bellerive
Jan 19-22	WA vs SA	WACA
Jan 26-29	VIC vs SA	MCG
Jan 27-30	NSW vs TAS	*TBC
Jan 28-31	QLD vs WA	Gabba
Feb 9-12	QLD vs SA	Gabba
Feb 9-12	WA vs NSW	*TBC
Feb 12-15	TAS vs VIC	Bellerive
Mar 1-4	NSW vs QLD	SCG
Mar 1-4	VIC vs WA	MCG
Mar 1-4	SA vs TAS	Adelaide
Mar 8-11	TAS vs NSW	Bellerive
Mar 8-11	SA vs WA	Adelaide
Mar 8-11	QLD vs VIC	Gabba
Mar 19-23	*FINAL*	**TBA*

2006/07 ONE-DAY DOMESTIC SERIES

DATE	GAME	VENUE
Oct 11	QLD vs TAS (D/N)	Gabba
Oct 13	WA vs VIC (D/N)	WACA
Oct 15	NSW vs SA	*TBC
Oct 25	QLD vs NSW (D/N)	Gabba
Oct 27	WA vs TAS (D/N)	WACA
Nov 4	TAS vs QLD	Bellerive
Nov 8	SA vs NSW (D/N)	Adelaide
Nov 12	VIC vs TAS	*TBC
Nov 17	WA vs QLD (D/N)	WACA
Nov 19	TAS vs NSW	Bellerive
Nov 22	NSW vs WA (D/N)	SCG
Nov 29	VIC vs QLD (D/N)	MCG
Dec 3	TAS vs SA	*TBC
Dec 3	VIC vs WA	*TBC
Dec 6	NSW vs QLD (D/N)	SCG
Dec 8	QLD vs VIC (D/N)	Gabba
Dec 10	NSW vs VIC	*TBC
Dec 13	SA vs QLD (D/N)	Adelaide
Dec 17	TAS vs WA	Bellerive
Dec 20	VIC vs NSW (D/N)	MCG
Dec 23	SA vs VIC (D/N)	Adelaide
Jan 17	WA vs SA (D/N)	WACA
Jan 24	NSW vs TAS (D/N)	SCG
Jan 25	QLD vs WA (D/N)	Gabba
Jan 31	VIC vs SA (D/N)	MCG
Feb 3	SA vs WA (D/N)	Adelaide
Feb 7	WA vs NSW (D/N)	WACA
Feb 14	QLD vs SA (D/N)	Gabba
Feb 17	TAS vs VIC	Bellerive
Feb 21	SA vs TAS (D/N)	Adelaide
Feb 25	*FINAL*	**TBA*

ICC CRICKET WORLD CUP
WEST INDIES 2007
March 13-April 28, 2007

The ICC Cricket World Cup will be held in the West Indies in 2007, with Australia aiming to win the prestigious one-day title for the third consecutive time.

Having triumphed in England in 1999 and again in South Africa in 2003, the Aussies are favourites for the 2007 event, but will face stiff opposition from England, South Africa, New Zealand, Sri Lanka, Pakistan and the host nation.

The tournament officially gets underway when the West Indies play Pakistan in Jamaica on March 13 (after a week of warm-up matches), with the final scheduled to be played in Barbados on April 28.

How does the tournament work?

The 16 competing countries have been split into four groups, with each team to play three matches against the other countries in their group.

The top two teams from each group will then progress to the "Super Eight" stage, playing each of the other six teams they have yet to meet.

The top four performing teams will then progress to the Semi-Finals, with the two winners to meet in the Final.

HONOUR BOARD - ICC Cricket World Cup

YEAR	WINNER	HOST NATION
1975	WEST INDIES	England
1979	WEST INDIES	England
1983	INDIA	England
1987	AUSTRALIA	India/Pakistan
1992	PAKISTAN	Australia/New Zealand
1996	SRI LANKA	India/Pakistan/Sri Lanka
1999	AUSTRALIA	England
2003	AUSTRALIA	South Africa

WHO'S COMPETING IN 2007?

GROUP A
Australia (1)
South Africa (5)
Scotland (12)
The Netherlands (16)

GROUP B
Sri Lanka (2)
India (8)
Bangladesh (11)
Bermuda (15)

GROUP C
New Zealand (3)
England (7)
Kenya (10)
Canada (14)

GROUP D
Pakistan (4)
West Indies (6)
Zimbabwe (9)
Ireland (13)

*Note: World ranking in brackets.

Did you know?

Since the first World Cup in 1975, only five countries have tasted success!

Australia has won three times, the West Indies twice, while India, Pakistan and Sri Lanka have all triumphed once. England, South Africa and New Zealand are notable absentees from the honour board.

www.ashes06.com

ICC WORLD CUP SCHEDULE

WARM-UP MATCHES

DATE	GROUP WA (Trelawny, Jamaica)	GROUP WB (St Vincent)	GROUP WC (Trinidad & Tobago)	GROUP WD (Barbados)
Mon 05 Mar	West Indies vs Kenya	England vs Bermuda	South Africa vs Canada	Sri Lanka vs Scotland
Tue 06 Mar	India vs The Netherlands	Australia vs Zimbabwe	Pakistan vs Ireland	New Zealand vs Bangladesh
Thu 08 Mar	Kenya vs The Netherlands	Zimbabwe vs Bermuda	Ireland vs Canada	Scotland vs Bangladesh
Fri 09 Mar	India vs West Indies	Australia vs England	Pakistan vs South Africa	New Zealand vs Sri Lanka

*OPENING CEREMONY - SUN 11 MAR

GROUP STAGE (STAGE 1)

DATE	GROUP A (St Kitts & Nevis)	GROUP B (Trinidad & Tobago)	GROUP C (St Lucia)	GROUP D (Jamaica)
Tue 13 Mar				West Indies vs Pakistan
Wed 14 Mar	Australia vs Scotland		Kenya vs Canada	
Thu 15 Mar		Sri Lanka vs Bermuda		Zimbabwe vs Ireland
Fri 16 Mar	South Africa vs The Netherlands		England vs New Zealand	
Sat 17 Mar		India vs Bangladesh		Pakistan vs Ireland
Sun 18 Mar	Australia vs The Netherlands		England vs Canada	
Mon 19 Mar		India vs Bermuda		West Indies vs Zimbabwe
Tue 20 Mar	South Africa vs Scotland		New Zealand vs Kenya	
Wed 21 Mar		Sri Lanka vs Bangladesh		Zimbabwe vs Pakistan
Thu 22 Mar	Scotland vs The Netherlands		New Zealand vs Canada	
Fri 23 Mar		India vs Sri Lanka		West Indies vs Ireland
Sat 24 Mar	Australia vs South Africa		England vs Kenya	
Sun 25 Mar		Bermuda vs Bangladesh		

SUPER EIGHT (STAGE 2)

DATE	TEAMS	VENUE	DATE	TEAMS	VENUE
Tue 27 Mar	D2 vs A1	Antigua & Barbuda	Tue 10 Apr	D2 vs A2	Grenada
Wed 28 Mar	A2 vs B1	Guyana	Wed 11 Apr	C2 vs B2	Barbados
Thu 29 Mar	D2 vs C1	Antigua & Barbuda	Thu 12 Apr	B1 vs C1	Grenada
Fri 30 Mar	D1 vs C2	Guyana	Fri 13 Apr	A1 vs D1	Barbados
Sat 31 Mar	A1 vs B2	Antigua & Barbuda	Sa 14 Apr	A2 vs C1	Grenada
Sun 01 Apr	D2 vs B1	Guyana	Sun 15 Apr	B2 vs D1	Barbados
Mon 02 Apr	B2 vs C1	Antigua & Barbuda	Mon 16 Apr	A1 vs B1	Grenada
Tue 03 Apr	D1 vs A2	Guyana	Tue 17 Apr	A2 vs C2	Barbados
Wed 04 Apr	C2 vs B1	Antigua & Barbuda	Wed 18 Apr	D1 vs B1	Grenada
Sat 07 Apr	B2 vs A2	Guyana	Thu 19 Apr	D2 vs B2	Barbados
Sun 08 Apr	A1 vs C2	Antigua & Barbuda	Fri 20 Apr	A1 vs C1	Grenada
Mon 09 Apr	D1 vs C1	Guyana	Sat 21 Apr	D2 vs C2	Barbados

SEMI-FINALS

DATE	SEMI-FINAL 1 (JAMAICA)	SEMI-FINAL 2 (ST LUCIA)
Tue 24 Apr	2nd vs 3rd	
Wed 25 Apr		1st vs 4th

FINAL

DATE	BARBADOS
Sat 28 Apr	FINAL

HOWZAT!
ASHES TRIVIA CHALLENGE]

Q1. What is the name of the cricket club in England which houses the famous Ashes urn?

Q2. To coincide with the 2006/07 series, the Ashes urn returns to Australia for just the second time in history. In what year was its only previous visit?

Q3. Who scored his debut century for Australia in Adelaide during the 1990/91 Ashes series?

Q4. Who was captain of the England team during the infamous "Bodyline" series of 1932/33?

Q5. Who was awarded "Man of the Series" in the 2002/03 Ashes contest?

Q6. Which England bowler took a hat-trick at the SCG in the 1998/99 Ashes series?

Q7. What was the name given to the Australian team that toured England in 1948?

Q8. In 2005, Australia lost the Second Ashes Test at Edgbaston by two runs, but how many did tailenders Brett Lee and Michael Kasprowicz put on for the final wicket - 39, 49 or 59 runs?

Melbourne Cricket Ground.

www.ashes06.com

Q9. How many wickets did Shane Warne take at The Oval in the Fifth (and deciding) Ashes Test in England in 2005?

Q10. Who scored the most centuries during the 2005 Ashes series between Australia and England?

Q11. Which English bowler took 6/60 to lead his team to victory over Australia in Melbourne during the 1998/99 Ashes series?

Q12. Who topped the batting averages for England in the 2005 Ashes series?

Q13. In what year did Shane Warne bowl Mike Gatting around his legs with what later became known as "the ball of the century"?

Q14. What was Don Bradman's batting average in Ashes Tests - 58.65, 89.79 or 99.94?

Q15. Australia and England played seven Tests during the 1970/71 series. How many were drawn?

Q16. During which famous Ashes series did Adelaide Oval record its largest ever cricket attendance of 50,962?

Q17. In what year was the WACA first used to play an Ashes Test?

Q18. Who was the Australian batsman who smashed five boundaries off one Tony Greig over during the 1977 Centenary Test at the MCG?

Q19. Who captained Australia during the 1989 Ashes series in England?

Q20. In what year did Australia and England last draw an Ashes series?

ANSWERS:

Q01. Marylebone Cricket Club (MCC).
Q02. 1988.
Q03. Mark Waugh.
Q04. Douglas Jardine.
Q05. Michael Vaughan (England).
Q06. Darren Gough.
Q07. The Invincibles.
Q08. 59 runs.
Q09. 12.
Q10. Andrew Strauss (England).
Q11. Dean Headley.
Q12. Kevin Pietersen.
Q13. 1993.
Q14. 89.79.
Q15. Five.
Q16. "Bodyline" 1932/33.
Q17. 1970.
Q18. David Hookes.
Q19. Allan Border.
Q20. 1972.

[AUSSIE SLANG

It doesn't matter whether you're English or Australian, it's worth brushing up on your Aussie slang before heading to the cricket. Here's a quick guide to deciphering the lingo:

A
Amped - Excited
Akubra - Hat worn by farmers
Arvo - Afternoon

B
Banana Bender - Someone from Queensland
Battler - Someone who tries hard but struggles
Bloody oath - Definitely
Bludger - Lazy person
Blue - Fight
Bogan - "Bludger" who takes little pride in appearance
Bonzer - Great
Boogie board - A half-sized surfboard
Boomer - A large male kangaroo
Booze Bus - Police random breath testing van
Bottle-O - Liquor shop/Off-license
Bottler - Excellent
Buckley's - No chance
Budgie smugglers - Male bathing costume
Bundy - Popular brand of rum made in Queensland
Butcher - Small glass of beer in South Australia

C
Cactus - Dead, not working
Chock-a-block - Full
Chunder - Vomit
Cobber - Friend
Cockie - Farmer

Coldy - Beer
Corker - Brilliant
Corroboree - Aboriginal dance festival
Countery - Pub meal
Crikey - Exclamation of surprise
Croweater - Someone from South Australia

D
Damper - Bread made from flour and water
Dead horse - Tomato sauce
Deadset - True
Digger - Soldier
Dinky-di - The real thing, genuine
Divvy van - Police vehicle
Drop Bear - Imaginary Australian bush creature
Dunny - Outside toilet

E
Esky - Insulated container to keep drinks cold

F
Fair dinkum - True, genuine
Fit as a mallee bull - Fit and strong
Flat out like a lizard drinking - Busy
Fremantle Doctor - Afternoon breeze in Perth

G
Galah - Silly person
G'day - Hello
Get on it - Start drinking alcohol
Give it a burl - Try/attempt

Good onya - Well done
Grog - Alcohol
Grouse - Very good
Grundies - Underwear

H
Hooroo - Goodbye
How are ya? - Standard greeting

I
Icy pole - Frozen snack
Iffy - Questionable/unsure

J
Jackaroo - Male farm hand
Jillaroo - Female farm hand
Jocks - Men's underpants
Joey - Baby kangaroo
Jumbuck - Sheep

K
Kelpie - Australian sheepdog
Knackered - Very tired
Knocker - Someone who criticises

L
Larrikin - Funny bloke/mischievous
Little ripper - Excellent
Longneck - 750ml bottle of beer in South Australia

M
Maccas - McDonald's
Mad as a cut snake - Very angry
Middy - 285ml beer glass in New South Wales
Milk Bar - Corner shop/general store

AUSSIE SLANG

Have a ripper of a time travelling around Oz, and be sure to mung on some grouse Aussie tucker before getting on it with a few coldies at the pub. But don't get too wasted or you'll be knackered the next day and labelled a piker by ya mates!

Mongrel - Bad person
Mozzie - Mosquito

N
Nipper - Young lifesaver
Not within cooee - A long way away
No worries - You're welcome/no problems

O
Ocker - Unsophisticated Australian
Op Shop - Second-hand clothing shop

P
Pavlova - Australian dessert
Perve - To look with lust
Pie floater - Upside down meat pie in pea soup
Piker - Someone who leaves party early
Pot - 285ml beer glass in Queensland and Victoria

R
Rack off - Go away
Ridgy-didge - Original, genuine
Ripper - Great
Rip snorter - Great

S
Sandgroper - Someone from Western Australia
Sanger - Sandwich
Schooner - Large beer glass in Queensland, medium beer glass in South Australia
Session - Period of drinking alcohol
She'll be right - No problems
Shonky - Dubious 
Slab - A carton of beer
Snag - Sausage
Spewin - Very angry
Spit the dummy - Get very upset at something
Stoked - Very pleased
Strewth - Exclamation of surprise
Stroppy - Miserable/ill-tempered
Stubby - A 375ml beer bottle
Surf'n Turf - Steak topped with seafood
Swag - Rolled up transportable bedding

T
Tallie - 750ml bottle of beer
Tall poppy syndrome - Tendency to criticise successful people
Thongs - Cheap rubber footwear
Tinny - Can of beer, small aluminium boat
Too right - Definitely
Top End - Far north of Australia
Toy - No good/weak
True blue - Patriotic Australian
Tucker - Food
Two pot screamer - Someone who gets drunk easily

U
Ute - Utility vehicle

W
Whacker - Idiot
Whinge - Moan/complain
Whoop-whoop - Outback/far away

X
XXXX - Brand of beer made in Queensland

Y
Yabby - Inland freshwater crayfish
Yobbo - Uncouth person
Yonks - A long time

EXTRAS

NEW YEAR'S EVE 2006

What better way to see in the New Year than with a fireworks extravaganza on Sydney Harbour!

This year, more than one million people are expected to converge around the foreshore, with some 3000 boats crammed into the harbour.

New Year's Eve in Sydney. Photo: Tourism New South Wales.

www.ashes06.com

NEW YEAR'S EVE

At this year's New Year's Eve celebrations in Sydney, there willl be two fireworks displays - at 9pm and midnight - plus a "Harbour of Light Parade" which will see 50 invited vessels decorated with ropelight sail from Rose Bay to Birchgrove.

Getting around...
Many roads are closed in and around North Sydney, the CBD and foreshore on New Year's Eve, however extra trains, buses and ferries will operate.
Note: It is illegal to drink alcohol on public transport.

VANTAGE POINTS ON SYDNEY HARBOUR
There are many vantage points to view the Sydney New Year's Eve celebrations, with fireworks erupting along the harbour from Cockatoo Island in the west to Point Piper in the east.
Note: Popular sites tend to fill by early afternoon!

Most areas permit alcohol, either for sale on site or BYO, but be mindful that many of the popular vantage points prohibit glass - so stick to cans for the night!

KEY VANTAGE SPOTS:
· Bicentennial Park, Glebe
· Blues Point Reserve (no BYO)
· Bradfield Park, Milsons Point (no BYO)
· Bradley's Head
· Clarke's Point, Hunters Hill
· Cremorne Point
· Embarkation Park
· Mrs Macquaries Point (no BYO)
· North Head
· Sydney Opera House (no BYO)
· Tarpeian Precinct, Macquarie St Lawns (no BYO)

CRUISING ON THE HARBOUR
Celebrate New Year's Eve aboard the brand new "Bella Vista" for a first-class evening of opulence on magical Sydney Harbour.

Offering 360-degree views, modern bars, luxurious lounges and an open starlight deck ensuring excellent viewing of the fantastic fireworks display, the Bella Vista has organised a six-hour New Year's Eve party package for Sydney visitors.

For $600 (£250) per person, enjoy a continuous cocktail menu, open bar, DJ and light show. For more information phone (02) 9211 3192 or visit sydneynewyearseve.com.au.

IF YOU'RE IN MELBOURNE ON DECEMBER 31...

Make your way to the banks of the Yarra River and marvel at the fireworks spectacular at midnight. The City of Melbourne has also organised free entertainment at various sites throughout the city.

TIP! XMAS IN MELBOURNE

So you've arrived in Melbourne for the Fourth Test and need some inspiration on how to spend Christmas before the cricket begins on Boxing Day.

Many restaurants close their doors on December 25, and prices tend to skyrocket in the ones that don't, so why not organise a picnic hamper and head to the Royal Botanic Gardens in South Yarra or St Kilda beach. You'll have a great time and it won't cost you an arm and a leg!

NEW YEAR'S EVE 2006

Celebrate in style

Join Sydney in the celebrations as we welcome in the New Year aboard Sydney's BRAND NEW & stylish vessel, the 'Bella Vista'. Offering 360-degree views, modern bars, luxurious lounges & an open starlight deck for prime viewing of the spectacular New Year's Eve fireworks.

Where will you be when the countdown begins? Book your first class seat on the 'Bella Vista' for a glittering, & simply extravagant night on magical Sydney Harbour.

NEW YEAR'S EVE PACKAGE

- 6 Hour Party Cruise on Sydney Harbour
- Delicious cocktail menu all night long
- Open bar including, house spirits, sparkling wine, beer, bottled red & white wine, soft drinks & juices
- DJ, dancing & light show
- Party streamers & hats
- Spectacular New Year's Eve fireworks display at 9pm & midnight

BELLA VISTA

New Year's Eve Cruise	AUD $600pp
Departs	Darling Harbour

* Conditions apply. Tickets are non-refundable. No reserved seating.

BOOKINGS ESSENTIAL

Ph 61 2 9211 3192   info@atstravel.com.au
www.sydneynewyearseve.com.au

[BEER DRINKER'S GUIDE TO OZ

There is a bewildering variety of beer glass names and sizes in Australia, which differ from state to state.

Order a "schooner" in Brisbane and you'll get a 425ml (15oz) glass, but the same command in Adelaide only results in a 285ml (10oz) glass!

Similarly, a "middy" in Sydney and Perth (285ml) equals a "pot" in Melbourne, and don't bother asking for either in Adelaide where you're better off requesting a "butcher" or "pint".

So unless you're planning on buying jugs throughout your travels, which is the only standard beer size across the country (1140ml/40oz), the following list is worth reviewing so you know exactly what to ask for when you sidle up to the bar...

GLASS NAMES & SIZES

BRISBANE, QUEENSLAND
Five	140ml	5oz
Glass	235ml	8oz
Pot/Middy/Ten	285ml	10oz
Schooner	425ml	15oz

*Local beers: XXXX Bitter, XXXX GOLD

ADELAIDE, SOUTH AUSTRALIA
Pony	140ml	5oz
Butcher	200ml	7oz
Schooner	285ml	10oz
Pint	425ml	15oz
Imperial Pint	575ml	20oz

*Local beers: Coopers Pale Ale, West End Draught

PERTH, WESTERN AUSTRALIA
Shetland	115ml	4oz
Pony	140ml	5oz
Bobby	170ml	6oz
Glass	200ml	7oz
Middy	285ml	10oz
Schooner/Pint	425ml	15oz
Pot	575ml	20oz

*Local beers: Emu Bitter, Swan Draught

MELBOURNE, VICTORIA
Pony	140ml	5oz
Small glass	170ml	6oz
Glass	200ml	7oz
Pot	285ml	10oz
Schooner	425ml	15oz
Pint	568ml	20oz

*Local beers: Victoria Bitter, Carlton Draught

SYDNEY, NEW SOUTH WALES (& ACT)
Pony	140ml	5oz
Glass/Seven	200ml	7oz
Middy/Half pint	285ml	10oz
Schooner	425ml	15oz
Pint	568ml	20oz

*Local beers: Tooheys New, Hahn Premium

HOBART, TASMANIA
Small beer	115ml	4oz
Six	170ml	6oz
Seven	200ml	7oz
Eight	225ml	8oz
Ten/Pot/Handle	285ml	10oz
Pint	425ml	15oz

*Local beers: Boags Draught, Cascade Premium

DARWIN, NORTHERN TERRITORY
Six	170ml	6oz
Seven	200ml	7oz
Handle/Pot	285ml	10oz
Schooner	425ml	15oz

*Local beers: Victoria Bitter (VIC), XXXX GOLD (QLD)

[CHECK OUT THE WEBSITE]

ashes06.com

Convert English pounds into Australian dollars.

Check to see what time it is back in England.

Log on for updated Ashes info.

GIFT IDEA!
Buy a guide online.

XXXX ALE HOUSE BREWERY TOURS

Receive a FREE STUBBY COOLER with a full priced ($18) adult Ale House Brewery Tour ticket.

XXXX Ale House Brewery Tours visit www.xxxx.com.au.

STUBBY COOLER

STORY BRIDGE HOTEL

Join us for a cleansing ale "under the bridge". Buy one pint of XXXX or XXXX GOLD and get a second one FREE.

Double Decker Bus Service to and from the Gabba each day.

FREE BEER

OXFORD HOTEL

The Famous Oxburger & Tooheys Extra Dry Stubby, all for $9.90! (Chicken Burger or Vege Burger also available).

Famous Oxburger & Tooheys Extra Dry Stubby.

BURGER & BEER

WORLDSEND HOTEL

Come in to enjoy a 10% discount off all main meals either for lunch or dinner. Get two pints of tap beer for the price of one.

10% off all main meals (lunch and dinner).

10% OFF

OXFORD HOTEL

The Famous Oxburger & Tooheys Extra Dry Stubby, all for $9.90! (Chicken Burger or Vege Burger also available).

Famous Oxburger & Tooheys Extra Dry Stubby.

BURGER & BEER

WORLDSEND HOTEL

Come in to enjoy a 10% discount off all main meals either for lunch or dinner. Get two pints of tap beer for the price of one.

10% off all main meals (lunch and dinner).

10% OFF

Address:	200 Main St, Kangaroo Point
Phone:	07 3391 2266
Web:	www.storybridgehotel.com.au
Email:	info@storybridgehotel.com.au
Conditions:	Not valid with any other offers. Must be over 18 years of age. One voucher per person only. At the Story Bridge Hotel we practice responsible service of alcohol.

Address:	Corner of Black & Paten Streets, Milton, Brisbane
Phone:	07 3361 7597
Web:	www.xxxx.com.au
Conditions:	Not to be used in conjunction with any other offer. Stubby cooler valued at $4.50. Offer only valid on presentation of an original voucher. One cooler per voucher. One voucher per person.

Address:	208 Hindley St, Adelaide
Phone:	08 8231 9137
Web:	www.worldsendhotel.com.au
Email:	worldse@bigpond.net.au
Conditions:	These offers are not valid with any other offers.

Address:	101 O'Connell St, North Adelaide (minutes from Adelaide Oval)
Phone:	08 8267 2652
Email:	oxford@boozebros.com.au
Conditions:	Offer available 27th November to 15th December 2006. Conditions apply.

Address:	208 Hindley St, Adelaide
Phone:	08 8231 9137
Web:	www.worldsendhotel.com.au
Email:	worldse@bigpond.net.au
Conditions:	These offers are not valid with any other offers.

Address:	101 O'Connell St, North Adelaide (minutes from Adelaide Oval)
Phone:	08 8267 2652
Email:	oxford@boozebros.com.au
Conditions:	Offer available 27th November to 15th December 2006. Conditions apply.

GLOUCESTER PARK
Relax under the stars on our huge lawn area, enjoy live harness racing, or eat out at one of our 6 bars and restaurants, there is something for everyone at Gloucester Park, located opposite the WACA.

Show your Perth Ashes ticket for FREE ENTRY on Friday 15th December. — **FREE ENTRY**

GLOUCESTER PARK
Perth's Largest Entertainment Complex, there is something for everyone at Gloucester Park, located opposite the WACA.

Show your Perth Ashes ticket for FREE ENTRY on Saturday 16th December. — **FREE ENTRY**

JAMES SQUIRE
Present this voucher to receive a free pint of any James Squire beer with every main meal purchased.

Free pint of any James Squire beer with every main meal. — **FREE PINT**

ELEPHANT & WHEELBARROW
Patrons can purchase discounted pints and half pints of the nominated 'Beer of the Month'.

Discounted 'Beer of the Month'. — **CHEAP PINTS**

BARCODE SPORTS BAR
Come in to Barcode to watch the 3 mobile Ashes series and purchase 1 beer and receive 1 beer free.

Buy 1 beer get another beer FREE. — **FREE BEER**

MOUNTAIN VIEW HOTEL
A NEW beer garden overlooking the MCG offering 10 beers on tap including Boddingtons & Becks. Six big-screen TVs with surround sound. Voted Richmond's "Best Parma" - an iconic Melbourne dish.

Buy one get one free beer, wine or soft drink. — **FREE DRINK**

Address:	Nelson Crescent, East Perth WA 6004
Phone:	08 9323 3555
Web:	www.gloucesterpark.com.au
Conditions:	Show your Perth Ashes ticket or this voucher for FREE ENTRY after the game! Valid on Saturday 16 Dec. All rooms, undercover areas, grandstands and majority of viewing areas are smoke free - No BYO Alcohol - No Glass

Address:	Nelson Crescent, East Perth WA 6004
Phone:	08 9323 3555
Web:	www.gloucesterpark.com.au
Conditions:	Show your Perth Ashes ticket or this voucher for FREE ENTRY after the game! Valid on Friday 15 Dec. All rooms, undercover areas, grandstands and majority of viewing areas are smoke free - No BYO Alcohol - No Glass

Address:	94-96 Bourke Street, Melbourne VIC 3000
Phone:	03 9639 8444
Conditions:	Patrons can purchase discounted pints and half pints of the nominated 'Beer of the Month'. Offer valid any time throughout the 06/07 Ashes series.

Address:	115 - 127 Russell Street, Melbourne VIC 3000 (cnr Little Collins Street)
Phone:	03 9654 5000
Web:	www.portlandhotel.com.au
Conditions:	Offer valid any time throughout the 06/07 Ashes series.

Address:	70 Bridge Road, Richmond
Phone:	03 9428 6654
Conditions:	One voucher per person per day. Not valid with any other offer. Valid for a drink of equal or lesser value.

Address:	Level 1, Crown Entertainment Complex, 8 Whiteman Street, Southbank
Phone:	03 9694 1280
Web:	www.barcodebar.com.au
Conditions:	1 per person per day. Not valid with any other offer. Valid for a drink of equal or lesser value.

SHARK DIVE XTREME
1 adult FREE entry to Oceanworld with every Shark Dive Xtreme booked.

FREE entry to Oceanworld. — **FREE ENTRY**

MOUNTAIN VIEW HOTEL
A NEW beer garden overlooking the MCG offering 10 beers on tap including Boddingtons & Becks. Six big-screen TVs with surround sound. Voted Richmond's "Best Parma" - an iconic Melbourne dish.

Buy one get one free beer, wine or soft drink. — **FREE DRINK**

MATILDA CRUISES
What better way to experience Sydney's vibrant outdoor atmosphere than to set sail for a leisurely cruise - complete with fascinating commentary and a delicious morning tea.

Discount applies to Sailing Coffee Cruise departing 10am. — **15% OFF**

SYDNEY TOWER + OZTREK
From the golden beaches to the distant Blue Mountains, Sydney Tower takes you to the highest point above Sydney Australia for breathtaking 360-degree views of our beautiful harbour city.

Discount applies for adult and child admission. — **15% OFF**

CAPTAIN COOK CRUISES
Cruise in first-class style aboard Sydney's most prestigious cruise ship, MV Sydney 2000. Includes full morning tea featuring freshly brewed coffee, handmade cakes and pastries. Fully narrated.

Discount applies to Sailing Coffee Cruise departing 10am. — **20% OFF**

SKYWALK
With an adrenalin rush you can enjoy spectacular views of all landmarks including the Sydney Harbour Bridge, Sydney Opera House, Sydney Harbour, and all the way to the Blue Mountains.

Discount applies for adult and child admission. — **15% OFF**

Address:	70 Bridge Road, Richmond		Address:	Oceanworld Manly, 200m from Manly Ferry Wharf, West Esplanade, Manly
Phone:	03 9428 6654		Phone:	02 8251 7877
Conditions:	One voucher per person per day. Not valid with any other offer. Valid for a drink of equal or lesser value.		Web:	www.oceanworld.com.au
			Conditions:	Present this voucher on entry to Oceanworld. Not valid in conjunction with any other offer, including family and group rates. Valid until 28/02/07.

Address:	Centrepoint Podium Level, 100 Market Street, Sydney		Address:	Pier 26, Aquarium Wharf, Darling Harbour, Sydney
Phone:	02 9333 9222		Phone:	02 9264 7377
Web:	www.sydneytoweroztrek.com.au		Web:	www.matilda.com.au
Email:	towersupervisor@skywalk.com.au		Conditions:	Valid for travel to 28 February 2007. Not valid with any other offer.
Conditions:	Discount applies off full adult & child prices. Not combinable with family, group or concession tickets, nor with any other discount or offer. Promo code SYDT105, valid to 31 January 2007.			

Address:	Sydney Tower, Centrepoint Podium Level, 100 Market Street, Sydney		Address:	No. 6 Jetty, Circular Quay, Sydney
Phone:	02 9333 9200		Phone:	02 9206 1111
Web:	www.skywalk.com.au		Web:	www.captaincook.com.au
Email:	towersupervisor@skywalk.com.au		Conditions:	Valid for travel to 28 February 2007. Not valid with any other offer. Not valid on special event cruises.
Conditions:	Discount applies off full adult & child prices. Not combinable with family, group or concession tickets, nor with any other discount or offer. Promo code ASH15, valid for Skywalks departing to 31 January 2007.			

SYDNEY AQUARIUM

Sydney Aquarium – Australia's #1 attraction! Present this voucher to receive 15% off adult and child admission tickets. Offer ends 28 February 2007. Open 9am – 10pm every day.

Discount applies for adult and child admission. — **15% OFF**

AUSTRALIAN TRAVEL SPECIALISTS

10% off Day Tours to the Blue Mountains, Hunter Valley & Port Stephens.

Valid for adults travelling with AAT Kings Tours. — **10% OFF**

TARONGA ZOO

Taronga Zoo is home to 2,000 unique Australian animals on the shores of Sydney Harbour, just 12 minutes from the city by ferry. Get up close with kangaroos, koalas, wallabies, echidnas and other Aussie natives.

Discount applies to adult and child admisssion prices only. — **15% OFF**

SYDNEY WILDLIFE WORLD

Experience a real Australian adventure, without having to travel all around Australia. See over 6,000 animals living in their natural habitats and ecosystems, where you can take a walk on the wild side with the yellow-footed rock wallabies, or meet our cutest national icon, the koala.

Adult & Child Admission Tickets to Sydney Wildlife World. — **15% OFF**

BAR CLEVELAND

Come in to receive 50% off any meal purchase when you spend $15.00 or more at this great establishment.

50% off all main meals at Bar Cleveland. — **50% OFF**

OCEANWORLD MANLY

Save 20% on each adult & child entry to Oceanworld with this voucher.

Adult & Child Admission Tickets to Oceanworld Manly. — **20% OFF**

Address:	Harbourside Shopping Centre, Darling Harbour, opposite Wharf 6 Circular Quay		Address:	Aquarium Pier, Darling Harbour, Sydney
Phone:	02 9211 3192		Phone:	02 8251 7800
Web:	www.atstravel.com.au		Web:	www.sydneyaquarium.com.au
Conditions:	Valid for adults travelling with AAT Kings Tours.		Conditions:	Offer not valid with any other offer, group, family or concession rate. Offer ends 28 February 2007.

Address:	Aquarium Pier, Darling Harbour		Address:	Bradleys Head Road, Mosman - Travel to the Zoo by ferry from Circular Quay
Phone:	02 9333 9288		Phone:	02 9969 2777
Web:	www.sydneywildlifeworld.com.au		Web:	www.zoo.nsw.gov.au
Conditions:	Valid to 28 Feb 2007. Offer is not valid with any other offer, group, family, concession or combined tickets.		Conditions:	Offer valid from 1st July 2006 until June 2007. Not valid with any other existing Zoo offer including pre-paid tickets, concession tickets or transport passes, including ZooPass. Not redeemable or transferable for cash.

Address:	Oceanworld Manly, 200m from Manly Ferry Wharf, West Esplanade, Manly		Address:	433 Cleveland St (Cnr Bourke), Surry Hills
Phone:	02 8251 7877		Phone:	02 9698 1908
Web:	www.oceanworld.com.au		Web:	www.barcleveland.com.au
Conditions:	Present this voucher on entry to Oceanworld. Not valid in conjunction with any other offer, including family and group rates. Valid until 28/02/07.		Conditions:	50% off any meal purchase when you spend $15.00 or more. Maximum of $20 discount applies. Not valid with any other offers.